BLACK FOLK HERE AND THERE

Afro-American Culture and Society
A CAAS Monograph Series
Volume 9

The Academic Editor for this Monograph was
Claudia Mitchell-Kernan.

BLACK FOLK HERE AND THERE

An Essay in History and Anthropology

ST. CLAIR DRAKE

VOLUME 2

CENTER FOR AFRO-AMERICAN STUDIES
UNIVERSITY OF CALIFORNIA, LOS ANGELES

Library of Congress Cataloging in Publication Data

Drake, St. Clair.
   Black folk here and there.

   (Afro-American culture and society, ISSN 0882-5297; v.9)
   Includes bibliographies and index.
   1. Racism—History. 2. Blacks—History. 3. Blacks—Nile River Valley—History.
4. Nile River Valley—History. 5. Afro-Americans—Race Identity.
I. Title. II. Series: Afro-American culture and society; v.7, etc.
CB195.D72   1987   305.8′96   86-16045
ISBN 0-934934-28-2 (set)
ISBN 0-934934-29-0 (pbk.: set)
ISBN 0-934934-20-7 (v. 1)
ISBN 0-934934-21-5 (pbk.: v. 1)
ISBN 0-934934-30-4 (v. 2)
ISBN 0-934934-31-2 (pbk.: v. 2)

CB
195
.D72
1987
V.2
C.2

Center for Afro-American Studies
University of California, Los Angeles

Library of Congress Catalog Card Number:
ISBN: 0-934934-30-4
      0-934934-31-2 (pbk)
      ISSN: 0882-5297
Printed in the United States of America

Designed by Rosalind Nzinga Vaughn
Maps by Timothy Seymour
Produced by UCLA Publication Services Dept.
Typography: DynaType

CONTENTS

ILLUSTRATIONS

Plates

PREFACE

Black Folk Here and There is a work that attempts to combine symbolic anthropology and comparative history in a study of the Black Experience from the beginning of literate cultures to the advent of the transatlantic slave trade and the White Racism that quickly developed as its ideological support. This is the second and final volume. We began with an examination of ancient Nile Valley civilizations, where black people held political, military, and sacerdotal power. We now proceed through the Judaic, Greek and Roman cultures to European Christendom and the Muslim World in the period before the great diaspora from Africa to the West began in the sixteenth century A.D.

The author's preface to the first volume related the circumstances under which a decision was made to write the book. It also positioned *Black Folk Here and There* as the most recent branch on a tree of "black vindicationist" writing that extends back to the days of slavery in the United States. While the polemical tone of volume 1 is much less pronounced in this second volume, the author consciously and deliberately makes whatever sacrifice of academic "objectivity" is needed to present this subject from a black perspective.

The first volume began by establishing conceptual guidelines: distinguishing, for example, between White Racism, which attaches innate inferiority to the Negro phenotype, and color prejudice, which may disparage dark skin color but does not necessarily imply a social or cognitive deficit. In thinking about the transatlantic trade in African slaves that began in the fifteenth century, it occurred to me that the most relevant theoretical and practical problems are concerned not with the derogation of dark-skinned people in general but, rather, with disabilities imposed upon those defined as "Negroes," those whose dark skin is only one feature in a *gestalt*— dark skin color plus frizzled (or kinky) hair plus flat nose plus alveolar prognathism (protruding jaw). *Negroidness*, not blackness in general, became the focal point of my inquiry.

Considerable attention was given in volume 1 to an examination of various theories that have been developed in the West to explain what happens when black people and white people interact and why color prejudice may arise. Some of these theories view color prejudice as an attitude transmitted by the culture, purposefully or not, and susceptible to change by situational changes and other processes that alter cultural norms. Some consider prejudice against black people to be instinctive among those lighter in skin color. Others view color prejudice as a response to early childhood experiences that are said to universally associate the color "black" with undesirable qualities.

A major purpose of both volumes is to test against the empirical data provided by history certain propositions that gained currency during the 1960s and early 1970s. These ideas had been advanced by two eminent American scholars, historian Carl Degler and social psychologist Kenneth Gergen.[1] Gergen suggested the high probability that in all times and places people tend to "look down" upon those who have darker skins than their own. Degler asserted it emphatically. Both men implied that if the symbol system of a society contrasts the colors black and white, disparaging black and blackness, such an appraisal at the abstract level will "carry over" to people with black skin color. Other scholars, some black and some white, have argued that the Negro phenotype has become the Other against which European Caucasians define themselves, imputing to the darker Other numerous undesirable characteristics.

There are alternative contemporary models to this "New Manichaean" belief. We republish here two diagrams from volume 1 that helped us to focus our attention in carrying out an inquiry on the meaning of blackness and the Black Experience in historical and comparative perspective. Chart 1 outlines the range of reactions that may occur when different cultural or racial groups confront each other. It incorporates ideas advanced by sociologist Herbert Blumer and social psychologist Gordon Allport, the latter emphasizing the fact that group prejudices and stereotypes may be positive as well as negative. Blumer notes that racial and ethnic hostility and negative prejudices are most likely to arise in situations where a dominant ethnic or racial minority feels threatened by a majority that it holds in subjection. Such situations occurred in the plantation areas of the Caribbean and the southern United States when masses of sub-Saharan Africans were forcibly transported to the Americas as slaves after the fifteenth century. They arose, too, in parts of Africa where Europeans established colonies. Chart 2 emphasizes the fact that while evaluations of blackness as a color may affect social relations, such evaluations also appear in contexts that have nothing to do

CHART 1. TYPES OF INSTITUTIONALIZATION: ATTITUDES EXPRESSED IN
INITIAL CONTACT BETWEEN INDIVIDUALS OF DIFFERENT RACIAL GROUPS

Basic Cognitive Reaction	Range of Possible Attitudes when Initial Contact Occurs (Individual)	Types of Possible Group Reactions after Contact	Possible End Results of Contact (including Institutionalization)
	Psychological rejection	Extirpation of one group	No incorporation into a single social system
cultural component — Evaluation according to some esthetic, ethical, and utilitarian norms and values		Expulsion of One Group	
		Enslavement	Systems of Color-Caste
AWARENESS OF DIFFERENCE IN SKIN-COLOR	FEAR DISGUST/ REPUGNANCE DISLIKE CURIOSITY INDIFFERENCE CURIOSITY EXOTIC APPEAL ADMIRATION CONFIDENCE	Acceptance with Inferior Status, but not in Kin Groups	Systems of Color-Class
cultural component — Evaluation according to some esthetic, ethical, and utilitarian norms and values			Systems Where Color is Not a Status Marker
	Positive Identification	Acceptance with Inferior Status in Kin Groups	Disappearance of differences due to complete amalgamation
		Egalitarian Acceptance	

SOURCES: Blumer, "Nature of Race Prejudice"; Allport, *Nature of Prejudice*.

CHART 2. THE NAMES OF COLORS AS VERBAL SYMBOLS
WITH MULTIPLE REFERENTS

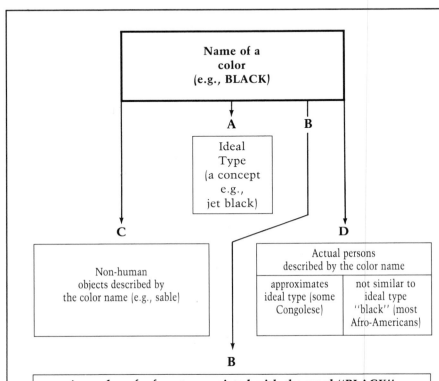

A number of referents associated with the word "BLACK"					
Positive Value		Neutral Value		Negative Value	
"Black is Beautiful" or "Black is spiritually powerful" or "in the black" (accounting)	Black Beauty, a horse in a story — Black Madonnas in Europe	"Black as Night" or black as absence of color in color spectrum	color of an auto or a dress — "Black Holes" in space	"Black is Evil" or "Black is Ugly"	Black cat in European folklore — Some devils — Some human races
abstract concept	empirical referent (in a context)	abstract concept	empirical referent (in a context)	abstract concept	empirical referent (in a context)

1. The term *Black*, in the chart above, has as referents:

    (A) an ideal type concept of what "*Black*" is

    (B) a number of referents that are imputed to the word, "Black," and that presumably evoke emotions, sentiments, etc. (connotations)

    (C) inanimate objects described by the name of the color

    (D) individuals or groups of people referred to by the color name; they may, or may not, approximate the ideal type in actuality

2. The crucial question is: "When one referent of the color-name is a characteristic or group of characteristics, is it possible that these characteristics are not necessarily imputed to *people* who may be called by the color name?" Is it possible that a distinction is drawn as between color to designate abstract qualities and color to designate skin-color?

with evaluations of human beings. The anthropologist Edmund Leach, citing examples, stresses the point that "black" and "white" may be organizing labels for social dichotomies without any fixed, necessary meaning and affect. Context and situation may generate meanings in one society that are different from those in another society, as anthropologist Victor Turner has pointed out.

Clarification of one concept is important in examining the behavior of those who are reacting to "Negroes" in varied social situations. The term "looking down upon" black people is too imprecise for our purposes. If used at all, it should be applied only within certain "domains." The ones we have chosen are: the *esthetic*, the *erotic*, the *religious/mystical*, and the *status-allocating*. People do not "look down" upon others in some generalized sense, but in interactions within these and other "domains." In many first-contact situations in Africa (and in New World plantation areas) white males did not "look down upon" black women in choosing sexual partners, i.e., in the *erotic* domain. But they might have defined some of these same women as "ugly," thus looking down upon them in the *esthetic* domain. Accepting black women as marriage partners was usually out of the question, this being behavior in the *status-allocating* domain. These same women may, however, have been thought of as having unusual capabilities in the *religious/mystical* domain, for beneficent or malevolent ends. In this volume, for several geographical areas and time periods, an attempt is made to analyze relations between black and white people using the concept of "domains."

As we began to test the Degler-Gergen propositions against the evidence supplied by comparative history, it became clear that negative prejudices against sub-Saharan Africans—"Negroes"— antedated the rise of mercantile capitalism and the modern expansion of Europe overseas. A second question for our inquiry naturally arose: "Where and when did the derogation of sub-Saharan Africans and the Negro phenotype first appear in the written record?" The conclusions that we reach in this volume seem likely to have a disquieting effect upon adherents of both the Judaic and Islamic religions. Early Christian theologians also espoused derogatory attitudes soon after their religion was founded. We have tried to search out the reasons why adherents of the three great religions deviated in this regard from the universalistic ideals of their founders. The only blame adhering to modern practitioners of these religions will be when they fail to face up to the deviations and to correct them in practice.

In developing an analysis of the meanings associated with black as a color, and of the effect that people defined as black elicit from others (and vice versa), we view what we are doing as an exercise in symbolic anthropology (broadly conceived) carried out within a framework of comparative history. The largest units within which analysis is attempted—such as medieval European Christendom or the Muslim World—are similar to what Arnold Toynbee, in *A Study of History*, calls "civilizations." Within each of these are sub-units based upon ethnicity and social class. A common language and scale of values unify the elite groups within a "civilization." They are participants in a "high culture," while there is great diversity at "lower" cultural levels.

In volume 1, we presented one historical case: "Nile Valley Civilizations." We concluded that blackness was not evaluated negatively in any of the domains over several millenia. Indeed, were it not for intervening centuries of White Racism, it would not be necessary to point out that surviving depictions of Egypt's political and spiritual leaders often bear a striking resemblance to the Negro phenotype. In certain periods, the nation was governed by full-blooded black Africans. Only after settlement by Greeks and Romans in the Nile Valley did light skin color come to be salient in status-allocation, and even then, it was not so in the religious/mystical domain.

A Hebrew civilization developed in Palestine just north of Egypt, and volume 1 discussed some of the relationships that it had with the Nile Valley civilizations. Volume 2 describes the Hebrew civilization in far more detail. We emphasize the fact that anti-black prejudice as well as skin color consciousness in general does not appear to have developed in the Palestinian Judaic tradition. However, after the defeats of Judah and Israel by the Assyrians and Babylonians, a variation of Hebrew civilization developed among those captives carried off to the Mesopotamian diaspora. The Talmudic tradition among the exiles differed significantly from the Palestinian biblical tradition with regard to black people. We suggest some reasons for derogatory attitudes toward black people that developed in the Mesopotamian diaspora but were not evident in the older biblical tradition of the Jews.

The Roman empire eventually engulfed the Palestinian Judaic settlements and portions of the Nile Valley. It was within the Palestinian segment of this empire that a Jewish religious sect developed into a proselytizing religion, Christianity. The Church Fathers synthesized Greco-Roman philosophical ideas and Judaic social ethics, both of which had assimilated some Persian values, especially the concept of a Manichaean cosmic struggle between Light and Darkness. In this volume, we note that the missionary efforts of the earliest Christians were directed at two groups of "pagans." To the North were the Caucasian "barbarians"; to the south the sub-Saharan Africans. In the North African church, the skin color of what they called "Ethiopians" assumed high symbolic significance, becoming equivalent to "sin." Making Christian converts demanded "washing the Ethiopian white"; the "degenerate" condition of their cultures must be transformed by Christianity. These theological attitudes toward blackness and black people were retained as the Church grew, but so was the insistence that black *people* could be "redeemed."

In the seventh century A.D., cultures on both shores of the Mediterranean that had been assimilating Christianity were subjected to a basic transformation by invaders bearing a new religion, Islam. The area of Mediterranean Christianity was transformed into one citadel of Islam, while another arose in Mesopotamia and Persia. Simultaneously, an area that might be defined as European Christendom was consolidating its gains in Frankish and German lands and imposing Christianity on the Slavs by force.

Some striking contrasts emerge from a comparative analysis. The pre-Christian Mediterranean civilizations in Greece accorded a high status to Ethiopians in several domains, a position that was reversed with the triumph of Christianity. Ethiopians became "sinners" to be converted. Yet, in the medieval Christendom of Western Europe, where there was very little actual face-to-face contact between black people and white people, a surprisingly high status was allocated to the few Blacks who were present and a mythology emerged in which Black Madonnas and black Christian military heroes were venerated. Concurrently, within the Muslim World, where thousands of sub-Saharan Africans were in contact with people of the Middle East and North Africa in the role of slaves, pejorative aspersions were often cast upon the Negro physical type by the elites even though the status-allocating norms allowed some Negroes to achieve prominence in the army or civil government. Esthetic derogation was widespread in elite circles despite erotic attraction exemplified by black women in harems or as concubines. A stereotype of special black capacities for piety took root in the Central Islamic Lands.

From the eleventh century through the fifteenth century, color consciousness increased markedly in European Christendom but without an increase in negative appraisals so marked as to eliminate favorable stereotypes of black people. A prolonged conflict—the Crusades—made brown and black people highly visible as the Enemy. Among the most important factors generating color consciousness in Europe was this conflict with Muslims in the Middle East. But the color awareness also had a positive aspect. A legendary African king, Prester John, became the symbol of what French scholar Henri Baudet calls *le bon éthiopien*, and a black military man, St. Maurice, was widely revered. Black Madonnas proliferated. By the end of the fifteenth century the image of the Black in European Christendom was definitely a more favorable one than that in Middle Eastern Islam. But forces were at work which would destroy this benign European attitude toward black people. The rise of the transatlantic trade in African men and women condemned to be enslaved on New World plantations meant that the system of multi-racial slavery, the norm in the Mediterranean, gave way to *racial* slavery in the Americas. A doctrine of White Racism was gradually elaborated to defend this practice as well as European colonial imperialism. This was a conscious and deliberate process of degrading Africans for economic and political ends.

The chapters in this volume dealing with these varying appraisals of blackness and black people envision the sixteenth century as a watershed in race relations, the beginning of the massive Black Diaspora into the Americas. The experience of black people in slave systems of the Western Hemisphere is a story that will be familiar to most readers. Thus, *Black Folk Here and There* deals with Black Experience in less familiar times and places. This volume has been made possible because, for over two millenia, scores of literate observers—philosophers, historians, geographers, theologians, and writers of poetry and fiction—have recorded reactions to sub-Saharan Africa and its people, as well as meanings associated with blackness. They also reveal their own attitudes.

However, one difficulty is almost insuperable when examining periods prior to the sixteenth century A.D. as we do. Those who wish to describe the past are, to a great extent, at the mercy of these individuals, who knew how to write and who left observations that can be read. However, the overwhelming majority of the people in the civilizations we examine were illiterate. Members of the literate elite were not, on the whole, interested in finding out and recording what ordinary people thought about anything, and certainly not about racial and ethnic relations. Anthropology as a discipline devoted to recording the thoughts and actions of non-literate peoples was not invented until the latter part of the nineteenth century. With one or two notable exceptions, novels and short stories are a relatively recent mode of imaginatively reconstructing, through invented characters, what a wide variety of people think. What blackness meant to ordinary people who were not defined as having black skins, and what it meant to people who were so defined, does occasionally emerge from folklore including tales and songs, but only occasionally. Inferences can also be made from the popularity of characters in sagas that were handed down from generation to generation by tellers of tales. An occasional proverb may also give us a clue to ethnic and racial relations and attitudes. In the Muslim World there are accounts of mutinies and revolts in which white and black soldiers or peasants occasionally collaborated, and of other cases in which Blacks and non-Blacks were in opposition. Such accounts are available, too, for those post-sixteenth century extensions of European power into Asia, Africa, and the Americas, but not for medieval Europe.

As we moved through history and from culture to culture, we made an effort to discuss different aspects of the symbol "black" in various social contexts where it constitutes a cue that "triggers" actions. In drawing conclusions about the presence of various attitudes toward the color "black" in a culture, it has often been assumed uncritically that these attitudes automatically "carry over" to the skin color of people. We take the position that this should be a hypothesis open to examination and not a dogmatic assertion. Research by social psychologists as well as ethnographers is necessary.

A thorough understanding of the functions of blackness in social relations requires statistically controlled research in social psychology using samples of people drawn from contemporary societies. Cross-cultural comparisons of the historical type used in our two volumes can only suggest hypotheses derived from an examination of a number of relevant situations. It is clear from our analyses that black as a color is polysemic. It means different things in different contexts within, as well as between, specific ethnic and national groups. Chart 2 displays a wide range of possible attitudes toward blackness, and still does not include the fact that "black" as a word spoken and heard has a different effect from the word "black" written and read. Studying who speaks the word to whom, in what contexts and with what effects, requires careful experimental designs.

Analysis of the status of Blacks in the past is not irrelevant to the present. It gives us a baseline against which to measure change. By looking into the history of the Black Experience we are led to face certain contemporary problems with a greater sense of their cultural tenacity and with a better understanding of areas where induced change may be necessary. For instance, we contrast the symbolic meanings and status of black people in biblical Palestine and the symbolism and treatment of Blacks in the Jewish Mesopotamian diaspora, where the influential Babylonian Talmud was produced. We are led to ask, "To what extent do pejorative statements about black people that appear in the Babylonian Talmud still persist uncriticized as a part of modern Jewish education?" Islam incorporated non-Koranic derogatory black stereotypes and reinforced them during centuries of slavery. Will status-allocation systems in North Africa and the Middle East eventually advance black people to positions of public and private responsibliity in accordance with their numbers in the population? In pursuit of their economic goals, white Europeans institutionalized an elaborate system denigrating black Africans to justify enslaving them on New World plantations. Can Western Christendom achieve the same degree of respect for black people that existed in medieval Europe or classical Greece?

ACKNOWLEDGMENTS

In assembling the documentation that made this book possible, I owe a debt of gratitude to the community of scholars who devoted themselves to patiently studying the role of blackness in European Christendom and in the Muslim World. I have acknowledged the efforts of some of them in the bibliographic comments preceding each chapter's endnotes. Some of my fellow scholars have been especially cooperative in directing me to source material for volume 2. Among them are Professor Martin Kilson of Harvard University and Professor Sylvia Wynter of Stanford University. A colleague, Sotere Torregian, has had a long-term interest in this project. He has offered the benefit of his encyclopedic knowledge of Sufism as well as insightful comments on medieval Christianity. I have acknowledged the cooperation of others in volume 1.

What began as a sprawling manuscript whose bulk and diffuseness made it too unwieldy for the general reader to handle was given a greater degree of coherence and readability by an experienced editor whose devotion to the task merits a statement of profound gratitude. Ms. Jacqueline Tasch, an author in her own right, took on the task of tightening up and improving my original draft. She is not, of course, responsible for any inaccuracies in the text which still remain.

Rick Harmon and Sabrina Gledhill gave advice on early versions of volume 2, as they did on volume 1. Ms. Marcelle Fortier retired as CAAS managing editor before this volume was prepared for the press, but we appreciate her participation in early stages of planning. Ms. Mona Merideth, who now serves as editor in the Center, has been equally zealous and knowledgeable about the fine details of book production. She has assisted in the design of maps and charts as well as attended to editorial minutiae that would have escaped a less discerning eye. We are grateful to them all.

Dr. Claudia Mitchell-Kernan, for this volume as for the first, was the Academic Editor whose patience knew no bounds in its willingness to accommodate my idiosyncrasies. As a fellow anthropologist, she also made substantive suggestions that were very welcome. It was her faith in the project that made both volumes possible.

The following publishers are among those which have generously given permission to use quotations from copyrighted works: From Louis Auchincloss, *Motiveless Malignity.* Copyright ©1969 by Louis Auchincloss. Houghton Mifflin Company, 1969. Used by permission of the publishers. From Georges Balandier, *Daily Life in the Kingdom of the Kongo: From the Sixteenth to the Eighteenth Century,* Helen Weaver, trans. Pantheon Books, 1968. Used by permission of Georges Borchardt, Inc. From Henri Baudet, *Paradise on Earth: Some Thoughts on European Images of Non-European Man,* Elizabeth Wentholt, trans. Yale University Press, 1965. Used by permission of the publisher. From Roland Mushat Frye, *Shakespeare's Life and Times: A Pictorial Record.* Copyright ©1967 Princeton University Press; Princeton Paperback, 1975, section 35. Reprinted by permission of Princeton University Press. From Heliodorus, *An Ethiopian Romance,* Moses Hadas, trans. Copyright ©1957 The University of Michigan Press. Used by permission of the publisher. From Paul H. D. Kaplan, *The Rise of the Black Magus in Western Art.* Copyright ©1984 by Paul H. D. Kaplan with permission from UMI Research Press, Ann Arbor, Michigan. Excerpts from James Kritzeck, ed., *Anthology of Islamic Literature.* Copyright ©1964 by James Kritzeck. Reprinted by permission of Holt, Rinehart and Winston, Inc. From Bernard Lewis, *Race and Color in Islam.* Copyright ©1970, 1971 by Bernard Lewis. Used by permission of the author. From Fernando Ortiz, *Cuban Counterpoint: Tobacco and Sugar,* Harriet De Onís, trans. Copyright ©1947 Alfred A. Knopf, Inc. Reprinted by permission of Alfred A. Knopf. From Ruth Pike, *Aristocrats and Traders: Sevillian Society in the Sixteenth Century.* Copyright ©1972 by Cornell University. Used by permission of the publisher, Cornell University Press. From J. Spencer Trimingham, *A History of Islam in West Africa.* Copyright © 1962 by Oxford University Press. Used by permission of the publisher. From Charles Verlinden, *The Beginnings of Modern Colonization.* Copyright ©1970 by Cornell University.

4. BLACKNESS IN THE CHRISTIAN SYNTHESIS OF JUDAIC AND GRECO-ROMAN TRADITIONS

In volume 1 we described the destruction of the Egyptian city of Thebes by the Assyrians as the nadir of "Black Power." Seven hundred and thirty years after this climactic event involving the shrine city of Amon in Africa, the Romans captured Jerusalem and destroyed the Temple, the site of sacrifice to Jehovah. In the thirty-five years preceding that catastrophic event, a small millenarian Jewish sect based in Jerusalem was gradually transforming itself into a "world religion," Christianity.

During its first twenty-five or thirty years, the small Christian community had no sacred writings other than those that Christians refer to as the Old Testament of the Holy Bible. Much of this body of ethical philosophy, historical chronicles, songs, proverbs, and myths was now reinterpreted as prophetic of the coming of Jesus Christ, the Messiah.

But the Old Testament also contained books such as Leviticus and Deuteronomy, books that laid down precise laws for individual behavior and collective rituals that Jews were expected to observe. The members of the original Christian community in Jerusalem, most of them converted Jews, were divided by practical problems arising from this portion of their biblical legacy. As it has been recorded in the New Testament, the dispute was between the followers of Peter, an uneducated Jewish fisherman who had been a disciple of the founder, and Paul, a well-educated Jewish convert trained in both the Jewish law and Greek philosophy, a native of Tarsus, a city in Asia Minor.

Peter contended that it was necessary to become a member of the Jewish ethnic community before becoming a Christian. Men would have to be circumcised, and families would be required to keep the laws regarding clean and unclean foods. Paul insisted that "the law killeth." Baptism—not circumcision—was the initiation rite of the new religion, he argued, making each individual "a new person in Christ Jesus." One's status as Jew or Gentile, Greek or barbarian, was irrelevant. Judaic ethical principles, but not the laws regulating the minute details of daily existence, were to be adopted. Paul won the

1

argument, and began a missionary crusade to convert non-Jewish pagans in Asia Minor, Rome, and several Greek cities. A number of letters to these churches are included in the New Testament.

This was a crucial moment in the development of Christianity. As a result, Judaic prophecy and ethics became merged with elements of Greek philosophy to form the first systematic Christian theology, what might be called the Pauline synthesis.

Following the destruction of the Temple, and especially after the subsequent defeat of the Jewish nation by Emperor Hadrian in A.D. 135, tens of thousands of Jews were sold into slavery in Egypt, North Africa, and elsewhere around the Mediterranean. With them went the seeds of the new religion. During the next century, the spiritual and intellectual home of Christianity shifted away from Jerusalem to the great Hellenistic intellectual center of Alexandria and to other North African cities. Paul had boasted of his knowledge of Judaism, of being a "Pharisee of the Pharisees." He displayed some acquaintance with Greek philosophy. Subsequent theologians were deeply influenced by the Hellenistic type of thought that was predominant in the academies of Alexandria, incorporating some Roman and Persian ideas with traditional Greek concepts.

During the same period, Jewish rabbinic scholars were establishing centers of learning in Judea and in a number of Mesopotamian cities. In these, folklore and legend, as well as Hebrew theological traditions that had not been included in the Old Testament (Greek Septuagint version), were being systematized and embodied in the Midrash, the Jerusalem Talmud and the Babylonian Talmud.[1] These were finally available in manuscripts by the fifth and sixth centuries A.D. The biblical tradition is a Palestinian tradition; the most influential Talmudic tradition is a product of the Jewish diaspora in Mesopotamia, where a culture far different from that of the Jewish homeland had developed. While the Old Testament was the principal Judaic component in the Christian intellectual heritage, some parts of the nonbiblical Jewish oral tradition may have had an indirect influence. The Palestine biblical tradition contained no pejorative references to Negroes. The nonbiblical Mesopotamian tradition did.

By the time the Talmudic manuscripts began to circulate beyond the boundaries of the Jewish communities, however, Christian conceptions of blackness and black people had become established. These were based upon biblical stories and attitudes, Greek and Roman classical literature, and first-hand experiences with Blacks, both pagan and Christian.

For the next three centuries, the Church Fathers—St. Augustine,

Origen, Jerome, Tertullian, and other Christian scholars—continued the process of interpreting the Old Testament and merging it with elements of Greco-Roman philosophy to reinforce the teachings of the Apostles. Sharp and acrimonious debates occurred periodically, and polemical writing flowed forth continuously. Alexandria, Antioch, and Rome became cities where debates about Christian belief and practice were carried on and scholarly work in church history and theology was produced.

The initial Christian goal had been to create communities in which considerations of race and ethnicity would be subordinated within a universal fellowship of believers. However, by the middle of the fifth century A.D., St. Augustine was verbalizing a philosophy that provided some room for color prejudice to be expressed while still retaining the universalist ideal. By the time the Christian church, having become the official state religion of the Roman Empire, launched a missionary crusade south into Ethiopia, the skin color of the pagans there had become a symbol of what was defined as their sinfulness.

This chapter first describes the legacy of attitudes about black people and blackness that was available to Christianity from the Judaic and Greco-Roman traditions. It examines how this legacy was incorporated into Christian faith, practice, and intellectual activity. Finally, it studies the other ideological and social factors surrounding the developing Church in an effort to discover how color prejudice took root in what had begun on a virtually prejudice-free foundation.

BLACKNESS AND THE OLD TESTAMENT LEGACY

Genesis contains origin myths that Hebrew priests, scribes, and prophets had selected from numerous legends common among people of the Near East. Transformed during many centuries in the Hebrew oral tradition, these stories were finally set down in writing by priests between 450 B.C. and 300 B.C. According to the canonical Hebrew story, all human beings are descended from a single ancestral pair, Adam and Eve, whom Jehovah and his angels created out of "the dust of the earth." They lived in the Garden of Eden where several rivers had their source; one was said to be the Euphrates and another, which "compasseth the whole land of Ethiopia," was presumably the Nile.[2]

The Old Testament also contains the story of the Fall, which was necessary for understanding the doctrine of Original Sin and the divine plan for Redemption; the account of the Flood that destroyed sinful mankind and a rainbow promise that it would never be repeated; and the tragedy of Sodom and Gomorrah, guilty of homosexuality, which were wiped out by fire and brimstone, a prototype of the final punishment of the sinful world. All of Jewish history up to the conquest of Judea by the Romans was present here to be studied and invested with symbolic significance: the enslavement in Egypt, the Exodus led by Moses, the national tragedy that befell both Israel and Judah, experiences in Judean and in Mesopotamian exile under Babylonians and Assyrians, and the Messianic Promise.

From its belief that all races had common parents, and through a history that makes frequent references to black individuals and black nations, the Old Testament transmits a legacy that, while not color blind, does not denigrate Negroes.

After a brief examination of color symbolism in the Old Testament, we shall turn to what the Bible tells us about attitudes among the Jews of Palestine toward black nations and black people. Finally, we will examine the Old Testament story that purports to explain the origins of the world's diverse peoples, a story that later generations would revise as they sought justifications for racial slavery.

We must begin with the caution that the Old Testament represents the views of a literate class among the Palestinian Jews. An oral tradition that was turned into written documents at a later date in the Mesopotamian diaspora will be examined separately. Of course, some concepts and attitudes among the common people may have escaped all recorded histories and legends, and thus are lost to us.

Color Symbolism in the Bible

As we pointed out in volume 1, some scholars have argued that people universally make negative associations with the color black and "blackness." Prominent among these were social psychologist Kenneth J. Gergen and Pulitzer prize-winning historian Carl Degler. They believed that negative associations with blackness are probably translated into a *universal* color prejudice against dark-skinned people. The Old Testament offers us some evidence to the contrary.

The word "black" is occasionally used to refer to depressed psychological states and to mourning attire, but there is no consistent presentation of white and black as polar opposites in the Old Testament.[3] Much of the discussion about the presence of such a contrast in biblical symbolism fails to distinguish between color— black and white—and brightness—light and dark. The former deals with *hue*; the latter with *degree of brightness*.[4]

Of the twenty-one instances where the words black, blacker, or blackness appear in the Bible, only six refer to people, and then not to race but to a mood, such as gloom. Twelve references—slightly more than half—might be termed negative. White is used far more frequently, a total of sixty-nine times. It rarely refers to skin color, and when it does the connotation is negative: white is used to designate leprosy.[5] Twenty-eight of the references to white are negative, compared to ten that are neutral. Of thirty-one positive mentions, many refer to white garments as a symbol of cleanliness and purity.[6]

Blackness is seldom used as a symbol of sin and evil. In fact, one Prophet is quoted as saying, "Though your sins be as *scarlet* they shall be white as snow."[7]

Black Nations in Jewish History

The people whom the Greeks named "Ethiopians," or "people with burnt faces," were actors in the great drama of Jewish history as it unfolds in the Old Testament. The Jewish people called them "Cushites." There is a clue that the Jewish people recognized a difference in complexion between these people and themselves in Jeremiah's rhetorical question, "Can the Ethiopian [i.e., Cushite] change his skin? Can the leopard change his spots?"[8] The Old Testament makes no other reference to the color of the Ethiopians' skin or to that of the Egyptians, pejorative or otherwise. And there is nothing pejorative about Jeremiah's query itself, but only the recognition of a sharp contrast in skin color. The overall message about race and color in the Old Testament is that the Jews recognized a striking physical difference between themselves and Ethiopians, but atttributed no social salience to the fact.

It is significant that the compilers of the Old Testament did not record the existence of any color-conscious attitudes of hostility or revulsion toward Egyptians and Ethiopians that might have arisen when soldiers from these areas invaded the kingdoms of Israel and Judah, as they frequently did.

One of the first and most brutal invasions was led by Shoshonk, who sacked the Temple after Solomon's death. According to the biblical record, his army included Libyans and Ethiopians, as well as Egyptians. Following this defeat, while King Asa and his people were fortifying the cities of Judah, it is reported that "there came out against them, Zerah, the Ethiopian with a host of a thousand thousand and three hundred chariots . . . the Lord smote the Ethiopian before Asa and before Judah; and the Ethiopians fled . . . They were destroyed before the Lord and before his host." The army of

Judah had evened the score for its defeat at the hands of Shoshonk. As the compilers of Chronicles tell the story, neither the Lord of Hosts nor his victorious Chosen People expressed antipathy toward the defeated foes by ridiculing their physical appearance. There was no display of color prejudice or Negrophobia. The rejoicing was of the same character as that voiced when Philistines fell or when Amalekites and Jebusites were defeated in battle.[9]

If there were popular expressions, in the oral tradition, of dislike or disgust for Ethiopians—and particularly for Ethiopian military leaders and their soldiers—they were not integrated into Old Testament accounts of relations between the Hebrews and the Africans.

To the Jewish leaders caught between the rampaging military powers of Babylon and Assyria to the north and east and Egypt and Ethiopia to the south, this question became urgent: "With which powers, if any, should alliances be made?" The biblical accounts of these events reveal a deep rift between what might be called the "African faction" and the "Mesopotamian faction" among the kings' advisers in both Israel and Judah. The version of the dispute that has been handed down in the biblical books of Jeremiah, Ezekiel, Isaiah, and other Prophets has an "I told you so" tone, expressed by the pro-Mesopotamians after a series of disastrous events. The African faction at the courts had pressed constantly for alliances with black and brown neighboring peoples to resist the Mesopotamian invaders and was willing to trust Egyptian/Ethiopian promises of aid. The Prophets warned repeatedly against such alliances and against trusting Egypt. To see this struggle through the eyes of the Prophets is to emphasize the manner in which the ancient Jews launched their criticisms on religious grounds and kept them free from derogatory remarks about race and color. This absence of anti-Negro attitudes was part of the Old Testament legacy handed on to the Christian sect.

For instance, Ezekiel, in prophesying doom for Egypt during Judah's alliance with the Ethiopian dynasty, had been particularly abusive. But there were no references to race or color. He claimed that Jehovah said to him in a vision:

> Son of man, set thy face against Pharaoh, king of Egypt and prophesy against him, and against all Egypt. Speak and say . . . Pharaoh king of Egypt, the great dragon that lieth in the midst of his rivers . . . I will put hooks in thy jaws. . . . I will bring thee up out of the midst of thy rivers. . . . I have given thee for meat to the beasts of the field and to the fowls of the heaven.[10]

The reference was to Taharka of the XXVth Dynasty, whose sculptural likenesses, as noted in Chapter 3, are manifestly Negro. There is no evidence, however, of the prophet having any *racial* animus against him in the strictures, and the king was cooperating with him.

The African faction in Judah, the southern kingdom, had been strengthened when the Assyrians "came down like a wolf on the fold" and besieged Jerusalem. Taharka (the Tirhakah of the King James version of the Bible) marched against the Assyrians and temporarily defeated them, while his allies in Judah were aided by some mysterious disease or other disaster that struck the Assyrian forces and caused them to withdraw from the siege of Jerusalem. But Sennacharib, the Assyrian king, had previously warned King Hezekiah of Judah not to form an alliance against him, saying, "Lo, thou trusteth in the staff of this broken reed, on Egypt, whereon if a man lean, it will go into his hand and pierce it. So is the [Ethiopian] Pharaoh, King of Egypt, to all that trust him."[11]

But the king of Judah chose the African alliance. The Assyrians then invaded, looting, burning, and taking captives. They proceeded to strike southward into Egypt, moving swiftly up the Nile where they sacked and burned Thebes, the city called No by the Hebrews. One of the minor Prophets, Nahum, reflecting on the fall of Thebes, predicted that one day Nineveh, capital of Assyria, would share a similar fate:

> Art thou better than populous No [Thebes] that was situate among the rivers, that had the waters round about it, whose rampart was the sea, and her wall was from the sea? Ethiopia and Egypt were her strength, and it was infinite; Put and Lubim [other African peoples] were thy helpers. . . . Yet was she carried away. She went into captivity: her young children also were dashed in pieces at the top of all the streets; and they cast lots for her honorable men, and all her great men were bound in chains. . . . O King of Assyria, thy nobles shall dwell in the dust.[12]

The biblical document attributed to Jeremiah, like the one said to be Ezekiel's, prophesied that Jehovah would use the Babylonians to punish the Egyptians and the Assyrians for their manifold iniquities. Any alliance of Judah with Egypt would thus be considered interference in God's plan. According to Jeremiah,

> Pharaoh, King of Egypt is but a noise; hath passed the time appointed. . . . Egypt is like a very fair heifer, but destruction cometh; it cometh out of the north. The Lord of Hosts, the God of Israel, saith: Behold I will punish the multitude of No [Thebes],

> Pharaoh and Egypt, with their gods and their kings; even Pharaoh
> and all that trust in him; And I will deliver them into the hands of
> those that seek their lives and into the hands of Nebuchadnezzar,
> king of Babylon.[13]

Eventually, when Babylon defeated Assyria, Judah was required to
pay tribute. Then, when King Joachim rebelled against Babylon in
597 B.C., the Babylonian king, Nebuchadnezzar, invaded Judah and
carried off a large group of upper-class people into slavery.

During the many years of dispute between Prophets and kings of
Israel and Judah over the advisability of African alliances, there were
no recorded imputations of inborn deficiencies of intellect to either
Egyptians or Ethiopians. When the Prophets assailed them, it was as
pagans whose acts were offensive to Jehovah, and whose influence
corrupted his Chosen People. Ezekiel, Isaiah, Jeremiah, and some of
the minor Prophets constantly assailed the inhabitants of Egypt for
being idolators, and, by implication, the Ethiopians also fell under
such condemnation. No exclusive association was made, however, between brown or black people and idolatry or lubricity
("whoredom"), a major target of prophetic wrath, nor were Egyptians
and Ethiopians considered the major embodiment of evil, perhaps
because the prime targets of prophetic wrath were nearer home—the
Semitic worshipers of Baal and Ashtaroth in Canaan. Thus evil
people, as presented in the Old Testament, were not exclusively
Egyptians and Ethiopians.[14]

There is no difference in tone or choice of words in the invective
hurled at the Africans and that used to castigate the rulers of
Babylon and Assyria. Jehovah was portrayed as determined to punish
the arrogance of the black rulers just as he was the overweening
ambition of the Mesopotamian rulers.

The prophecies attributed to Ezekiel were eloquent in their
prediction of doom for Assyria, Babylon, and Egypt. Jehovah would
destroy Egypt first, using Babylon for this purpose:

> I will set fire in Egypt. Sin [a Nile Valley city] shall have great pain
> and No [Thebes] shall be rent asunder. . . . I shall put my sword into
> one hand of the King of Babylon and he shall stretch it out upon the
> land of Egypt. And I will scatter the Egyptians among the nations.[15]

Ezekiel is depicted prophesying a similar fate for his own people, by
that same sword. But both would be rescued eventually, restoring
the Chosen People to eminence. As for Egypt:

> Yet, thus saith the Lord God, at the end of forty years I will gather
> the Egyptians from the people whither they were scattered . . . and

will cause them to return. . . . They shall be there a base kingdom . . . for I will diminish them; they shall no more rule over the
nations.[16]

But this was not to last forever. Several generations of Afro-
American preachers have treasured a prediction in the Psalms that
promises a higher status for Egypt and includes in the "redemption"
another part of Africa: "Princes shall come out of Egypt and Ethiopia
shall soon stretch forth her hand unto God."[17] They thereby
developed a doctrine of hope—"Ethiopianism."

One of the minor Prophets, speaking of the days when Israel's
punishment would be over and the Jewish people would again be in
possession of their promised homeland, expresses Jehovah's love for
his people in words that have been considered enigmatic by some
scholars: "Are ye not as the children of the Ethiopians unto me,
Oh children of Israel? saith the Lord." Most African and Afro-
American Christians take the passage at face value and see in it an
expression of affection and compassion on the part of Jehovah for
Ethiopians as well as Jews. Some Jewish scholars advance a different
interpretation.[18]

The relations of Israel and Judah to Egypt and Ethiopia were, as we
have noted, suffused with tension because of the disagreement
between Prophets and kings over military strategies. But the
relationships also involved military cooperation from time to time,
even though that partnership was sometimes disastrous for the Jews.
These were relations between rulers who apparently respected each
other. The Old Testament accounts are free from pejorative comments based upon color prejudice. That Ethiopians and many
Egyptians were Negroid seems to have been accepted as one of the
facts of life during the period of the great power conflicts, like
variations among the fauna and flora. Attitudes, of course, may have
been otherwise at other times, and in other places, or among other
social strata during this period, but the equal-status contacts among
those in high places provide important empirical data in examining
theories of race relations which suggest that light-skinned people
always "look down upon" those with darker skin.

Black Individuals in the Old Testament

Antagonism toward the rulers of Egypt and Ethiopia on the part of
the Prophets found forceful expression from time to time, but it did
not include derogatory expressions about their color or physiognomy.

The names of a few black military leaders appear in historical accounts in the Bible, designated sometimes as Ethiopians and sometimes not. These are matter-of-fact accounts of successes or failures in battle, unaccompanied by blasts of prophetic wrath. In all of the cases—historic allusions and prophecies—ethnic origin is mentioned, but no adjectives are employed to describe the color of the actors' skins. The few individual Ethiopians mentioned as living in Judah and Israel are not identified by direct allusion to skin color. The absence of references to skin color and Negro features is significant if compared with certain statements in the Hindu sacred Vedic literature.[19] The comparison of the two sacred scriptures highlights the difference between a situation in which black people were military allies and one in which they were a conquered enemy.

One Ethiopian living in Judah during these critical times became a symbol of piety and loyalty to the Jewish people. The figure of Ebed-melech is etched sharply in the biblical record and is the subject of much comment in the Talmud. He was an influential eunuch at the court of King Zedekiah. When the enemies of the Prophet Jeremiah had him thrown into a dungeon, Ebed-melech interceded with the king on his behalf. The Ethiopian received permission to remove Jeremiah from the pit, and the Prophet promised Ebed-melech that when the day of doom arrived for Jerusalem, he would not be enslaved. Some rabbis considered Ebed-melech to be one of the nine persons who were given the honor of being transported to Paradise without having to die. Among the others was the Prophet Elijah, who was taken up into the heavens in a chariot. Some contemporary cynics see sinister significance in the fact that it was a black eunuch who was so highly regarded. But that Ebed-melech was a eunuch and not a virile warrior may not have had the invidious implications in ancient Judah that it would have in modern Europe or America.[20]

Moses and the Ethiopian Wife

In our discussion of Egypt, we summarized the biblical account of how the Jewish people happened to go there and eventually become enslaved, and of their Exodus under the leadership of Moses, who became both culture hero and legendary law giver to the Hebrew nation. This story became an integral part of the Christian heritage, prized for its value as an allegory and for didactic moral instruction. Out of the Exodus experience came the Ten Commandments, and a lesson for all was present in the punishment given to Moses for impatience and for losing his temper. He saw the Promised Land only from afar. Jehovah did not permit him to enter.

Nothing in the Old Testament account suggests that the exile in Egypt would have given the Jews any reason either to look down on people darker than themselves nor to attribute any kind of cognitive deficit to them.[21] They may have hated the Egyptians as oppressors, and they very likely preferred their own somatic norm image and harbored esthetic prejudices. However, it is very unlikely that they had the type of attitudes and behavior toward Egyptians that we call "racist."

However, there are some troubling implications to the story of Moses' marriage to an Ethiopian woman. In the Old Testament account, Miriam, along with her brother Aaron, a high priest, are portrayed as "speaking against" their brother Moses because he had married a Cushite woman.[22] The biblical story implies divine approval of the marriage: Miriam is punished with leprosy for her criticism. But it gives no reason for the opposition, other than that the woman was an Ethiopian. An inquiry such as ours would like to know whether Miriam and Aaron objected to her because she was a foreigner or because she was black. Miriam's reputed reaction could be linked to ethnocentrism, rather than racial or antiblack prejudice. Contradictory forces have often coexisted in ancient Jewish history: on the one hand, group exclusivism verging on chauvinism, and on the other, absorption and assimilation of outsiders through intermarriage.

A study of the Hebrew sacred literature at various periods reveals shifts in social attitudes over the centuries, including attitudes toward non-Jewish ethnic groups. The first scriptural canon took form during a period of national recovery from the trauma of Babylonian captivity. The "remnant" that returned to Jerusalem tried to rebuild national consciousness by stressing the preservation of the traditions of the Chosen People: e.g., taboos on intermarriage and warnings against fraternization with surrounding peoples, who worshipped idols and whose rituals introduced sexuality into the heart of religious ceremonies. Such behavior was defined as an "abomination" by both priests and Prophets. Yet not only did ordinary members of the Jewish community have a tendency to participate in the worship of fertility gods "in the high places" (the shrines in the mountains), but some prominent individuals, including kings, actually built shrines to the gods of foreign wives and concubines. Thus, holding the line against intermarriage with foreign women became a cardinal value at certain periods in Jewish history.

In general, it was not intermarriage per se that was opposed from time to time, but intermarriage that was thought to bring more harm than potential benefit to the Hebrews. The high visibility of black people made them potentially vulnerable when ethnocentric feeling ran high; but in only one instance, the case of the marriage of Moses, is a black person (or group) specifically designated as a target in the legends. In this case it is not clear whether calling the woman an Ethiopian was merely an identifying label for a member of an out-group or a statement of objection to her because she was black. Evidence against a finding of antiblack prejudice may be seen in the fact that the memory of Ebed-melech was carefully preserved. He had rescued the prophet Jeremiah from a life-threatening situation by an appeal to King Zedekiah. Admittedly, being a eunuch, this Ethiopian could not have been a threat to a policy against intermarriage, but his reputed position of trust at the court of King Zedekiah indicates that blackness itself was no barrier to confidence and respect in the kingdom of Judah either at the time when the story was recounted or later.

The Girl in the Song of Solomon

There is one other instance of possible skin color prejudice in the Old Testament. Like the story of Moses' Ethiopian wife, it involves man-woman relations and could conceivably reflect esthetic, erotic, or status-allocating appraisals.[23] Church Fathers, beginning with Origen in the latter part of the first Christian century, assumed that both cases indicated the existence of color prejudice against Ethiopians (i.e., Negroes) among the ancient Jews, and they used the cases for allegorical interpretations in their own writings.[24] But these Church Fathers may have been reading the values of their own period—the late Hellenistic—back into ancient Jewish history.

In the Song of Solomon (or Song of Songs) a peasant girl is competing with other women for the affections of the king. The possible implications of this encounter for the self-image of the dark woman were discussed in the previous volume. Most familiar to the English-speaking world is the King James version, which renders the incident in the Latin Vulgate translation from the Hebrew, made during the fifth century A.D.

> I am black, but comely, O ye daughters of Jerusalem, as the tents of Kedar, as the curtains of Solomon. Look not upon me, because I am

black, because the sun hath looked upon me; my mother's children were angry with me; they made me the keeper of the vineyards.[25]

We do not know when this song, which existed originally in the oral tradition, was first written down and became sacred instead of secular. It is significant, however, that the Septuagint translation into Greek from Hebrew, which was made earlier and which the Christians used during the first three centuries, read, "I am black *and* comely." Either way, however, the girl would be pointing to some esthetic or status "disability" connected with dark skin color. Some modern scholars have argued that the passage intends to point out only that darkness of skin comes from working outdoors, in contrast to the lighter skin of leisure-class women. From a modern reader's perspective, it is significant, not that the girl referred to her own dark skin color, but that she did not let it inhibit her from competing aggressively for the king's favor against those with fairer skins.

Noah and the Origin of Diverse Peoples

The diversity of nations and peoples is discussed in the story of Noah and his sons, Ham, Shem, and Japheth. Generations of rabbinic scholars combined facets of this story (and fanciful versions of it) with environmental theories to account for differences in skin color as well as ethnic temperament. The biblical version of the story of Noah and his sons says nothing about the color of Noah or his children and grandchildren.

As the Old Testament tells the story of Noah,[26] the descendants of Adam and Eve had become so wicked that Jehovah (God) decided to destroy them by a flood, allowing only Noah and his family to survive. From this righteous man a new group of men and women would be born. Noah and his family were allowed to survive the Deluge in the Ark, a boat prepared according to Jehovah's instructions. After forty days and forty nights of rain, the Ark was said to have landed on Mount Ararat (in what is Soviet Armenia today). Sometime after their landfall, God allocated various portions of the Earth to each of Noah's three sons, Ham, Shem, and Japheth. These lands were subsequently inhabited by their descendants.

The Table of Nations

The account in the Old Testament is sometimes referred to as the "Table of Nations" (see chart 3). Japheth's descendants, including the Greeks, lived north of the Mediterranean. Shem was father both to the Jews and to the Assyrians and Persians who would at times

CHART 3. TABLE OF NATIONS: BIBLICAL VERSION

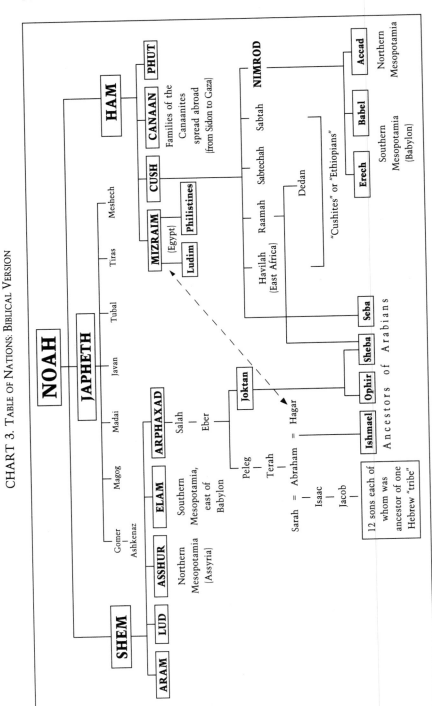

[NOTE: One non-biblical tradition places Cush as a *son* of Canaan. Hagar's Egyptian ancestry is the basis of an Arabian claim to a connection with Egypt.]

conquer them. Ham's sons settled other parts of Arabia and Mesopotamia, along with North Africa and East Africa. Ham's son Cush gave birth to the people who would later be called Ethiopians. Cush was also father of Nimrod, the progenitor of the Babylonians.

In setting up this line of ancestry, the writers of the Old Testament created what biblical scholars, even today, define as a puzzling contradiction: if the ancient Cushites were the same people whom the Greeks named "Ethiopians," why were the contemporary Babylonians then not Negroes? It is a question that Jewish historian Flavius Josephus may have been attempting to resolve when he put forward another version of the ancestral lineage in his *Antiquities of the Jews* (A.D. 93) (see chart 4).[27] The most striking differences between his Table and the biblical version appear in the lineage of Ham. Josephus makes Nimrod the progenitor of the Babylonians, as the biblical Table does, but he lists Nimrod as a brother of Cush, not as his son. Other apologists have used migration and miscegenation to explain why most of the ancient descendants of Cush were African and Negro, while others had the appearance of Arabs or ancient Sumerians.

CHART 4. TABLE OF NATIONS:
FROM FLAVIUS JOSEPHUS

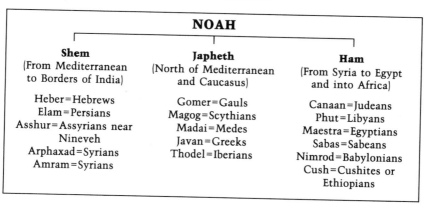

NOAH		
Shem (From Mediterranean to Borders of India)	**Japheth** (North of Mediterranean and Caucasus)	**Ham** (From Syria to Egypt and into Africa)
Heber=Hebrews Elam=Persians Asshur=Assyrians near Nineveh Arphaxad=Syrians Amram=Syrians	Gomer=Gauls Magog=Scythians Madai=Medes Javan=Greeks Thodel=Iberians	Canaan=Judeans Phut=Libyans Maestra=Egyptians Sabas=Sabeans Nimrod=Babylonians Cush=Cushites or Ethiopians

The apparent anomaly in the biblical "Table of Nations" was a matter for heated debate among abolitionists and defenders of slavery in North America during the nineteenth century. It is of some relevance today to the claims of those black vindicationists who use biblical support for their contention that the founders of the Mesopotamian civilizations were black, i.e., that Cush *was* the father of Nimrod, a legendary figure who has generated numerous legends over many centuries.[28] Until recently, linguists have classified the languages of Europe, the Middle East and northern Africa under the rubrics Semitic, Hamitic, and Japhetic, despite the fact that neither version of the Table of the Nations coincides with data supplied by physical anthropologists and culture historians. And the Table also excludes many societies that we, unlike Josephus, know existed contemporaneously with the ancient Hebrews.[29]

As the tale is told in the Bible, the classification of nations according to the sons of Noah reveals the ethnocentrism of the Hebrew people among whom it originated. They classified themselves as descendants of Noah's son Shem. Much of the Old Testament revolves around their claim to the area bounded by Syria to the north, Egypt to the south, the Mediterranean Sea to the west, and the Arabian Desert to the east. Also living in this area were the Canaanites, whom the Old Testament places in the line of Ham. According to Hebrew tradition, the Canaanites were heathen peoples who seized their land while the sons of Abraham were in Egypt. Upon their return, the Hebrews fought the Canaanites to reestablish their claim. Descendants of Ham through his son Canaan were said to have lost their right to the land through a curse laid upon them by Noah, the father of Ham, described in the Old Testament. Their expulsion or subordination could thus be seen as being in accord with God's will.[30]

The Curse of Noah

In the biblical story, Noah becomes drunk with wine made from grapes he planted in a vineyard after spending forty days and nights in the Ark. The King James version of the Bible states that Ham "saw the nakedness of his father," who was lying uncovered within his tent. Ham told Shem and Japheth, his brothers, what he had seen. They showed respect for their father and "took a garment and laid it upon both their shoulders and went backwards and covered the nakedness of their father." When Noah was sober, he punished Ham for his act of filial disrespect by placing a curse on Canaan, his youngest son—not on Ham himself, nor on Misraim, Put, or Cush, his other sons:

> Cursed be Canaan, a servant of servants shall he be unto his brethren, but blessed be the Lord God of Shem, and Canaan shall be his servant.[31]

It is understandable why the Jewish people, in their origin myths, portrayed the sons of Canaan as cursed to be their servants, whereas no reference was made to any such curse being placed upon those of Ham's sons who were specified as progenitors of Libyans, Egyptians, Sabeans, Babylonians, and Ethiopians. This curse on Canaan "legitimized" the Hebrew claim to the land they fought for and took after the Exodus. Focusing the curse on Canaan exempted from condemnation potential black allies in the struggle against the Canaanites and other enemies.

The biblical story of Noah's curse aims it squarely at the enemies close at hand—the Canaanites, worshipers of Baal, with whom the followers of Jehovah engaged in warfare for centuries. One rabbinic justification for taking the land of the Canaanites simply said, "What the slaves have belongs to the master." Another rabbi argued that because the descendants of Canaan hated work and loved to spend their time sleeping, they did not deserve what they had. Their masters, the Jews, in contrast, were an enterprising people who deserved the land they occupied.[32]

Centuries later, some of the followers of Islam and Christianity, in an effort to substantiate a claim for exercising hegemony over Negroes and enslaving them, turned the myth of a Noaic curse to their advantage. The biblical version, it must be remembered, justified Canaanite slavery but not Negro slavery. In fact, the biblical account makes no mention of skin color or facial features. No version of the biblical story speaks of any such curse being laid upon anyone other than Canaan.[33] Nor is there any mention of dark skin color being the result of a curse by Noah. Christianity did not inherit any such tradition from the Bible. However, certain nonbiblical Judaic versions of the Noah and Ham story have been used from time to time to derogate Negroes, and by those seeking to justify the enslavement of Negroes.

BLACKNESS IN JEWISH FOLKLORE AND THE TALMUDS

The story of Noah and his sons is revised in Jewish tradition outside the Old Testament to make black skin a curse that was pronounced as a result of the breaking of various sexual taboos. Both the Babylonian Talmud and the Midrash include stories about black skin as a curse. The Jerusalem Talmud does not. Whether these stories are Midrashic creations of the Talmudic epoch (A.D. 500 to A.D. 600) or very old legends handed down outside of the biblical tradition has not yet been systematically addressed by the scholars. The Midrash and Talmuds were being compiled during the first four Christian centuries, a considerable time after the Old Testament was written down. The unanswered question is, "How old were these stories?"[34]

The folklore that went into the Midrash had been accumulating since remote antiquity and was transmitted orally. Between 30 B.C. and A.D. 210, the scribes began to systematize this material, classifying it in relation to books of the Bible. Thus we have a Midrash Rabbah Genesis, a Midrash Rabbah Exodus, and so on. Some collections were organized around individuals prominent in biblical history—a Tanhuma Noah, for instance. Other folklore, referred to as the Agadic or Haggadic element, was incorporated in the Jerusalem Talmud and the Babylonian Talmud, which also contained rabbinic commentary and Jewish law. During the sixth century A.D., after the Talmuds had been produced in written form, Midrash manuscripts began to appear.

All folklore was subject to rabbinic editing; older rabbinic comment was subject to editing by later rabbis. This complicates the problem of dating the material. An Irish biblical scholar, in discussing rabbinic commentary on all of the nonbiblical literature, makes some important remarks:

> While receiving its final redaction in the Christian era, much of it can be presumed to go back to pre-Christian times. A large element of uncertainty remains, nonetheless, with regard to the dating of any particular passage. *As we have it, it came from Judaism as reorganized or in the process of reorganization, after the fall of Jerusalem in A.D. 70. The rabbis cited as authorities, or as the source of individual interpretations, are almost entirely from this later period. The actual interpretation they give is doubtless very often much older than their own day. Still we would like some proof that such is the case. We shall see later that much of it probably depends on older tradition found in the Palestinian Targum to the Pentateuch.* Another difficulty with rabbinic material is that it is linked with the Jewish schools; it need not necessarily have been known to the masses of the Jewish people, or if it was, this was probably from sources other than the scholastic discussions in which we now find it [italics added].[35]

Of crucial interest to our inquiry is whether this derogatory material about black people was widely known among the Fathers of the new Christian religion. We will examine this subject at greater length later. Most significant is the fact that none of these stories, including the legends of black skin as a curse, are referred to in the writings of the Church Fathers.

Here we will study those curse legends in detail, and then survey the body of Midrashic literature, which stands in sharp contrast to the biblical tradition. The color black is invested with a wider range of negative attributes, and some very derogatory material about Ham and his descendants, not present in the Bible, is included. In this literature, descriptions of actual relations between Jews and Ethiopians do not include denigrating references.

These derogatory images of black people did not find their way into the Old Testament or into the Jerusalem Talmud being compiled by the scholars in the Judean academies; yet they did appear in the Mesopotamian compilation, the Babylonian Talmud. This suggests that the negative tradition may have evolved in Mesopotamia, where relations between Jews and black people were far different than in Palestine. We will conclude our discussion of nonbiblical Jewish traditions with an examination of this possibility.

Legends of Black Skin as a Curse

Stories about black skin being a curse on Ham, and through him on all (or some) of his descendants, are a ubiquitous part of the nonbiblical Jewish heritage. In some versions believed to be the earlier ones, such a curse is placed on Ham and all of his descendants, whereas in other versions it is placed only on his son Canaan, and thus presumably leaves Egyptians and Ethiopians—sons of Misraim and Cush—"untainted." They do not remain completely exempt, however, for one set of stories makes Cush the son of Canaan, not his brother!

In one story, Noah, the patriarch, sought sexual intercourse with his wife in her tent after he became drunk. Ham saw him enter. Some accounts say that Ham's son Canaan told him that Noah had entered the tent and that this information led to Ham's act of voyeurism. Other accounts charge Ham with trying to castrate his father when he saw Noah preparing to have intercourse with his wife, Ham's mother. In defense of such a drastic act of filial impiety, Ham said, "The first man had but two sons and one slew the other; this man, Noah, has three sons, yet he desires to beget a fourth beside." Ham then told the other sons that their father was trying to increase the number of progeny with whom they would have to share the inheritance. When Noah found out what Ham had done, he cursed him.[36]

The thought of castrating a naked, aged father and then shaming him in front of his other sons is only one of the Talmudic stories emphasizing Ham's aberrant sexuality. Taken as a whole the various stories and rabbinic comments link the curse laid on Ham and/or one or another of his descendants with the traditional priestly and prophetic horror expressed within Judaism over "licentiousness," the breaking of sexual taboos, and over sodomy, incest, and bestiality. In some versions of the story, Noah had placed a taboo on the act of sexual relations between any of the living things on the Ark, all of them in pairs. The taboo was purportedly broken by the dogs, the ravens, and one of the four pairs of human beings—Ham and his wife. (All of the animals that fornicated with each other were punished.)[37] One Talmudic interpreter gave sodomy, not the act of human connubial incontinence, as the taboo that was broken.[38] Blackness becomes a punishment for these sexual delinquencies in some rabbinic comments.

One view of the rabbinic discussion that has become familiar to the English-speaking world in the twentieth century[39] is in a passage from the Midrash Rabbah Genesis. It contains the opinions of six rabbis on the text "Cursed be Canaan" (Genesis 9:25). It was customary for individual rabbis to use folklore in their preaching and teaching, sometimes adding additional elements of their own. Also comments by the more prestigious rabbis found their way into the written record. This passage, which did not appear in written form until after the time of St. Augustine, that is, after the fifth century A.D., reads as follows:

> R. *Berekiah* said: Noah grieved very much in the Ark that he had no young son to wait on him, and declared, 'When I go out [of the Ark] I will beget a young son to do this for me.' But when Ham acted thus to him [i.e., castrated him], he exclaimed, 'You have prevented me from begetting a young son to serve me, therefore that man [your son] will be a servant to his brethren! R. *Huna* said in R. *Joseph's* name: [Noah declared], 'You have prevented me from begetting a fourth son, therefore I curse your fourth son.' R. *Huna* also said in R. *Joseph's* name: You have prevented me from doing something in the dark [i.e., cohabitation], therefore your seed will be ugly and dark-skinned. R. *Hiyya* said: Ham and the dog copulated in the Ark, therefore Ham came forth black-skinned while the dog publicly exposes its copulation. R. *Levy* said: This may be compared to one

who minted his own coinage in the very palace of the king, where-upon the king ordered: I decree that his effigy be defaced and his coinage cancelled. Similarly, Ham and the dog copulated in the Ark and were punished [italics added].⁴⁰

It is significant that Rabbi Huna's comment, in some versions, simply mentions "ugly" and omits "dark-skinned." In any serious study of this passage, an attempt to date the rabbinic comments would be important, as well as a statement of the earliest date at which this Midrash Rabbah Genesis passage began to circulate in its entirety.

A popularized version of this passage was published in New York in 1968 by a Jewish organization, with a citation to Genesis Rabbah:

> The sexes of both man and the lower animals were meant to be separated in the ark during the deluge. . . . Ham among the human beings, and the dog among the lower animals, disregarded this injunction and did not separate from the opposite sex in the ark. The dog received a certain punishment, and Ham became a black man; just as when a man has the audacity to coin the king's currency in the king's own palace his face is blackened as a punishment and his issue is declared counterfeit.⁴¹

A passage from a Midrashic source describes a curse pronounced by Noah on Ham's son, Canaan, rather than on Ham himself. It was said to have made Canaan extremely ugly, to have changed his facial features and hair. But the story does not mention a change in skin color. It is significant of the vicissitudes of the story that some editors have added blackening of the skin in order to "round out" or complete what they interpret as the intention of the compilers of the Midrash to provide a total facial configuration. They have been sharply criticized by Professor Ephraim Isaac, a Jewish scholar of color (a former Harvard faculty member now at Princeton), for making such an addition.⁴² One widely quoted version of that passage, as translated in the United States by social worker Henrietta Szold and anthropologist Paul Radin and presented in the 1966 edition of Louis Ginzberg's *Legends of the Bible*, does not mention skin color and specifies that the curse passed through Canaan, not through Cush, the generally agreed-upon ancestor of the Blacks. It does not include blackening of the face as part of the curse:

> The descendants of Ham through Canaan therefore have red eyes, because Ham looked upon the nakedness of his father; they have misshapen lips because Ham spoke with his lips to his brothers about the unseemly condition of his father; they have twisted curly

hair because Ham turned and twisted his head round to see the nakedness of his father; and they go naked because Ham did not cover the nakedness of his father.[43]

Was this version edited to avoid Afro-American criticism? Or was a reference to skin color absent from the earliest version? If the Ginzberg version was edited in deference to Afro-American sensibilities, another version of this same story, published two years earlier, in 1964, by anthropologist Raphael Patai (with Robert Graves) showed no such concern. Unlike Paul Radin and Henrietta Szold, neither Patai nor Graves had any sustained relations with black Americans. Using the same Hebrew sources, Patai presents Noah as saying to Ham:

> "Canaan's children shall be born ugly and black! Moreover, because you twisted your head around to see my nakedness, your grandchildren's hair shall be twisted into kinks, and their eyes red; again, because your lips jested at my misfortune, theirs shall swell; and because you neglected my nakedness, they shall go naked, and their male members shall be shamefully elongated." Men of this race are called Negroes; their forefather Canaan commanded them to love theft and fornication, to be banded together in hatred of their masters and never to tell the truth.

A sentence is inserted, "Men of this race are called Negroes," which, as Isaac points out, did not appear in any of the original sources.[44]

It should be emphasized that reference to blackness as a curse in the Babylonian Talmud is only a minor matter for comment among very extensive rabbinic discussions on Noah and Ham. The most prevalent versions of the story, including the one that appears in the Old Testament, associate slavery with Canaan; the black-skin-as-curse myth is not mentioned at all.

The curse legends were used in rabbinic teaching for several purposes. One was as explanatory myth. They supply answers to why certain things are as they are. Why do dogs sometimes show certain peculiarities in the way the copulate? Why do male ravens reputedly have certain sexual peculiarities? Why are black people black? At another level the legends are allegorical, and the Talmud is full of statements that point out morals concerning drunkenness and sexual misconduct, and suggest parallels between the behavior of Noah and his sons and the behavior of God's Chosen People. It seems obvious, however, that the curse-of-blackness story is serving as more than an explanatory myth or allegory. It is also being used to confirm a stereotype, defining black people as unable to control their sexual impulses. In one version of the punishment, Ham's foreskin becomes elongated! In this complex of stories about Ham, we see an early form of the stereotype of Negro supersexuality that remained ubiquitous and tenacious in the Middle East and was transmitted to Mediterranean and European cultures.

The black-skin-as-curse version of the Ham story is relevant to our inquiry because of its use in varied socioeconomic contexts, widely separated in time and space, either to explain the dark skin color of black people or to justify exploitation of them, or to serve both functions. The explanatory function was dominant among whatever group of rabbis or early Church Fathers, if any, knew about and believed the story. However, it was not of any great importance in Christendom for either use until the sixteenth century.

Nonbiblical References to Blacks and Blackness

Evil in the Line of Cush

One Talmudic passage speaks of evil as manifest in the line of Cush, transmitted not because of Noah's curse, but because of paternal favoritism extending over two generations. As the story goes, Adam's legacy included a coat made of skins that passed through the ancestral line to Noah, who hid it on the Ark. Ham's sins began when he stole the coat from his father during the forty days on the Ark. He gave the coat to Cush, who gave it to Nimrod, a son conceived in his old age. The coat gave "strength and might; might as a hunter in the fields, and might as a warrior in the subjection of his enemies and opponents" to Nimrod, who is reputed to be the founder of the Mesopotamian city-states. Thus, "his wars and undertakings prospered until he became the king over all the earth . . . and at that time all the people of the earth were of one language and one speech."

Nimrod is a symbol of rebellion in all of the many Hebrew legends about him. According to one, he built a large walled town named Shinar, between the Tigris and Euphrates rivers, but "his prosperity did not regard the Lord." It is recorded that "he made gods of wood and stone and the people copied after his doings." Eventually all of the descendants of Ham, including the children of Canaan as well as Cush, joined under Nimrod in battle with the descendants of Japheth. Nimrod's forces decided to "build a city and also in its midst a tall tower for a stronghold which shall reach even to the heavens." They eventually decided to use the tower to "scale the heavens" and make war with God. So God said, "We will confuse their language."

Amid the confusion caused by the sudden diversity of tongues, the work ceased and the descendants of Ham began to fight each other. God punished them further, and those who were most rebellious "were changed in appearance and became like apes." One version of the story states that not only the most rebellious but all of those who were involved in building the Tower of Babel "became like apes."[45]

This story is the nonbiblical version of the Tower of Babel legend and functions as an explanatory myth for the diversity of languages in the world. It claims nothing about the origin of differences in skin color. The reference to some people being made to look like apes may, however, be a pejorative allusion to some unnamed ethnic group, probably sub-Saharan Africans who may have been popularly stereotyped as having a simian look.

Though most of the stories about Nimrod are negative, at least one represents an alternative view. In this nonbiblical legend, the survivors of the Deluge clung to mountain areas because they were afraid of another flood. It was only Nimrod who had the courage to come down into the plains of Shinar and to build cities. Some students feel that this is a Hamitic version of the Noah story, developed by agricultural peoples, and that the nomadic pastoral Semites developed the stories that depict Nimrod as a malevolent person rather than a hero. Relevant to our inquiry is the fact that both versions depict Nimrod as a descendant of Ham and therefore presumably "dark-skinned."

Blackness in the Midrash

Although the biblical tradition contains no consistent black vs. white symbolic contrasts, blackness, as we have mentioned, was often associated with death or sorrow. There was no evidence in the scriptural references that this symbolic contrast was "carried over" to the skin color of human beings. Midrashic literature does, however, contain some rabbinic elaborations that emphasize negative associations with black and blackness.[46] For instance, the Midrash on the Song of Songs contains a long section, with no attribution to specific rabbis, presenting comments on the passage, "I am black but comely," that illustrate rabbinic methods of interpretation as well as a generalized negative feeling about blackness. One set of comments stresses contradictions within the Jewish ethnic group's experiences:

(a) The Hebrews fleeing Egypt were blocked by the Red Sea because they were rebellious and this constituted a "black" experience, but their loyalty to God, at the same time, made them "comely."

(b) Moses was "black" at Marah when the thirsty people murmured against him, but he became "comely" when God provided sweet water for the people through a miracle.

(c) Moses was "black" at Shittim when "the people began to commit harlotry with the daughters of Moab," but he became "comely" in spirit when they were punished for it.

(d) Jehovah was made "black" through the behavior of the people of Israel (the northern kingdom that was destroyed by the Assyrians and its people exiled), but "comely" through the behavior of the people of Judah (the southern kingdom in which Jerusalem was located).

Significantly, the rabbis who are named are totally unconcerned with the actual color of the woman in love with Solomon, or even with the historicity of the event. The story serves, rather, as a parabolic or allegorical teaching device, a springboard for dispensing words of wisdom. Rabbi Joshua ben Levi commented that the passage applied to King Ahab, who was "black" when he was a sinner but became "comely" when he repented. This bit of exegesis comes closest to that of the Church Fathers, who later equated blackness with sin that could be washed away. However, it did not assume that Ahab was black in body color. Rabbi Levi ben Raytha commented that the passage meant Jews were "black" all the days of the week but were "comely" on the Sabbath, "black" all the days of the year but "comely" on the Day of Atonement, "black" in this world but "comely" in the world to come. In whatever manner the passage was interpreted, "black" was surely something thought to be undesirable.[47]

In discussing a reference to "the tents of Kedar" in the Song of Solomon, the Midrash Rabbah notes, "Just as the tents of Kedar, although from the outside they look ugly, black, and ragged, yet inside contain precious stones and pearls, so the disciples of the wise, although they look repulsive and swarthy in this world, yet have within them knowledge of the Pentateuch, the Scriptures, the Mishnah, the Midrash, Halachoth, Talmud, and Toseftas and Haggadah. . . . Also just as a curtain after becoming dirty can be washed, and can again become dirty and be washed, so although Israel are defiled with sin all the rest of the year, yet the Day of Atonement comes and makes atonement for them.'[48]

One somewhat labored Midrashic interpretation, in discussing the passage that asks, "Are ye not as the children of the Ethiopians unto me, O children of Israel?" (Amos 9:7), uses the same rationale as that used by some of the Church Fathers: when sinful, the Jewish people are "black" like the Ethiopians, but when they recognize their faults and repent, they are truly Children of Israel in Jehovah's sight. The contemporary editor of a 1966 edition of the Midrash has inserted an esthetic evaluation in a footnote explaining that " 'Children of Ethiopians' is understood as a synonym for persons lacking beauty." He thus adds a twentieth-century gloss on top of the rabbinic gloss, and both may be covering up the original meaning of the Song of Solomon!⁴⁹

Through a careful study, including his own translation of disputed Hebrew texts, Professor Isaac reports that some of the nonbiblical traditional Hebrew material invests blackness with positive associations, but that contemporary scholars ignore these passages in discussing Midrashic sources. He writes:

> What really impressed the rabbis about Cush's blackness was rather its distinctiveness. Canaan's dark complexion, which was not unlike that of the Israelites, was said to be ugly; *Cush's blackness, on the other hand, which was deep and distinguished, had no such stigma attached to it. To the contrary Cush's blackness in its distinctiveness is associated with beauty and purity of heart and good character.* Thus Moses' wife, who was a Cushite woman, was so-called because her actions were as distinctive as her beauty. King Solomon had two Cushite scribes who were very beautiful; at their death, Solomon thought that the beauty of these two Cushites affected even the angel of death who felt sorry that he had to take their lives . . . It is interesting to note that in some Jewish sources both the children of Shem (including the Israelites) and the children of Ham were described as black; the first as "black and beautiful," the latter as black like a raven [italics added].⁵⁰

Professor Isaac points out that at least one source specifically refers to the ancestors of the Jews as black, and this leads him to suspect that a nonbiblical passage referring to a curse that turned Canaan "black and ugly" has been tampered with, the world *black* being added at a later period. His assumption is that the above-quoted passages attributing beauty to blackness may come from a very early layer of folklore.

Eldad-ha-Dani and Stories About Africans

Most of the Talmudic and Midrashic legends that deal with Blacks

are probably a product of exiled Jews living in the Mesopotamian
diaspora. One of these legends tells of Alexander the Great, "with all
his host," invading the land of Kush with three hundred ships.[51] This
is a reference to an event that occurred some time after the deportation of Palestinian Jews to Assyria and Babylon. Kush is defined as a
"country that is near the ten tribes," meaning the Jewish people from
the kingdom of Israel who had been exiled to Mesopotamia. According to the legends, long before Alexander left for Kush, some intrepid
Jews had gone there.

One story tells of Eldad-ha-Dani, "a nobleman of the tribe of Dan,"
who tells "all the Children of Israel who are dispersed in Exile" about
some of the tribes who had found their way to Africa after a dispute
with other Jews in Israel, prior to the exile by the Assyrians. He said
that when he and a fellow Jew from the tribe of Asher went on a
trading expedition, a storm blew their boat ashore among a people
known as Rumrum. He described them as "tall black men of Kush
without any cloak or garment upon them, for they resemble beasts
and they eat humankind."[52] We are not told the location of this
shore, but the area specified matches descriptions of the East African
coast given by Romans and Persians through the eleventh century
A.D. However, these references do not speak of cannibalism among
the people. Eldad continued:

> When we came upon their land they seized us. They saw that my
> companion was healthy and fat and appetizing, so they slaughtered
> him and ate him up, but he cried, "Woe is me that I came to know
> these people and that the Kushim should eat my flesh."[53]

Eldad claimed that the African "Rumrum" put him in a fattening
pen but that he managed to avoid eating the food delivered to him
and so never gained enough weight to satisfy his captors. Eventually,
a group of people whom Eldad described as "fire worshipers"
(presumably Zoroastrians from Persia) attacked this part of Kush,
and he returned with them to Mesopotamia.

There were legends about other Danites, too, who lived permanently in Kush. One story states:

> Our rabbis tell us . . . the sons of Dan went up toward the River
> Kishon, riding their camels until they reached the river of Kush.
> There they found a fat, good, and spacious land, fields and vineyards,
> gardens and orchards. Nor did the inhabitants of the land prevent
> the Children of Israel from dwelling together with them but made an
> alliance with them.[54]

These camel-riding Hebrew nomads, confronting peaceful black people who were different from the uncivilized Rumrum, turned on them and managed to conquer them: "So the men of Kush used to pay them a tax and dwelt together with them for many years until they increased and multiplied exceedingly."[55]

The next passage describes marauding expeditions into East Africa:

> Then after the death of Sennacherib [the Assyrian ruler who attacked Jerusalem] three tribes of Israel journeyed to join them [i.e., the sons of Dan], these being Naphthali, Gad and Asher. They journeyed and camped until they reached the borders of the men of Dan, where *each of the tribes slew men of Kush for three months of the year and took the spoils for his own tribe* [italics added].[56]

If this legend has a kernel of truth, some breakaway tribes from Israel went to Africa where they began to harass Blacks who lived outside of the "civilized" portions of Egypt and Ethiopia, in a land rich in "gold and silver and precious stones and flocks and herds and camels and asses in exceedingly vast number."[57]

The black-skin-as-curse story could have been used ideologically to justify the raids of the Danites on the people of Kush. We have no way of knowing if the legend was actually used—or perhaps even created—for this purpose. But we have seen that the curse-on-Canaan story served a similar function for the Palestine Jews. Some rabbis quite explicitly state that justification for conquests explains why the biblical story has the curse being laid on Canaan rather than on Ham himself.[58]

Influence of the Mesopotamian Diaspora

If we examine the social functions of Jewish myths, it is important to note that the story of black skin as a curse was not dignified with a place in the Old Testament or the Jerusalem Talmud. It would have had no function in the Palestinian situation. But it does appear in the Babylonian Talmud, which was compiled in the Mesopotamian diaspora. It is possible that the curse story existed as a folktale in Palestine before the first exile of Jews to Mesopotamia in the eighth century B.C., or arose in Judea after the Babylonian captivity and was deliberately excluded from Jewish traditions as compiled in Palestine.[59]

I would advance an alternative hypothesis, suggesting that the black-skin-as-curse idea is a rabbinic construct reflecting interests and values of the literate and landed Jewish classes in the Mesopotamian diaspora, that it functioned as ideology as well as explanatory myth. This theory assumes that special conditions in Mesopotamia generated rabbinic stories associating Negroidness with excessive and aberrant sexuality and Noah's curse. Note that Mesopotamia was also the source of the stories about the alleged cannibals of Kush, a people whose description was far from the mainstream *biblical* image of black people—sometimes respected, sometimes honored.

The Hebrew people of the Mesopotamian diaspora inherited the biblical images of an Ethiopian woman married to their great hero, Moses; of Ebed-melech, the pious eunuch who aided the Prophet Jeremiah; and of Ethiopian soldiers who tried to help them resist Assyrian conquest. But the Jews of Mesopotamia encountered other types of Blacks in other roles and experienced other types of social relations likely to excite negative prejudices against Negroes. In the biblical story, Ham's son Canaan had been cursed; in these stories it is the sons of Cush. Were there conditions conducive to the emergence of a derogatory image of black people between the exile of Israel to Mesopotamia in 731 B.C. and the final editing of the Babylonian Talmud in A.D. 500, conditions that did not exist in Judea and that could have inspired rabbinic stories about a curse? There were some.

When the kingdom of Judah was conquered by the Babylonians, the exiled Jews were taken to the lands between the Tigris and Euphrates. Extensive irrigation works were necessary before this land could be farmed. The slaves who worked on these projects, in agriculture, and on the docks of Persian Gulf ports were black slaves from inner Africa, bought from settlers on the eastern coast. The Arabs who imported them from the coast of Africa called them Zanj, a word meaning "southerners" that assumed pejorative connotations. The Zanj were quite different in culture and reputation from the Ethiopians and Egyptians who were familiar to Palestine Jews. Later Arabic descriptions of them refer to facial scars, filed teeth, scanty clothing, and even cannibalism. They were easily stereotyped as "undesirables," and may have incited fear, dislike, or even contempt among the Jewish exiles.[60] The variable of wide cultural differences was present in this situation. It was absent in Palestine, or even in Egypt.

In addition to the cultural differences, there was, as time went on, a status differential, too, between Mesopotamian Jews and the masses of Africans with whom they were in contact. Some members of the Jewish community participated in the direct exploitation of

Zanj, and some Jews had a stake in maintaining slavery. They were not just supervisors of slave labor; eventually, they became slave owners and dealers in the slave trade. A diaspora Jewish culture, with values quite different from those in Palestine, developed.[61] Ethnic and racial evaluations were, inevitably, different. Denigration of black slaves was quite consistent with Mesopotamian Jewish social stratification.

It is possible that some of the more sensitive students of Torah and Oral Law in the Babylonian academies felt the need to dissolve the cognitive dissonance between Jewish precepts of justice and the behavior of some members of the Jewish community toward black people.[62] Certain strata among Mesopotamian Jewry could use a derogatory myth to "sanctify" their own privileged position in the social order. Conceivably some of the Noah/Ham stories reflect guilt as well as contempt. A certain amount of projected guilt seems to be present in the repeated statements that Ham was the progenitor of Nimrod, who introduced the enslavement of people throughout the area. In this version of events, most of the wickedness in Mesopotamia, including the building of the Tower of Babel, resulted from the acts of Ham's descendants and not from the assumed progenitors of either the Assyrians or Babylonians—Semitic groups who had enslaved the Jews. Enslavement of Blacks was, to some extent, interpreted as punishment for the sins of Cush and Nimrod.

Thus, it is possible and plausible, although as yet unproven, that the belief in black skin as a curse provided an ideology to justify the enslavement of the Zanj, although curiously the curse in Talmud and Midrash, unlike the biblical curse on Canaan, does not doom the sons of Ham to servitude. It only makes them a degraded variety of human being. This explanatory myth certainly assumed social significance in Europe, during the sixteenth century when it was used as an ideology to defend a system of *racial* slavery, a fact we shall discuss in Chapter 7.

In the meantime, it is important to recall that not all the images of Blacks in nonbiblical Jewish sources are negative.[63] It should also be noted that the amount of material in Midrashic sources that refers to Ham and Noah, Cush, Ethiopians, and similar subjects is quite small as compared with the amount dealing with other subjects. The biblical attitudes toward black people, not the Midrashic and Talmudic stories, were synthesized with Greco-Roman images and attitudes by early Church theologians.

THE CLASSICAL GREEK COMPONENT IN THE CHRISTIAN SYNTHESIS

The Apostle Paul, whose writings showed familiarity with pre-Talmudic Jewish thought, also displayed knowledge of Greek philosophy and religion.[64] Until the development of Christian educational institutions, all of the educated church leaders were men who had been socialized in the Greco-Roman tradition. In fact, after the first century, Christian congregations were made up largely of converted Gentiles, rather than converted Jews. As a result, Christianity was strongly influenced not only by the Judaic biblical tradition as presented in the Greek Septuagint translation of the Old Testament, but also by the Greco-Roman intellectual tradition. The Christian synthesis included some aspects of classical Greco-Roman attitudes toward blackness and black people, although these, like the Judaic traditions, would undergo extensive change during the first five centuries of Christian history. Some were expressed in the writings of the philosophers, others in poetry and drama.

Our survey of the Greco-Roman elements that may have been influential will move from the connotations of color in Greek poetry, through mythological and artistic depictions of black people, to what we know of actual interactions between Greco-Roman civilization and black nations and individuals. As we noted in our consideration of the biblical tradition, recorded history and folklore may not provide an adequate picture of relations among the unlettered, but, unfortunately, it is all we have. In considering the Greco-Roman legacy, we will reserve discussion of the Hellenistic culture in North Africa to place it in the context of the early Christian Church.

Blackness and Black People in Greek Literature and Art

Color Connotations in Greek Poetry

Alice Elizabeth Kober, in a doctoral dissertation at Columbia University in 1932, presents an analysis of color terms used by Greek poets from Homeric times to 146 B.C. according to "the type of object to which the word applied," these being specified as human beings, animals, plants, minerals, natural products, and natural phenomena. She also studied metaphorical usage. Words referring to the following colors were used by the poets: purple, violet, blue, green, white, black, dark, grey, yellow, and brown/smoky. All except the first four were applied to people. Forty-two years later, Eleanor

Irwin published *Color Terms in Greek Poetry*, confirming most of
Kober's earlier generalizations, contributing new insights, and
relating her research to recent trends in semiotics.

Both of these scholars are in agreement on one point that would
seem to support, in part, the Degler-Gergen views about negative
values assigned to blackness as a color, though not necessarily their
views about carry-over to black people. Kober and Irwin indicate that
the abstract symbol system of both Greeks and Romans tended to
invest blackness with undesirable characteristics. Kober notes that
"Evil and misfortune are very often characterized by *melas* [one of
the Greek words meaning "black"] . . . Not only death itself, but
everything associated with death and the dead is called *melas* . . . the
gods of the underworld . . . the abode of the dead . . . ghosts,
dreams . . . the silence of oblivion."[65] Irwin points out that "the
brightness of life and happiness were in sharp contrast to the
darkness not only of death but of sadness and gloom. . . . In Homer
we find pain described as 'dark' . . . grief as 'a dark cloud'. . . .
Oedipus' curse is dark.'[66]

*However, both analysts point out that positive associations with
blackness exist side by side with negative connotations, a fact that
seriously weakens the Degler-Gergen contention about the universality of negative associations with the color black.*

Kober notes that when it is used metaphorically, "'black' stands
for all that is terrible and fearful, but also for bravery."[67] Both she and
Irwin point out that men were being complimented when they were
referred to as "dark" or "black." To speak of them as "white" or "light
skinned" was to imply that they were effeminate or cowardly.

> The association of white with cowardice probably arises from the
> fact that the face becomes pale from fear, and also that a white skin
> is effeminate. Blackness of complexion on the other hand results
> from an outdoor life which brings out the masculine virtues of
> courage and strength, and also from hairiness, which the Greeks like
> most ancient peoples associated with manliness.[68]

Elaborating on the meanings associated with white, Kober noted
that sometimes white seems to carry the connotation of "beautiful"
or "lovely," and that this is because "a pale skin was so much
admired in women and in boys." But in addition to its negative
meanings when applied to men, white is "used also of the pallor due
to illness or to lack of exposure to the sun."

When used to refer to a person, and not in a metaphorical sense,
the Greeks usually chose the root word *melas* (which occurs in the

English word *melanin*) for "black." Kober writes that

> the adjective may refer to the actual blackness of the skin. . . .
> Usually, however, mere darkness of skin is meant. This may be a
> racial characteristic, as of the Egyptians . . . But more often it is
> used of individuals who are white naturally, but have been browned
> by the sun, or are of a darker complexion than others. . . . That this
> darkness was considered a sign of beauty in men is evident.[69]

How much "blackness" in a Greek man could be accepted as
handsome is not clear.

At times the "blackness" that referred to a dark Greek man was
distinguished from the "blackness" of men outside of the ethnic
group by calling the latter "Ethiops," or "those with burnt faces."
This designation was gradually restricted to people living in Africa
south of Egypt, but had formerly been applied to Egyptians and to
people in southern Persia and India as well. Yet some Greek poets
referred to "Ethiops" by the term *melas*, too. "Ethiopian" only
gradually became a synonym for "Negro."

Kober concludes that, on balance, "melanos is associated with
undesirable qualities." Irwin, however, questions such a sweeping
conclusion. Her study suggests that in the ancient pre-Homeric
cultures of Greece, words meaning dark may not have had any strong
pejorative associations at all.[70] Those gods who lived underground
were dark like the earth, whereas those who lived in the sky were
white or bright. Both were worshiped and cherished.[71] The Indo-
European invasions of Greece brought new religious concepts with
an emphasis on sky gods, as well as a new word for "black," or "dark,"
that had unsavory associations. Thus *melas* is related to the Hindu
Vedic word *mala*, which means dirt or smut. Some Greek words
related to *melas* mean to stain, sully, defile, or corrupt.[72] Semantic
changes continued to take place long after the initial Indo-European
invasions of Greece, between 1900 and 1600 B.C. The poets of the
Homeric age spoke of the "black-hearted" and the "black-livered" as
people to be praised. It was not until after the sixth century B.C. that
the dramatists drifted in the direction of current English usage and
spoke of the "black-hearted" as being evil.[73]

In summary, Eleanor Irwin's study suggests that in some Greek
literature, color codings were the reverse of those in the Indo-
European tradition generally and in our modern European and
American linguistic heritage particularly:

> When the poets were writing of the inner man, they regarded
> darkness as the normal state. It is difficult for us to equate good (or

normal) with blackness, because of the Judaeo-Christian influence in our background where, in matters of the heart, white is good and black evil. This association is supported by the figure of cleansing resulting in purity or whiteness and connections between blackness and dirt or sin. This view is foreign to the early Greeks; they thought of darkness as the normal state of the internal organs. . . . Whiteness of the internal organs was indicative of abnormality.[74]

It is reasonable to assume that the first generation of Christian theologians and prelates were aware of these Greek conceptions of blackness.

The Mythological Ethiopians

The Greek philosophers, poets, and dramatists of the Golden Age (fifth and fourth centuries B.C.) inherited a body of legends and folk tales that derived, in part, from the works of the poet Hesiod, who lived between 900 B.C. and 800 B.C., just before the great struggle between the Assyrians and the kings of Egypt and Ethiopia described in volume 1. Most treasured, however, were the tales told by Homer, to whom authorship of the *Illiad* and the *Odyssey* is attributed in the period between Hesiod and the cultural efflorescence in the sixth century B.C. People described as Ethiopians appear in Homer's pages as actors in great events that involve both gods and men. Eurybates, a loyal friend of Odysseus, is described in terms that suggest he was an Ethiopian.[75]

As the *Odyssey* begins, all of the gods except Poseidon sympathize with Odysseus, who wants to return home to his wife after the Battle of Troy but is being held captive by the powerful and beautiful goddess Calypso. When the gods and goddesses met to discuss his fate, the one unsympathetic deity was absent, for he had gone to visit "the distant Ethiopians, the farthest outposts of mankind, half of whom live where the Sun goes down, and half where he rises." It was not unusual for the gods to visit the land of the "blameless Ethiopians" and to banquet with them. Poseidon had gone "to accept a sacrifice of bulls and rams, and there he sat and enjoyed the pleasures of the feast."

Mythology placed some black people at the center of the stage in ancient history, playing honored and heroic roles. Ethiopia was linked to Egypt, Greece, and Asia Minor as a participant in a common Mediterranean and Middle Eastern "high culture" that was shared by the more sophisticated people. Some elements of it gradually became the possession of the common folk through drama and spoken poetry. The image of Ethiopians was, on the whole, favorable.

Ethiopians varied in features and body build, but they had one thing in common: the trait that gave them their name. "Ethiop" meant "people with the burnt faces." There is some evidence that, in mythological times, the term "Ethiopian" was applied to people with very dark skin from India and some areas of the Middle East. During the classical period, the name was gradually being restricted to parts of Africa south of Egypt, and neither Indians nor Egyptians were being called Ethiopians.

People of this physical appearance are depicted as having beauty as well as other merits. The ghost of Agamemnon, reflecting on the death of Eurypylus at the Battle of Troy, remarks that "he was the handsomest man I ever saw, next to the godlike Memnon." The latter was the Ethiopian hero who, according to the legend, brought ten thousand troops to aid his uncle, Priam, against the Greeks during the Trojan War.[76] In the myth Memnon's mother was Aurora (Eos), goddess of the dawn, and his father was a mortal, the king of some Middle Eastern city. Dew found in the morning represents the tears shed by Memnon's mother when her son died on the plains of Troy. The Roman poet Virgil told the Memnon story in the *Aeneid* many centuries after the Battle of Troy and spoke of Memnon as the "handsome Ethiopian."[77]

Frank Snowden, distinguished Afro-American professor of classics at Howard University, has pointed out that some important changes in interpretations of mythological events had taken place by Roman imperial times, when the earlier Christian theologians were writing.[78] A Roman poet "attributes the fall of Troy to Priam's acceptance of ill-omened assistance from Memnon and his black troops," Snowden notes in his definitive vindicationist work, *Blacks in Antiquity.* Another battlefield report in Roman times claims that "ill-starred persons were known to have seen an Ethiopian before their misfortunes."[79] However, in the Greek legend, Penelope viewed Odysseus' herald, Eurybates, with his Ethiopian visage and hair, as an omen of good fortune. Despite these changes, as Greek culture was absorbed into the Greco-Roman synthesis, Snowden is convinced that "the classical evidence as a whole . . . indicates that *serious evaluations of dark or black skinned persons were not affected by beliefs that the Ethiopian's skin was ominous or that black was a symbol of evil or death"* [italics added].[80] That is, in his view, abstract evaluations of blackness did not necessarily carry over to people. Although these conceptions of blackness as bad luck may not have seriously affected race relations among the Romans, they were a part of the legacy of ideas bequeathed to the Christian founding fathers. But they existed side by side with a mystical/religious view that Blacks had apotropaic powers that warded off evil.[81] These were associated with a belief in sexual potency.

Paintings and Sculptures

In addition to literature and folklore, the visual arts conveyed conceptions of Negroes. While a portrayal of Memnon as black but not Negroid appeared on vases painted in Athens during the classical period, other paintings include Negroid Ethiopians depicted in a fashion suggesting they were viewed as an exotic people (see plate 1). Snowden stresses a point that impressed him as he examined sculpture and vase paintings of varied size and subject, as well as painted frescoes and mosaics in Greek and Roman ruins. He stresses the lively concern of artists with anatomical differences between Caucasians and individuals with varied degrees of Negro mixture from the fifth century B.C. through the period of the Roman Empire. This concern reflected an esthetic interest that sought to exploit the possibilities of contrast in color and features as well as a desire to leave a record of various public events that included Ethiopians.

Following a custom that began with Hesiod's poetry and continued in the literature and art of classical times, Ethiopian and Scythian physical types were contrasted. These were considered not only as the types most different from Greeks in appearance but also as most representative of the extremes among mankind—Scythians of the Eurasian north, Ethiopians of the African south. The contrast is frequently presented in painting and sculpture (see plate 2). Snowden is convinced that the intent is primarily esthetic, that the contrast was thought to be dramatic and pleasing to the eye. He does not view the contrasting of types as being necessarily derogatory to black people.[82]

On the other hand, Professor Joseph Harris, one of Professor Snowden's colleagues at Howard University, considers some of the depictions of Negroes in the illustrations provided in *Blacks in Antiquity* to be demeaning caricatures. While Snowden admits that some of the representations involve caricature, he does not see either malicious intent or racial prejudice in this fact.[83] Yet it is clear from the sculpture of classical Greece that Greek artists cherished their own somatic norm image, and little of their sculpture attempts to present the unmixed Negroid physical type in a form apt to make it appear especially pleasing.[84]

On the other hand, some of the Roman sculpture depicting Blacks may indicate that the artists were trying to judge black beauty by norms inherent to the subject and not by Roman norms (see plate 3).[85] Even if an objective analysis by art critics eventually demonstrates the existence of esthetic biases against the Negroid physical type among Greeks and Romans, this does not seem to have determined individual choices in the erotic domain, nor did it carry an imputation of intellectual deficiency. Negative esthetic appraisals may exist side by side with positive evaluations in the erotic, status-allocation, and religious/mystical domains.

Black People in Greco-Roman Society

For most ordinary Greeks and Romans, mythology, literature, sculpture and painting constituted the primary source of knowledge about black people, in the absence of actual personal contacts, until after the the fifth century B.C. There is evidence that a few Negro Ethiopians—as distinct from Indians who were sometimes designated as such—lived among the populations of the Greek city-states, and that not all of them were slaves. Some were culturally assimilated, and, if the legend can be given credence, Aesop of the fables was one of these. There were enough such individuals to set off some speculation among philosophers over why black people were black and what the outcome of miscegenation would be.[86] Undoubtedly contact with Negroes was more frequent in Ionia, Crete and Cyprus than in European Greece. It is in Ionia that the first records of Greek philosophers visiting Egypt appear, and they would certainly have met Negro physical types there. Pythagoras was reputed to have studied in various Egyptian temples for over fifteen years.[87]

Greco-Roman Accounts of Africa

Historians and philosophers, some of whom traveled to Egypt during the fifth century, picked up hearsay about Ethiopians and confirmed the existence of a generally favorable attitude there—verging on admiration—about the ancient Ethiopians, coupled with some ambivalence about contemporary Africans who lived far up the Nile. Herodotus and Diodorus, historians separated by several centuries, both stressed the intelligence and piety of the ancient Ethiopians. They joined the philosophers Pythagoras and Thales in being impressed by the intellectual contributions of Egypt, although some Greeks objected to the custom of wrapping ideas up in theological mystery. All Greek intellectuals recognized their debt to

Egypt, and Ethiopians were frequently referred to as "civilizers" of Egypt.[88]

These travelers wrote within the context of an ongoing contest for power between the Persians and the Greeks. As the struggle proceeded, the Egyptians and Ethiopians ceased to be abstractions to Greeks. Ionians and Athenians now met numerous Blacks in the flesh in situations outside of the city-states. Instead of hearing about mythological Blacks in armies at the Battle of Troy, they now confronted real Ethiopians as foes in the armies of Xerxes and Cambyses. According to some accounts, Blacks from the Nile Valley fought at Marathon.[89] Later, cities of the Attic League were allied with Egypt. Descriptions of the behavior of Ethiopian soldiers concede their skill as archers and their bravery but also express some condescension at what must have struck the Greeks (as well as the Romans, later) as barbaric ceremonies during preparation for battle.[90] These contacts did not, however, lead to a stereotyping of all Ethiopians, for Herodotus and other scholars drew distinctions between "civilized" and "uncivilized" Ethiops. Plato and Aristotle, however, preferred to stress the distinction between all Greeks and all barbarian Others.[91] In both cases, culture not race was the basis for evaluation. This remained the essential element in Mediterranean appraisals of sub-Saharan Africans well into the fourteenth century A.D.

"Civilized" vs. "Uncivilized" Africans

During the Roman imperial period, attitudes were affected by the continuous warfare with Ethiopians along the Egyptian-Nubian border and by the slaves who were purchased or secured as prisoners of war. The contrast between "civilized" and "barbarian" Blacks was thereby underscored.[92] During these wars, however, Rome's "civilized" allies in southern Egypt were as black as the "uncivilized" Blemmyes against whom they fought. Culture not biology was crucial; behavior not color or features was what mattered in dealing with Blacks. From the time of Herodotus well into the Roman period, a variety of Ethiopian cultures and peoples were written about—all people "with burnt faces." Herodotus had described, in addition to the cultivated people of Meroë, some cave-dwelling Ethiopians who ate snakes and lizards and "whose language was like the squeaking of bats."[93] Diodorus wrote very favorably of the highly regarded kingdom of Meroë near the sixth cataract of the Nile, contrasting the civilized Ethiopians there with others who were said to keep their nails long like wild beasts.[94] Diodorus described physical types as well as cultures, commenting that the majority of the Ethiopians who dwelt in the Nile Valley were black, flat-nosed, and had kinky hair. He drew no conclusions of a derogatory nature from their physical traits, but Agatharchides, writing in the second century B.C., described an African group living south of Egypt as having noses so flat they looked like apes.[95] The idea of sub-Saharan Blacks as "strange" became the basis for a stereotype.

Face-to-Face Encounters

The Greeks were the first Europeans to encounter Ethiopians in considerable numbers. They did so when serving as citizen-soldiers against the Persians, or when employed as mercenaries fighting for the Egyptians against the Ethiopians during the sixth century B.C.[96] Blacks were on both sides in the latter case, but we have no record of what ordinary Greek soldiers thought of the Ethiopians either as friends or foes. At the same time, a few Ethiopian civilians were entering the cities of Greece, probably by way of Naucratis, the Greek colony in the Egyptian Delta. It is known that Ethiopians were present there in considerable numbers during the fifth century and after.

From the fifth century B.C. until the Roman conquest of Egypt during the first century B.C., relations between that part of Africa and Greece were very close. Egyptians became the allies of Greece in a joint struggle against the Persians, and under the Ptolemies, Alexander the Great's successors who ruled Egypt, they maintained close ties with a Greece that had lost its power and prestige but was still a trading partner and an intellectual "homeland." Alexander himself had been declared a pharaoh, and his body had been brought for burial to Egypt from Persia, where he had died. The legend was spread widely that he was actually the son of Nectanebo, the last Egyptian pharaoh. Both the Alexandrine Empire and the Ptolemaic regime that succeeded it maintained diplomatic and commercial relations with the Ethiopian kingdom of Meroë. Philosophers continued to speculate about the origin and meaning of skin-color differences, but this did not preclude egalitarian relations between individuals within the Mediterranean population and some Ethiopians of similar status.[97] Color awareness did not have invidious discrimination as an inevitable result.

While the Greeks and Romans successively conquered Egypt, Egyptians and Ethiopians were appearing in Europe in greater numbers. Snowden, after a careful assessment of the literature, states that "the exact number of Ethiopians who entered the Greco-Roman world as a result of varied military, diplomatic, and commercial activity is difficult to determine, but all the evidence suggests a sizeable Ethiopian element, especially in the population of the Roman world." And he concludes that "their presence, whatever their number, constituted no color problem."[98] This, of course, did not mean a complete absence of negative evaluations of black people.

Slaves, Slavery, and Prejudice

Commenting on the institution of slavery in the Greek city-states, William L. Westermann, a distinguished classicist, makes an observation of some importance to students of race relations:

> Granting that slave status in general was an unenviable condition, there are many indications that deeper racial and class antipathies, such as those based upon differences of skin coloring, were totally lacking in the Greek world.[99]

Absence of "antipathies" did not preclude expression of color preferences in some domains. However, when Greeks became involved in the imperialism of the Ptolemaic period in Egypt, and after the spread of the Roman Empire resulted in large-scale movements of people and an increase in the volume of slaves throughout the Mediterranean world, conditions were still not such as to generate in the mind an equivalence between blackness and slavery. Although most Blacks were slaves, most slaves were not black. African slaves were highly visible, but Westermann disagrees with Snowden when he reminds us that, "the number of Aethiopian or Negro slaves provable for the Roman Empire was small even in Egypt where they should be found in largest numbers."[100] Slaves in the Greek city-states and their appended hinterlands were overwhelmingly white, as they were in Rome.

Even if blackness had become associated with slavery, this would not necessarily have held the Ethiopian population up to contempt or contumely. Slavery was demeaning but not degrading in the Greco-Roman world. Most slaves were employed in households in every kind of pursuit from tutoring children to cleaning and carrying. While some women were respected concubines, the female slave population also included the women of the state-owned brothels. The dramatists of the classical period contributed to a stereotype of slaves as doltish malingerers who made up a crude element in the body politic. This was not true of all slaves and was not a racial stereotype.

There are some suggestions in Greek classical literature that slavery was unethical or undesirable. However, Aristotle represented the consensus when he spoke of slavery as a necessity for a well-ordered community. Other philosophers questioned both the ethics and the necessity of slavery.[101] Eratosthenes advanced the idea that instead of drawing distinctions between "slaves" and "free men," it would be better to make distinctions according to "virtue" and "vice." He declared, too, that not only were many Greeks undesirable but many barbarians (i.e., those without Greek culture) were "refined." Epictetus asserted that "all men derive their descent from God. . . . Slavery is not a question of descent from servile parentage or of races, but a matter of character and excellence."[102] There is just a hint in this remark that individual slaves might have done something to deserve their fate or might lack traits that would make them desirable free men and citizens. Aristotle thought some ethnic groups were "born slaves" but he did not specify Negroes as such a group.

Although the Greeks and Romans did not make race or color a basis for enslaving people or justifying their enslavement, the classicist A.N. Sherwin-White points out that thinking in narrow *ethnic* terms was a deeply rooted custom in the Greco-Roman world. It is reflected in the remarks of Greek and Roman authors when commenting on the European tribal peoples, on various ethnic groups in the Mediterranean basin, particularly the Jews, and, less frequently, on Africans. He notes that "racial prejudice against the northern barbarians existed in the Roman mind over a long period of time and could focus on details of character, physique and customs." It was not skin color, however, but body build and hairiness that excited the prejudices of Roman soldiers against tall and brawny Britons and Gauls.[103]

Roman generals and government officials considered some ethnic groups more amenable to civilization and assimilation than others. In discussing the antagonism of Romans toward Greeks and of Greeks toward Jews, Sherwin-White interjects a note of caution:

> I have called this antagonism racial for convenience. But this is misleading. Though Greeks and Latins refer to the Jews as *ethnos* or a *natio* or a *gens*, i.e. a folk or tribe, there is no genuinely racial or racist connotation. The distinction is political, social and religious, national rather than genetic.[104]

Environmental Explanations for Ethnicity and Temperament

There is abundant evidence of a Greco-Roman belief that certain traits of temperament and ability were associated with specific ethnic groups. Occasionally writers in antiquity spoke of physical traits as an index to temperament or ability. As Snowden points out, and stresses, these differences were thought to be the result of differences in the environmental setting in which the ethnic group had developed. These environmental differences were, in turn, sometimes linked to mythological events. Thus Greek myths explained in this way the "burnt faces" of those they named "Ethiops": Phaeton, the son of Helios, the sun god, drove his father's chariot wildly across the sky, swooped too low in some places, and scorched the earth, and in doing so created the deserts and blackened the faces of some men.

After the fifth century B.C., Greek rationalists, questioning the authenticity of the myths, began to develop an environmental theory that became characteristic of classical Greek explanations of differences as taught by most of the philosophers.

Snowden has given us a glimpse of the Roman synthesis of various Greek theories and their own thought, a synthesis that represented the dominant view during the period when the Church Fathers wrote:

> The Ethiopians are obviously, in Pliny's view, burnt by the heat of the sun near them and are born with scorched complexions and frizzly hair, whereas the races in the opposite regions of the world have straight yellow hair and white frosty skins. . . . Climate also explains the habits of the population of Scythia and Ethiopia, for, according to Ptolemy [Claudius Ptolemaeus], the Ethiopians are for the most part savage because their homes are oppressed by the heat and the Scythians are savage because their dwelling places are continually cold.[105]

Hippocrates, Aristotle, Polybius, Posidonius, Strabo, and Pliny contributed to this theory, prevalent among Greco-Roman intellectuals, that climate and the associated environment were responsible for differences in physique, temperament, and culture. Pliny and Ptolemy helped to fix in the minds of literate people the extreme contrast between Scythians to the north and Ethiopians to the south. Snowden summarizes the views of Ptolemy:

> The inhabitants of the region from the equator to the summer tropic, known by the general name of Ethiopians, have black skins and thick wooly hair, are shrunken in stature and sanguine in their nature because they are burnt by the sun which is over their heads.

Those in the more northern parallels, on the other hand—designated by the general name of Scythians—are white-complexioned, straight-haired, tall and well nourished, and have a more abundant share of moisture, and are somewhat cold by nature, since they are far removed from the zodiac and the sun. Climate also explains the habits of the population of Scythia and Ethiopia.[106]

Hot climates, for instance, were associated with a high degree of sensuality that was attributed to the "nature" of Ethiopians. The Roman upper class used the belief to sanction a cult of black sexuality. Some students of the period have stated that after the Roman conquest of Egypt,

> the increasing interest in phallic art and the myths and legends about the African's eroticism led wealthy Romans to new adventures in sex. They began to import black mistresses. Sometimes they bought black women at high prices from traders along the shores of the Mediterranean, or from army generals returning from the wars. Other times they traded white women for black women, dealing with the Turkish or North African sea captains. . . . Big black men were brought from Africa to provide the desired pleasures for women in private chambers and at gaudy banquets that frequently degenerated into more licentious orgies.[107]

Blacks generally ranked low in the esthetic and status-allocation domains but high on the erotic scale. One student of homosexual practices in the Middle East and the Mediterranean has reported that "among the aristocrats the richest men kept harems of boys. The favorites were usually recruited in Africa."[108] Pliny the Elder told the story of a Roman general who sent a black man with an extremely large phallus to a lady friend, and of a consul in a foreign land who sent a similar gift to his wife to keep her from committing adultery, while he was away, with a certain political enemy of whom he was suspicious.[109]

The environmental interpretation of group differences reinforced stereotypical thinking, exemplified, for example, by Aristotle's assertion that both the wooly-haired and the excessively fair were cowardly as compared with the warriors of the Athenian temperate zone.[110] But it left open two questions: what happened when people born in one area grew up in another and what fundamental changes among people within a given geographical setting could be affected by changes in culture? Christians were convinced they could effect fundmental changes in Ethiops as well as others.

The significant fact about Greco-Roman intellectuals was not that they elaborated ethnic stereotypes, but that they debated the causes of group differences and were generally skeptical of theories of biological determinism. Against environmental determinism and the ethnocentrism it reinforced, as well as the danger of incipient racism it embodied, were the arguments of men like Menander, who wrote: "the man whose natural bent is good . . . though Ethiop, is nobly born."[111] The Sophists, particularly, emphasized the idea that traits of individual character and intelligence were more important than any kind of status divisions, and that such traits were not determined by climate.

As late as the time of imperial Rome, the old Greek belief that Ethiopians were a special breed of men characterized by unusual piety and a sense of justice existed side by side with beliefs that no men, Greek or Ethiopian, had a monopoly on virtue, and that skin color had nothing to do with a man's worth even if it might be an index to the climate that shaped some aspects of his temperament. Men like Ephorus insisted that the bizarre and strange should not be emphasized at the expense of recognition that opposite behaviors exist within a stereotyped group. He singled out the Scythians as an example.[112] Christian theologians could assimilate all of this, as well as Seneca's admonition to remember that "the color of the Ethiopians among his own people is not notable and . . . among the Germans red hair gathered into a knot is not unbecoming a man." However, as dedicated leaders of a missionary movement they would have to draw the line at the cultural relativism implicit in Seneca's injunction: "You are to consider nothing in a man odd or disgraceful which is characteristic of his nation."[113] No believing Christian fired up with missionary zeal could accept this philosophy.

COLOR EVALUATION AND EARLY CHRISTIANITY

Using the Old Testament as the fundamental text, the early leaders of Christianity blended some of the ideas they found there with selected concepts from Greek philosophy to formulate a Christian position that was fundamentally egalitarian. After conversion, all men and women—Greeks, Jews, slaves and intellectuals—were "one in Christ." As "civilized" and "uncivilized" had been the basic poles of judgment for the Greeks and Romans, "believer" and "pagan" now became the relevant dichotomy of the new era—not differences in skin color. But there were problems.

A system of hermeneutics emerged that treated much of the Old Testament, including stories about Ethiopians, as allegory. Concurrently, contrasts of black with white came to be used symbolically in a manner that tended to identify blackness with sin. The Christian concept of sin was alien to Greco-Roman religion and philosophy. It was unique to Judaism and the evolving new religion. The Manichaean contrast derived from Persia portrayed darkness and light as polar opposites. This was not incompatible with Christian symbolism of Sin and Righteousness. For the first time, too, a Greek philosopher appeared who associated the concept of a cognitive deficit with the Negro phenotype. This was Galen.

These influences were in conflict with the traditional Greco-Roman evaluations of black people, and Christian theologians were not isolated from them. However, the social context in which the Church in North Africa was growing up was probably decisive in shaping attitudes toward black people during the first five Christian centuries. In Egypt under Roman rule, a social structure inherited from Greek colonizers tended to equate upper class with light skin color. Then, too, as the world became more and more Christian, "pagan" came to be equated with sub-Saharan African cultures by North African Christians. Dark skin color became a symbol of the undesirable.

After a brief consideration of how the Judaic and Greco-Roman traditions were blended in the ideology of early Christianity, we shall examine the crucial first five centuries of the new religion for any evidence of color prejudice and discrimination among its practitioners.

The Christian Synthesis

Christians were taught that "Jews after the flesh" had rejected Jesus Christ on his first appearance, but that the Christians, "Jews after the spirit," had a mission to "go into all the world" preaching the gospel (i.e., "good news") of His imminent second coming. It was to be preached to all nations. When Christ came a second time, "Jews after the flesh," having returned to Palestine by then after centuries of suffering in exile, would recognize Him as the rejected Messiah. Justice would then flow out from Jerusalem like a mighty stream and would cover the earth. The Millennial Kingdom would bring peace and plenty to all mankind. This is reflected in Paul's letters to the new congregations.[114]

Problems of survival for the new Christian sect, as well as for Pauline theology, created a climate that was unfavorable to discrimination on the basis of skin color. Their apocalyptic, eschatological perspective envisioned an imminent return of Christ to establish his Millennial Kingdom. Converts were gripped by a sense of being "in this world but not of it," and an "interim ethic" emerged that included social norms and values suited to a temporary sojourn while awaiting The Coming. Thus Paul advised against marriage, calling it a necessary evil, at best, for the Christian. Undue concern with a desirable somatic norm image would certainly have constituted a display of interest in "things of this world" inconsistent with the belief that soon the dead would be resurrected and the bodies of the living would be "changed in an instant" into an "incorruptible" form. It is highly probable that nothing could have been of lesser consequence for those who held such beliefs than whether or not a Christian's body was black or white or yellow.[115]

Following the injunction, "Go ye into all the world and preach the gospel," Paul promised forgiveness and willing acceptance to all who had been "born again" and who no longer worshiped idols or engaged in the practices of their pagan neighbors. In all this it is easy to see the imprint of the Greek Sophist concept of "a community for all men despite racial and cultural differences." Seneca, the Roman Stoic, had also contributed, with his idea that all men were equal, including slaves. Neither the Stoics or Sophists made the abolition of slavery either mandatory or desirable. Some of the teachings did attempt to lessen the social distance between slaves and free men, however, and Christianity gave emphasis to this conception of the relations between men.[116] The Greco-Roman influence was so strong that one influential school of early Christian writers known as the Apologists took as its task the intellectual defense of Christians persecuted by Romans.[117] Their main line of argument was that Christianity was in accord with the spirit of the greatest Roman and Greek philosophers and that it did not teach treason and sedition.

The Greek Septuagint version of the Old Testament constituted the body of Jewish literature accepted by the Apostles and the Church Fathers as sacred, inspired, and revealed, until St. Jerome completed the Vulgate translation directly from the Hebrew language into Latin in A.D. 404. The Pentateuch, or the first five books of the Old Testament, attributed to Moses, were deemed especially sacred by both Jewish and Christian theologians. The prophets Isaiah and Ezekiel, as well as some of the minor prophets, were prized for their ethical teachings.

The Church Fathers diligently reviewed the Old Testament for statements that could be interpreted as prophecies predicting that Jesus Christ would be born, crucified, resurrected, and taken up into heaven, from whence he would return to inaugurate a millennial age. Early churchmen sometimes treated Old Testament episodes as allegories, and dark skin color began to assume symbolic significance in the cases of the woman in the Song of Solomon, Moses' wife, the Queen of Sheba, and the Ethiopian eunuch. The use of biblical characters as subjects for allegorical interpretation, and of Ethiopia as a metaphor for black pagans, was the focus of theological interest in the Black Experience during the first three Christian centuries. These allegorical interpretations made black skin color a symbol of sin that could be "washed away."

Professor Louis Ginzberg, a distinguished Talmudic scholar, is convinced that some of the early Christian theologians and commentators on the Scriptures were aware of nonbiblical legends about Noah and his sons, as well as other legends, and that they occasionally reveal such familiarity inadvertently. The Church Fathers do not seem, however, to have taken the nonbibilical stories seriously enough to use them in their homilies and arguments. The descendants of Cain, the first murderer, not Nimrod, son of Cush, are blamed for a multitude of evils relating to the beginning of "civilization" in Mesopotamia.[118] This is the "mainstream" biblical tradition, and it reinforces the role of the curse-on-Canaan story in deflecting derogatory stereotypes and attitudes away from Ethiopians, who were believed to be the sons of Cush, Canaan's brother.

The synthesis of Greek philosophy and various aspects of Old Testament history, ethics, and eschatological thinking during the first five Christian centuries involved very little contact between Christian and Jewish scholars that would have effectively passed on Jewish oral tradition to the Christians. It is possible that ordinary Jews among the early Christian converts were familiar with some of the derogatory Jewish legends about black people, if any were in existence at the time, especially outside of Mesopotamia. Jewish converts may occasionally have transmitted some of this lore to non-Jewish fellow Christians.

But it was not what the Jewish masses may have discussed and transmitted that affected the development of Christian thought and practice; rather it was what the priests, scribes, and rabbis had written down. The Babylonian Talmud and the Midrash, with their stories of black skin as a curse and other tales derogatory to Negroes, were not available in writing until the fourth and fifth centuries, after the formative years of Christianity. The Christian theologians did not refer to the sexual sins of Ham as the cause of the Ethiopian's color.

Louis Ginzberg, by minute and sometimes ingenious textual comparisons, argues convincingly that some of the early Church

Fathers, including Jerome, were aware of some of the legends that eventually found a place in Midrashic manuscripts and in the Talmuds. It was pointed out that early church leaders may have been exposed to some of the nonbiblical stories through the works of historian Flavius Josephus (e.g., Theophilus of Antioch) and philosopher Philo Judaeus (e.g., Clement of Alexandria), both of whom were Jewish scholars and writers of the first century.

Not all of the legends were negative. For instance, in *Antiquities of the Jews*, Flavius Josephus presents a lengthy, highly romantic account of how Moses came to marry his Ethiopian bride. He describes an incident in which the daughter of the king of Ethiopia fell in love with Moses when an Egyptian army he led besieged her father's capital city. They were married, thus ending the war and cementing friendship between Egypt and Ethiopia. The Josephus account, current during the early Christian period, does not mention disapproval of the marriage by the brother and sister of Moses at all!

Philo Judaeus presented a nonbiblical Jewish tradition, probably of Mesopotamian origin, in which Nimrod, the son of Cush, the son of Ham, was said to have founded the cities of Babel, Erech, and Accad. Nimrod is represented as the acme of evil, the prime example of impiety, arrogance, and rebelliousness. Philo Judaeus speaks of Cush as "the eldest offspring of evil," that is, Noah's son, Ham. Of Cush he says further that "the name is a clear indication of the thing signified for it is to be translated as 'Ethiopian-pure evil' that has no participation in light but follows night and darkness." Here Judaeus is making "Ethiopian" equivalent to evil sometime before Paul began writing the epistles to the European and Asian churches. One recent scholar is convinced that these derogatory comments were not in the original Philo version.[119]

The extent to which the nonbiblical Jewish tradition affected Christian theology and folklore is a subject that deserves full monographic treatment. Dr. I. Epstein, a leading twentieth-century authority on nonbiblical Jewish literature, mentions Church Fathers of the third, fourth and fifth centuries whose writings, in his opinion, show some familiarity with the Midrash. The scholars he names are Eusebius (260-340 A.D.), Chrysostom (347-407 A.D.), and Augustine (354-430). The great first- and second-century Apostolic Fathers and Apologists do not appear on this list, but Epstein states that the New Testament itself "abounds with Midrashic elements."[120]

The tradition was set early, however, of rejecting from the approved canon what St. Paul had called "Jewish fables," and presumably nonbiblical accounts of the Noah, Ham, Cush and

Nimrod stories were among these. Most significant is the fact that none of the Church Fathers refers to any of the black-skin-as-curse stories; nor do they mention various rabbinic comments about the Song of Solomon or the negative references to Cush and Ethiopia; nor, finally, do they cite the nonbiblical Jewish references in their allegorical contrasts of white and black.

The Church Fathers had either never heard of the black-skin-as-curse theory, or, if they had, they did not deem it worthy of comment. We assume that they accepted the Greek and Roman environmental explanations to account for the physical differences among various human groups, and they did not find it necessary to supplement these theories with theological folklore.

Blackness in the Early Church

The fusion of Old Testament ideas and Greco-Roman philosophy developed in a matrix of Pauline doctrine. Paul's letters to individuals and to churches in Greece, Asia Minor, and Rome became a part of the New Testament, the non-Jewish portion of the Christian's Bible, which also contains the Acts of the Apostles, four gospels, and The Revelation of St. John the Divine. There are few references to Africa or Africans in these writings, in contrast to the Old Testament: Mary and Joseph are said to have taken the child Jesus into Egypt to avoid Herod's "slaughter of the Innocents"; one Simon of Cyrene is said to have assisted Jesus in carrying his cross when he stumbled; an Ethiopian government official is described as an early convert baptized by the Apostle Philip. These few references, and no more.

Presumably there were very few Blacks among the members of the congregations to which Paul's epistles were written. Most of the first group of new converts were from the urban artisan and merchant class and not from among slave strata, insofar as a judgment can be made from the letters of Paul to the churches. One student of Greco-Roman slavery notes that "the early Christians admitted slaves into their midst as readily as free persons. The number of slaves to be found in any group of converts would presumably approximate the proportion of slaves to free which existed in the particular town or city of each Christian congregation. This is necessarily an opinion only; but the rationalization is at least a sensible one."[121] Greater use of black slaves in Italian cities in late Roman Empire times, as well as increased exploitation of all slaves, may have made Christianity attractive to this stratum, and may have resulted in churches north of the Mediterranean that were more multiracial and multiethnic than those of the earliest period of Christian growth.

In stressing the all-inclusive nature of the new Christian community, Paul did not specifically mention Ethiopians when he spoke of "barbarians" generally. Ethiopians were probably omitted because they were not present in great numbers in Asia Minor or on the northern side of the Mediterranean Sea, where Paul concentrated on spreading the gospel. Nevertheless, in Paul's statement that God had made of one blood all men on the face of the earth, Ethiopians were, of course, included as potential members of the broader Christian community.

Frank Snowden, impressed with the extent to which the Romans were influenced by the Greeks and the early Christians by both, has emphasized that skin color prejudice and discrimination were largely rejected by the early Christians:

> Those Greeks who first described and depicted dark or Negroid peoples did so without bias. . . . The early, unbiased approach toward colored peoples adumbrated what was to follow. Long after the Ethiopian was divested of any romanticism stemming from a mythological aura and long after he was well known to the Greeks and Romans, whether in Africa or in various parts of the classical world, antipathy because of color did not arise. *The Greco-Roman view of blacks was no romantic idealization of distant, unknown peoples but a fundamental rejection of color as a criterion for evaluating men.* . . . Both the devotees of Isis and the converts of Christianity continued the tradition of Homer's gods, who knew no color line [italics added].[122]

In one sense this continuation of an old tradition by both pagans and Christians is undeniable. For the priests and priestesses of Isis during the Roman imperial age, the most relevant question would have been, "Is the worshiper completely devoted?" For the Christian, it was, "Is this person a 'believer,' saved from sin?" As in the past skin color was a less important consideration than certain beliefs and modes of behavior. The crucial question to be asked in evaluating a person was still some variation of the query, "Is he civilized or uncivilized" not, "What is the color of his skin?"

In words attributed to St. Paul, a continuing community-based focus was given to egalitarian sentiments that were manifested symbolically and temporarily in the Greco-Roman world only upon certain festive or ceremonial occasions: "There cannot be Greek and Jew, circumcised and uncircumcised, barbarian, Scythian, slave, free man, but Christ is all and in all."[123] Among North African Church Fathers, Ethiopians were included with Scythians when speaking in this all-inclusive fashion.

Changes in Attitudes Toward Race and Color

The concept that all men and women are potential members of the Christian community after they have been "redeemed from sin," since all are descended from common parents, Adam and Eve, became a matter for serious discussion in the fourth century A.D. when it was challenged by the Roman emperor in Constantinople. He was known as Julian the Apostate because, although he had been reared as a Christian, he tried to reinstitute paganism as the state religion when he came to power. He argued that the wide range of physical differences among men was inconsistent with the theory of a common ancestor:

> For different natures must have existed in all those things among the nations that were to be differentiated. This, at any rate, is seen, if one observes how different in their bodies are the Germans and Scythians from the Libyans and Ethiopians.[124]

Christian ranks remained solid in defense of what is now called a monogenetic theory of origin, and, in the fifth century, St. Augustine made a statement that remained definitive for Western Christendom, declaring that all human beings, including "freaks" and "monsters," were "of the stock of Noah's sons," and that

> whoever is born anywhere as a human being, that is, as a rational mortal creature, however strange he may appear to our senses, in bodily form or colour or motion or utterance, or in any faculty, part or quality of his nature, whatsoever, let no true believer have any doubt that such an individual is descended from one man who was first created. Yet there is a clear distinction between what has by nature persisted in the majority, and what is marvelous by its very rarity.[125]

Not only were black people "strange" in the eyes of Imperial Rome's nonblacks, the term "decolores" used for mulattoes indicated a feeling that dark skin color was "unnatural."[126] Augustine's distinction between what "by nature persisted in the majority and what is marvelous by its very rarity" left the door open for an ethnocentric defense of ethnic and racial discrimination within specific cultures but at the same time, conceded the humanity of all people. It is significant that Augustine himself called Ethiopians "the remotest and blackest of men," revealing his own reaction to them as "strange."[127]

St. Augustine elaborated a doctrine that both accommodated prejudices and subordinated them to a basic Christian doctrine of the unity of mankind. His remarks can be seen as a continuation of a trend begun by Origen, writing during the first Christian century. This early Church Father used biblical references to Blacks as allegories. He wrote that Moses' marriage to the Ethiopian woman, the visit of the Queen of Sheba to Solomon, and Ebed-melech's kindness to Jeremiah, all involved color symbolism, that all of these Blacks had "white souls within their black bodies," and that Christ could produce more people like them. Christianizing Ethiopians would fulfill a prophecy: "Princes shall come out of Egypt, and Ethiopia shall soon stretch forth her hand unto God."

Origen not only used the Ethiopian cases as allegory in his teaching and preaching. He also used the story of Moses and his wife as a defense of the interracial marriage, apparently accepting the story as historic fact, not only as a teaching parable.

> And never did Moses, in spite of his many splendid achievements, receive from God such high praise as when he married the Ethiopian woman . . . You see what punishment the detractors got for themselves, and what praise for him whom they criticized: Shame for them, honor for him; leprosy for them, glory for him; reproach for them; nobleness for him—this is what they got for him.[128]

Following Origen, the Church Fathers reflected upon the implications of biblical references to black people for missionary work among contemporary Ethiopians, as well as the repercussions of transferring to black people in the flesh ideas and emotions about blackness in the abstract. Snowden feels that none of this preoccupation with the color, physical features, and customs of Ethiopians resulted in social discrimination against them, and that the euphoria of the Christian brotherhood prevailed. His chapter, "The Early Christian Attitudes," is as eloquent as it is scholarly. Nevertheless, while Snowden's generalization may have been generally applicable to the Christian communities of the first Christian century, his own research turned up some evidence that this situation did not always prevail.

Snowden presents evidence that from the second Christian century on, the skin color of Ethiopians was being used as one term in a Manichaean dichotomy between white, symbolizing purity, and black, symbolizing impurity and sin. Some of the early Christian exegetes used the Ethiopians' skin color as a symbol of those sinful impurities that Christ's blood would wash away, leaving the saved person "white as snow." Ezekiel had said, "Though your sins be as scarlet . . . ." Now the statement became, "Though your skins be as black as the Ethiopian's skin." Paulinus of Nola referred to "Ethiopian peoples burnt not by the sun, but black with vices and dark with sin." Gregory of Nyasa wrote that "while we were sinners and black, he made us radiantly bright and resplendent with grace."[129] A Byzantine Menologium [collection of lives of the saints] also expressed this widespread idea. Christianity could "wash the Ethiopian white." Snowden feels that, all things considered, these "variations of the imagery of spiritual blackness and whiteness,"[130] did not affect social relations in any serious way. He cites Father Moses as a test case, a not entirely convincing example.

Father Moses was the slave of a man who worshiped the sun, but Moses yearned to know the "true" God, and having heard that there were monks in the desert of Scete who "knew God," he fled there and was baptized. Moses became a monk, and "Satan warred upon him because formerly he used to eat to excess and commit fornication." Moses became very sick, but "God saw his endurance and healed him of his disease, and removed the sickness and the attacks of Satan." Moses had made it a habit to voluntarily fill the water pots of the old men at night, and this act of devotion had won him friends and much admiration. When he was almost miraculously cured in body and soul, five hundred of his brethren decided to make him a priest and their abbott.[131]

There are two slightly different versions of the archbishop's reaction to their decision. In the first,

> the archbishop of Alexandria, wishing to test Moses, instructed the clergy to drive him out of the sanctuary and to observe him. As they rebuked him and exclaimed "begone Ethiopian," he was heard to say, "they have treated you rightly, sooty-skinned black man. You are not a man. Why did you enter among men?"[132]

Another version shows the archbishop in a more plain-spoken mode:

> And when they set him in the sanctuary, the archbishop wished to try him, and to get knowledge of his spiritual fight. And the archbishop said unto the holy old men, "Why have ye brought this black man here? Take him away." And Moses went out reproaching himself, and he said, *"They have treated thee rightly, Oh black man, O thou whose face is horrible,"* and after this the archbishop called him and laid his hand upon him, and made him a priest. And the archbishop said unto him, "Behold, *thou hast become white, all of thee within and without"* [italics added].[133]

Father Moses was said to have accepted this treatment with Christian humility, replying to the bishop, "Outwardly holy, father;

would that I were inwardly, too." In contemporary racist societies, for a black person to act in this fashion would be demeaning. It would earn the derogatory Afro-American epithet, "Uncle Tom." Perhaps it did not result in personality damage in a non-racist society.

Snowden places the treatment of Father Moses in the context of "the well known Christian symbolism of spiritual blackness and whiteness."[134] But Moses' tormentors and his own reactions reveal attitudes and behavior that deviate markedly from what Snowden calls the "traditions of Homer's gods who knew no color line" and from the Christianity preached by Paul. What could possibly account for such behavior by a member of the Alexandrian clergy? Why would an archbishop subject a fellow Christian to such abuse, even if it were only a "trial"? Furthermore, why did some of the monks in the Egyptian desert actually begin to have visions of "Ethiopian imps" leading them into temptation and to conceptualize the devil himself as black?

We must attempt to explain why some Church Fathers acted as they did, having inherited a tradition of favorable attitudes toward blackness and the Ethiopians from the Bible and the Greek poets. They did not derive a sharp symbolic contrast between black and white from either source. Why then did they display such a contrast in their writings and exhibit a negative attitude toward Ethiopians in the flesh? While negative attitudes toward Blacks were to be found in the nonbiblical Jewish tradition, the Church Fathers either were not exposed to these specific legends or did not take them seriously. We must look elsewhere.

The Impact of Persian Concepts

The cosmic struggle between Darkness and Light is not waged in the Old Testament. Rather, this was a Persian concept that inculcated a habit of thinking in terms of binary oppositions in the minds of its Zoroastrian and Manichaean devotees. Insofar as Light= purity=white skin color and Darkness=evil=black skin color may have been set up as subliminal equivalences, racial prejudice against Negroes was reinforced. This was a widespread thought style in Mesopotamia, where one group of Jewish thinkers lived. The Dead Sea Scrolls, dated in the first century B.C. and the first century A.D., reveal that some Jewish cult groups in Judea fostered essentially Persian religious concepts at this time. Such ideas, in the form of Gnosticism, were prevalent in educated circles throughout North Africa and spread rapidly after A.D. 300, in the form of Manichaeism.[135] Augustine, the great fifth-century theologian, was a believer in Manichaeism before he became a Christian convert.

The old Zoroastrian doctrine conceived of a great cosmic struggle between Good symbolized by Light and Evil by Darkness. Between A.D. 230 and 274, Mani interpreted the concept to include the idea that various groups and individuals have differential amounts of the light that lifts them out of Darkness. It is not clear whether Mani taught that dark-skinned groups had less Light, but women as a group were believed to have more Darkness (i.e., sin and evil) than men. Sexual intercourse was evil, though necessary for procreation, and therefore women were thought to be "corrupting" and "seductive." Manichaeans prized asceticism, and the chosen elite among them who taught mankind how to "free" the Light captured by "the Darkness of their bodies" were expected to live ascetic lives.[136] St. Augustine writes at length about his own early attachment to Manichaeism and seems to have retained some of his earlier views. Manichaean concepts reinforced Pauline ideas about the undesirability of sexual relations for the "saved."

Although Persian thought styles in the form of Manichaeism did not affect Alexandrian and North African intellectuals until after the third century A.D., other aspects of Persian esoteric doctrine had been influential in that region from the time of the first Persian conquests of Egypt in the sixth century B.C. As we have seen, early Church Fathers were familiar with the work of Philo Judaeus, the Hellenized Jewish scholar who combined some aspects of Persian thought with Platonic philosophy and Judaism during the first half of the first Christian century.

Philo Judaeus lived in Alexandria and wrote in Greek. In his color symbolism, white represented "living carefully with simple elegance," something greatly to be desired. At one point Philo Judaeus asked, "What is simpler [and therefore better] than the color white?" and in response, his translator posits a material equivalence with a highly prized type of cloth—fine linen. However, Philo Judaeus did not conceptualize a clear-cut Manichaean-type dichotomy in which an undesirable "spiritual blackness" was contrasted with "spiritual whiteness." His translator implies that he did not exclude blackness or brownness from the realm of the "good," since he "appropriates concepts and materials from the Isis-Osiris cycle for the formulation of his theology."

Although the hue white is not contrasted with a negative hue, black, Philo Judaeus draws a sharp contrast in the brightness dimension between Light and Darkness that seems definitely

Persian in its origin. So different is this emphasis from other portions of Philo's work that the translator considers the Light/Darkness contrast a corruption of the text, not present in the original and an addition "evidently from a Christian hand." Philo Judaeus also equates Negroidness with undesirable traits.

Many adherents of earlier dualistic heresies—Docetists, Marcionites, and Gnostics—were attracted to Manichaeism before church authorities declared it a heresy. However, the influence of Manichaean thought cannot alone account for the casting of Ethiopia and the Ethiopians in the role of symbols of sin. In fact, Manichaean ideas that contrasted Light with Darkness were themselves pagan ideas, suspect because of their origin, even if they did have profound influence on Christian thought. Modified Persian thought styles were undoubtedly important in structuring thought about black people, but, in all probability, Manichaean thinking served as a reinforcement rather than as a primary cause in making "spiritual blackness" a concept interchangeable with skin-color reference.

Galen and the Belief in Cognitive Deficit

Not all Greek scholars were tolerant philosophers who stressed the brotherhood of all mankind. One learned scholar who was reputed to have admired the Christians and who spoke out against cruelty to slaves referred to black people in a manner that was alien to both the biblical and the older Greco-Roman tradition. Born of Greek parentage in the city of Pergamum in Asia Minor, educated there and in Rome, Galen became the greatest physician of his time. Writing between A.D. 122 and A.D. 155, he produced a textbook on anatomy that profoundly influenced medieval Islamic and Christian medical practice.[137] His works included a list of traits he claimed were found combined together in black men exclusively. He projected an atypical Greek point of view, stating that Blacks inherited defective brains.

Insofar as Galen's views were taken seriously by any of the Church Fathers, they would have been available to sanction and reinforce pejorative attitudes and discriminatory behavior toward Ethiopians. The probability is high. He described ten traits as characteristic of black males:

(1) thick lips
(2) broad nostrils

(3) frizzy hair
(4) black eyes
(5) furrowed hands and feet
(6) thin eyebrows
(7) pointed teeth
(8) smelly skin
(9) long penis
(10) great merriment.[138]

Galen was here describing not the Ethiopian-type Negro known to the Mediterranean region, but the African of the centuries-old travelers' tales who was said to live south of the Sahara Desert and the kingdom of Kush. This physician had some first-hand experience with sub-Saharan Africans of this type.

For twenty years Galen was the official doctor to the gladiators in the circus at Pergamum and may have had a similar function for a time in the circus at Rome. His sample of Blacks may have been confined to those selected to fight in such shows. Some of these were very probably men whom the Mesopotamians called "Zanj" and about whom the early Muslim travelers wrote at length. Some people with pointed teeth were definitely located by later writers in eastern Africa south of Ethiopia. The characteristics of smelly skin and long penis became components of a stereotype about Blacks that persisted in Mesopotamia. These traits could have been generalized from actual experience with a few eastern African pastoral peoples, whose body anointments may have been offensive and whose males had genitalia that matched their very tall physique or who wore "penis sheaths."

But while Galen may have been accurately describing a specific kind of black male whose anatomy he had examined, he then overgeneralized to include all varieties of black men. Modern anthropologists would also criticize Galen for mixing physical traits and presumed psychological characteristics in his classifications. Not only did he list "merriment" as a trait but he asserted that it " . . . dominates the black man because of his defective brain, whence, also the weakness of his intelligence." This is perhaps the earliest statement on record alleging that Blacks have an organically based cognitive deficit. Such a belief may have been widespread in North Africa and the Middle East, but for a prestigious learned man like Galen to espouse it added an atypical element to Hellenistic scholarship.

Galen's demeaning of Blacks, with its strong racist potential, does not appear in any explicit statements in early Christian literature, but his ideas may have influenced attitudes and stereotypes, unconsciously, that men of learning developed toward Negroes.[139]

Sexual Stereotypes of Blacks

Neither Persian concepts nor the ideas of Galen had the type of impact upon Christian theologians that certain aspects of paganism did. As we have seen, one of the stereotypes about black people that was already prevalent in Greco-Roman times was supersexuality. The Jewish tradition, except for views about religious vocations of certain types, did not embody puritanical attitudes toward sexuality. However, Judaism has always been opposed to sexual activity as a part of religious worship. Christianity inherited the Judaic point of view and added monastic asceticism to it. The Apostle Paul focused his fire upon pagan religious worship that incorporated orgiastic displays, gluttony, and drunkenness. Fornication was assailed, and Paul made severe strictures upon another aspect of Greek culture— the acceptance and even lauding of male homosexuality.[140] Celibacy was considered the most appropriate state to maintain while awaiting an imminent millenium.

Because asceticism involves negative attitudes toward sexuality, stereotypes of supersexuality about Ethiopian pagans tended to reinforce the association of black people with sin. Dreams and apparitions of ascetics may reveal fears, wishes, and apprehensions of much larger groups of believing Christians. Thus R.E.L. Masters, in *Eros and Evil* (1962), states that the desert anchorite St. Macarius the Younger reported in the fourth century A.D. that he saw "little demons 'like foul Ethiops' flying around a gathering of monks." These little imps were substituting lumps of coal for the host at Holy Communion. Abbot John of Lycus in the fifth century said that the demon Zabulus took the form of a "hideous Ethiop."

Both of these men may have been influenced by leading Christians who preceded them. Origen, who had himself castrated as a demonstration of his own asceticism, not only used Ethiopians as symbols of sin but stated explicitly that "black is the color of sin." Jerome (A.D. 347-420), one of the four great doctors of the Western church, was obsessed with the problem of the relationship between sexuality and living the Christian life. He lived as a hermit in the desert for a period and was celibate, although he did not go so far as Origen. In commenting on one of the psalms, Jerome, who translated the Scriptures into Latin, wrote, "Cushi in Hebrew means Ethiopian, that is black and dark, one who has a soul as black as his body . . . Cushi, this Ethiopian, is no other than the devil."[141]

The Social Environment of the North African Church

The earliest Christian church contained within its congregations Jewish-Gentile tensions, but there was no hierarchy in which an educated clergy was integrated into a social-class system characterized by color prejudice against a dark-skinned lower class. Such a system emerged in the Greek and Roman colonies of North Africa. It provided the context within which North African theologians lived.

After the Greeks penetrated Egypt they built up the city of Alexandria on the Mediterranean coast as the greatest Greek commercial and intellectual center in the world. It was also the center of North African intellectual life. Other Egyptian cities fell under Greek domination, too, including the ancient shrine cities of Memphis and Thebes.[142] The ideals of classical Greece did not dominate this Hellenistic milieu. As one student of ancient Egypt has phrased it, the Ptolemaic Greek rulers of Egypt, in establishing their dominance,

> were faced with the same problem as so many conquerors of old civilizations: maintenance of rule by a very small minority of a foreign race and culture over the great mass of a conquered people. . . . In order to prevent the destruction of this ruling class in Egypt the mingling of the two peoples was strictly forbidden. The new masters settled in closed groups and they alone were allowed to bear arms. Mixed marriages were forbidden.[143]

As in many other cases, such rules proved to be not only unenforceable but actually dysfunctional. As time went on,

> it became necessary to take Egyptians into the army; the order against mixed marriages was forgotten; a large class of mixed race grew up; and many Egyptians exerted great political and financial influence.[144]

The Greeks living in Egypt became a very different group in speech and custom from the Greeks in Greece. They developed a *colon* mentality. The masses of the people were exploited Egyptian peasants. The ruling class evolved as a polyglot mixed group in which Egyptian Greeks predominated but which included some assimilated Egyptians.

However, with the Roman conquest in 30 B.C., Augustus Caesar deliberately set up a divide-and-rule system in the form of "insur-

mountable barriers between the two peoples of the Nile Valley."
All Egyptians were classified as *dedicti,* which made them "legally
no more than serfs . . . the property of the emperor." The Greeks
were classified as *foederati* ("confederates"). The reasoning behind
this classification had nothing to do with beliefs about racial or
color superiority, but the objective result was to create a status
division that roughly coincided with a difference in physical type.
The same was true throughout northern Africa, where brown-
skinned Berbers were "second-class citizens" under Roman rule.[145]
As for Egyptians:

> Any possibility of rising higher in the social scale was prohibited by
> law. It was completely out of the question for an Egyptian to gain
> Roman citizenship. . . . Egyptians could not be taken into the armed
> forces because this automatically brought Roman citizenship.[146]

Egyptians were also barred from attendance at the Greek schools
(the gymnasia) and thus from the university in Alexandria. They
were shut out from all the higher official posts.[147] Greeks were the
large landowners, and few Egyptians could acquire enough wealth or
political patronage to enter that class. The Roman government laid a
heavy tax on all segments of the population, although the wealthy
Greeks were quite adept at evading it. It has been noted that "over
these two completely divided parts of the population was now placed
a handful of Roman soldiers and officials. . . . They were certainly
the most highly privileged class in the Roman Empire."[148] These
rulers and the wealthy Greeks associated socially.

The Romans also revived and tightened the neglected Greek law
against intermarriage and reversed the trend toward assimilation
and amalgamation. People of mixed blood thereby suffered.

> How to classify the progeny of mixed marriages? Up to now they had
> been tacitly reckoned among the Greeks; more important, they
> themselves considered that they belonged to them. . . . [Emperor
> Augustus] brought the pretensions of the half-castes abruptly to an
> end; they were decreed to be on the level of the Egyptians, and like
> them completely debarred from every possibility of improving their
> social position.[149]

In the social order of Hellenistic Egypt, the only people "below"
Egyptians in power and prestige were enslaved Blacks from Ethiopia.

Changes had occurred as well in views held about the once
"blameless" Ethiopian. Between A.D. 100 and A.D. 200, the old image
of "civilized" Ethiopians residing in Meroë came in competition

with another image generated by chronic warfare between the Roman legions and tribes on both sides of the borders of the kingdom of Meroë. Blemmyes and Nobatae together constituted a black enemy attacking Rome's friendly black state, Meroë. It is also possible that enough Blacks were appearing as captives and mercenary soldiers in Egyptian and North African cities to excite general comment about "wild" and "uncivilized" black men as compared with the more acculturated resident black populations.

The word "Ethiopian" referred to two quite distinct entities during this period. On the one hand, there was a turbulent but brave mass of black people divided into a number of ethnic groups, some of whom were as savage as the white Scythians in northeastern Europe. On the other hand, there were rulers whose history stemmed from a glorious past and who were trying to restore the order that had once prevailed. Meroë was continuing the task of "civilizing" other Africans that some believed had begun in remote antiquity with Osiris and his wife, Isis.

As the evangelization of the upper Nile valley proceeded, a work of fiction written in Greek during the third century A.D. became popular among literate Christians. It romanticized the past and had as its hero an Ethiopian king who became a reformer and who began to lead his people along a path that suppressed old savage customs. The romance was *Aethiopica*, authored by one Heliodorus and reissued in English by the University of Michigan in 1957.[150]

Some literary critics believe that the author of *Aethiopica* was a Stoic philosopher or a Gymnosophist trying to make the point that wisdom and sentiments of humaneness are to be found among all races of men, not among Greeks alone. Others think Heliodorus was a Christian bishop interested in converting Ethiopians and bent upon convincing those who had prejudice against them that there was nobility among them as well as barbarity. And some students of the subject are convinced that whatever the religious or philosophical orientation of Heliodorus, he was probably a man of color.[151]

As the plot unfolds, the black queen of Ethiopia, giving birth to a white daughter, fears that the black king will accuse her of adultery. She has the girl spirited away to Greece, where she grows up at the shrine of Delphi and falls in love with a Greek nobleman. When her mother sends for her to come home, the couple return together. As they reach the border between Egypt and Ethiopia, they find themselves in the middle of a battle between Persian invaders and soldiers of the girl's father. The story gives high praise to the

Ethiopian warriors:

> The Persians thought it was sheer madness for so small a group to charge a force so much larger and so perfectly equipped. Thinking such foolhardiness was a godsend to them and would enable them to sweep the enemy away at the first encounter, they charged the more furiously. But when the Blemmyes [an Ethiopian tribe] were within reach and all but impaled on the spears, they crouched down, supporting themselves on one knee, and avoiding the horses' hoofs they thrust their heads and backs under the horses' bellies. This unexpected maneuver worked great carnage.[152]

Others were praised for their archery, the famous "eye piercers."

When the battle is won, the victorious king's daughter and her lover are caught up among the prisoners of war. They are about to be sacrificed, according to Ethiopian custom, when she claims her noble lineage. Her father, King Hydaspes, although astonished, accepts her. Reflecting on the death he had almost caused, the black king abolishes human sacrifice and extends mercy to the Persian commander.

Moses Hadas, in the University of Michigan's translation, gave the following opinion on the significance of the book:

> In effect the book is a glorification of a dark-skinned race and an obscure sect. It is easy to believe that the author was a colored man; it is clear that he was attached to the gymnosophist cult. . . . The Ethiopian king is a model of wisdom and righteousness, and his people are highly cultivated. The author's concern for these matters goes far beyond romantic requirements, and the episode at Delphi takes on special significance in this connection. Here . . . a descendant of Achilles himself falls in love with an Ethiopian girl who is shown to be fully his social equal. Recognition in the most ancient and highly regarded sanctuary of Greece is a sufficient victory; minorities wish only equality, not superiority.[153]

However, the positive attitudes held by some Greeks, Romans, and Egyptians toward individuals like King Hydaspes and the educated minority in Meroë existed side by side with negative stereotypes about ordinary Ethiopians handed down in the works of historians and geographers, and gleaned from watching them in gladiatorial combats or viewing them as prisoners of war paraded through the streets of cities in the Roman Empire.

In North Africa Ethiopians of the Diaspora were functioning in a color-based social structure. Their situation was worsened when the Christian church reinforced the negative attitudes about Ethiopians by making their skin color a symbol of sin.

Blackness in the Christian Confrontation with Paganism

We have mentioned that some of the earliest Church Fathers made allegorical use of stories about Ethiopians in both the Old and New Testaments and set the goal for Christianity of "washing the Ethiopian white." This goal was implicit in the concept of spreading the Gospel throughout the world and establishing communities of the "saved" within which converted Ethiopians would be the equals of any other men and women. The historian of classical antiquity, Westermann, has contrasted this ideal with the practice of other religions with which Christianity was competing:

> The belief that all men were of one human brotherhood was nothing new or startling. In pre-Christian days it had already been expressed in the ancient world, notably as a dogma of Stoic thought. A new element was, however, injected into the Christian concept of the brotherhood of all men. . . . There came into the Christian relationship between men and their God an intimacy which cut across all lines of caste or status. This had been absent from the pagan worships.[154]

The egalitarian ideal had to be adjusted to customs and social structures of the many varied concrete situations in which Christian congregations existed, and to beliefs about ethnicity and race that were already operating when the new faith began to replace paganism in specific areas. Under Roman imperial rule, Christians lived in societies in which slavery was considered normal but was not restricted to any single racial or ethnic group. The story of Onesimus in the New Testament is Paul's defense of a Christian runaway slave returning to his master. His subordination to a master did not alter his equality "in the sight of God" or in relations with his Christian brothers and sisters, according to Paul. There are no biblical sanctions for keeping Blacks in slavery because they are black, but there is no opposition to slavery.

Christians did not use nonbibilical Jewish supports to justify slavery and the slave trade until after the fourteenth century, when those institutions were being confined exclusively to Negroes. Failure to use the Mesopotamian Jewish tradition earlier is significant in view of the fact that the Church Fathers had defined the Ethiopians south and east of Egypt as the main target of their missionary efforts and used "Ethiopia" as a metaphor for sin, especially sexual sin. The noncanonical nature of Talmud and Midrash may have been the crucial factor in not using them.

Attitudes toward sub-Saharan Africans under imperial Rome, though not as favorable as those of classical Greece, were relatively positive. However, the colors black and white in the dominant symbol system during the Roman imperial period stood in Manichaean contrast to each other. North African and Egyptian theologians, as well as some in Asia Minor began to equate the color "black" with impurity when contrasted to the color "white." In Egypt and other North African areas this evaluation was "carried over" to the appraisal of skin color. Theologians viewed sub-Saharan Africans, i.e., "Ethiopians," as living symbols of sin, and their cultures were believed to encourage sexual excesses. An obsession with sexual behavior during the first five centuries of Christian thought and practice (remember, Origen had himself castrated!) contributed toward entrenchment of negative attitudes toward the peoples and cultures of "black Africa." The close proximity of Egypt to Ethiopia focused the attention of Church Fathers and desert ascetics there upon sub-Saharan Africans to an extent that did not occur elsewhere.

In becoming Christians sub-Saharan Africans had to be persuaded to conceive of their own cultures as depraved and of themselves as needing "cleansing," symbolically by baptism, from the contamination of their pagan societies. In theological parlance they had to be "born again of the spirit and the water."

Although there are no recorded accounts of these conversions, the first black Africans to become Christian were probably Ethiopians and Negroid Egyptians living in the Middle Eastern and Mesopotamian Diaspora in the days of imperial Rome, mainly as slaves. These may have joined Christian congregations in cities along the North African littoral and on the northern side of the Mediterranean as far west as Italy. Some were probably present, too, in the Asia Minor churches of such cities as Antioch, Thyatira, Smyrna and Pergamos, out of which the Nestorian branch of Christianity grew early in the fifth century A.D. and spread into Mesopotamia, Persia, and parts of India and China. The Black Experience in Nestorian communities still awaits research. Christian communities in Mesopotamia were operating within a social system that gave rise to the antiblack Zanj stereotype and that propagated the Manichaean contrast between Light and Darkness. Soon after these communities were established the black-skin-as-curse belief emerged in the culture surrounding them. How seriously black communicants were affected by these structures and ideas is, at this point, a question that cannot be answered.

Black experience with Christianity is usually thought to have begun with the conversion and baptism by the Apostle Philip of an

Ethiopian official who was riding in a chariot back to his homeland up the Nile, after a visit to Jerusalem to offer a sacrifice. This story, embedded as it was in the New Testament (Acts of the Apostles 8:26-40), became widely known throughout Christendom. Less widely known was the persistent belief in Egypt that Christianity was introduced into that country by St. Mark, and that he was martyred and buried there.[155]

Whatever its origin within Egypt, Christianity spread rapidly in that country, taking root in a population subordinated by Greco-Roman elites who kept themselves separate from the darker-skinned masses, but who assimilated a few persons of color into the highest strata. Historians agree that sometime during the first hundred years of the Christian Era, churches were established in the Egyptian city of Alexandria, and that a group of intellectuals associated with the well-educated, sophisticated Greek population of this multiethnic, multiracial city became involved in the theological speculations that later made the North African church famous.[156] Alexandria also became the site of one of the most important bishoprics, along with Rome and Constantinople. The extent to which clergymen of color were involved in the continuous disputations about the more esoteric aspects of the faith is, at this state of our research, unknown. The experience of Father Moses is testimony to the fact that the Christian hierarchy in Alexandria was not completely free from the skin-color prejudice that existed among the Greco-Roman elites in the Egypt of the Roman imperial period. It was a prejudice that persisted into the period of rule by the representatives of the Byzantine Roman Emperor in Constantinople.

Egyptian Christians expressed their resentment and sense of ethnic solidarity by forming the Coptic Orthodox Church, which maintained its own hierarchy apart from the bishopric at Alexandria. As a result of numerous theological disputes and several ecumenical church councils, some consensus in both the Roman Catholic and the Eastern Catholic communions was reached. However, the Coptics remained theologically outside of that consensus as did the masses of the North African Berber Christians in the Maghreb west of Egypt, who expressed their hostility toward dominance in religious affairs of both Rome and Constantinople by giving their allegiance to the Donatist heresy.

Augustine was made Bishop of the North African church in A.D. 396 and became the most influential theologian within the western Latin Catholic patriarchate centered in Rome. He did not refrain from using the power of the state against the Pelagian heresy as well as the Donatists. However, he had no jurisdiction over Coptic Egyptians. As to pagan Africans south of Egypt, they were covered by his remarks about the proper Christian assessment of "strange" human beings. During the century when Augustine made his observation about all men, "however strange," being members of the human family, Christianity was already firmly established in the urbanized areas of North Africa as well as of Egypt. Acrimonious disputes were going on about varied interpretations of the Scriptures. These reflected ethnic and national conflicts as well as theological differences. As a native of a North African city, Augustine had no doubt seen black people with Negroid features who had adopted Berber customs. But he, like other North Africans, had to depend upon hearsay about the customs of the Blacks residing on the oases in the vast Sahara and Libyan deserts, and those who lived in the savannah, sahel, and forest lands below those deserts. Augustine referred to Ethiopians as "the blackest of men" and the "remotest of men." Their black color and Negroid features signified the "strange" customs that characterized their societies. Despite the veneration of feudal European critics for St. Augustine, their remoteness from the "remotest of men" did not prejudice them against sub-Saharan Africans. For Augustine himself, another group of "strange" people constituted an immediate threat, European barbarians from Europe, the Vandals who swept through Spain and then eastward across North Africa. They captured Hippo, the seat of Augustine's bishopric, just after his death in A.D. 430.

Unlike Origen, Tertullian, and Jerome, Augustine never addressed himself to the conversion of Ethiopians. During the century after his death the bishops in Alexandria, Egypt, and in Constantinople assumed the task, anxious to win a wider following for the competing varieties of Christian doctrine they espoused. While Ethiopians were the "remotest of men" to Augustine the Tunisian, to his Egyptian neighbors they were very close, not separated by a desert. From pharaonic times Egyptian rulers had made war on the "uncivilized" Blacks who lived on both sides of the Nile and far south of the "civilized" Blacks in the kingdoms of Napata and Meroë with whom the pharaohs cooperated from time to time. (See section on the Nile Valley civilizations in volume 1.) The kingdoms of Nobatae (Nubia) and Makuria replaced these ancient kingdoms, and their troops occasionally invaded Egypt, sometimes as allies of rebel groups. Christians in Egypt considered their pagan customs a constant threat. Of particular concern were what rumor inaccurately described as "orgiastic rites" connected with the worship of the goddess, Isis, who was very popular in Egypt and much of the Mediterranean world as well as in Nobatae. The Coptic Christians in Egypt, many of whom, in physical type, were similar to the Ethiopians, showed no enthusiasm for mounting a crusade to "wash the Ethiopian white."

The first breakthrough into the lands of the black pagans did not occur in the kingdoms immediately adjacent to Egypt but rather on the Red Sea coast of East Africa. Early in the fourth century, a Syrian Christian named Frumentius was made a prisoner after a shipwreck at a Red Sea port. Through the influence of Christian traders settled there, he was able to travel to the capital of the king in the highlands. Frumentius converted the king to Christianity, and the faith spread among some of his pagan and Jewish subjects. Eventually an indigenous church hierarchy emerged. At first it claimed legitimacy by giving allegiance to the patriarch in Constantinople. Later, it affiliated itself with the Coptic bishopric in Egypt as the Ethiopian Orthodox Church. High church dignitaries, frequently distinctly Negroid, participated in pilgrimages to Jerusalem and went to conferences in Rome. However, the so-called Solomonid Dynasty, claiming descent from Solomon and the Queen of Sheba, shaped the style for Christian artistic representations. The somatic norm image of the upper-class Amharic ethnic group still predominates in religious paintings—the light-brown person with Mediterranean-type features and straight or wavy hair.

The overwhelming majority of the subjects of the Amharic kings were, and are, "black" as Latin Americans define that term, that is, dark brown with Negroid features and hair. Nevertheless, people of their type seldom appear in the beautiful narrative paintings that illustrate the myth surrounding the visit of the Queen of Sheba to King Solomon. They are believed to have had a son, Menelik, who brought the Ark of the Covenant to the East African highlands. Nor does the Negro physical type appear in depictions of the Madonna and Child and the apostles and angels.

A skin-color preference is plainly evident in hagiography and it reflects the preference in the social relations of the ruling circles— brown skin rather than either white or black. In actuality an occasional Negro was present within the ruling stratum, and much more frequently in the church hierarchy. Black skin color had a religious/mystical significance that it lacks in the other domains. A similar color preference to that in Ethiopia has been evident among the Coptic Christian leaders in Egypt. Nevertheless, one painting has been found in an ancient monastery near Cairo that depicts both the Virgin Mary and the infant Jesus with Negroid features.

The Blacks of Ethiopia were accepted as full-fledged members of eastern Christendom. During the sixth century A.D. the patriarch of Constantinople appealed to the rulers of Ethiopia to cross the Red Sea to invade Yemen in southern Arabia to punish the Jewish rulers who were accused of mistreating Christians, in events that will be discussed in Chapter 5. Historians agree that what took the form of a religious conflict in this south Arabian region was really a struggle for control of the trade routes from Asia to the Middle East through Arabia.

Reinforcing esthetic preferences in the elite circles of the Ethiopian highlands was the transfer of antiblack biases from the early Alexandrian church leaders that had become a part of the Coptic liturgy used in the Ethiopian Orthodox Church. This despite the fact that many of the church leaders were black. The legend of Father Moses appears in one of the readings used in worship. It perpetuates stereotypes about what constitutes a "good" Negro and a "bad" Negro. In the reading for the liturgy, Father Moses is mentioned a number of times as "Moses the Black," with the same mixture of awe and condescension that appears in the quotations cited previously from the Menalogium.

In the Ethiopian church, the reading for the Tenth Month, June 5-July 4, after "In the Name of the Father and the Son and the Holy Ghost, One God," notes that "on this day Saint Abba Moses the Black became a martyr." The reading tells the story of Moses' flight from slavery to monks in the desert of Scete, his conversion, his "war" with Satan, and his selection as abbot by the brethren. It recounts the "test" in which the archbishop first scorns Moses ("Why have ye brought this black man here? Take him away") and then makes him a priest: "Behold, thou hast become white, all of thee within and without."[157] Eventually some unnamed barbarians attacked the monastery. Abba Moses decided that he had been called to martyrdom: "For it is written, He who hath slain with the knife shall die by the knife." All the brethren, except he and seven others, fled as he advised them to do, "and he went out to the barbarians and they killed him."

The reader of this lesson in a church would then end his account of the martyrdom with a word to the Ethiopian faithful:

> Observe, O our brethren, the power of repentance and what it doth. It changed a man who was an infidel, and a murderer, and a fornicator, and a thief and made him a father, and a teacher, and a comforter, and a priest, and one who laid down the rule and Canon of the monks, and one who is mentioned at the altar in all the churches.

And his body abideth to this day in Dabra Badremos, and many signs and miracles are made manifest through it. Salutation to Moses the Black.[158]

The message of the Father Moses legend is clear—Christianity is necessary to "wash an Ethiopian white." Whether when presented in this fashion it is inimical to the self-esteem of black people who read these words or hear them read—in the presence of lighter-skinned fellow worshippers—is an as-yet-unanswered question. Negroidness is explicitly devalued. Calling him "the Black" in a church ceremony emphasizes the undesirable somatic image. Snowden states that newly converted black Christians who were Father Moses' contemporaries accepted the view that black symbolized sin in an allegorical sense without feeling any personal shame. They "found it inoffensive to their blackness," he insists.[159] Perhaps in a society that was not basically racist this was possible; but in our own post-sixteenth century world culture such a reaction is inconceivable.

Christianity had been the state religion in highland Ethiopia for over a century by the time the Faith became institutionalized in the nations of Nobatae (Nubia), Makuria, and Alwa, immediately south of Egypt. In A.D. 540, Justinian, Emperor of the Eastern Roman Empire, which had become the secular arm of Christianity, struck a dramatic blow on behalf of the faith. He sent his troops to the first cataract of the Nile to demolish the shrine of Isis, the popular goddess, which attracted pilgrims seeking holy water from as far away in the west as Italy. This pagan cult was in competition with the Church in Egypt which was nominally Christian, and in Nobatae and Makuria, where the bishops of both Alexandria and Constantinople wished to spread the faith. The black goddess was dethroned. Some students feel that after the destruction of the Isis shrine and the carrying away of her image to Constantinople, Isis worship continued, in an attenuated and disguised form, in the veneration of the Madonna and Child, and that Black Madonnas in Europe may be remnants of Isis worship.

In A.D. 540 the king of Nobatae became a Christian and used his power and influence to spread nominal Christianity among his subjects. In A.D. 580, the king of Makuria south of Nobatae became a Christian. The process of "washing the Ethiopian white" proceeded rapidly within the Nile valley of these kingdoms but less rapidly among the tribesmen of the desert on both sides of the river valley. The American anthropologist William Y. Adams, who has authored a book on Nubia, is convinced that the Nile valley people were anxious to become affiliated with the wider world and joined the church without compulsion. The Afro-American historian Chancellor Williams feels that the price may have been too high. The Nubian written language was ignored in favor of Greek and Latin. A nonblack hierarchy was imposed upon Africans, and they had to fight that elite to secure an indigenous clergy. No schools for training black aspirants for the ministry were opened. He charges anti-Negro prejudice verging on White Racism.

Studies of murals in churches that have been uncovered as part of a UNESCO project reveal pictorial representations that were not typical of the black majority but were not white. For instance, Bishop Kyros (A.D. 879) and Bishop Petros (A.D. 975) are both painted as light brown with Negroid features. One archaeologist reports that Nubian frescoes dated as of the eleventh century A.D. always show Christ, the Virgin and the saints as white.[160] This might be interpreted as an attempt to make an historically accurate statement by people who had different color and features from those in Palestine, but the practice could mean adoption of Coptic and Byzantine practices in religious painting. When the Muslims invaded Egypt in A.D. 640 they made no serious efforts to conquer the kingdoms south of Egypt, which remained Christian for over 600 years. Studies of the art for the period after the tenth century A.D. are not available.

Summary

The founding fathers of the Christian religion, which gradually became the integrating ideology in Western Europe and the Near East, carried on their debates and disputations, their exhortations and admonitions, within a framework of mythic history that they invested with rich spiritual meanings. In the Judaic Old Testament, they found a legacy that, while not color blind, is not prejudiced against Africans because of their skin color. The biblical tradition does not present derogatory stereotypes of black people, nor does it speak of Ethiopians in terms more disparaging than those used to describe other "heathens" and sometimes-enemies, sometimes-allies who surrounded Israel and Judea. Even as the Prophets abused African rulers for their idolatry and "abominations," Jewish kings were exchanging emissaries and fighting side by side with them against the Assyrians.

There was a universalistic note in some of the Prophets that transcended Hebrew ethnocentrism, and this appealed to the Church Fathers. It was a tone they also found in some aspects of the Greco-Roman tradition. The classicist Westermann stresses the fact that Christian leaders incorporated the most humane aspects of the pagan philosophies in their concept of a Christian community where even slaves were to be welcomed as "brothers and sisters."[161]

Early Christian theologians were exposed to the literature and folklore of classical Greece (i.e., Athens), and of Roman philosophers, historians, essayists and playwrights as part of their education. Favorable attitudes toward Ethiopians were a part of this tradition. Greek tradition provided a history of color symbolism that was polysemic. When referring to temperament and behavior, the early Greeks had considered the "dark heart" as the normal passionate and compassionate condition of a person, while the "white heart" was equivalent to our expression, "cold-hearted." Even in classical times, darkness was considered a positive attribute in men, and whiteness could be a symbol of cowardice.

Yet first-hand contact with increasing numbers of sub-Saharan Africans introduced some negative esthetic and status-allocating evaluations. Also, meanings would change with time due to the influence of Persian ideas about a cosmic struggle between the forces of Light and Darkness. Even positive attitudes toward the mythical Ethiopians would change, so much so that Memnon, a hero in Greek mythology, had become a symbol of bad luck by Roman times. However, the Homeric myth that spoke of Ethiopians as a people highly favored by the gods did not disappear.[162]

As encounters between Greeks and real Ethiopians became more frequent, the evaluation of Africans in terms of "civilized" versus "uncivilized" became the basic consideration in dealing with black cultures and individuals. The philosophers of the Greek Golden Age were not color-blind; rather, they were intrigued by the existence of many varieties of mankind and theorized about the causes and implications of these differences. They speculated, too, about why some men were slaves and about the ethics of holding fellow men in bondage. Color or "blackness" was never cited as either a reason or a justification for enslavement.[163] *Racial* slavery, in which all slaves were of one racial group and all masters of another, was never institutionalized.

However, the Greek explanation of the origin of skin color differences opened the door to deterministic theories that intermixed physical characteristics with personality traits. Ethiopians were black, the Greeks said, because they lived in a hot climate, a situation that was also believed to result in heightened sexuality. The Church Fathers accepted the environmentalist theories, and concurrently developed a symbolic system that equated black skin color not just with inordinate sensuality, but with evil generally.

Prejudice against black skin color, and even some discrimination against individual Ethiopians, developed among North African church officials. This is typified by the case of the martyred Father Moses, described by his fellow Christians as "a man whose body was black but whose soul was brighter than the splendor of the sun." The contempt expressed for the color of Father Moses' integument has deeper roots than the allegorical interpretations of "spiritual blackness" and "spiritual whiteness" stressed by Professor Frank Snowden in *Blacks in Antiquity*. The evidence in his case reveals that it was coupled with discriminatory behavior.

The preoccupation of North African Christian churchmen with the color symbolism of Ethiopian bodies arose in the cultural context that produced the fundamentally racist ideas of Julian the Apostate and Galen the physician—a multiethnic Roman Empire that was bringing people of different racial groups into contact on a scale never before seen, thus exacerbating ethnic and class tensions. It is also related to the social and economic structure of Hellenistic Egypt.

All students of ancient Alexandria stress the extent to which both the social structure and the ecology of the city reflected a high degree of ethnic separatism. Roman conquerors established strict class barriers along color lines in a society where upper status Greeks and Egyptians had intermixed with less rigid social distinctions. However, the Greek monopoly of opportunity within the educational process made negligible the flow of young Egyptian and Ethiopian scholars trained in Greek thought styles into the ranks of the intellectual elite. This and other factors limited Egyptian and Ethiopian upward mobility within Egyptian society, thus accentuating the stereotyping of Blacks as an inferior group. In a society structured in this fashion, Ethiopians, most of them slaves, were powerless aliens at the bottom of the heap.

For Christians, black skin came to symbolize more than depressed social status, which existed in the whole North African Diaspora, as well as in Egypt. It also symbolized the paganism of African homelands, a condition that must be wiped out by the spread of the Gospel. The missionary movement based, as it was, among lighter-skinned Christian theologians in Egypt and Byzantium, with the goal of converting darker-skinned "heathens" in Africa, probably reinforced the tendency existing in the Christian symbol system to equate blackness with sin. This began with the allegorical use of biblical stories about Ethiopians, but was intensified by Persian intellectual influences, spreading rapidly in educated circles throughout North Africa and the Middle East.[164] In Paul's time, white skin and European paganism were correlated in Christian social perceptions, but by the time a serious effort was made to establish the church in Africa, dark skin color had come to be associated with paganism.

Black *people*—Ethiopians—became a symbol of sin. A black person could be "saved." However, it was necessary to "wash the Ethiopian white" through the rituals of conversion and baptism. What had been a Judaic sect evolved into a world religion during the first five hundred years of the Christian Era. These ideas about blackness and black people spread with it.

The color prejudice against Ethiopians that evolved in Hellenistic Egypt was in contradiction with the ancient Greek tradition. Neither did it have roots in the Old Testament adapted from Judaism, although some elements of the Judaic oral tradition would have supported such prejudice. In Midrashic and Talmudic tradition, black skin was the result of a curse, and the enslavement of black people was to some extent a punishment for the sins of their ancestors. There is little to support the idea that these Midrashic and Talmudic stories, which are nowhere mentioned in the writings of the Church Fathers, had any strong influence on early Christianity. The Talmud manuscripts did not become available until the sixth century A.D. The biblical story of Noah's curse on Ham does not mention color.

In assessing the role of myths and ideologies discussed in this chapter it is important to emphasize time and place as factors operating to make them socially salient. Christianity arose in Judea, a Near Eastern province of the Roman Empire where black people were not numerous. One Judean experience with large numbers of Blacks under the empire was traumatic. During Trajan's reign, a Moorish general, Lusius Quietus, was sent with African troops to put down a rebellion (A.D. 105-106). The soldiers exhibited unusual brutality in doing so. We have no record of the impact of these Moorish soldiers on the Christian communities in Judea or of how ordinary people in Palestine reacted to this brutal repression. The Babylonian Talmud mentions the incident but without any reference to the race of the soldiers and their leader. The Jews of the Mesopotamian diaspora were exposed to a less harsh experience. Exiled and harassed during the formative years of Christianity, the Jewish people were most secure in Mesopotamia where, ironically, the black-skin-as-a-curse legend became embedded in the nonbiblical written tradition.

Some emphasis has been placed in this chapter upon the difference in the kind of experience with black people that the Jewish people had in the Mesopotamian diaspora as contrasted with experience in the Palestinian homeland. There is no indubitable evidence of racial prejudice toward black people in the sacred literature of Palestine. In the literature of Mesopotamia, there definitely is. There is some support for a theory that such anti-Negro sentiments were generated in the Mesopotamian diaspora, where exiled Jews came in contact with African "Zanj," who differed markedly from the "civilized" Ethiopians and Egyptians present in Palestine. Also, as the Mesopotamian Jews eventually came to participate in the exploitation of the Zanj as slaves, it is possible that legends about a curse of blackness proved useful in justifying their activities.

Pointing out this contrast is intended not merely to highlight the situational contrast within Judaism—Palestine versus Mesopotamia—but also to indicate how a given set of myths and legends can become salient at one historic period and not at another. For centuries, Christian theologians did not utilize the pejorative material from nonbiblical Judaic sources, even after it was widely circulated. The "black-skin-as-curse" theory was certainly known to some Christians by the twelfth century A.D., since the Pope found it important enough to denounce. As we shall see in Chapter 6, positive attitudes toward black people that were also a part of the Christian tradition were dominant in Europe during this time. It was not until the sixteenth century, when a printed version of the Babylonian Talmud became available in Europe, that a few English scholars began to discuss the "curse of blackness" concurrent with the involvement of Britain in the transatlantic slave trade. Some scholars and theologians used it only as an explanatory myth for differences in skin color, but others used it for ideological purposes, as justification for the enslavement of Africans, a massive trade in black bodies sanctioned by Church and State. It was its social salience for the defenders of slavery that finally brought prominence to this relatively inconspicuous myth from the Hebrew Mesopotamian diaspora.[165]

It is ironic that the myth was spread throughout the Middle East not by the Jews, but by the intellectuals of the religion that replaced Christianity throughout that area. At the outset its leaders boasted that they had no prejudice against Negroes. An episode in the Muslim conquest of Egypt reveals their claim as well as the extent to which, by the seventh century A.D., a high church dignitary was deviating from the earliest Christian rejection of color prejudice.

The Egyptian masses, some of whom were certainly Negroid during the fifth and sixth centuries, clung to their Coptic variety of Christianity even after the country was made part of the Eastern Roman Empire, and Constantinople named the official church dignitaries. We have no record of the state of race relations in the Eastern Empire during this period but have some evidence that not all of its functionaries were free of color prejudice. It is possible that negative attitudes toward Negroes may have contributed to the hostility that had grown so strong that the Coptic Christians welcomed the invading Muslim Arabs in 640 A.D.

A tradition has been preserved by Muslim scholars that purports to contrast the skin-color prejudice of the Christian archbishop in Alexandria with their own abhorrence of such attitudes. Acting on behalf of the established Catholic church, the archbishop was authorized to negotiate with the Muslim Arabs who had invaded the country. According to one account:

'Amr [the Arab leader] accordingly deputed ten of his officers, headed by a powerful negro (sic) called 'Ubadah ibn as-Samit. . . . The Arabs were ferried across to Raudah . . . when 'Ubadah was ushered into the presence [of] the Roman archbishop the latter was shocked and exclaimed ''Take away that black man: I can have no discussion with him.'' But the Arabs explained that 'Ubadah was one of their most trusted and capable leaders, and that 'Amr had commissioned him personally to treat with the Romans. To the Archbishop's further astonishment, they added that they held negroes (sic) and white men in equal respect—that they judged a man by his character, not his colour. And 'Ubadah, when bidden to speak gently, so as not to frighten the delicate prelate, replied, ''There are a thousand blacks, as black as myself, among our companions. I and they would be ready each to meet and fight a hundred enemies together. We love only to fight for God, and to follow His will. We care nought for wealth, so long as we have wherewithal to stay our hunger and to clothe our bodies. This world is nought to us, the next world is all.'' This profession of piety moved the Archbishop. ''Do you hear this?'' he said to his companions; ''I much fear that God has sent these men to devastate the world.'' Then turning to 'Ubadah, he remarked, ''I have listened, good sir, to your account of yourself and your comrades, and I understand why your arms so far have prevailed. I know also that the Romans have failed by caring overmuch for earthly things. But now they are preparing to send against you immense numbers of well-armed battalions. Resistance will be hopeless. But for the sake of peace, we will agree to pay a sum of money at the rate of two dinars a head for every man in the Arab army, a hundred dinars for your commander, and a thousand for your Caliph, on condition that you return to your own country."

To this 'Ubadah answered, "Do not deceive yourselves. We are not afraid of your numbers. Our greatest desire is to meet the Romans in battle. If we conquer them it is well; if not, then we receive the good things of the world to come. Our prayer is for martyrdom in the cause of Islam, not for safe return to wife and children. Our small numbers cause us no fear; for it is written in the Book, 'Many a time hath a small company overcome a great host, by the will of God.' "[166]

In the next chapter we shall discuss this new religion that inspired 'Ubadah and examine the extent to which the egalitarian ideal was realized as Islam continued to spread.

5. THE BLACK EXPERIENCE IN THE MUSLIM WORLD

During the eighth and ninth centuries A.D., for the second time in five hundred years, a new crusading religion transformed the intellectual and moral life of Mesopotamia, the Middle East and North Africa. Both religions had profound implications for black people. The first transformation was due to Christianity, and what that meant for black people during the first four or five centuries of its growth has been discussed in the previous chapter. The second was Islam (a term meaning that the believers had surrendered themselves to the will of Allah, the Arab word for God). The episode recounted at the end of Chapter 4 documents a significant encounter between leaders of an Islamic army and a functionary of the Byzantine Christian empire. It is significant for what it tells us about the Black Experience in the formative stages of Islam, several centuries after the birth of Christianity.

Between A.D. 630 and A.D. 730, bands of warriors, missionaries, and settlers from Arabia, urged on by the cry, "There is no God but Allah and Mohammed is his prophet," swept through the southern portion of the Byzantine Christian empire and the western part of the Sassanian Zoroastrian empire. In the former they began to replace the governmental institutions and religious beliefs and practices that had developed from the impact of Christian values on Hellenistic and indigenous African and Middle Eastern cultures.

By the end of the eleventh century the Muslim world and European Christendom were engaged in a military contest that began with the First Crusade and did not end until the defeat of the Ottoman Turkish Empire by a group of Western powers in the early twentieth century.

Black people were present in both the Christian and Islamic armies during the first phase of the long struggle between the two faiths. The reluctance of the Byzantine Christian leader in Egypt to surrender to a black follower of Mohammed documents the fact that although Christianity still proclaimed a doctrine of the equality of all men, some six hundred years after the birth of that religion not all of its leaders were adhering to that doctrine. This chapter discusses the manner in which Islam, which began with a similar doctrine, deviated from it when Islam was adopted by people in cultures that carried racial and ethnic stereotypes, or when the economic and political interests of various groups profited from invidious discrimination based upon ethnic and racial differences.

Within a few centuries after its founding Islam became the faith of tens of thousands of black people as well as hundreds of thousands of brown, yellow and white people. It provided a socio-political matrix within which they lived their lives. People of color have always taken the egalitarian teachings of Mohammed seriously. Others have not always done so. Absence of color prejudice has remained an ideal within Muslim societies, but has frequently not been realized in practice. We shall be concerned with the conditions under which deviations have occurred and the circumstances under which attempts have been made to re-emphasize egalitarian values by various groups of Muslims. Negative color prejudice sometimes emerged in inter-ethnic conflicts, but it was directed primarily against Negroes, not dark-skinned people in general, and only occasionally against lighter-skinned Europeans and Asians. We shall note the extent to which skin-color prejudice operated in the esthetic, erotic, status allocating, and religious/mystical domains, noting that the high values attached to military prowess in Muslim societies often operated to the advantage of individuals from Africa south of the Sahara.

Although most Blacks in the Islamic Middle East came into those cultures as slaves, not all slaves were black and in some situations slavery did not necessarily imply a degraded condition. A number of sub-Saharan kingdoms became a part of the economic and cultural nexus of the Muslim world after the eleventh century A.D., and today, all of Africa north of the equator has been profoundly affected by the southward spread of Islam.

In examining the Black Experience in the Muslim World between the seventh and sixteenth centuries A.D., a time frame that facilitates comparison with medieval Christendom, map 1 will be useful. The Middle East and Persia might be defined as The Central Islamic Lands, those areas in which Islam first struck deep roots and which formed the core of the Abbasid Caliphate, an organized empire that lasted from A.D. 750 until A.D. 1258.

A western periphery might be defined to include North Africa west of Egypt and Andalusia or Muslim Spain. This part of North Africa, sometimes called the Maghreb, was inhabited by the Berbers, a group of dark-skinned, tribally organized people who, through the

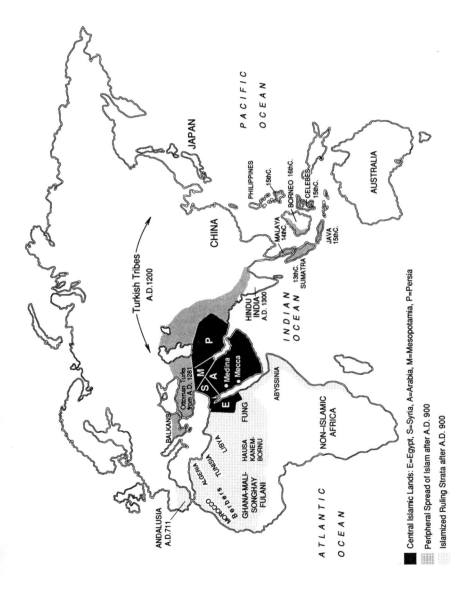

MAP 1. The Central Islamic Lands and the Peripheries in Medieval Times
Cartography based on a concept of the author.

centuries, had absorbed the genes of various European groups who came as conquerors and sub-Saharan Negroes, who came as slaves and warriors attached to Berber armies. When the Arabs began to invade this area during the eighth century, the Berbers of the coast were practising the Donatist variety of Christianity while those of the Atlas Mountain hinterland and portions of the desert were "pagans." Both groups resisted Arab conquest, but eventually accepted Islam and carried the faith southward into the kingdoms of the savannah lands: Ghana, Mali, Songhay, Hausa, Kanem-Bornu, and Fulani. During the eighth century, three-quarters of the Iberian peninsula became Andalusia or Muslim Spain and Portugal.

An eastern periphery was gradually Islamized and included parts of the Asian grasslands and of the Indian subcontinent as well as the Anatolian highlands (Turkey). There were scores of ethnic groups in this area which developed their own distinctive varieties of Islamized culture, but with a fundamental core of beliefs based on the Koran and a few rituals that were adhered to everywhere. A literate minority using the Arabic language provided a high degree of cultural homogeneity among elite groups throughout the Muslim world. (The Latin language played a similar role in European Christendom.) People of all races contributed toward the development of a civilization that made significant contributions toward the evolving civilizations of Western Europe during the same period when the Muslim World and Christendom were locked in combat during the Crusades (A.D. 1096-1365).

Chart 5 is provided for reference from time to time as the Black Experience is described in this chapter. Certain areas have been presented in such a manner as to relate events in one area to events happening at other places in the Muslim world at the same time, and to allow the tracing of events through time in each of the areas.

THE BIRTH OF ISLAM

Mohammed as Reformer and Synthesizer

The religion of Islam was born of the fervent preaching, physical courage, and organizational skill of Mohammed, an Arab orphan and caravan trader who today is revered by 580 million people of various races and ethnic backgrounds. During the seventh century A.D., he launched a verbal attack against polytheism and what he considered social injustice in his native city of Mecca (see map 2). Islam subsequently became one of the world's great religions.

CHART 5. COMPARISON OF KEY EVENTS IN OLD WORLD HISTORY
RELATED TO RACE RELATIONS

Date	West Africa	Spain & Portugal	The Maghreb	Egypt	Mesopotamia/ Persia
16th c.	Morocco defeats and conquers Songhay, which had replaced Mali as major Sudanic kingdom.	Small black settlements in Lagos, Lisbon, Seville, Cadiz; import of Guineans began in 1440s.	Sub-Saharan Africans used as concubines and domestic servants; over 100,000 Blacks in armies.	1517: Ottoman Turks begin 381 years of rule. White mamelukes curb power of black eunuchs, soldiers, and concubines.	Continued use of Sub-Saharan Africans as concubines and eunuchs in Baghdad area; continued use of East African Zanj in Persian Gulf area.
1495	Pilgrimage of Askia the Great, ruler of Songhay, to Mecca.	First African settlements in Iberian peninsula about 40 years old.			
1320	Pilgrimage of Mansa Musa, ruler of Mali, to Mecca.		Ibn Khaldun denounces black-skin-as-curse theory.		
12th c.		1148: Almohades from Morocco enter Spain.	Almoravids and Almohades conquer Maghreb.	1169: Black eunuchs lose power to Saladin.	
11th c.	1076: Almoravid Berbers conquer Ghana.	1086: Almoravids from Morocco enter Spain.		Fatimids take power with aid of black troops.	
10th c.	Ghana is dominant kingdom; gradually Islamized.	Gradual assimilation and amalgamation of few Blacks who came as soldiers and domestics.		Black vizier conquers Syria; conflict between black and white troops.	Recruitment of Blacks into caliph's army; subordinated by Turks. Turkish soliers usurp power.
9th c.	Kingdom of Ghana evolving since 4th c. A.D. on Soninke Negro base with Jewish and Berber influences.		Gradual Islamization of Berbers after wars of conquest by Arabs.	Conflict between Turkish and black soldiers.	868-883: Revolt of the Zanj. Rise of Abbasid caliphate
8th c.		711: Berbers and Arabs into Spain.			
7th c.		Visigoth Kingdom	Invasion of Maghreb by Arabs.	Egypt conquered by Arabs.	

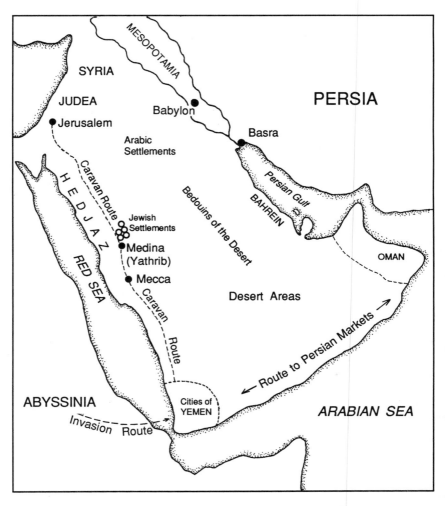

MAP 2. THE ARABIAN PENINSULA IN MOHAMMED'S DAY
Cartography based on a concept of the author.

According to his most reliable biographer, Mohammed, when a child, was sent to live for a while among the rural Bedouin tribesmen who were his kin. Like the Jews, the Bedouins of northern Arabia regard Abraham as their founding patriarch. According to the Hebrew tradition, Abraham's wife Sarah had a servant named Hagar who bore his first son, Ishmael, with Sarah's consent, she being barren. Sarah later bore a son, Isaac, through divine intervention. When Sarah and Hagar quarrelled, Abraham took Hagar and the infant Ishmael away from his homestead, leaving them with some bread and water at Beersheba, in the Negev desert.

As the Arabs tell the same story, Hagar was Abraham's second wife and a daughter of the Pharaoh, allowing them to claim a heritage of Egyptian royalty. Abraham escorted Hagar and their child to the very spot where the city of Mecca now stands. There, a well known as Zem Zem miraculously sprang up for their refreshment.[1] Both Jewish and Arab stories tell how Abraham returned regularly to check on the welfare of Hagar and Ishmael, who became the ancestor of the Arab people, as Sarah's son Isaac was ancestor of the Jewish people.

During these visits, according to the Arab tradition, Abraham built a house of worship that became known as the Kaaba. Ishmael's descendants allowed various other Semitic groups to settle around the well, Zem Zem. All of the people were idolatrous, and many were wicked. The Kaaba eventually became a shrine where the idols of many tribal gods were worshipped, as well as the god of Abraham.

Looking back on his childhood experience among tribal kin, Mohammed recalled being deeply impressed by an uncle who upbraided him for eating meat that had been sacrificed to idols in the city of Mecca. Mohammed never ate such meat again or made any offering to the idols in the Kaaba. This uncle had been ostracized for his beliefs. When Mohammed declared himself the Prophet of the new religion of Islam around A.D. 622, his self-proclaimed mission was to cleanse the Kaaba, destroy the idols, and restore the shrine to its original state of purity.

Mohammed's tribesmen, the Koreish, collected fees and gifts as custodians of the Kaaba. It is no mystery why they considered Mohammed a traitor to both his religion and his tribe. They said he had been led astray by Christians and Jews, and indeed these two religions were the major sources of the new synthesis Mohammed made.

Mohammed claimed to come with a message from God that confirmed the writings revealed to the Jews and Christians, according to Alfred Guillaume, professor of Arabic at the University of London.[2] The spirit of monotheism that animates the earlier religions breaks forth in the poetry of the first Sura (i.e., chapter) of the Koran: "In the name of God, the Compassionate and Merciful, . . . the king of the day of judgment . . . direct us in the right way." An echo of Christian Gospel teachings and of the Old Testament prophets can be found elsewhere in the Koran, where the sins of the new religion are made clear: "But ye know not the orphan / Nor urge ye one another to feed the poor / And ye devour heritages, devouring greedily / And ye love riches with exceeding love." The punishment for serving false gods and for social sins was not to be the national disaster that the Prophets foretold for the ancient Jews but rather individual consignment on the Day of Judgment to a Hell of intense pain. As time went on, Mohammed began to predict that the worst punishment was reserved for Unbelievers, that is, those who rejected his "revelation." For believing males a very enjoyable Paradise was promised.

Mohammed's wife was his first convert, and in the beginning only some members of his immediate family and some slaves and ex-slaves listened to his preachings. There were many unbelievers among the prosperous citizens of Mecca. They did not welcome Mohammed's call for an end to the idolatry represented by the Kaaba and for humane treatment of the poor people among them. Some abused him for preaching to what they considered the "rabble" of the city.[3] Some even instigated violence against the small band of believers that gradually formed.

If his tribe accused him of being led astray by Jews and Christians, they had reason for their charges. Mohammed was, indeed, familiar with some of the traditions and teachings held by followers of Judaism and Christianity, and perhaps with some of their rituals. It is highly probable that he had met and conversed with Jews and Christians during his journeys as the husband and trusted employee of a wealthy caravan trader. He may also have spoken with monks from some of the Christian religious communities in central Arabia and with residents of the Jewish villages that had been scattered here and there throughout the area for centuries. Textual criticism of the Koran has led some experts to conclude that Mohammed had either a Jewish audience or a circle acquainted with the broad outlines of the Old Testament stories.[4]

Blackness in the Koran

The Holy Koran is the result of Mohammed's brooding over what he knew of these religions, combined with original interpretations of what he had assimilated and flashes of insight that display shrewd and intelligent judgment as well as deep sincerity. In the beginning, he received what to him were "revelations" during trances while meditating in the mountains near Mecca. These were written down on leaves and skins, forming the basis for Islam's holy book. Later, they were more formally transcribed.

Like the story of Abraham and Hagar, the legend of Noah and his sons was part of accepted Arabic traditional lore. Arabs believed that they, like the Jews, were descendants of Noah's son Shem. The story of Noah and the Flood is told in the Koran, and additional details about Noah's family appear in the commentaries on the Koran.

Some of his opponents at Mecca accused Mohammed of "writing down old stories and fables told him by foreigners."[5] He apparently was familiar with some nonbiblical Jewish lore, but he did not include in the Koran any stories from the Babylonian Talmud or the Midrash about Noah's curse, or about black skin being a punishment for Ham's sexual delinquencies. Neither of these stories appears to have been part of northern Arabian folklore either, although both would appear later in the Muslim world.[6]

There is one Koran text that speaks of how the faces of the righteous would be turned white on the day of judgment, a concept not unlike the idea of Christian Church Fathers that conversion would "wash an Ethiop white." In the opinion of Arabist Bernard Lewis, the usage is purely symbolic, and such a belief did not automatically carry over to people. Opponents of color prejudice could quote Sura XV of the Koran, wherein Allah says, "We created man of dried clay, of black mud, formed him into shape; and we had before created the devil of subtle fire." The Koran also tells that when Elbis, the rebellious angel, said, "It is not fit that I should worship man whom thou hast created of dried clay, of black mud," Allah responded, "Get thee therefore hence . . . and a curse shall be on thee until the day of judgement."

The Koran teaches that all men are made of one substance—black mud. Apparently there was no negative connotation to black as a color. In early Islam, there were positive associations with blackness, as for instance the Kaaba stone of pre-Islamic devotion, and the tradition that the Prophet's turban was black as were the banners carried by adherents of the Abbasid caliphate. In the folklore of many areas, however, some unsavory supernatural beings such as evil *jinn* and *ifrits* were thought of as black. There is no reason to assume that either the positive or negative associations with the color black carried over to the skin color of human beings. However, rural segments of northern tribes—nomadic Bedouins—seem to have had negative reactions toward Negroes since their status among them was that of slaves. In Mecca, on the other hand, Abyssinians from across the Red Sea seem to have been used as a protective garrison for the city. It seems likely that the kind of social relations that existed in specific times and places in Arabia, rather than abstract conceptions of color values, were decisive determinants of concepts about black people and attitudes toward them.

There are no pejorative remarks about Ethiopians or other Africans in the Koran, and Mohammed insisted upon the brotherhood of all believers in his teachings and in his practice. There were a few Blacks among the original circle of believers, including a freed Abyssinian slave named Bilal, whose freedom was bought by Mohammed's wealthy uncle after his master mistreated him for following the Prophet.[7] Bilal became one of Mohammed's first Companions, and later was celebrated for his exploits as a warrior in the conquest of Syria, an image sharply at odds with that of the obsequious Father Moses.

When persecution of the new religion in Mecca became intense, Mohammed arranged for some of his followers to cross the Red Sea to the Christian kingdom of Abyssinia in the East African highlands, where they were offered refuge.[8] Thus Abyssinia, or Ethiopia, became one of the cherished symbols of Islam in its formative years, just as Ethiopia had become a Christian symbol due to the story that the Apostle Philip converted the Candace's treasurer. Bilal and the friendly king of Abyssinia gave "blackness" a favorable connotation among the first Muslims.

Mohammed incorporated Negroes into the new Islamic communities as equals. Voluntary emancipation of slaves was encouraged. This meant freedom from bondage. Some ex-slaves were thus made equal to their former masters within the community of Believers, and were even given the opportunity to exercise authority over any former masters who also became Muslims. From the beginning, there was some opposition among those who viewed Negroidness as a mark of low social status and lack of full membership in the tribal community. Thus, favorable associations with "blackness" co-existed in Arab cultures with derogatory assessments of enslaved Africans. But in first-generation Islam, the solidarity of brothers-in-arms outweighed any racial and ethnic prejudice.

The Jihad Ethic and Black Warriors

The society of northern Arabia was composed of settled communities at well-watered spots along the caravan routes to Palestine and Syria and bands of Bedouin nomads who kept camels and small animals. A tribe of Bedouins would have an urban and a rural segment. Feuds between kinship groups were endemic, involving in-town relatives as well as nomadic bands. Towns were sometimes embroiled in warfare with each other. Disputes between pagans, Christians, and Jews within the same town were not always resolved peacefully. In time, the teachings of Mohammed would unify a large area, extending the possibilities for peaceful intercourse and trade.[9] But his immediate impact was to exacerbate the conflicts.

Facing opposition from his kinsmen as well as his pagan neighbors, Mohammed sent some of his followers to Ethiopia. Others withdrew from Mecca to the town of Medina about 250 miles away. In A.D. 622, after an assassination attempt, Mohammed accepted an invitation from the citizens of Medina to come there as an arbiter in disputes between clans that grew dates on neighboring oases, and between some of them and three Jewish tribes in the region. The date of the Prophet's Hegira, or flight to Medina, is the Islamic Year 1.

Mohammed proved to be an able and just administrator whose judgment was respected.[10] He developed a system of jurisprudence for the small theocracy he created at Medina. Bilal, the black ex-slave who was now one of his Companions, had a melodious voice. He was given the privilege of making the calls to prayer from atop the house of worship.[11]

Mohammed expected the Jews to accept him as the last and most important in a line of Prophets that began with Abraham, and in which his most recent predecessor had been Jesus. But the Jews, who comprised half the population of Medina at the time, ridiculed his claim. A number of the Suras in the Koran express his indignation at this rejection. Acrimonious arguments put his authority at risk, and open warfare broke out between Mohammed's followers and members of the Jewish community. The battles were savage and bloody. Where honor and prestige were at stake, Arab tribesmen had always considered battle legitimate. Now, issues defined as "right" and "wrong" in religious belief were at stake, rather than clan or tribal prestige. Victory in battle was accepted as proof of Allah's blessing. The worst sinners were Unbelievers and war against them was a just war. The "jihad ethic" was born.

The first generation of Christians had adopted passive resistance as a technique and nonviolence as a philosophy. Paul's injunction to "love ye one another" had survival value for the small groups of ostracized and persecuted Christian believers scattered throughout the Greco-Roman world, waiting for what they believed was the imminent Second Coming of their crucified Jewish teacher. They practised what theologians call an interim ethic while waiting for the return of Jesus.

During the first three hundred years of Christian expansion, nonviolent missionary evangelism was the sole means of winning converts. However, the admonition to "love your enemies" did not ultimately prevail. By the time Islam emerged, Christianity had been adopted by rulers of the Roman Empire's successor state, the Byzantine Empire. With Constantinople as its seat, it had been fighting paganism with arms as well as words for three hundred years. It would present a formidable enemy to Islam, when the new faith tried to spread out from Arabia. Christians interpreted "love your enemies" as an injunction for reducing conflict among themselves, not as a guide for dealing with pagans and Infidels.

The Islamic experience was quite different. The use of force from the outset to defend and expand the faith became a cornerstone of policy.[12] Mohammed actually led his armies into battle. During the first six years after the Hegira, the Prophet devoted much of his time and energy to organizing military operations against hostile Jewish settlements and against the city of Mecca. Passages in the Koran vividly reflect these conflicts.[13] However, there was nothing *racial* about Mohammed's hostility toward Jews—or any other opponents. The issues were ideological.

Mohammed's victories during these years in Medina attracted numerous nomadic Bedouin Arabs to his ranks, some out of conviction that his teachings were true and some because there was loot to share after successful battles, one-fifth to the cause, the rest for themselves.[14]

In A.D. 630, Mohammed made a triumphal return to Mecca, leading ten thousand devotees who destroyed the 366 pagan images that had been erected in the Kaaba. The sacred old black Kaaba stone was spared and reconsecrated to the one god, Allah.[15] Mohammed's biographers stress his compassion and mercifulness on the occasion of Mecca's conquest. He drew a distinction between those killed in the heat of battle and those executed after the victory was won. Only four persons were in the latter category. All erstwhile opponents who embraced the Faith were forgiven.[16]

Professor Guillaume, discussing Mohammed in his role of Warrior, explains the origin of the concept of jihad or "holy war:"

> It was evident that Muhammed believed that his message was for all Arabs—perhaps for all mankind—and it had now become clear that they could be made to listen by force. There could be no compromise with idolatry. Therefore, it followed that all those who refused to believe in Islam must be quelled. Idolators whose very existence was an insult to the one true God would have to acknowledge their inferiority by paying a special tax. This became the established principle of Islam during the few years of the prophet's life. . . . It was put into effect in the whole of the Arab empire in the century that followed.[17]

This principle affected race relations profoundly, for no inferiority based upon race or color could place a man so low as inferiority based upon refusal to believe in Islam. Conversely, acceptance of Islam could erase an inferiority previously based upon ethnicity, race, or color. Or at least so Islamic doctrine taught. Often it was actually so in practice.

There was never any dispute among the Companions and the Followers, as there had been among the Apostles and the first converts to Christianity, over whether or not a convert had to become a member of the Arab ethnic community before being accepted into the new religious community. In fact, since the Arab religious tradition was pagan and idolatrous, any such requirement would have been illogical. Islam was not a development out of Arabian religion as Christianity was from Judaism. Islam involved a rupture with the traditional religion, rather than an adoption of ethical and theological principles derived from it.

The implications for race relations were that lineage solidarity and lineage pride that might have excluded and stigmatized Negroes, marking them as highly visible "outsiders," were declared un-Islamic. The solidarity of the jihad warriors replaced the solidarity of clansmen; color was inconsequential within their ranks.

Mohammed died peacefully in A.D. 632 in the arms of his youngest wife, Aisha. Before his death, he had sent a letter to the head of the Byzantine Christian empire calling upon him to repent of his sins and to accept the teachings of the Prophet. His advice was, of course, ignored. A similar call to the Zoroastrian ruler of the Persian Sassanian empire was also disregarded. Mohammed's successors carried the jihad outside of Arabia. They knew that both the Byzantine Christian empire and the Sassanian Zoroastrian empire were weak—overextended, riddled with corruption, and subject to rebellion by dissatisfied ethnic groups they had conquered.[18]

The Jews could understand the jihad when it was directed against idolatrous pagans. Their ancestors in Palestine had often made war against the idolators around them, tearing down sanctuaries to Baal and Astarte and putting both the "false prophets" and their worshipers to the sword. Having "cleansed" their own land, however, the ancient Jewish prophets did not preach a crusade against the surrounding nations in an effort to convert them to monotheism and social reforms. The followers of Mohammed, however, were determined to move into the realms of the Christians and the Zoroastrians and to either make Muslims of them or reduce them to tribute-paying inhabitants of an Arab-dominated empire.

In A.D. 634, Mohammed's successor, Abu Bakr, having put down tribal revolts and completed the unification of Arabia under the banner of Islam, dispatched three thousand troops to take Syria away from what they called the "Greeks," whose Byzantine Christian empire controlled Syria, Palestine, and Egypt. He died before the conquest was completed, but his successor, Omar, wrested not only Syria but also Egypt from the Byzantine grasp.[19] The Coptic Christians of Egypt welcomed the Arab Muslims as "liberators" from what they considered the tyranny of their fellow Christians in Constantinople.[20]

Omar's troops also broke the power of the Persian Sassanid empire and proceeded to annex Iran and Iraq to Arabia. Garrison towns were established throughout Mesopotamia, and systematic tax-gathering procedures were established in order to funnel one-fifth of the wealth collected back to Mecca and Medina. By A.D. 644, Omar's troops stood on the borders of India and, during the next hundred years, under his successors, Muslim power would sweep along the Mediterranean coast of Africa and into Europe as far as southern France.

Military force in the form of the jihad could not, by itself, have achieved such victories. The beliefs and practices of the new religion—simple monotheistic worship and concern for women and the poor—had a powerful appeal for thousands of people throughout an area where both Christianity and paganism were prevalent.

Tradition maintains that Mohammed insisted upon acceptance of Negroes as equals within the ranks of the Companions. The jihad ethic reinforced this disapproval of color discrimination, even if it did not abolish individual color prejudices. Evidence of the presence and equal status of Blacks in the jihad armies is indicated in the story about the surrender of Egypt related at the end of the previous chapter.

A similar story has been handed down about the surrender in Damascus. There, Mohammed's black Companion, Bilal, fought in the ranks of the invading armies and was given the honor of taking the surrender. Prince Constantine, like his "Greek" counterpart in Egypt, considered this an insult. He is reputed to have said, "I will have nothing to do with that black slave."[21] Muslims have conserved laudatory legends about Bilal, including the story that he never made the call to prayer after the death of his beloved Mohammed until he felt inspired to sound the call after the victory in Damascus. The tomb of Bilal, who died in Damascus, became a shrine for pilgrims. The legends about his role in the conquest of Syria became an enduring Islamic tradition—along with those about a few other black warriors in Islamic armies.[22]

The faith continued to spread, making the claim of being a universalistic religion and stressing the equality of all believers. However, insofar as the majority of its carriers were Arabs, this ideal was modified by their ethnic chauvinism.

Ethnic Politics and Early Islam

In Islam, as in Christianity, there has always been tension between its universalistic teachings and their application in concrete situations. Local ethnocentric attitudes have had a powerful effect. Western Arabia was the dynamic center of the faith at the time of Mohammed's death in A.D. 632, and Arabs led the jihad that spread quickly throughout the Middle East in the years that followed. Although the brotherhood of the Companions and the Followers welcomed people without regard to race or color, some practices of Arab armies inevitably led to structured social inequality. Victorious warriors not only demanded the right to booty in the form of available goods and women, but some of them also laid claim to land in conquered territories. Within Arabia, this tended to disintegrate tribal structures without introducing ethnic stratification. In other lands, Arab conquerors formed a landed aristocracy extracting wealth by taxation from a free peasantry that was often ethnically different.[23]

Mohammed had proclaimed the equality of all believers; less than a decade after his death, a hierarchy was institutionalized under Omar. In the new Muslim states, Arabs enjoyed the highest degree of prestige and honor, with non-Arab Muslims ranked below them, and "Unbelievers" at the bottom. Moreover, the Arab-led jihad carried more than the new religion. It also took with it an ethnic Arab legacy that included some prejudice against Negroes.

Bedouin Pride and Prejudice

Although their origin myths say they are descendants of Shem, and thus aligned with a wider Semitic grouping, the nomadic Bedouin tribes of northern Arabia were extremely conscious of clan and lineage. There is also some evidence that prejudice against Negroes existed within the tribal societies that surrounded Mecca and Medina[24] and included members within these cities.

A tenth-century anthologist notes that a group of pre-Islamic poets was given the name *aghribat-al-'Arab* or "crows of the Arabs." A prominent ninth-century literary figure repeated a legend about a sheikh and one of these "crows" that suggests both the presence of color prejudice and the argument employed on occasions when color was ignored in favor of merit. A poet had written an ode to a sheikh, who rewarded him lavishly with gifts. Someone asked him, "Why do you treat a fellow like this so handsomely—a negro and a slave?" The sheikh answered, "If his skin is black, yet his praise is white and his poem is truly Arabian. . . . He gave an ode fresh and brilliant and praise that will never die." The query implies that the poet had two handicaps to overcome, being black and being a slave.[25] At the symbolic level "white" meant "excellent."

Professor Bernard Lewis, an outstanding Arabist, in commenting on the "crows," reveals the reason why lavish material rewards could not always satisfy a gifted black poet among the Bedouins, even if he were not a slave:

> Some of them—*mostly pre-Islamic*—were Arabs of swarthy complexion; others were of mixed Arab and African parentage. For the latter, and still more for the pure Africans [i.e., those with Negroid physiognomy], blackness was an affliction. In many verses and narratives, they are quoted as suffering from insult and discrimination, as showing resentment at this, and yet to some extent as accepting the inferior status resulting from their African ancestry [italics added].[26]

Lewis seems to concede here that some Bedouin color prejudice and discrimination were pre-Islamic, but he is inclined to interpret this as a manifestation of ethnocentrism and scorn for slave status, not as racial prejudice.[27]

However, if only Bedouin snobbery and pride of lineage had been involved in the experiences of the "crows," whether before or after the advent of Islam, "blackness" would not have been an "affliction," as Professor Lewis terms it, and the poets expressed it. The complexity of the situation is well-illustrated by the facts and legends about the best-known of the "crows," Ibn Shaddad al-'Absi, or 'Antar. A much-celebrated legend has grown up around the beloved seventh-century poet, who was the son of a Bedouin chief and an African slave woman. 'Antar and 'Abla, his father's brother's daughter, were in love, but the girl's family opposed their marriage.

Because of the rejection, 'Antar refused to ride into battle when the tribe was attacked, although he was a daring and brave warrior. Then as defeat for his tribe was impending, he abandoned his protest, flung himself into the fray, and helped to bring victory to his father's tribe. He was given the hand of 'Abla in gratitude and admiration for his bravery. Prowess in battle and skill in poetic improvisation were highly valued by Bedouin Arabs.

Some observers, including Professor Lewis, think that in forbidding 'Antar to marry his paternal first cousin—a prized marriage among the Bedouin—the tribal elders were expressing their disdain for his lowly origin as the son of a slave woman and their disapproval of a concubine's child being given the kind of rights that should go only to a legitimate wife's child. But 'Antar himself charged color prejudice. As the saga is told, the Arabic stories do not deny color prejudice but emphasize the point that being a warrior-poet could overcome both this disability and the fact that his mother was a slave.[28]

Because Bedouin society was patrilineal, and one's identity was derived from one's father, the son of an Arab man and a black slave woman was considered an Arab, as was 'Antar. Girls with Arab fathers and black slave mothers were classified as Arabs, too. There is some evidence that males like 'Antar were pressured to seek wives among them. These families formed a separate, caste-like segment of some Bedouin camps.[29]

Two considerations may have been operative in trying to prevent Negroes and mulattoes from marrying Bedouin women with no slave ancestry. One was a status consideration. *As nomads with a warrior tradition, slavery was a condition repugnant to the Arabs, signifying either defeat by their enemies or purchase in a slave market.* Descendants of slaves were customarily absorbed into a family lineage over several generations, and when the slaves were other Arabs, this happened with little comment. However, Negroid features "advertised" the presence of slaves in one's lineage. Color, hair, and features, even of light-skinned quadroons, constituted a signal—"Some slave ancestry there!" Because the overwhelming majority of Bedouin slaves were black, the word 'abd came to mean "a black person" as well as "slave."

The second consideration was the esthetic component of Arab ethnic chauvinism. A non-Negro somatic norm image of what constituted a "typical" or "pure" Arab and therefore desirable male or female prevailed in pre-Islamic and early Islamic days. Some of the first-generation progeny of Arab males and Negro concubines, as well as some of the progeny of two mulattoes, fell within this range, but those with more Negroid features not only excited suspicion about slave ancestry, they were also considered "ugly."

Marriage between mulattoes who were classified as Arabs resulted in occasional recombinations of genes that produced a Negroid physical type. Although the Prophet's complexion was described as "red," the tradition was handed down in some Muslim circles that one of Mohammed's grandfathers was a Negro.[30] However, Negroidness remained associated with low status. Nothing approaching a random distribution of Negro genes throughout the population could occur because of marriage restrictions preventing slaves from marrying unmixed Arab women and the fact that the introduction of new full-blooded Blacks as slaves was constantly taking place.

Arab dislike of the Negro phenotype, or its association with negative meanings such as "ugly," "alien," "slave," "inferior," "pagan," or "uncivilized" was no barrier to miscegenation. Erotic evaluations often overrode esthetic or status concerns.[31]

Islam should have meant the end of the agony of the "crows," but it did not. Within Mohammed's inner circle, color prejudice may have become irrelevant, but legends are preserved of the resistance the Prophet met when trying to insist upon the primacy of piety and merit over Negro ancestry.[32] A story about Mohammed suggests that he hoped to discourage belief in the purity of "blood lines" among Arabs. He was asked if the birth of a black child to a white woman was certain evidence of adultery. He asked the suspicious husband, "Have you any camels?" When the man said he did, Mohammed asked, "Do any ash-colored ones appear among them?" (Another version explains that the herd was red.) When the man answered "Yes," Mohammed said, "How is that?" The man answered, "Something in the blood made that happen." Mohammed then replied, "Perhaps something in the blood made your child black." The story only makes the point if it is assumed that Arab males believed *their* "blood" determined the characteristics of their children.[33]

Some of the custodians of Islamic tradition claimed that the Prophet wanted to remove the bars against intermarriage between Arab males and black women. One student of the matter reports that Mohammed "encouraged miscegenation in order to improve the social and spiritual state of humanity," and cites a tradition that "the prophet of Allah set an example in Arabia by taking several Ethiopian females into his harem—as well as Greeks, Persians, Jews, and other 'Infidel' women." Another legend, however, suggests that the Prophet opposed marriage between Arabs and Negroes.[34] These stories reflect social divisions among Muslims and the use of legends to sanction their differing beliefs.

Complex Racial Patterns in Yemen

There was another strong tradition within early Islam, from Yemen in southern Arabia, a culture where patterns of race relations were more diverse than among the Bedouin Arabs. The peninsula is separated from Africa by the Red Sea, a relatively narrow body of water constricted to a 22-mile strait at its southern extremity, where the modern state of South Yemen is located. In historic times, boats have moved freely in both directions, carrying troops and slaves (see map 2).

This area of Arabia had been "civilized" for centuries before becoming either Christian or Muslim. Soon after the Neolithic Revolution in the Middle East about eight thousand years ago, Semitic-speaking immigrants brought knowledge of cultivation into the fertile highlands, and large urban communities grew up.[35]

These legendary "civilizers" were called the Adites. The West African scholar, Cheikh Anta Diop, in *African Origin of Civilization*, suggests that the Adites were Blacks tracing their genealogy to Cush, a son of Ham. The ninth-century Arab historian Mas'udi traces the Adites to Shem, not Ham, an interesting point of view, since the Koran states that the wickedness of the Adites brought a disaster to southern Arabia. In Mas'udi's story of the Adites, it was Shaddad, son of Shaddid, a Semite, who brought the disaster.[36] There are two Muslim traditions, however. *The Arabian Nights* says that these wicked Adites who "once ruled all mankind" were sons of Ham; and his descendants are described as Blacks.[37]

If Blacks were not present in Yemen in the beginning, they certainly were as time went on. During the fourth century A.D., the Abyssinian kingdom of Axum across the Red Sea conquered southern Arabia and thus acquired control of the trade flowing between India and the Mediterranean. The soldiers must have left Negro genes in the population. The southern Arabs or Yemenites, with help from Persia, threw off this Abyssinian dominance around A.D. 375. The ruling strata subsequently adopted Judaism. When reports reached Byzantine centers that these Jewish rulers of Yemen were persecuting Christians, the king of Constantinople urged the Abyssinian king to cross the Red Sea again, this time to protect his fellow Christians, and incidentally to reclaim the trade routes.

The Africans reconquered Yemen in A.D. 520. A few years later, Abraha al-Ashram, a Negro leader among the invaders, led a coup that made him emperor. He was considered a humane ruler, devoted to developing a prosperous Yemen.[38] He married into the Jewish royal family. But successors were not so highly regarded, and soon those Jews who had fled into exile began plotting to overthrow the African king's regime.

The Byzantine emperor in Constantinople turned down their appeal for help: "You are Jews. Abyssinians are Christians. . . . We do not give aid to adversaries against our coreligionists." According to Mas'udi, the pagan Zoroastrian king of Persia, Chosroes Anouchirvan, saw things differently: "This is the white skin against the black race. I am closer to you than to the Abyssinians."[39]

The Persian ruler formed an invasion army of criminals freed from prison and confronted the black king, who is said to have ridden a war elephant at the head of a hundred thousand soldiers. The Persians won, and a victory poem begins: "We have crossed the waters to free Himyar [southern Arabia] from the tyranny of blacks."[40] There is no way of knowing whether the Arabs and Persians of the time actually conceived of this as a *racial* struggle, or whether Persian Muslims several centuries later—at a time when color consciousness was running high—put these words in the mouth of the Persian king. Even if the struggle was conceived of as racial, it did not involve the kind of racism we have come to know, for the first black king was praised, he married into the previous royal family, and the cruelty of his successors was not attributed to their race.

It is significant that Abraha, one of the first African kings of Yemen, had engaged in a military confrontation with Mecca that must have been fresh in the memory of Bedouins when Mohammed began preaching racial equality. It was certainly part of tradition at the time, and Mohammed devotes Sura CV of the Koran, known as "The Chapter of the Elephant," to it. The incident was said to have occurred in the year of Mohammed's birth. George Sale, the English translator, presents this note to Sura CV:

Abraha Ebn al Sabah, surnamed Al Ashram, i.e., the Slit-nosed, king
or viceroy of Yaman [i.e., Yemen], who was an Ethiopian, and of the
Christian religion, having built a magnificent church at Sanaa, with
a design to draw the Arabs to go on pilgrimage thither, instead of
visiting the temple of Mecca. The Koreish, observing the devotion
and concourse of the pilgrims at the Caaba [i.e., Kaaba] began
considerably to diminish, sent one Nofail, as he is named by some, of
the tribe of Kenanah, who getting into the aforesaid church at night,
defiled the altar and walls therof with his excrements. At this
profanation Abraha being highly incensed, vowed to the destruction
of the Caaba, and accordingly set out against Mecca at the head of a
considerable army, wherein were several elephants, which he had
obtained of the king of Ethiopia, their numbers being, as some say,
thirteen, others mention but one. The Meccans at the approach of so
considerable a host, retired to the neighboring mountains being
unable to defend their city or temple; but God himself undertook the
protection of both.[41]

According to the Koran, a miracle sent the invaders fleeing back to
Yemen. Significantly, Mohammed does not refer to Abraha as "the
Ethiopian," nor does he ridicule him as "the slit-nosed." In fact,
although he had doubtless heard the legend as a child, he bore no
animosity toward Ethiopians and sent some of his followers to
Abyssinia for refuge.[42] It is possible, however, that this encounter
embedded anti-Negro prejudices in the popular mind.

After a brief jihad, Islamic relations with the kings of Eastern
Africa were free of overt conflicts for over a thousand years.[43] In
Yemen, an occasional black ruler would appear under Islam, but this
time in a fashion that became characteristic of Muslim states. For
example, when his master, the sultan, died, Husayn ibn Salamah, a
Nubian slave, took over the business of governing, at the sultan's
daughter's request. Among his accomplishments as *wazir* were "the
construction of great mosques and lofty minarets along the road
from Hadramaut to the city of Mecca."[44]

But Blacks in Yemen faced ambivalent attitudes. For instance, a
distinguished and wealthy Abyssinian living in Yemen was abused
as a "mutilated negro [sic]" (i.e., a castrated Black), by an angry
traveler whom he had befriended. To cement an alliance with Ibn
Ziyad about A.D. 969, the Abyssinian king provided an annual levy of
a thousand "head" of slaves, "whereof five hundred of them were
Abyssinian and Nubian female slaves." Some stories indicate the
presence of "wild" Blacks from inner Africa. Thus, Blacks functioned

in a wide range of roles in Yemen, and whatever color prejudice was present was not institutionalized.[45]

Yemen was at first the target of the Bedouin-led jihad, but later its own warriors were among the armies of Islam as they swept onward to other lands. According to tradition, five thousand of the warriors who invaded Egypt were Yemenite cavalry, among them the black leader who took the surrender, 'Ubadah.[46] As time went on, the Yemenites and the Arabs would not always fight on the same side.

Ethnic and Theological Rifts Divide Islam

During the first thirty years of the growth and expansion of Islam, leadership of what was then still a movement was in the hands of four individuals, each of whom succeeded the other. The Companions selected Abu Bakr of Mecca when the Prophet died; he was called *khalifat rasul-Allah*, or "successor to the Messenger of God." Those who claimed leadership of all Muslims thereafter bore the title of caliph.

Abu Bakr served only two years before he was succeeded by Omar, whose military exploits over the next ten years became the subject of a great body of oral tradition. As the empire spread to Syria and Persia under his leadership, discontent also became widespread. His Arab ethnocentrism contradicted some of Mohammed's values. One result was his assassination by a disgruntled Persian.

Actual revolt broke out under 'Uthman, the third caliph. He was also slain, in this case by a group of assassins carrying out the will of theologians who considered 'Uthman a perverter of the Prophet's teachings, but who also expressed the resentment of discontented ethnic groups. The assassins installed 'Ali, the husband of Mohammed's daughter, Fatima, as the fourth caliph. Then open warfare broke out between 'Ali's supporters and another group of the Prophet's relatives based in Syria.

The two factions decided to settle the matter by arbitration. The anti-'Ali faction was victorious. The Umayyad caliphate was established, and headquarters of the faith was moved from Arabia to Damascus in Syria. 'Ali accepted the verdict, but not all of his followers were agreeable. Some became known as "the seceders" or the Kharijites. They immediately became the standard bearers of opposition to the northern Arab oligarchy; prominent among these were Yemenites. A number of groups who had grievances of a social nature flocked to their ranks.

That some Arab followers of the Prophet were now holding

Negroes in contempt was evident from the way in which the stand for egalitarianism was phrased during the dispute. Guillaume notes that:

> They [the Kharijites] maintained that any one, even a Negro slave, could be elected as the head of the Muslim community if he possessed the necessary qualifications. . . . Purity of life was the only test. . . . As upholders of the democratic principle they attracted many who were dissatisfied with the government for one reason or another. For instance, the Berbers [in North Africa] found their doctrines agreeable in their revolt against the Umayyad governors [of Syria] . . . they [the Kharijites] split up into numerous parties in the early days and lost the superficial unity which was based as much on negation as on positive principles [italics added].[47]

The phrase "even a Negro" reveals the existence of some prejudice—even among the Kharijites, who were nonetheless more favorable to black aspirations than their opponents.

The new Umayyad caliph based in Syria launched a vast expansion of the Arab empire deeper into Persia and westward into Spain. Then he tried to wipe out the last remnants of the 'Ali faction, but instead elicited a counteraction: the two strongest sectarian movements in Islam, the Shiites and the Fatimids. Both became champions of non-Arab peoples. Both also fostered a distinctive Islamic form of messianism, mahdism.

The descendants of one of Mohammed's uncles formed the nucleus of a far-flung clandestine movement dedicated to overthrowing the Umayyad caliphate. Early in the eighth century, its two great centers of strength were in North Africa and in Persia, where ethnic grievances against Arab invaders—especially manifestations of Bedouin pride and prejudice—were pronounced. The tenets of this new movement included belief in the coming of a *mahdi* who would "fill the earth with justice as it is now filled with violence and iniquity."[48]

In A.D. 743, the leader of the movement sent a holy man named Abu Muslim to an area of Persia which seemed ripe for rebellion, and he recruited a number of wealthy landowners who resented high taxation. A rebellion broke out that was supported by Yemenites throughout the Umayyad caliphate, after Shiites unfurled the black banner that was believed to symbolize the imminent coming of the precursor of the mahdi.[49]

Abu'l-'Abbas, a grandson of 'Ali, proclaimed himself to be that precursor. His followers declared him caliph and set out for Damascus to install him in the seat of power. After the people of Damascus opened the gates to the rebels the Umayyad caliph and his relatives were hunted down and killed.

The Abbasid leaders established a new capital in Mesopotamia on the banks of the Euphrates in the village of Baghdad, which eventually became a brilliant intellectual center. But discontent among the poor and among non-Arab ethnic groups continued. Also, the Shiites who had supported 'Abbas felt betrayed by the conservative actions of the new caliphate, and were active in many of the sporadic rebellions that followed.

While none was successful in either Mesopotamia or Persia, the heartland of the Abbasid caliphate, a North African revolt detached a large portion of territory from the Baghdad caliph's realm. British historians Oliver and Fage have related the story succinctly:

> It must be appreciated that the Abbasids had risen to power with Shiite support, but that once they had established themselves as Caliphs of all Islam, they had kicked away this ladder in the fear that others too would seek to climb it. The Shiites who survived their persecution naturally redoubled their clandestine efforts against the establishment. At the end of the ninth century, one of their missionaries was sent from Yemen to the Maghrib [in North Africa]. There he was so successful among the Kutama, a Berber tribe of the Kabyles who had always been hostile to settled administrations, that Ifriqiyah was overrun and its Aghlabid government overthrown. The Mahdi of the time soon arrived from the Yemen himself to exploit the situation. In 910 his proclamation as Caliph made it clear that he wanted much more than the leadership of a mere Berber tribal movement. The aim of the Fatimids, as the new dynasty was called, was nothing less than the mastery of all Islam.[50]

It is significant that this Yemenite mahdi, leading Berbers among whom matrilineality was strong, fought under the banner of Mohammed's daughter, Fatima, not her husband, 'Ali. Within sixty years the Berber Fatimid armies had conquered Egypt, and soon thereafter both Syria and northern Arabia acknowledged the Fatimad caliph in Egypt instead of the Abbasid caliph in Baghdad.

The Fatimids proclaimed no jihads against the black Christian kingdoms just south of Egypt. Instead, the recruitment of troops from that area, as well as the taking of concubines by officials and the use of Nubian eunuchs at court, opened doors of opportunity to Blacks to an extent found nowhere else in the Muslim world. The concept of mahdism was cherished by Sudanese Blacks after they adopted Islam. The mahdis best-known to the West have been Africans, and in this regard it is significant that Ibn Khaldun, the distinguished fourteenth-century Tunisian scholar, said that according to the original Shiite tradition, the mahdi was expected to be "very dark."[51]

An understanding of these conflicts between Arab and non-Arab factions within Islam is crucial to understanding the Black Experience in the Abbasid empire. Defeats of Blacks in political struggles, more than Bedouin Arab color prejudice, may have accounted for the low Negro status in some ethnic hierarchies. Also playing a role in status allocation affecting Blacks were pre-Islamic stereotypes and attitudes in the countries that came under Muslim rule.

The conquered cultures adopted the Arabic language along with the Muslim religion, and thus contributed to an international "Arabic" culture that was distinct from an "Arabian" culture characteristic of the Arabian peninsula. But each culture added its own values and practices. For instance, there was a hedonistic ethos in the life style of the Baghdad court that was far removed from Bedouin austerity. Architecture in Muslim Spain combined Middle Eastern and Moroccan esthetics. Artists in Persia, Turkey, and Muslim India suffered no reprisals for depicting the human form, which was tabooed in other areas.

Where skin-color prejudice existed before Islam, as in India and in parts of Christian North Africa, conversion to Islam did not automatically eliminate it, any more than it had spelled an end to Bedouin ethnocentrism. However, the coming of an Islamic "high culture" did have a tendency to transform color prejudice into an attitude that was subordinated to other values.

BLACK PEOPLE IN THE MUSLIM WORLD

A pronounced increase in the number of Negro slaves, as compared to the number of white slaves, occurred throughout the Muslim world after the seventh century A.D. According to Bernard Lewis:

> There were black slaves in the Hellenistic and Roman worlds—but they seem to have been few and relatively unimportant. *The massive development of the slave trade in black Africa and the large scale importation of black Africans for use in the Mediterranean and the Middle Eastern countries seem to date from the Arab period. Inevitably, it influenced Arab (and therefore Muslim) attitudes to peoples of darker skin whom most Arabs and Muslims encountered only in this way* [italics added].[52]

Because Islam encouraged the freeing of slaves, and also because it placed a taboo on enslaving fellow Muslims, continuous raiding occurred outside of Islamized areas. Until they were converted, Berbers were enslaved by Arabs in North Africa. Afterward, they supplied sub-Saharan Africans to the market. By the tenth century, most black people in Central Islamic Lands were slaves, recently emancipated slaves, or the descendants of slaves. *Although most Blacks were slaves, not all slaves were black* (see plate 4).

Most of the Africans who were carried off into the North African and Middle Eastern Diaspora between the eighth and the sixteenth centuries were women destined to become concubines, prostitutes or entertainers.[53] Many of them became the mothers of children who would be classified in the contemporary United States as "Blacks" or "Negroes" but not all of whom were so classified in the Muslim communities where they were born. The patrilineal system of the Bedouins became the Islamic standard, and children of concubines were considered Arabs. In this way, sons of black female slaves sometimes became political leaders, particularly in Egypt and the Diaspora of North Africa and in Muslim Spain. They were assigned the status of their Arab fathers.

Occasionally the mothers exerted considerable influence through their sons. Only in Egypt under the Fatimids, however, did a black concubine—a Sudanese slave who was the caliph's mother—exercise power in her own right. In Muslim Spain, in contrast to Central Islamic Lands, black women were sought after as wives as well as concubines, but they still had no direct influence in political affairs.

Some black men achieved great power on their own. Some were soldiers, others were emasculated males—eunuchs—serving in household roles as guards of the harem, but others were given civilian posts of considerable responsibility and influence.[54] Occasionally, they actually ruled when their former owner died, or they served as regent for a child. Arab caliphs in Mesopotamia limited influential administrative posts to Turkish slaves whom they trained for such roles.

Given the constant warfare that became associated with the spread of the Abbasid empire, it was not long before the armies of jihad volunteers gave way to mercenary troops. Most enslaved black men were used as soldiers. African foot soldiers had a long and well-chronicled pre-Islamic history, with a high reputation as accurate archers. Although the status of black soldiers waxed and waned relative to larger power struggles within Islam, a few black military leaders emerged in these armies composed largely of Arabs, Turks, and Berbers.

Many black soldiers and a few black caliphs, viziers, and concubines played prominent roles in power struggles within the Central Islamic Lands, North Africa, and Muslim Spain until power was seized by various groups referred to as "Turks" (Kurds, Armenians, as well as several varieties of Turks). Cultural and political environments varied substantially within this area. In general, opportunities for black achievement increased with distance from the Central Islamic Lands, except in Egypt.

We must keep these ecological and cultural variables in mind, as well as the historical overview previously discussed, as we examine the roles that Blacks played in various places and times within Islam (see chart 5). Access to political power has been selected as a major theme: to what extent did Negro individuals and groups attempt to gain and maintain economic and political advantages through competition and conflict? How well they succeeded, and to what degree color prejudice affected their achievements, are our major concerns.

Black Soldiers in Islamic Power Struggles

Ethnic and doctrinal divisions within Islam, and the conflicts they created, had a great impact on black soldiers, who were often caught up in factional disputes. The jihad armies that erupted out of Arabia had black warriors in their ranks. When they reached Persia, they found that large numbers of black and white troops were counterposed to each other in the armies of the Sassanian Empire.[55] The conquerors adopted this biracial pattern and passed it along to Cairo and Damascus. Muslim leaders soon came to depend upon mercenary troops or "slave soldiers," and Muslim historians constantly differentiate between "white" and "black" troops.[56]

"Black" troops were at first almost exclusively secured from African areas immediately south of Egypt, from the pool of soldiers whose reputation for bravery and martial skill stretches back as far as pharaonic times. Later, they came from the western Sudan and eastern Africa. "White" troops were Turks, Armenians and other people from the Caucasus area and Kurds; at times they also included Germans, Franks, and Albanians.

The Turks quickly became dominant in the armies of Central Islamic Lands. Beginning in the ninth century, the Abbasid caliphs decided to utilize them in large numbers to lessen dependence upon Arab and Negro soldiers in suppressing revolts. This brought the

Turks into conflict with black soldiers, who in turn attempted to use their numbers and strategic position to fight Turkish attempts to depress their status, both in Baghdad and in Cairo. A similar situation obtained in Muslim Spain, where the so-called "saqalibah," drawn from among European and Asian slaves, were used by Berbers and Arabs to checkmate each other, and by both to prevent black soldiers and sultans from increasing their power.

Eventually, the term "Turk" came to include Kurds, Albanians, and other non-Arab groups who seized power in Egypt, the so-called mamelukes or nonblack slave soldiers. The black contest for power against "Turkish" soldiers is a significant case of an objective situation where people differing sharply from one another in physical traits were deliberately pitted against each other by power holders.

'Amr ibn Bahr-Jahiz, one of the greatest tenth-century intellectuals writing in Arabic, suggests the presence of incipient racism in the Abbasid caliphate. He implies that charges were made in some Mesopotamian quarters—especially among Turkish leaders—that Blacks were poor combat troops, and he rises to their defense. He quotes a black poet El-Haiqutan, "My color does not prevent my being valiant with my sword in battle," and another well-known poet, Nusaib ibn Riah, who said, "If you ever met the Negroes in battle, you found them valiant and strong." Al-Jahiz added a comment by Nusaib that "the mulatto children of the Negro women are fully as brave as the blacks." Jahiz notes of the Arabs that "You even have sayings in your language which vaunt the deeds of our kings—deeds which you have often placed above your own."[57] No such questions about black soldiers were raised in Egypt, North Africa and Muslim Spain.

Two geographical areas in which tension between "Turks" and black soldiers assumed historical importance were Mesopotamia and Egypt.

In Mesopotamia: The Turks Take Over

Early in the ninth century, Caliph al-Mu'tasim assembled the most powerful army ever recruited by a caliph in order to fight off Byzantine Christian invaders on his northwest borders. He utilized a large number of Turkish cavalrymen from the Eurasian grasslands, who had been prisoners of war or were bought as slaves. These troops were subsequently used against dissident Arabs and Alid and Shiite rebels—Arab and Negro—in the Middle East.

As caliphs continued to build up armies that would be loyal to them personally and would resist schismatic trends within Islam, they began to send their armies to systematically raid the Turkish lands north of Mesopotamia and Persia for more slave soldiers. The warlike horsemen of the Asian plains were incorporated into the caliph's armies by the thousands. The Turkish soldiers became the caliph's personal slaves, but slaves with special privileges.[58] Schools were set up to train them for administrative tasks, and their families were accorded special food and education. Some of their descendants became administrative officials at the palace, and eventually these Turks took power away from the caliph.[59]

Black soldiers, who had been a traditional part of the Arab armies, were gradually pushed into a subordinate position, barred from cavalry units by the proud Turkish horsemen. Without the special training Turks received, the black soldiers were placed in a disadvantaged position. The Turks were determined to maintain hegemony. They became part of a new aristocracy of cavalrymen from the steppes that was establishing its power from Vienna to Peking,[60] and they were ruthless in keeping Blacks from developing any competing cavalry units.

In A.D. 836, the caliph left Baghdad to escape the continuous struggles between Sunni, Shiite and other sectarian groups. The Turkish military leaders soon became involved in political intrigue. They assassinated four caliphs one after the other in order to bring individuals to power who would grant them favors. A new form of government gradually emerged, with a Turkish *emir* installed by the army holding effective power under the caliph and ruling through a *vizier*. In A.D. 892 the capital was moved back to Baghdad, still the center of constant intrigue and conflict.

In A.D. 930, a fight broke out between the Turkish cavalry and a group of black infantrymen over a differential in the increased pay that soldiers had been granted. As an elite military group, the Turks had insisted on higher pay than footsoldiers of any race. Now they demolished the homes of the officers of the complaining black soldiers and burned down the troops' barracks. The black soldiers retreated to a provincial town, accompanied by some disaffected white soldiers. The Turkish troops pursued and slaughtered them.[61]

During the tenth century, the Seljuk Turks gained effective power throughout all of Iraq and most of Iran, although the caliph was still the nominal ruler. Social and religious conflicts continued among the populace and occasionally involved some elements of the army. Blacks, in spite of the inequity of their treatment, proved as loyal as any of the other military units, an inconsistent record at best.[62]

By the eleventh century, the tide was running strong against black access to military power in Mesopotamia. Bernard Lewis notes that, eventually, in Baghdad,

> the black infantry . . . were attacked and massacred by the white cavalry, with the help of other troops and of the populace, and their quarters burnt. Thereafter black soldiers virtually disappear from the armies of the eastern caliphate.[63]

The Turkish soldiers, once they had seized power in Baghdad from the Arabs, were determined not to tolerate the Blacks as competitors. That the populace helped the Turkish troops to massacre the black troops in Baghdad contrasts sharply with other places in Mesopotamia in which the common folk assisted black troops.[64] Not color per se but unique situational factors of time and place are necessary to explain the difference in behavior in various areas of the caliphate.

In Egypt: Blacks vs. Mamelukes

The Islamic conquest put brakes on the "whitening" process that had prevailed in Egypt since Greco-Roman times, a process we discussed in volume 1. However, power moved into the hands of Arab and Berber "browns," not sub-Saharan "Blacks." The Arab empire builders made no serious attempt to convert Egypt's Christian Copts to Islam. Instead they imposed a higher tax than on Muslims. This practice bred rebellions. These taxes were in addition to other "revenues" extracted from North Africa, and slaves from Nubia. Discontent festered.

A Turkish peace-keeping force, under a Turkish administrator named Ahmad ibn Tulun, was sent to Egypt by the Baghdad caliph to "pacify" the country. Tulun adopted the old Mesopotamian pattern for organizing an army: two ethnic groups serving as counterweights to each other. According to Bernard Lewis, "These were organized in separate corps, and accommodated in separate quarters at the military cantonments."[65]

Tulun did not invoke any racist theories to justify the segregation nor did he express any color prejudices. Separating black troops from white was partly a concession to differences in life styles of tropical African and Central Asian troops. It was also necessary for carrying out a policy of divide and rule.[66] But the practice generated stereotypes. When Tulun became suspicious that the Turks who had come with him from Baghdad were planning his overthrow, he sent them to Syria to fight. Meanwhile, he strengthened his personal bodyguard with black soldiers.

Neither Tulun nor his successors sent any of the revenues back to Baghdad. This de facto Egyptian independence was tolerated for a time because the caliphate was engaged in a two-front war and faced constant rebellions from Shiite opponents. Egyptian loyalty on the southwestern front more than made up for the loss of revenues.[67] But in A.D. 905 another group of Turks was sent to Egypt to oust the Tulunites.

This Ikhshidid dynasty extended the Egyptian sphere of influence to include Mecca, Medina, and Yemen. A eunuch of either Nubian or Abyssinian origin, Abu'l Misk Kafur, a slave of the dynasty's founder, led the army that captured the city of Aleppo in Syria and served as tutor of his master's two sons. He was appointed guardian of the sultan's oldest son, and in the struggle for power after the master's death, this black "slave-soldier" became Egypt's ruler, a rare occurrence. Abu'l Misk Kafur became famous throughout the Muslim world, and some historians view him as one of Egypt's best post-pharaonic rulers. He was a genuine scholar, a patron of scholars, and is said to have been a poet.[68]

After Misk Kafur's death, the dynasty weakened, and Shiite jihad warriors, the Fatimids, moved in. In A.D. 973, the Fatimids, having already secured the Nile Valley, Mecca, Medina, and Yemen, began to occupy their new city, built on the Nile near the site of the ancient holy city of Memphis. They named it Al Qahira (Cairo), "The Victorious." The new capital soon began to compete with Baghdad for power and prestige. The Fatimid dynasty lasted from A.D. 961 through 1171.

Professor Herbert S. Deighton, an Oxford historian, notes that "The Fatimid era vividly impressed itself upon contemporary Islam and left a strong imprint upon Egyptian civilization." That these rulers did not preside over regimes able to "rival the high culture of the great Arab rulers of Spain" was, he thinks, due to the fact that "the dynasty was heretical in the eyes of the great majority of Muslims, and scholars from the far larger Sunnite world shunned these gifted heresiarchs and damned their works."[69] Oliver and Fage put the Fatimids in this perspective:

> Under the Fatimids and their successors, especially the Ayyubids, Egypt entered upon one of the more glorious periods of her history. The revenues of the state were efficiently organized; trade flourished. . . . One of the most notable buildings was the new mosque of Al-Azhar, under the arches of which a great theological school was to develop. If the heterodoxy of the Shiia caliphs initially somewhat discouraged scholarship, it proved a great stimulus to literature and

the arts bringing in rich influences from Persia and Byzantium. Although the power of the Fatimids rested largely on Africa troops, initially Berbers from the Maghrib, and later Negroes from the Sudan, theirs was essentially an oriental regime embroiled in the affairs of nearer Asia, as was inevitable with their claim to supremacy throughout the world of Islam.[70]

Shiia heterodoxy also provided an atmosphere favorable to black aspirations.

The Fatimid caliphate required a large body of soldiers, but the loyalty of Turkish mamelukes that the caliphs had inherited from previous regimes was suspect. Thus, they were inclined to rely primarily on black troops. But ideology, not color, was the issue involved. The first Fatimid ruler, Muhammad ibn Sulayman, considered the hundreds of black troops in the army of the previous Ikhshidid ruler to be untrustworthy. So he "gave orders to slaughter them and they were slaughtered in his presence like sheep" and their quarters were burned to the ground. New black units were then immediately formed. By the time his successor, Hakim, repressed a Fustat rebellion, he had organized a loyal Shiite black garrison in Cairo.[71]

Occasional conflicts between black troops and the populace must have left a residue of antiblack sentiments in the Cairo population. Civic disasters also raised the level of prejudice, for at one point, when there was a severe famine in Cairo, hostility to the black troops mounted. They became highly visible scapegoats, and some were accused of cannibalism—but so were some non-Blacks.[72]

Whatever the popular attitudes toward them may have been, the black soldiers were a crucial factor in offsetting pressure from mameluke troops on the weak caliph, al-Mustansir. When he vested both civilian and military power in the hands of a single mameluke, Blacks moved to thwart him. For a while, the real ruler of Egypt was the weak caliph's mother, a Sudanese slave.[73] Clashes between black regiments and those of other races occurred frequently at the middle of the eleventh century, with black and Asian troops expelled from the city in turn.

Then the Fatimid caliphate was threatened from outside by a warlike Turkish tribe, the Seljuks, who detached Syria from the Fatimid sphere in 1078 and moved on Palestine, triggering the first of the Crusades to "rescue" the Holy Land. Battles raged among the Seljuk Turks, the Egyptians and the Crusaders, in various combinations. Through palace intrigue during these critical years, the Blacks in Cairo strengthened their position and blocked mameluke maneuvers.

As Lewis points out, "By the time of the last Fatimid caliph, al-'Adid, the blacks had achieved a position of power. The black eunuchs wielded great influence in the palace; the black troops formed a major element in the Fatimid army."[74] This was a critical moment in Egypt's history, for the Crusaders from Europe had invaded Syria and Palestine.

With the connivance of a traitorous vizier, the historic task of expelling the Crusaders from Egypt fell to nonblack soldiers sent by an emir from Syria who was officially a subordinate of the Fatimid caliph in Egypt but who was openly a partisan of the Abbasid caliph in Baghdad. The Cairo caliph appointed the leader of the victorious Syrian troops as his new vizier. When this man died, his nephew, Saladin, an officer in the army from Syria, was installed as vizier. He immediately abolished the Fatimid caliphate and brought Egypt back into the Sunni Baghdad fold.

Saladin began a purge of Fatimid elements that led to a confrontation with black troops and the elimination of Negroes from the Egyptian army. One episode precipitated an actual battle between Turkish troops and Blacks. The chief eunuch, a black man, was accused by Saladin of colluding with the Crusaders to overthrow him, and, according to one account:

> The offender was seized and decapitated; and replaced in his office by a white eunuch. The other black eunuchs of the caliph's palace were also dismissed. The black troops in Cairo were infuriated by this summary execution of one whom they regarded as their spokesman and defender. Moved, according to a chronicler, by "racial solidarity" (jinsiyya), they prepared for battle. In two hot August days, an estimated 50,000 blacks fought against Saladin's army in the area between the two palaces of the caliph and of the vizier.[75]

The reprisals taken against these black rebels were draconian. When the black soldiers heard that an order had been given to burn down their homes with their families in them, they broke off the battle and tried to return to defend their families. They were massacred. The battle is known in Arabic annals as "the battle of the blacks" or "the battle of the slaves." One scholar suggests that "the conflict was not primarily racial" but that it "acquired a racial aspect."[76]

After several pro-Fatimid revolts that required forceful suppression, Saladin disbanded the black regiments entirely.[77] He incorporated the Fatimid caliph's white "slave soldiers" into his army.

When Saladin took Egypt out of the Shiite camp and accepted the authority of the caliph in Baghdad, the nominal leader of the Sunnite faithful, thousands of Fatimid officials and soldiers fled. Judges, malams, and influential people at the court took refuge in Upper Egypt and Nubia. Amid the resulting tensions, both the Nubians and Saladin's forces took agressive actions, but the fighting was indecisive and quickly broken off.[78]

Saladin's cruel purge of black soldiers from his army and his two invasions of the black Christian kingdom south of Egypt did not necessarily signify either personal prejudice against black people or contempt for Negroes. He was protecting his regime from possible internal subversion and external invasion. He was also attempting to build a more effective machine for fighting the Venetian navy, and the Frankish infantry and cavalry, and stopping the Mongols who had fought their way from the plains of Eurasia to the Mediterranean Sea. Relations with the highland kingdom of Ethiopia that posed no military threat were free of any antiblack *animus*. Thus, as Oliver and Fage point out,

> even during the Crusading period, Ethiopian bishops were conse-
> crated in Cairo, and Ethiopian pilgrims, thousands at a time,
> marched through Egypt on visits to the Holy Land, with drums
> beating and flags flying; and with regular halts for the celebration of
> Christian worship.

After the Crusaders had been expelled from Jerusalem, "it was Saladin, the greatest opponent of the Western Christian Crusaders who gave the church of the Invention of the True Cross to the Ethiopian Christians as their religious centre in Jerusalem."[79]

The five Ayyub sultans who followed Saladin continued his policy of relying upon mamelukes rather than black soldiers for the military strength needed to keep at bay the Mongol invaders from Asia who had now come as far as Syria, and to continue the wars against the Crusaders. By 1226 the soldiers of the Sixth Crusade had recaptured Jerusalem from the Muslims, who had previously taken it back from the Franks. In 1244, a group of Asian Turks invited in by the Egyptian Ayyub sultan expelled the Crusaders from Jerusalem again. Meanwhile a bitter struggle was raging in Egypt between the mamelukes and the family of the sultan. The latter had close ties with the family ruling Syria. The mamelukes felt that this family had interfered too much in Egyptian affairs during the years after it sent Saladin's uncle to defeat the Crusaders. Now at the center of the struggle was al-Salih, the mulatto sultan of Egypt. Haughty and ambitious, but also sagacious and brave, according to the chronicles, his mother was a black slave, the favorite concubine of his father, the previous sultan of Egypt.[80] Saladin and his immediate successors had allowed no Blacks to bear arms but did not bar black women from the royal harem. However, since no black soldiers from Nubia were present in the palace guard, black concubines could not wield the kind of power they had sometimes enjoyed in the past in collusion with black soldiers and black eunuchs.

Under al-Salih's regime, the Egyptian armies scored some impressive victories against the forces of Louis IX of France, who invaded the delta, and against Crusader armies in Egypt and Palestine. The vizier who managed state affairs was a Turk in whom the mamelukes had confidence. The sultan chose a slave girl for his wife, but she was either Kurdish or Armenian, not a black woman like his mother. She called herself Shadjar al-Durr (the String of Pearls). After winning a victory against the Crusaders in Syria the Turkish mercenaries murdered the sultan in an attempt to seize power in Egypt. The String of Pearls immediately proclaimed herself the sultana and rallied the mamelukes to her side against the mutinous Turks whom they considered outsiders. She was able to inspire the army to administer another defeat to the Crusaders. Now she proclaimed herself "Queen of the Muslims," and had her own coinage struck. The Syrian branch of the Saladin family objected to a woman playing such a prominent role and insisted that she marry a man whom they designated. A lover of intrigue, she did not object but still clung to her title and her power. This husband was eventually murdered in a dispute with a group of mamelukes, reputedly on orders from The String of Pearls. She, in turn, was battered to death by harem women who were loyal to the sultana's mulatto first husband.[81] Amid this turmoil, the mamelukes were preparing to dispense with the Ayyub dynasty entirely. In 1260, they did so, installing a sultan from within their own ranks. They would now keep control of the Egyptian government for 257 years. They did not relinquish power until the Ottoman Turks invaded the delta in 1517.

The victory of the mamelukes over Crusaders, Seljuk Turks, and Mongols was a further setback for Blacks. During the century before the Ottoman Turks took power in Egypt, the mamelukes, recognizing the fact that Blacks were likely to be pro-Fatimid, continued a policy of barring them from armed units, but used them as slaves in caring for the horses and quarters of the cavalry. It was not long before the Fatimid religious leaders who had been displaced by Saladin's purge began to conspire with the resentful black ex-soldiers who, in an attempted revolt, seized horses and arms and attacked the Cairo citadel. Reprisal was swift. The mameluke cavalry "rode in, surrounded them and shackled them; by morning they were crucified outside the Zuwayla gate."[82] There was ironic symbolism in the spot chosen for this merciless, gruesome punishment. It was through this gate that the Berber and black horsemen rode into Fustat (Old Cairo) when they established Fatimid rule in Egypt. Having made an example of the Blacks who tried to revolt, the mamelukes continued to use docile unarmed Negroes as menials in the Egyptian army. Black eunuchs and concubines had no masses of black soldiers with which to intrigue as they had done in the days when the black mother of the mulatto caliph, Mustansir, dominated Egypt.

After 1382 the "Turks" brought in new recruits for their ranks from the Caucasus, preferring Circassian slaves to members of Turkish tribes. Except for an occasional raid into Nubia, the mameluke rulers steered clear of military operations outside of Egypt.

An unusual occurrence took place in 1446 that emphasizes the difference between Egypt and the western Sudan, where black kings ruled. Some discontented elements among the black slave-soldiers who had been reduced to horse grooms and body servants began to fantasize about black sovereignty. They rebelled, established an outlaw community, and invented rituals that expressed their suppressed desires. As Lewis tells the story:

> Some five hundred slaves, tending their masters' horses in the pasturages outside Cairo, took arms and set up a miniature state and court of their own. One of them was called Sultan, and installed on a throne in a carpeted pavilion; others were dignified with the titles of the chief officers of the Mameluke court, including viziers, the commander in chief and even the governors of Damascus and Aleppo. They raided grain caravans and other traffic and were even willing to buy the freedom of a colleague. They succumbed to internal dissentions. Their sultan was challenged by another claimant, and in the ensuing struggles the revolt was suppressed. Many of the slaves were captured and the rest fled.[83]

Not long after this pathetic caricature of state-building was being acted out by Blacks in Egypt, Cairo was host to the second real black sovereign to make a pilgrimage to Mecca. This was Mohammed Touré, known as Askia the Great, the king of Songhay.

The episode of the revolt of the black horse grooms in 1446 was not the end of the story of conflict between mamelukes and Blacks attached to the Egyptian armies. According to Lewis, when a technological innovation in warfare was introduced that most of the mamelukes considered beneath their dignity to use, their leader decided to adopt it but to have the porters, grooms, and menial servants—all Blacks—trained in its use. Firearms had become available and it seemed wise to organize a musket corps. A black man named Farajallah was made chief of the firearms personnel of the Cairo citadel. The sultan in Cairo, anxious to have the complete loyalty of this newly created military functionary, honored him. He presented him with a beautiful Circassian slave girl from the palace as a wife, and he permitted him to wear the short-sleeved tunic that only mamelukes had previously worn. The mamelukes complained to the sultan, and a battle broke out between them and the black "slave-soldiers," who numbered about five hundred. The Blacks retreated and gathered in the towers of the citadel from which they fired at the royal mamelukes. The Turkish soldiers marched on them, killing Farajallah and about fifty of the black "slave-soldiers"; the rest fled. Two royal mamelukes were killed.[84]

According to Ansari, whose account is cited by Lewis, the sultan's maternal uncle intervened and was promised that the black slaves would be sold off to the Turks. He does not tell us whether the mamelukes then decided to handle firearms themselves, but we are informed that they never again recruited any Blacks for combat duties.[85]

Meanwhile, a new wave of invading Asians not averse to using firearms had been moving southward from Anatolia throughout the late fifteenth century. In Anatolia, small fanatical warlike bands of authentic Turks came raiding inland close to Christian and pagan territory hoping to extend the faith and secure loot, gradually transforming themselves into a well-disciplined war machine under a man whose name they took, becoming the Ottoman Turks.

About A.D. 1500 they adopted the new technology that the mamelukes in Egypt and other warrior traditionalists scorned, the use of firearms. In 1512 they stormed Cairo and took the city, establishing the dynasty of Ottoman Turkish mamelukes, who ruled the country either directly or indirectly until the Ottoman Empire collapsed during World War I. They used black soldiers as well as black eunuchs in high places, although most of the troops were white slave-soldiers. Some of the eunuchs supervised the harem of the sultan of Constantinople, and others were in charge of the shrines in Mecca and Medina.[86]

A combination of fast-moving cavalry, an infantry adept at besieging cities as well as fighting in the field, and proficiency in use of firearms made the Ottoman Turks an invincible force. Historian William H. McNeill notes that, after 1438, the Ottoman leaders had begun to recruit a military slave corps from among the white Christian subjects of the expanding empire, especially from the Balkans. This, added to a high degree of toleration of Christians within its boundaries, speeded up successful expansion.[87]

Viewed from the standpoint of contemporary Islam in which, except for Persia and Yemen, Sunnite theology and political theory have prevailed over Shiism in the Central Islamic Lands, the breakup of the Fatimid caliphate was fortunate. Viewed from a black perspective, however, the defeat of the Fatimid caliphs in Egypt meant a victory for forces that were determined to eliminate Blacks from influential sectors of the military and political life of Islam. The restoration of Egypt to the Abbasid Sunnite fold by Saladin made it imperative, from the caliph's perspective, that any possibility of a Fatimid comeback be prevented, and there were possibilities of that occurring through a coalition between black viziers, Negro concubines, and black soldiers acting in concert with the Christian kingdoms of Makuria and Alwa, south of Egypt, all allied with disgruntled Coptic Christians in Egypt. The mamelukes also feared such a coalition and concentrated upon keeping Blacks attached to the army, but disarmed. The recruitment of a black corps to use firearms was a potentially self-destructive act in which feudal pride dictated giving the new technology to a subordinated group. The mamelukes quickly realized this and disarmed the black soldiers.[88]

Oliver and Fage detect a special service rendered to Africa by Saladin and the mamelukes who succeeded him, arguing that when Saladin and the Ayyub dynasty drove the Seljuk Turks out of Syria and Palestine they "confirmed that Egypt's main service to Africa was one of shielding the continent from foreign invasion."[89] Presumably the reference is to invasion by the Seljuk Turks and the Mongols, and perhaps to the fact that they "absorbed" the Ottoman invasion and blunted it. Yet one foreign invasion they did not prevent was the devastating impact of a massive Arab Bedouin invasion from the middle of the eleventh century through the fifteenth. In fact, Egyptian rulers assisted it in its early stages, encouraging the Bedouins to move westward into Berber territory. In any event the question might be asked, from a black perspective, could not black sultans and viziers using black troops have performed what Oliver and Fage call the "main service" to Africa?

The fighting ability of the foot soldiers in Egypt does not appear to have been questioned by either their leaders or their foes. And the Farajallah episode indicates their readiness and ability to use the new gunpowder technology. For Blacks to have seized the leadership, however, would have demanded a defeat of Saladin after his two preemptive strikes against the Christian kingdoms in Nubia. Divided among themselves and harassed by invading Bedouins, no leaders emerged in Nubia at this point who could have assembled the vast number of cavalrymen needed on the fertile plains near the sixth Nile cataract and transported them and masses of footsoldiers north to attack the rear of Saladin's forces while he was engaged in the Middle East, thus duplicating the feats of the Seventeenth and Twenty-fifth Egyptian dynasties. There is no evidence that there was any strong desire to do so.[90] By the end of the sixteenth century the cavalry power of the Kanem-Bornu kingdom allied with the black sultans of Fung and the sultans of Darfur might have been able to assemble forces equal to those of the Ottoman Turks coming down from the north. A famous *mahdi* engaged them successfully in the nineteenth century. The eleventh and twelfth centuries were too early, however, for such a mobilization of power in Bilad al-Sudan to take place.

In the Periphery: Muslim Spain

Illuminated manuscripts of the eleventh century depict Negro soldiers in the army of Islamic Arabs and Berbers that Tarik led across Gibraltar into Spain in A.D. 711.[91] The Umayyad caliph still ruled from Damascus when Syrian soldiers were dispatched to help Arabs put down rebellions in Morocco and Spain. After helping defeat the Berbers in Muslim Spain, the Syrian soldiers were drawn into the struggle for control between northern Arabs and Yemenites who were settling in Spain.

In a battle for the capital city of Cordova in A.D. 747, the Syrian Abu'l Khattar joined forces with the Yemenite Horaith in an attempt to overthrow the northern Arabian emir, Yusuf. With help from Cordova's citizens, the emir won and both Abu'l Khattar and Horaith were beheaded. But first, the Syrian turned on his ally of convenience and abused him as a "son of a negress." Abu'l Khattar, the Syrian, knew that elders in the joint force had decided to make the Yemenite mulatto, not him, emir if they won. He resented the choice of the Yemenite. So as they both faced death he verbally abused him by casting aspersions upon his ancestry. The significant fact for our inquiry, however, is not the Syrian's use of race as a weapon of verbal abuse, but rather the selection by the elders of a mulatto to rule all of Muslim Spain. The absence of color as a determinant in power allocation, despite the presence of color prejudice in the culture, makes this a very different situation from the system of color-caste that would eventually develop in the New World Diaspora.

Although the chronicles do not always single out black troops for comment, an occasional description shows that Blacks were used frequently and were highly regarded by some rulers of Spanish cities, but the populace did not always view them favorably.[92] The king who confronted the forces of Charlemagne used black soldiers in the army he organized to hold off the Frankish invaders and to cope with occasional Norman raids. These may be the legendary Blacks who are spoken of in *The Song of Roland*, an epic we shall examine more closely in the next chapter.

By A.D. 1000, the prevailing image of the black soldier in the Middle East was that of a skilled archer, but in Muslim Spain, Blacks were also appreciated for their skill on horseback. Some Blacks were jihad warriors, some were slaves or freemen fighting for a share of the loot, and others saw themselves as clients of a powerful patron, whom they followed and fought for. In A.D. 1090 thousands of Negroes entered Spain with the Almoravid armies from Morocco. When the Almohade dynasty replaced this one in A.D. 1121 more black troops came. The ruling class during the twelfth century was a mixture of Berber brown and sub-Saharan black. It laid the foundation for the "Empire of the Two Shores."[93]

In Mesopotamia and in Egypt, there was one army, with counterbalanced black and white units. In Spain, the ruler of each city had his own army, and the overall ruler tried to coordinate these forces with Cordova as the capital. Arabs, both Syrian and Yemenite, were distrustful of Blacks, because they maintained close relations with Berbers. But the Berbers also distrusted Blacks, as a result of their experiences with well-armed independent black states south of the Sahara.[94] During their conflicts with the Berbers, some of the Arab rulers of Spanish city-states began to rely on white soldiers, or *saqalibah*, for their palace guards and advisers. Although *saqalibah* is sometimes translated as "Slavs," they were prisoners of war or purchased slaves of various European origins. Eventually Arab rulers, distrustful of both Blacks and Berbers, bought white children, raised them as Muslims, and prepared them for sensitive and influential posts as administrators, advisers, and top army officers.

The saqalibah did not bar Blacks from the cavalry in Spain, but Negroes were effectively blocked from access to leadership posts in the armies, as they were elsewhere. Late in the tenth century, the saqalibah also made a bid for political power, as the Turks had in Baghdad and Cairo.[95] They were defeated, and their power was diminished until resistance to a Fatimid attempt to control Muslim Spain strengthened their position again vis à vis black troops. Thus black, Berber and white troops were continuously counterposed in these power struggles. The forces of Christian Spain would eventually capitalize on this disunity to push the Muslims back across the straits to Morocco. There are no recorded attempts of black slave revolts or mutinies in Muslim Spain.

Black Slaves Stage a Revolt in Mesopotamia

Relatively few black slaves were crucial to the process of production in the Muslim world. Some of these were on sugar estates; others were used on date farms along the Persian Gulf and others toiled on *latifundia* in the Tigris-Euphrates Valley. A group of these slaves conducted a rebellion against their masters during the ninth century that lasted fifteen years and at its height threatened the capital itself. This revolt was the first massive attempt by a group of Diaspora Africans to use force to free themselves from slavery under either Islam or Christendom. It is of theoretical importance in studying conditions under which slave revolts occur.

We previously mentioned the black slaves of this area as we examined the highly pejorative images of Blacks in the Babylonian Talmud. Among these was the belief that black skin resulted from a curse on Ham's descendants because of his sexual sins. We noted that these stories appeared in the Babylonian Talmud, not in the Jerusalem Talmud or the Old Testament, which were composed in Palestine. We speculated that the pejorative legends may have been, in part, an attempt by Mesopotamian Jews to justify their involvement, along with non-Jewish owners of large estates, in the enslavement of Blacks.

The Persians were still in power when Arab Muslims established a beachhead near the mouth of the Tigris and Euphrates rivers close to the Persian Gulf and founded a city there named Basra. It became a commercial center and military citadel under the first caliphs.

The Basra area became a stronghold for Shiite forces during rebellions against the Damascus-based Umayyads who finally defeated the Persians. Blacks who were recently freed slaves participated in these rebellions and were among those slaughtered as a result. There is some evidence that a class-stratified black community developed in Basra as a result of ongoing assimilation,[96] but it was not the incipient black bourgeoisie that made history in southern Mesopotamia. It was the black underclass, which for centuries had worked the area's farms, that left its mark on the Muslim world, Mesopotamia's "wretched of the earth."

Early Arab caliphs attempted to maximize the potential of the southern Mesopotamian lands, which were dependent upon a system of irrigation. Masses of "uncivilized" Africans were imported to repair the water control system that was damaged in the Muslim takeover and to labor in the restored agricultural operations.[97]

The ethnic origin of these laborers is hard to determine. They were called "Zanj," a term that was originally quite neutral, designating people from the southern part of Africa, as in the word Zanzibar. The Zanj became the objects of a derogatory stereotype of Blacks. Emaciated, clad in rags, and stinking from the sulphurous mud of the salt flats, these "Zanj" were not an attractive people. They were very different from "civilized" Blacks of Egypt or Ethiopia or Baghdad. The Zanj were people from "inner Africa," the so-called "barbarians" whom Ibn Qutayba said lived on fish, sharpened their teeth, and were "ugly and misshapen."

The new slaves were brought into an area where rebellion was already commonplace. Discontent among artisans and peasants because of low wages, inflation, and loss of land was expressed throughout the ninth century by schismatic religious movements. The introduction of slave labor on large estates is said to have degraded the standing of free labor, yet the rebel forces included "fair-skinned people" as well as Blacks.[98]

Many of the latifundia in southern Mesopotamia were operated by *wakil* or appointed overseers because the owners preferred to live in Baghdad, Basra, and other cities. The agents of these absentee landlords are said to have been brutal, and some scholars have compared the conditions on Iraq's large farms with those in ancient Rome or on plantations growing cotton or sugar in the Americas.

Although the conditions of the black agricultural workers had led to sporadic rebellions in the past, the great rebellion in the late ninth century began among black workers engaged in the back-breaking task of preparing the ground for new farms. Professor Lewis has summarized the conditions existing among this particular group of Zanj:

> Their task was to remove and stack the nitrous top soil, so as to clear the undersoil for cultivation, probably of sugar, and at the same time extract the saltpetre. Consisting principally of slaves imported from

East Africa, and numbering some tens of thousands, they lived and worked in conditions of extreme misery. They were fed, we are told, on "a few handfuls of flour, semolina, and dates."[99]

These men worked in gangs of from five hundred to five thousand, and in one extreme case, a gang of fifteen thousand is mentioned.[100]

Most scholars do not describe the revolt of the Blacks that began in A.D. 868 as a spontaneous uprising, but rather as one "instigated" by an Arab who felt he had a mission to oppose the caliphate. According to this view, he exploited the grievances of the black workers and persuaded them to follow him. That they did so readily, and in a well-organized, disciplined fashion, proves the value of preparatory work involving a black leadership group, including one Soleiman, who is mentioned as the most capable and courageous of the leader's supporters.[101]

Al-Burku'i or 'Ali, who appeared in the vicinity of Basra sometime during A.D. 868, had recently joined the Kharijite sect and had tried unsuccessfully to persuade the Zanj on the island of Bahrein in the Persian Gulf to join in an insurrection.[102] He preached "equality of the races within the faith," in accord with the original Kharijite teaching that "the best man should always be the caliph even if he were an Abyssinian slave."

Unlike their fellows in Bahrein, the Zanj near Basra accepted his leadership, and the rebellion quickly spread to other agricultural slaves, to runaways from the towns and villages, and beyond. As Lewis tells the story:

> The black troops of the imperial army sent against them deserted to them, enriching them with arms and trained manpower, while the prospect of booty brought them the support of the neighboring Bedouin tribes and of the marsh Arabs. Some free peasants of the area are said to have rallied to the Zanj leader and helped him with supplies. There is little sign of support from discontented free elements in the towns, though the sources tell us that two of 'Ali's lieutenants were a miller and a lemonade seller.[103]

The rebels raided some farms to capture horses, and thus were able to organize a rudimentary cavalry. The battle strategy of the Zanj was to place the people with horses and captured weapons in the front ranks; people with rebel-made clubs followed, and troops wielding large branches of trees brought up the rear. Professor Lewis concludes:

> The military record of the Zanj was brilliant. One imperial army after another suffered defeat, enriching them with slaves, booty, and

especially arms. . . . the Zanj built themselves a new capital city known as Al-Mukhtara . . . On the 19th of June, 870, the Zanj captured and sacked the flourishing commercial seaport of Ubulla, greatly strengthening their forces with liberated slaves. Shortly after they expanded into southwest Persia, capturing the city of Ahwaz.

The Movement was by now a major threat to the Empire. It dominated important areas of southern Iraq and southwest Persia. . . . On the 7th of September, 871, they captured and sacked Basra itself but wisely evacuated it immediately after. Meanwhile, they had defeated several more Imperial forces, and in 878 captured the old garrison city of Wasit. By the following year, they were within seventeen miles of Baghdad.[104]

Now, at tremendous cost, the brother of the caliph organized an expedition that pushed the Zanj back from the vicinity of Baghdad and then advanced to the Zanj capital city of al-Mukhtara in the south with a river flotilla.

After a long siege, the city fell on August 11, A.D. 883. al-Burku'i's head was chopped off and carried triumphantly to Baghdad on a pike. We can safely assume that most of the Zanj who were captured were returned to their masters or assigned new ones. (Early in the struggle, owners of slaves tried to "buy" them from al-Burku'i, who refused such a deal.) It is probable that some, too, were able to flee into Oman and Bahrein in Arabia. Some leaders were, no doubt, executed. But many of the captives were taken into the caliph's army.[105]

The revolt of the Zanj took advantage of other conflicts that were distracting Baghdad's forces. Significantly, their Arab leader had tried to negotiate a formal alliance with the Persians, who were fighting against the caliphate in the Northeast. This bid was rejected. The Zanj were small in number fighting against the power of a centralized government. No kinsmen or fellow tribesmen could be mobilized to aid these aliens.

Relying uncritically on an account by Tabari, a pro-caliph Muslim historian, for both his details and his interpretation, French Arabist Gaudefroy-Demombynes dismisses these black rebels as "rabble," a "mob of drunken slaves" who were "good for nothing but to pillage, kill and ravage." Because most of the Zanj knew no Arabic, and the leader, al-Burku'i, had to speak to them through an interpreter, Gaudefroy-Demombynes concludes that the noble Kharijite sentiments passed over their heads. In his view, they followed their leader only because he promised them "community of women and of goods" in the future and allowed them to loot and rape in the present.[106] *The Encyclopedia of Islam*, however, does not evaluate them in the same cynical and hostile terms as Tabari does, but compares their rebellion to that of Spartacus and the Roman gladiators, and to the uprising of slaves in Haiti in 1791.[107]

Gustav von Grunebaum, a University of Chicago Orientalist, expresses surprise that "although a considerable proportion of the Zanj were themselves slaves, they showed no desire to abolish slavery but instead took to keeping slaves on their own."[108] He concludes correctly that the Zanj "desired betterment of their position, not a reorganization of society." Lewis also notes that the movement "had no real program of reform, no general aim of abolishing slavery," but was rather a revolt of specific slaves to better their conditions.[109] The Zanj rebellion was certainly not an antislavery crusade, and some of the Zanj rebels made slaves of their captives. But both Grunebaum and Lewis are judging these rebels by modern standards. It should be remembered that no Islamic reformers, or Christian ones for that matter, had yet declared slavery itself to be "sinful" or "unjust."

While the Zanj revolt was in progress one of the most radical Muslim groups, the Carmathians, established a communal settlement in Arabia just south of Basra. The settlement used 50,000 black slaves to make possible a model community. (The pattern of using black slave labor in southern Mesopotamia persisted into the nineteenth century.) Under medieval Islam, the specter of a revolt that menaced even the capital tended to make the caliphs distrustful of their black soldiers and increased their reliance on the Turks, even while incorporating defeated Zanj in the caliphate armies. In the capital, co-optation took another form.

Black Scholars and Artists

One of the most famous caliphs was Harun al-Rashid (A.D. 786-809), who presided over a Baghdad court that was the contemporary world's symbol of luxurious living. Both hedonistic behavior and scholarly pursuits flourished despite Shiite and Kharijite criticism. The reign of Harun al-Rashid is highly romanticized in *The Arabian Nights*, a work that is, on the whole, derogatory in its portrayal of Blacks. Not surprisingly, *The Arabian Nights* makes no mention of Ibrahim al-Mahdi, the caliph's beloved half-brother and a legendary figure in his own right.[110] But his fame was widespread.

Ibrahim's mother was Caliph al-Mahdi's favorite wife, a woman who, one tradition holds, was a Negro princess captured during a war against a kingdom in southern Persia (presumably Elam). Ibrahim was a mulatto but may have had a greater infusion of Negro genes, with some coming from the paternal line. Both Ibrahim and his half-brother Harun al-Rashid were well-educated. Ibrahim became an accomplished poet and musician. When Harun became caliph, he named Ibrahim ruler of Syria, but he gave up that post in order to make the pilgrimage to Mecca with al-Rashid.

When Harun al-Rashid died, his sons fought over the succession, and Ibrahim, their uncle, reluctantly accepted the caliphate in the interim. He is the only caliph of Negro ancestry to become well-known throughout the Muslim world. In Ibn Khallikan's widely circulated collection of biographies, compiled four hundred years after his reign, Ibrahim is depicted as a well-liked but irresponsible ruler who had to be replaced because of his incompetence.

In accordance with the prevalent stereotype of the tenth and eleventh centuries, the biographer stressed Ibrahim's gift for music and his love of it as the dominant aspect of his life.[111] Some chroniclers suggest that Ibrahim's easy-going and overly generous nature caused him to tolerate people whose corrupt practices discredited his rule and alienated the soldiers whose loyalty was the guarantee of any caliph's continuation in power. Whether these charges were justified is impossible to determine. Those who made them were ambitious men who never intended Ibrahim to be more than a caretaker caliph. One of his nephews, al-Ma'mun, organized the coup that overthrew him.

As soon as Ibrahim made it clear that he had no political ambitions, he was accepted back into court circles by al-Ma'mun. But as reigning caliph, al-Ma'mun sometimes ridiculed and embarrassed his uncle. In one sadistic jest, al-Ma'mun asked Ibrahim, "Art thou the *Negro* caliph?" Ibrahim replied in the words of a poet, "Though I be a slave, my soul, through its noble nature is free; though my body be black, my mind is fair." The nephew then said: "Uncle, a jest of mine has put you in a serious mood. Blackness of skin cannot degrade an ingenious mind, or lessen the worth of the scholar and the wit. Let darkness claim the color of your body; I claim as mine your fair and candid soul."[112] Besides showing the degree to which Manichaean concepts had pervaded a court whose intellectual circle was dominated by Persians, this exchange also proves that even high-status individuals were mocked for a Negro physiognomy and themselves apologized for it.

Rather than live in luxury at the court under the thumb of his patronizing nephew, Ibrahim eventually became a travelling concert artist, often singing his own compositions.[113] When this profession was criticized in later years, it became customary to ask, "Was not

Prince Ibrahim, son of al-Mahdi and a descendant of the Prophet, the first singer of his day?"[114]

Ibrahim's life story confirmed the prevalent belief that Blacks had a special gift for music. For us it provides support for the argument that Blacks became notable in certain fields because they developed the talents or skills they needed for the few avenues left open to their ambitions. Certainly black scholars were almost as rare as black caliphs during the 767 years of the Abbasid caliphate.[115] Color is mentioned in one or two recorded cases, proving that their occasional appearance was unusual enough to elicit comment. For instance, Zu 'n-Nun al-Misri, son of a Nubian slave, became noted for "his learning, devotion, communion with the divinity, and acquaintance with literature." Another black man, Khair al-Nassaj, is referred to as a "noted ascetic and Sufi doctor;" another was a prominent mathematician.

A success story from a period of early Islamic history, when Blacks, no doubt, had already acquired a favorable reputation for special skills in the field of music, is a black musician named Ziryab. His career began in Mesopotamia, and he became an influential and widely known personality at the court of 'Abd al-Rahman II in Andalusia. According to one account, Ziryab was introduced at court by an influential Jew. High honors were heaped upon him and he was given a palatial home and a fabulous salary. One account claims that his "influence at the court grew rapidly, and he was soon one of the ruler's favorites." It was stated that

> [his] greatest talent lay in singing, playing the lute, and instructing and training students. He is credited with knowing one thousand songs from memory. . . . He composed numerous songs. . . . He founded a conservatory of music in Cordova, the first of its kind.[116]

Who was this remarkable person? An answer to that question throws some light upon both the nature of slavery and the role of color in the early Islamic period. According to one account,

> 'Ali ibn Nafi', known as Ziryab (789-859) . . . was probably a client (mawla) who was brought up and educated in Baghdad. Acording to Ibn 'Abd Rabbihi, he was a black slave of the famous musician Ibrahim al-Mawsili, the leading musician of the day, who trained him in the arts of music and singing. He was so gifted that his special talents attracted the attention of the caliph Harun al-Rashid . . . his master became jealous and advised Ziryab in unmistakable terms either to leave the country immediately and settle in a distant land or to remain and suffer anguish and enmity.[117]

(Lewis states that antagonism toward black entertainers later became prevalent in some circles.)[118]

After spending some time in Egypt, Ziryab moved on to Spain at the invitation of the ruler there. His influence in Andalusia extended far beyond the circle of those who loved music for, being at court, "he introduced new fashions in hair styles, culinary arts, table etiquette, and dresses for every season and occasion."[119] It has even been said that it would require a whole volume to record his contribution to the evolution of Andalusian music. His work was continued by several of his children."[120] Ziryab encountered jealousy and intrigue in Andalusia, as he had in Baghdad, but the caliph protected him.

Al-Jahiz, introduced briefly as we mentioned his defense of black military prowess, probably had ancestors among Basra's assimilated Blacks. Joel A. Rogers states unequivocally, and Lewis less certainly, that al-Jahiz was part Negro. He became known throughout the Muslim world for his scholarship, and he wrote what is probably the first "vindicationist" work, *The Boast of the Blacks or The Superiority in Glory of the Black Race Over the Whites (Kitab fahr al-Sudan 'ala l-bidan)*. This aggressive polemical essay defended Negroes as a group against their critics, denounced the custom of derogating the Negro body image, and at the same time criticized those who judged all Blacks by the unsavory characteristics of some.[121]

Al-Jahiz himself had derided what he saw as culturally repulsive masses of "backward" Africans[122] and accepted the designation "Zanj" for these people. But he raised questions of his own about the query sometimes heard: "How is it that we have never seen a Zanj who had the intelligence even of a woman or a child?" In analyzing this charge of black stupidity, he called the middle class's attention to the fact that "the only Zanj they knew were slaves of low origin from outlying and backward areas." Al-Jahiz pointed out that the same people did not judge India by Indian slaves but by its intellectuals.[123]

Al-Jahiz claimed that Blacks were not only fine cooks and gifted singers, but "as for trustworthiness, they excel all others. The bankers confide their money and their businesses to them because they have found them more experienced and worthy of trust."[124]

Biographer Ibn Khallikan mentions less than a dozen Blacks among several hundred famous Muslims. Speaking of black achievements in the Central Islamic Lands, Professor Lewis notes, "the *emancipated* black slave was rarely able to rise above the lower levels . . . Muslim authors attribute this want of achievement by black slaves and freedmen to lack of capacity. The modern observer will recognize the effects of lack of opportunity" [italics added].[125] Slaves may have, on the whole, had an advantage over freedmen because they had owners who could profit from their skill, intelligence, and loyalty, as well as relatives, particularly fathers, who were interested and sometimes affectionate patrons. In kin-based societies such relationships were crucial. Kin ties could offset slave status.

Distance from Central Islamic Lands was also a factor in a black person's favor whether slave or free. Lewis noted that upward mobility was easier in some peripheral areas, where distance from the Arab/Persian centers of dominance widened the "space" for achievement. The classic case is that of Ziryab in tenth-century Muslim Spain. Lewis also detects increased anti-Negro behavior throughout Islam after the tenth century.[126]

Black Colonizers and Rulers in India

The first wave of the jihad moved rapidly eastward as far as northern India, where it carved out a beachhead in what is now Pakistan. Here, in this peripheral area, Blacks lived in a unique type of Diaspora, a place where the somatic norm image of many of the indigenous people was similar to that of Negro Africans, except for straight hair. Color prejudice was less important than religious and caste prejudices in India, although it influenced mating choices. In public life it was of little or no importance.

On the Indian periphery, Von Grunebaum notes, "a number of soldiers of African slave origin rose to high office, some even becoming rulers."[127] By the sixteenth century, one of the early emancipated slaves in the area east of Bombay had become prominent. Sa'id al-Habshi Sultani "became free, acquired property, and established a library that attracted scholars. He constructed the Siddi Sa'id mosque, which is still a permanent attraction in Ahmadabad,"[128] according to Professor Joseph Harris, the Afro-American scholar at Howard University who has made a detailed study of Africans who became leaders in India.

India provides other examples of Blacks who acquired power in a Diaspora country. The descendants of Africans had settled on the island of Janjira, where they participated in piracy as well as legitimate trade, and came to dominate the northwestern coast. These black seamen became important allies of Malik Ambar, one of the most important leaders of the resistance to the Mogul invaders who brought Islam to north-central India centuries after the Arab jihad (see plate 5). He had been an African slave. The Siddis of Janjira supplied the naval muscle for several successive groups of Hindu conquering rulers, but their first great thrust was in the move to assist Malik Ambar in fighting off the Muslim Mughal incursion. Of this black ruler, Harris has written:

> the most dramatic assertion of power by a single African in Indian history was that of Malik Ambar, an Ethiopian who was sold as a slave in Ethiopia, the Hejaz, al-Mukha, and Baghdad before finally reaching India. Ambar spent much of his life in Ahmadnagar, where there was a community of hundreds, or perhaps, thousands of Africans. Ambar himself recruited 1,000 for his guard. The greatness of Ambar stems from the fact that he became a commander of a large army for the king of Ahmadnagar and resisted several Mughal attacks. . . . He reigned supreme in the area around Ahmadnagar for nearly a quarter of a century (1602-26). During that time he founded towns, encouraged the construction of canals and irrigation schemes, stimulated trade with Asians and Europeans, attracted scholars and poets to his court, and fostered the construction of some of the most impressive buildings in the Deccan.[129]

Professor Graham Irwin, in *Africans Abroad*, presents a long excerpt written by Peter van den Broecke, a representative of the Dutch East India Company who sought Malik's aid. He complimented Malik for his intelligence, integrity and competent administration, although he called him "a black kaffir from the land of Habeeshi or Prester John's land." Irwin finds no corroboration for a story still told that Malik married the widow of an Indian king whose slave he had been, and later insisted that another king marry his daughter in order to seal an alliance.[130]

Professor Harris emphasizes the fact that Africans managed to win support and respect from diverse Indian groups while retaining a sense of their own identity. However, most of the descendants of the early Blacks were eventually absorbed by amalgamation, although some who arrived during the nineteenth-century slave trade still form separate groups in the population. Noteworthy though the black impact on western India was, the impact of Negroes was much stronger and persisted longer on the western peripheries than on the eastern edge of the Central Islamic Lands. Black military leaders are part of the history of the nation in Morocco, not merely of local areas as in India.[131]

Black Leaders in the Kingdom of the Two Shores

Andalusia, including parts of Spain and Portugal, was populated by a mixture of Celts and Romans, with a later influx of Visigoths. When Islamized a distinctive culture developed. On the other shore of the Mediterranean stood Morocco, its old Berber population heavily infiltrated with the genes of Negroes who had been imported as slaves for centuries. Romans, Vandals, and Goths had also left a stamp on the population, and Jewish communities were scattered here and there. Andalusia and Morocco were both on the western periphery of the Central Islamic Lands.

Disunity among the Berbers facilitated the Muslim conquest of Northern Africa. Far from the central core of Islam, Morocco and Andalusia developed separate Islamic cultures, but together after the eleventh century they formed the Kingdom of the Two Shores. The black population was rapidly absorbed in Andalusia, while Negro enclaves persisted in Morocco. Blacks moved into high positions in both regions. The union of Andalusia and Morocco brought unusual opportunities to Blacks.

The greatest of the Moorish rulers of Spain was popularly called "The Black Sultan," Ya'kub ibn Yusuf, better known as al-Mansur. The son of a partially Negro Berber and a concubine from one of the black kingdoms below the Sahara, he ruled Morocco from 1149 through 1189.

Twice al-Mansur invaded Andalusia for successful attacks, bringing home thousands of Christian prisoners. Then the kings of Leon, Castile, and Portugal decided to mount an offensive aided by the Crusaders to drive the Moors out of Spain. Mansur responded to their taunts and invaded a third time. The loot taken in the Moorish victory was immense. Mansur took his "fifth" and let his soldiers divide the rest. Most of the principal Christian cities were captured, and Toledo was besieged. He released 24,000 Christian prisoners and granted the Christians' request for a ten-year truce, returning to Morocco where he died in the fifteenth year of his reign.[132]

Mansur sponsored the building of mosques, schools, and aqueducts in cities on both shores of the kingdom, and one of the aphorisms attributed to him was, "A rich man who does not practice charity is like a tree that bears no fruit." A fourteenth-century historian wrote of The Black Sultan that:

> His reign was remarkable for the tranquility, the safety, the abun-
> dance, and the prosperity that reigned everywhere. . . . His govern-
> ment was excellent; he increased the treasury; his power was
> exalted; his actions those of a most noble ruler; his religion was
> sincere and deep; and he was a great benefactor of Islam.[133]

Nevertheless, the Christian Reconquest continued its persistent thrust southward. Cordova and Seville fell during the thirteenth century. In 1492, all Moors except those in the city of Granada would be expelled, and Muslim power in Spain would end. But during the fourteenth century African rulers made a final attempt to keep Spain as part of a Kingdom of the Two Shores.

Joel A. Rogers in *World's Great Men of Color* has described in some detail one Moroccan leader who made the effort. Like al-Mansur, Abu'l-Hasan was popularly known as the "Black Sultan." One biographer stated that "He got his name like his dark skin from his mother, who was an Abyssinian negress to whom in one of his inscriptions he paid a lofty tribute."[134]

In a maneuver that was not unusual in Muslim royal families, Abu'l-Hasan, with the aid of a faction in the armed forces, seized the throne from a brother who had succeeded his father, Abu Sa'id. The father had concentrated upon consolidating his power in Morocco and establishing peaceful relations with Algeria and Tunis, ignoring the Christian Reconquest that was whittling away Muslim territory across the straits. His son, however, was not prepared to cede Andalusia to the Christians.

Abu'l-Hasan took an expedition across to Spain that defeated the king of Castile in 1330 and recaptured Gibraltar. The Moroccan fleet also defeated the Christian fleet in the Mediterranean. However, Castile and Portugal, formerly enemies, now made an alliance and shattered the precarious Moroccan foothold in Spain. The black sultan returned to the policy of his father and concentrated upon making Morocco the major power in North Africa. Rogers notes that

> He was renowned in the annals of the East for his ambition, courage, and the fortitude with which he bore his reverses as well as for his patronage of art. Under him Moroccan art, architecture, and literature rose to the zenith of their splendor. . . . His colleges, upon which he lavished all the beauties of Moroccan art, are monuments to his highly civilized taste and love of culture.[135]

Abu'l-Hasan was also renowned for the encouragement he gave to artists and literary men. Incidentally, the favorite wife of this "Black Sultan" was a European named Shams-ed-Douha or "the Morning Sun," and his tomb and hers are among the architectural treasures of Morocco.[136]

During the fifteenth century, the Portuguese began to obtain a foothold on the coast of Morocco. In organizing resistance and mobilizing for sea raids against European shipping, a new dynasty assumed power in Morocco. It claimed Arab rather than Berber connections, but a number of black leaders quickly rose to the top.

Sultan Mulai Ismael, like Mansur and Hasan, also had a Negro slave for a mother, a woman referred to in some of the chronicles as "notoriously ugly." Mulai Ismael himself has been described as "almost black with a white mark near his nose." Rogers calls him "a strange mixture of excellent qualities and amazing defects." Mulai spent the first twenty-four years of his fifty-five-year reign on the task of expelling English, Spanish, and French forces from Moroccan soil, fighting off mountain Berbers who were attacking from the rear, and preparing to resist the Turks who were moving in from the east.

Like Abu'l-Hasan, Mulai Ismael had a reputation for extreme cruelty toward enemies. But he has also been remembered for the extraordinary refinement of his esthetic sensibilities. He was also remembered for something else: "The common people loved him; the rich he taxed heavily."[137] Europeans and colonials dubbed him "the Bloodthirsty," and legends proliferated about his cruelty to whites, whom he captured and enslaved, as well as about his prodigious sexual powers and the hundreds of children he fathered. That he was cruel and vindictive at times is not to be denied; that he was unusually cruel to whites does not seem to be a charge that can be sustained. He was too anxious to use their services in building up Morocco to have unduly alienated his prisoners of war.

One European scholar has made this assessment of him, which might be compared with Rogers's somewhat more laudatory profile:

> His mind is ever alert . . . He is very shrewd . . . intrepid and courageous in time of danger . . . He rules by the terror of his name . . . a strange mixture of excellent qualities and amazing defects. . . . He began by increasing the number of Bokhara composed entirely of full-blood Negroes, his bodyguard. There were 150,000 of these soldiers living in villages scattered about the country. He himself commanded 10,000 white Christian troops.[138]

The unified Morocco that was Mulai Ismael's legacy fell apart during thirty years of disorders that followed his death. Nevertheless, his dynasty remains in power to this day, although Blacks are no longer prominent in it. But the Black Guard still escorts the king.

ISLAM AND STATE BUILDING IN SUB-SAHARAN AFRICA

Blacks had already been barred from the armies and from key administrative posts in Egypt, when Mansa Musa, the black king of

Mali, passed through Cairo on his pilgrimage to Mecca. Basil Davidson describes his

> camel train and servants and his wives and gifts and arrogant horsemen, all the trappings of a king whose realm would soon comprise a land as large as Western Europe and as civilized as most of its kind in Europe.

Mansa Musa brought so much gold that it is said to have depressed the currency in the Middle East. The same mamelukes who had relegated Blacks to menial positions in the army greeted Mali's king as a fellow Muslim potentate, and we are told that the population of Cairo was impressed by the ostentatious display of his opulence.[139]

More than a century later, not long after five hundred disgruntled black grooms and servants in the Egyptian army tried unsuccessfully to set up a mini-state, Cairo was host to another black king on pilgrimage. Mohammed Touré, known as Askia the Great of Songhay, also brought with him a vast entourage and enormous quantities of gold, creating even more of a stir than Mansa Musa.

There were no mamelukes or saqalibah in West Africa to thwart the aspirations of Blacks. Berbers and Arabs at the courts of these independent states never achieved military and political power, even when they were employed as advisers. The black kings of West Africa wielded power to an extent that was not rivaled by Blacks elsewhere in the Muslim world until the Fung kingdom appeared in East Africa in the sixteenth century A.D.

If we survey the thousand years of black history between the sixth century A.D., when the Christian king of Axum in the Abyssinian highlands took southern Arabia away from its Jewish kings and made Abraha's attack on Mecca possible, and 1591, when the Muslim forces of Morocco swooped down across the desert and smashed the power of Songhay in West Africa, the most striking aspect of African history is the progressive involvement of the Sudanic kingdoms in the affairs of the Muslim world, culminating in Mansa Musa's visit to Mecca in 1324 and Askia the Great's pilgrimage in 1495, three years after Columbus reached the Caribbean.

All Africans north and east of the equatorial rain forest were pulled into the vortex of vast political and economic changes during these three hundred years. The changes were organized and expressed as a conflict between two competing world religions, Christianity and Islam, occurring simultaneously with the spread of Islam northward into the Turkish lands of the Eurasian plains. Economic interests were just beneath the surface in these religious conflicts.

Below the Sahara and Libyan deserts and west of the Nile Valley, on the great savannah lands north of the equatorial rain forest, Ghana, Mali, and Songhay emerged successively as black empires. By the thirteenth century, the region was becoming integrated into the Muslim *ecumene*. Writers from Muslim Spain and the Central Islamic Lands were praising some of the black West African kingdoms for having adopted Islam, while criticizing them for retaining many pagan practices, especially matrilineal descent and a degree of freedom in relations between men and women that the religious leaders of the Central Islamic Lands considered intolerable.[140] After four centuries of contact with Islam through Arabs and Berbers, the black sovereign kingdoms were not accepting orders, or even responding to nonmilitary pressures from Islamic states with whom they were in contact. Acculturation took place on their terms, not those of conquerors from Europe, Asia, or North Africa.

Independent black rulers used Islam in their own state-building processes and fought off the domination of non-Negro Muslims. Black self-assurance was exhibited by pagan rulers who resisted Islamization, especially when they suspected that it might mean Berber domination. For black rulers who eventually adopted Islam, that self-assurance was expressed in the ostentatious manner in which they made the pilgrimage to Mecca.

The aggressive initiative of African states after Islamization is manifest in their warfare against pagans within their own vicinity, not only for the ostensible purpose of extending the faith, but also in order to capture as marketable slaves those who refused the jihad option of adopting Islam. The black rulers never allowed sentiments of black solidarity to prevent the capture and sale of slaves, any more than the French, German, and Italian Christians allowed their common whiteness to interfere with the capture and sale of Slavs from the Caucasus and the Black Sea coasts, incidentally selling some of them to Muslims in Cyprus, Sicily, and North Africa. Thus, it is unlikely that Askia the Great experienced any sympathy with the Blacks whose rebellion in Cairo had been squelched. Indeed, his regime may have sent some of these Blacks north for sale. And he had African slaves in his own retinue.

Before contact with Islam, the great repository of manpower in sub-Saharan Africa had already been exploited by the black rulers who organized several pagan kingdoms on the sahel and savannah lands south of the deserts, in what the Arabs called Bilad al-Sudan, the "Land of the Blacks." This state-building had begun centuries before Islamized Berbers and Arabs began to settle in the area as missionaries and merchants. However, the scope and pace of state-building was accelerated by contact with Berbers and Arabs.

The Arab impact on Africa west of the Nile falls into two distinct periods. During the first four hundred years, that impact was almost entirely indirect. Arabs and Berber converts were carrying the jihad into Spain and Islamizing the old Christian Berber cities of North Africa.[141] Meanwhile, many Berbers who resisted Islamization moved deeper into the desert as camel nomads, often forcing indigenous Negroes on the oases to become serfs and compelling them to surrender a portion of their crops. During this period some Arabs settled in towns of the dominant black kingdom, Ghana, but they were outnumbered by Berber merchants and religious dignitaries.

The second period of Arab impact began in A.D. 1065, when the Fatimid caliph of Egypt encouraged invading Bedouin tribesmen from Arabia to leave Egypt and move westward into the Berber domains. By the thousands, families with their herds of small animals and their camels poured across North Africa to the Atlantic coast and then moved southward into what is now Mauretania. Some also trickled into the Libyan desert and mixed with black and Berber nomads.[142] Anthropologist George Peter Murdock believes that these Bedouins transmitted their concepts of pride and prejudice to the Berbers, who pushed deeper into the desert, where they exploited and enslaved the black oasis dwellers and eventually began to invade the territory of the black kingdoms of the savannahs.[143]

During this period, invading Arabs and Berbers had a marked effect on the black kingdoms south of the desert, setting off a wave of state-building activities that toppled the old kingdom of Ghana and saw it replaced by Mali and, later, Songhay. When the Arab Bedouins first arrived in the eleventh century, the major export of these kingdoms was gold. As time passed, the major export became human beings for use as slaves.[144] With Berbers increasingly being converted to Islam, they could not be enslaved by fellow Muslims. Pagan Blacks became the sole pool of potential slaves to meet an increasing demand in the Middle East.

We shall look first at the Arab and Berber impact on the emergence in the desert of what anthropologist Murdock calls the closest approximation to color-caste in the Islamic world. Then, we will turn to a more extensive examination of Islam in the kingdoms of Bilad al-Sudan, the "Land of the Blacks."

Berber Dominance in the Desert

Agricultural Blacks have lived in the Saharan and Libyan oases from time immemorial. Many of them, including those who live among the desert nomads, today speak languages related to those used by the Hausa people of the savannah lands. The American anthropologist George Peter Murdock concludes that

> with the exception of an uninhabitable section in the center, the western Sahara was originally inhabited exclusively by Negroes. They still survive there as the Haratin, a subject group of agricultural serfs whose status almost exactly replicates that of the Bella among the Tuareg and who are equally distinct from Sudanese slaves and their descendants.[145]

He should have noted that most, but not all, *Haratin* are black.

Arab intrusions into this contact zone after A.D. 700 resulted in increased competition between Berbers and Blacks for control of the oases. Between A.D. 800 and 900, while the Arabs were occupied in North Africa and Andalusia, three nomadic Berber tribes—Lamtuna, Masufa, and Godala—all units of the larger Sanhaja Berber group that roamed the fringes of the desert and controlled many of the oases, formed a confederation.

One section of the Lamtuna tribe gradually moved southwest into the area now called Mauretania. Historian J. Spencer Trimingham notes that

> In these regions lived many groups of black and white cultivators and the arrival of the nomads upset the whole western Sahara. . . . Continually in search of pasturage they roamed over the most suitable regions occupied by Negro peoples who either became their tribute-paying cultivators or were pushed toward the Senegal [river].[146]

In this area and others where the camel nomads moved in, a class called the *Haratin* arose, including Blacks and whites who were obliged to provide some produce and labor to the nomads. This was serfdom, not slavery. However, they did enslave Blacks from below the desert.

Anthropologist Murdock attributes the development of what he calls a color-caste system to the impact of those Bedouin Arabs who entered the Libyan desert and the western Sahara in great numbers during the eleventh century. He notes that their *shorfs* or nobles proceeded to exact tribute from other Arabs who had preceded them, as well as from Berbers and Negroes. They exercised the prerogatives of males in the Arabian social system—introducing slavery, polygyny and concubinage—within a framework that soon included four to six "castes" with black slaves near the bottom.

Murdock blames whatever is rigid and undemocratic in North African and desert social stratification on the Arabs rather than the Berbers, stating that the social system in these areas "rests on a caste stratification so extreme that it can be paralleled elsewhere in the world only in India and the Union of South Africa."[147] In the desert, eventually a variety of stratification patterns emerged; chart 6 shows a few existing today, as described by L. C. Briggs.[148] The ethnic groups are arranged in order of prestige and status from highest to lowest. In all of the cases, a slave stratum exists below the haratin, made up of Negroes captured in raids on caravans or purchased.

The Arab Bedouins who arrived during the eleventh century showed contempt for Berbers, whose variety of Islam was unorthodox. They also displayed the prejudices toward Blacks that Islam had never been able to eliminate from the Bedouin tradition in

CHART 6. Caste Stratification in the Sahara

WESTERN SAHARA (in Mauretania)	AMONG THE ZENATA (Central Sahara)	AMONG THE TEDA (Eastern Sahara)
Berbers or Arabs	All Zenata	Noble Berber clans
Assimilated Blacks	Islamized Jews	Commoners (vassals)
HARATIN	HARATIN	Hunters, artisans
Free descendants of domestic slaves	Slaves (Blacks)	HARATIN
Free descendants of laborer slaves		
Domestic slaves (Blacks)		
Laborer slaves (Blacks)		

Arabia. There, as we have mentioned, pride of lineage resulted in a subordinate status for children born to women slaves or serfs and a Bedouin father. If an Arab woman had a child fathered by a male of slave or serf status, it could mean death for the woman if adultery was involved or ostracism if she was single. In adjusting to new situations in Berber lands, changes were made in customs related to the place of concubines and their progeny in the social system. Bedouin practice injected a note of greater severity in some places while in others, Arab customs were softened by interaction with Berbers.

Briggs emphasizes the crucial distinction between marriage, which is controlled by status divisions in the society, and miscegenation, which frequently cuts across status lines but assures that the progeny will not disturb the family and kinship structure. In discussing race relations in the vast northwestern desert area, he writes:

> The various racial and social segments of the sedentary population of the desert naturally are not entirely shut off from each other biologically . . . On the contrary, more or less sporadic and usually clandestine interbreeding has been going on between them for centuries, regardless of theoretical prohibitions which are respected more or less strictly as the case may be. Marriage below the social rank into which one was born is unthinkable for almost every self-respecting native of the Sahara . . . In spite of this, however, continuing race mixture is widespread among the sedentary peoples of the area and presumably always has been.[149]

Marriage is controlled by rules and regulations interpreted to suit the best interests of kin groups. However, mating is determined by erotic proclivities and esthetic evaluations, the essence of personal attraction between the sexes. The institution of concubinage distinguishes between children of legitimate wives and those resulting from other sexual relations. There are no taboos based on color or Negroidness controlling the choice of concubines, and the male progeny can assume high status so long as their advancement does not jeopardize the kinship structure.

As Briggs explains:

> even among the notoriously puritanical inhabitants of the Mzab . . . one sometimes sees the face of a handsome Negro woman peering from the parapet of a housetop terrace down onto the street . . . She is probably a children's nurse or some other kind of household servant, and a slave or descendant of slaves, but she and others like

her have occasionally left the mark of their race clearly stamped on the features of both Moslems and Jews of the Mzab who firmly maintain, often no doubt in full sincerity, that they surely have no negroid, far less Negro ancestors.[150]

Some of the western Sanhaja Berbers would eventually organize what came to be known as The Desert Empire. It would challenge Ghana's control of the area around the southern terminus of the old Sijilmasa caravan route, and thus stimulate further state-building.

The Rise and Fall of Ghana

The caravan routes, which had existed since Roman days, were discovered by the first wave of Arabs who crossed North Africa and reached Morocco in the eighth century (see map 3). One route linked caravan assembly points near the Atlas Mountains with a region below the desert near the big bend in the Niger River. Traveling down this route, Arabs found cities where salt was mined and sent south to be traded for gold.

Berbers and Blacks had competed for control of the southern termini of the trade route for centuries. At the end of the fourth century A.D., several clans of the Soninke tribe of Mande-speaking Negroes had established a state near the southern terminus of the western caravan route. Their ruler was known as a *gana*. From his capital city, Kumbi-Saleh, the *gana* controlled trade between the Berbers of the desert and the Negroes of the gold-producing regions.

The Arab historian Ibn Khaldun, writing of the period of first Arab contact, stated that "When, after the conquest of North Africa, merchants penetrated into the western parts they found no Negro kingdom more powerful than that of Ghana [by then the Soninke term for king was applied to the state] whose domain extended westward as far as the Atlantic."[151] Ghana was composed of a Soninke core with numerous other ethnic groups being tribute-paying territories that were forced to give allegiance to the king at Kumbi-Saleh. Some of their subordinate kings and chiefs provided gold dust or gold nuggets in exchange for valuable salt as well as protection from rival kingdoms and desert marauders.

In A.D. 739, the Arabs sent a small expedition south from Morocco to take over the kingdom of Ghana. The black king's troops defeated the invaders, and another military conquest from the north was not attempted for over 230 years. However, as the eighth century moved forward, Arab merchants settled in the oases along the caravan

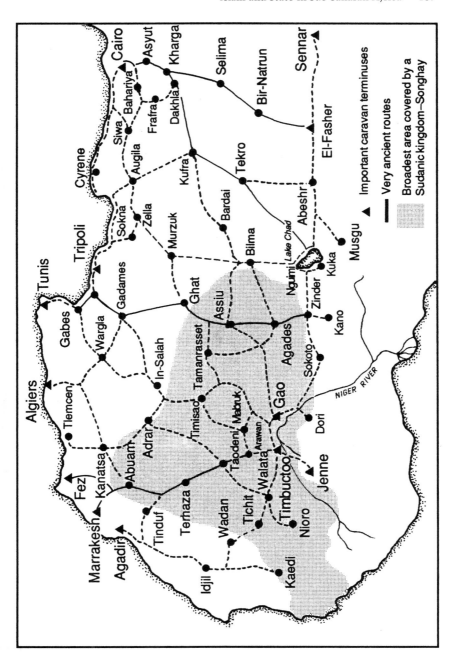

MAP 3. THE MAJOR TRANS-SAHARAN CARAVAN ROUTES
Cartography based on a concept of the author.

route, improving wells and other sources of water and taking charge of business transactions.

Missionaries established mosques and Koran schools, which were attended by some indigenous Blacks as well as newly arrived Arabs and Berbers. Some pagan customs were modified as a few converts were made. Travelers occasionally complained that black converts ignored proper Islamic practice and that Arab and Berber settlers were being "corrupted" by exposure to African customs.[152]

Meanwhile, the Sanhaja Berbers kept pressing south between the western caravan route and the Atlantic, eventually pushing most Negroes, except for *Haratin*, across the Senegal river. The first prize that pagan Blacks and Berbers fought over was the city of Audoghast, two hundred miles north of Ghana's capital in the fertile, well-watered valley just below the desert. (To the east of it was Walata, a well-known city in the area.)

Al-Ya 'qubi wrote in A.D. 891 that after passing the great salt deposits, "one comes to a place called Ghast, an inhabited valley in which are dwellings and a king of [pagan] Berbers who has neither religion nor revealed law. He raids the countries of the Negroes, whose kingdoms are numerous."[153] During the tenth century, the city attracted Koranic scholars and missionaries, as Berber chiefs began to adopt Islam.[154] Audoghast became an Islamic city, with mosques and calls to prayer five times a day, *cadis* to dispense justice and *malams* to teach and preach. By mid-century, there were mosques and Muslims in Kumbi-Saleh, as well, although Ghana's king was still pagan. Pagan Negroes and Muslims lived in separate quarters, which were architecturally distinct, but there apparently was no racial or religious conflict.[155]

The rulers of The Desert Kingdom, residing in Audoghast, tried to detach segments of the Ghana empire and thus gain control over the territory where northbound caravans were assembled. This would also eliminate middlemen in trade with gold-mining regions south of Ghana. Between A.D. 961 and 971, Audoghast sent the black king of Massina 50,000 camel-borne warriors to help him defeat another Negro kingdom east of Ghana. Al-Bakri, writing a century later, said the king's wives and concubines committed suicide "to avoid falling into the hands of white men."[156] Whether or not this interpretation of the alleged suicides was true, al-Bakri was not the only Arab writer who interpreted pre-Islamic conflict in this region in racial terms.

In A.D. 990, the king of Ghana, acting in his perceived economic interests, sent his armies into Audoghast, took control of the municipal administration, and appointed governors for all sections of the Berber empire.[157] Although a few Ghanaians, including one prominent family, were Muslims, the king remained pagan. The stage thus was set for the conflict between Berbers and Ghana to assume religious as well as economic significance.

In an effort to unite the Sanhaja Berbers against Ghana, leaders of the partially Islamized Lamtuna tribe and their largely pagan Godala and Masufa kinsmen decided to seek the sanction of the wider Muslim world for subduing the pagans of Ghana and extending the Faith to "uncivilized" pagan Blacks as well, some of whom were reputedly cannibals. The tribal leaders sent a delegate on a pilgrimage to Mecca. He was slain by non-Islamic Berbers whom he visited on the way home. He had tried to convert them and they resented the attempt.

The next delegation to Mecca not unreasonably decided to proclaim a jihad against pagan Berbers first, before launching any attack on Ghana. They persuaded a conservative *marabout*, Ibn Yasin, to accompany them but his fellow Berbers became hostile over the accusations that they were semipagan and corrupt. Yasin withdrew to an island in the mouth of the Senegal River and there established a *ribat* or retreat where potential jihad fighters—Murabitun—could be trained. When his recruits had reached a thousand in number, Yasin sent them out with the pre-jihad warning to all of the Berbers in The Desert Empire:

> Go under the protection of God (Allah) and warn your fellow tribesmen . . . teach them the law of God and threaten them with his chastisement. If they repent and return to the truth and amend their ways, then leave them in peace; but if they refuse and persist in their errors and infidelity, let us invoke the aid of God against them and make war upon them until God decides the issues between them.[158]

The warning had no effect. So, in 1042 the jihad warriors moved out from the ribat, called for volunteers along the way, and were able to defeat band after band of Berber tribesmen who had not yet adopted the faith. Gathering momentum, this band of warriors moved up the caravan route to Sijilmasa, and, having secured control of that city, started back southward to Audoghast. With greatly augmented forces the Berbers now expelled the black Ghanaian pagan rulers from this southern city that had once been a Berber stronghold. This movement of Murabits, usually referred to as the Almoravids, now split into two sections. The main body under

Tashfin moved north and established the city of Marrakesh. It was he who responded when the call came from a beleaguered group of Andalusian kingdoms to cross over into Spain to stem the tide of the Christian Reconquest. Black troops from below the Sahara as well as from the desert oases, both slave and free, were among the Almoravid soldiers who helped establish Morocco and to garrison Spanish cities between 1056 and 1147 in the European part of the Kingdom of the Two Shores.

Meanwhile, Abu Bakr, Yasin's co-leader, decided to pursue the battle against the black pagans in the south and this was, of course, a battle for control of the southern terminus of the caravan route, as well as a jihad. Some of the black tribes and kingdoms adopted Islam; others preferred to pay the *jizya* or tax laid on conquered people. The Ghana capital of Kumbi Saleh fell to the Berbers in 1076 (ten years after William of Normandy crossed the English Channel and invaded England).

Ibn Khaldun states that the attack on the Ghana empire was also motivated by the desire of Abu Bakr to find a way to divert the Sanhaja, Godala, Masufa, and Tuareg Berbers from fighting each other. The sack of Ghana offered booty.[159] The conquest was made easier by the fact that restless subordinate kings within the Ghana Empire were ready to declare themselves Muslims and to cooperate in an attack upon the king of Ghana. Also small ethnic states were now free to pursue their feuds against each other and to attempt to put together a state that would rival Ghana. The most ambitious leaders were among the Malinke and Songhay peoples along the Niger river. Trimingham, summing up the implications of the collapse of the Ghana empire, states that

> The sack of Ghana ended the long period during which this kingdom had dominated the Western Sudan. Its fall led to the political triumph of Islam throughout the Sahil region between the Senegal and Niger. The Soninke of Ghana were compelled to adopt Islam and they not only did so en masse but began to spread it amongst the many people over whom they still ruled. . . . The role of the Murabitun in the Islamization of the Sudan has been exaggerated. The peaceful penetration of Islam along trade routes into borderland towns had begun before this movement was born. Traders were allowed full liberty by the tolerant Negro rulers both to practice and propagate their religion. Ghana and other towns possessed Muslim quarters whilst the rulers of Takrur and other states had become Muslims. The Murabitum simply accelerated a process that had already begun, and their conquest was ephemeral because the

attraction of Morocco was stronger than that of the Sudan. The role of Ghana in the Sahil and southern Sahara was taken over by the Mande empire of Mali, but its function was much greater than that of a buffer-state and it rapidly became the greatest Negro state Africa has ever known.[160]

The Rise of Mali

Ghana's main export had always been gold acquired by barter from areas not under its control. When the Almoravid jihad destroyed the Ghana empire, the victorious Berbers found it profitable to encourage successor states to send raiding parties into areas south of the black kingdoms. As Trimingham describes it:

> as a result of the demand for slaves in North Africa the Sahilian states were no longer contented with the reduction of prisoners of war to slave and eventually to serf status within their own communities but made a regular practice of raiding these uncoordinated Lem Lem to obtain slaves for sale to northern merchants.[161]

Trimingham is here using one of the terms Arab travelers had used in referring to groups of Negroes living south of the black kingdoms. "Lem Lem" and "Dem Dem" were the equivalent in the west of "Zanj." It was believed that cannibalism was widespread among them.

Al-Idrisi not only described the Lem Lem (al-Bakri added Dem Dem and Nam Nam to the list of people raided, calling the latter cannibals) but also mentioned one of the few towns in this land beyond the black kingdoms' boundaries where there were "many Negro peoples entirely naked who marry without dowry or proper rites," and who "scarify the face and temples at puberty" and "are steeped in infidelity and superstition."[162] These pagans were of course fair game for jihad warriors, and like the "Zanj" in Mesopotamia, were sometimes used to stereotype all Negroes. Legends about this town, Malel, if true, indicate one way in which Muslims may have sometimes spread Islam.

According to tradition, a learned Muslim staying as a guest at the home of the ruler of Malel convinced him that if he became a Muslim their joint prayers could bring rain to break a persistent drought. The king began to take instruction in the Koran, and the two men prayed together. One day, "God enveloped the land with abundant rain" and, in gratitude, the king ordered the destruction in his kingdom of the idols, and the expulsion of "the magicians" from his country. An Arab commentator stated of the king of Malel that

"He is sincerely attached to Islam as are his heir and courtiers, but the people of his kingdom remain idolators."[163] Another tradition mentions a Mali king of this period who made the pilgrimage to Mecca. The Mali kings eventually made war on pagans, but not to convert them. They wanted soldiers for their armies, forced labor for their farms, and slaves for export. The conflict between Mali leaders who approved of the adoption of Islam and those who opposed such a move has been well-documented by Arab and Berber historians, and the story has been recounted in English in several places.[164]

Both the black kingdoms and the Tuareg nomads on the northern borders of the black states had a traditional system in which advancement from slave to serf to client was possible, with substantial increases in freedom. Now, the prisoners sent along the caravan trails into bondage faced a new form of slavery, outside of a kinship matrix. However, under Islam, adoption into lineages or families was possible.

The Berber jihad had not crossed the Niger into the land of the Mali kings, and no Berber armies ever would, although their missionaries traveled through Mali making converts. Eventually its ruling families were also Islamized,[165] so in the early fourteenth century, Mali's reigning monarch Mansa Musa felt the time had come to make the pilgrimage to Mecca, the first for a ruler from the western Sudan group of Negro nations. As we have seen, his visit in 1324 made a favorable impression in Cairo. Mansa Musa carried back manuscripts as well as scholars, but above all ideas about how a Muslim state should be governed, how an acceptable Islamic monarch should comport himself, and plans for erecting buildings.[166]

Within thirty years of Mansa Musa's return from Mecca, the Andalusian traveler, Ibn Battuta, toured Mali and was able to compare it with Muslim communities he had visited in the Indian Ocean area. Ibn Battuta spoke of the African kingdom with qualified approval: "These people are Muslims, punctilious in observing the hour of prayer, studying books and law, and memorizing the Koran. Yet their women show no bashfulness before men and do not veil themselves, though they are assiduous in attending prayer."[167]

He complained in a decidedly racist vein that Malians, including kings, did not know how to treat "white people" with respect. He expressed shock over what he considered laxity in applying Islamic decorum in relations between the sexes, and his own preference for white settlers whom he met on his journey (especially the women).[168] However, he was impressed by the government, commenting that "There is complete security in their country. Neither traveler nor inhabitant in it has anything to fear from robbers or men of violence.'' And speaking presumably of the people as well as their rulers he said that the Blacks are "seldom unjust, and have a greater horror of injustice than other people.''[169]

But Ibn Battuta was also taken aback by the fact that Mali had a greater tolerance for the customs of some of its neighbors in the forests to the south than he felt good Muslims should exhibit. He described a visiting dignitary from one of these regions as a cannibal whose menu preferences, he claims, were accommodated by his Mali hosts.[170]

Mansa Musa built a military machine that won control over the northern caravan routes as far as the salt mines and the crucial oases north of the former boundary of Ghana. He also extended his conquests southward to take in the gold fields, which Ghana had never controlled. His main source of revenue was still taxation of trade commodities, especially gold, passing over the caravan route to Morocco. But the backbone of financial stability was produce and tolls from plantations established in every province of the Mali empire and worked for the king by slaves.[171]

The Mali kingdom blended Middle Eastern Islamic principles of government and political economy with African practices. It achieved a remarkable degree of success. Before the fifteenth century ended, a map was being circulated in Europe that bore a drawing purported to be a picture of Mansa Musa, and under it the caption: "This Negro Lord is called Mansa Musa, Lord of the Negroes of Guinea. So abundant is the gold which is found in his country that he is the richest and most nobel [sic] king in all the land.''[172]

Professor Joseph Harris points out that something more significant than military conquests and the stepped-up procurement of gold had taken place:

> While on his pilgrimage the king persuaded a number of Muslim scholars, jurists, architects, and others to return with him to Mali . . . some of the Muslim teachers began establishing Koranic schools that taught reading, writing, and comprehension from the Koran. The great university at Timbuktu, Sankore, built by es-Saheli, attracted students and professors not only from the immediate area but also from northern Africa and the Middle East. Timbuktu thus emerged as a significant intellectual center of Muslim learning.[173]

As Harris sees it, "this was a golden age in Africa and Mansa Musa was part of it; but with his passing rivalry for rule, competition for wealth, and religious reform movements began to bring Mali to decline.''[174]

The Emergence of Songhay

The decline of the Mali empire was related in part to the rapid growth of one of its dependent ethnic groups, the Songhay people of Kaw Kaw, pagans not Muslims, who had developed a prosperous city on the Niger southeast of the big "bend" or "buckle." Here at Gao, an old caravan route through the Libyan desert to Cairo and Tunis terminated (see map 3). As the Fatimid caliphate had prospered, it generated a market for slaves to be distributed throughout the Middle East and Mesopotamia.

Songhay kings organized a well-disciplined army of paid troops to fight off the Berber Tuareg nomads who preyed on the caravans. Between 1464 and 1492, Sonni 'Ali began to conquer non-Muslim states adjacent to his own, and he championed the cause of those who resisted the growing Berber influence. He has been depicted in Islamic history as a brutal persecutor of the learned scholars and merchants of Timbuctoo, a city that he attacked as Berber Muslims increased their influence among members of the royal line. Soon after the attack on Timbuctoo, the Muslim faction at court managed to dethrone Sonni 'Ali.

His successor, Mohammed Touré or Askia the Great, inherited a kingdom that Sonni 'Ali had built on the ruins of the Mali empire. Eventually he extended it to reach from the borders of Morocco almost to Lake Chad, embracing the important Tuareg desert stronghold of Air (see map 4). Askia, unlike Sonni 'Ali, was a Muslim, and as Askia the Great, he made the pilgrimage to Mecca in 1495.[175] Like Mansa Musa before him, he carried vast quantities of gold and brought back scholars in his entourage as well as advisers on Islamic law.

A cultural revival took place at Timbuctoo and Jenne, two cities whose rivalry dramatizes how cultural differences between Berber Muslims and African Muslims heightened color consciousness. Timbuctoo became a symbol of "white" alien culture. Jenne was the symbol of indigenous African urban culture. Trimingham sounds a warning note:

> The role of Timbuctoo as a centre of Negro Islamic learning must not be exaggerated for Jenne was more important. . . . It is note-worthy that under Mali and the earlier period of Tuareg rule the imams of the chief mosque were Negroes. Afterwards all those appointed were whites and from then on Timbuctoo continues to be dominated by whites. . . . It never became a real city state and its people derived from heterogeneous sources, separated by caste like

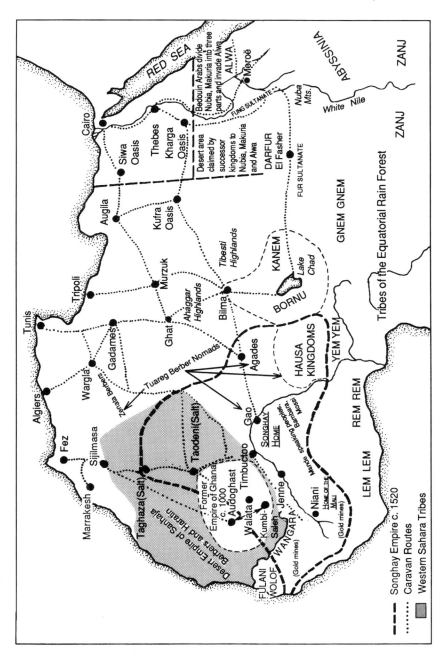

MAP 4. Africa During the Period of Songhay Hegemony
Cartography based on a concept of the author.

distinctions, never formed a real unity or achieved a form of municipal government.[176]

Timbuctoo was founded by Islamized Tuareg Berber nomads on the desert side of the Niger River bulge about twenty years after their Sanhaja kinsmen had sacked the capital of Ghana in the eleventh century. Amid the disorder that followed the fall of Ghana, the Tuareg were able to guarantee some safety. Timbuctoo grew rapidly as a trade center on the desert's edge. Farther up river, a prosperous city called Jenne emerged in an area where river commerce was important.

The Islamic scholars and missionaries who settled in Timbuctoo accepted the protection of the Tuaregs against neighboring pagan Blacks, but they did not urge their fellow Muslims to declare a jihad against Blacks, because they were their trading partners. The scholars were content to develop educational institutions in Timbuctoo, eventually making it a center of learning that attracted Blacks as well as Arabs and Berbers.

Meanwhile, some Muslims served as advisers to rulers of black cities and kingdoms, making such converts as they could. The Muslims scored their first important success in the upper Niger riverrain when the ruler of Jenne accepted Islam in A.D. 1200.[177] It took nearly three centuries after that before Jenne's officials decided its population was ready to accept the destruction of the city's sacred grove, symbolizing the triumph of Islam over indigenous pagan gods.[178]

Islamization was a prolonged and difficult process for Negro societies, because their cult of ancestors was very strong and was integrally related to the family and civic life of villages. The belief that spiritual forces animate nonliving objects, plants and animals, as well as human beings, was central to African religious beliefs. In the Middle East and North Africa, Judaism and Christianity had already weakened religious concepts of this kind by the time Islam came along, but remnants of them remained. They were viable in West Africa when the adoption of Islam was taking place and never disappeared.

By 1500, Jenne had overshadowed Timbuctoo as a commercial center. It had become to Timbuctoo what the capital of Ghana had been to Audoghast, a black city essential to the economic welfare of a Berber city. The rulers of the black kingdoms considered Timbuctoo a "white" city inimical to their interests, and both Mali and

Songhay incorporated it within their empires, but without changing its ethos. Trimingham notes of Jenne that *"in addition to its trade the town acquired renown as a center of Negro Islamic culture in contrast to Timbuctoo which was largely non-Negro* [italics added]."

During the period after Askia the Great's pilgrimage to Mecca in 1495, indigenous African writers published several important books: Ahmad Baba composed a number of works on Islamic law and compiled a dictionary of Muslim scholars. Thirteen of his works are still in use in parts of West Africa, according to historian Joseph Harris, who also mentions Mahmud al-Kati's *Ta'rikh al-Fattash* and 'Abd ar-Rahman as-Sa'di's *Ta'rikh as-Sudan* as "crucial documents for the reconstruction of West African history during the Middle Ages."[179] It is ironic that the intellectual potential of the first group of black literary men west of the Nile had just matured at the time Songhay was being destroyed.

That some Sudanese Blacks made contributions to Islamic "high culture" is becoming increasingly well-known. That they made significant cultural contributions at another cultural level is less well-known. After the third century of Islamic expansion a wide-spread mystical Islamic sectarian current began to well up. Western Africa made distinctive contributions that have been succinctly described by Professor H. A. R. Gibb:

> During the first three centuries of Islam, Berber reaction against Arab domination took the form of adhesion to the Kharijite or Shiite heresies, but the masses remained strongly attached to their primitive animistic beliefs, especially in the magical powers of "holy men". . . . the persistence of the old beliefs has given a characteristic feature to Berber Islam, the prevalence of "Maraboutism" or "the cult of living holy men," possessing magical powers (Baraka). The Sufi movement in the Barbary States . . . spread into the Negrolands on the Niger, where (with a similar background of animism) the local marabout (alufa) replaced the old "medicine man" of Negro Fetishism."[180]

In 1591, invasion from Morocco broke up the kingdom of Songhay. Its dissolution coincided with the beginning of the transatlantic slave trade that was destined to obliterate all memories of the existence of the Sudanic kingdoms from Western minds for several centuries.

As an integral part of the Muslim world, Songhay had played a major role in meeting the almost insatiable demand for slaves in

North Africa and the Middle East to serve as eunuchs, soldiers, and concubines. Professor Harris has made a sober appraisal of that fact:

> While this trade did not even begin to approach the volume of the Atlantic slave trade, it was nonetheless a brutal enterprise, with skeletons of Africans strewn across the Sahara. The heat, cutting winds, attacks by animals, raids by renegade slavers, thirst and hunger all took their toll in African lives; and yet men thrived on this kind of business which helped to make Songhai a great kingdom.[181]

Africanists and Arabists have always been quick to point out that the slavery within Muslim societies was relatively benign compared to the degradation of plantation slavery in the Americas. They are justified in doing so. But before reaching those societies, they had to endure the ordeal of the desert trek, which was comparable to the Middle Passage across the Atlantic.[182]

Limitations on Black Power

The opportunities for black sovereign states to exert power within the Islamic state-system did not arise until the sixteenth century. This was when Songhay was at its apogee. Later, Kanem-Bornu near Lake Chad offered possibilities for coalition with Nile Valley kingdoms (see map 5). The challenge had been posed by Turkish military elites. The response was never adequate for coping with Turkish power.

The relentless southward push of Turkish military leaders from the eleventh century onward constituted a threat to southeastern Europe and a potential threat to Africa. As late as the eighteenth century the Ottoman Turks were battling against the Venetian fleet in the Mediterranean. This chapter has depicted the triumph of Turkish soldiers over black troops in Mesopotamia and Egypt.

By the time the Ottoman Turks began to extend their power from Syria and Palestine into Egypt, a group of Islamized black kingdoms extended halfway across Africa above the equatorial rain forest and below the desert from the Atlantic Ocean eastward (see map 5). Songhay occupied most of this area, but the Hausa states and Kanem-Bornu in the direction of Lake Chad were also Islamized and maintained trading relations with Cairo and the Upper Nile Valley kingdoms. They had adopted the use of the horse in warfare and there is a modern reminder of this fact in the magnificent display that horsemen of the sahel and savannah lands put on at important ceremonies in northern Nigeria.

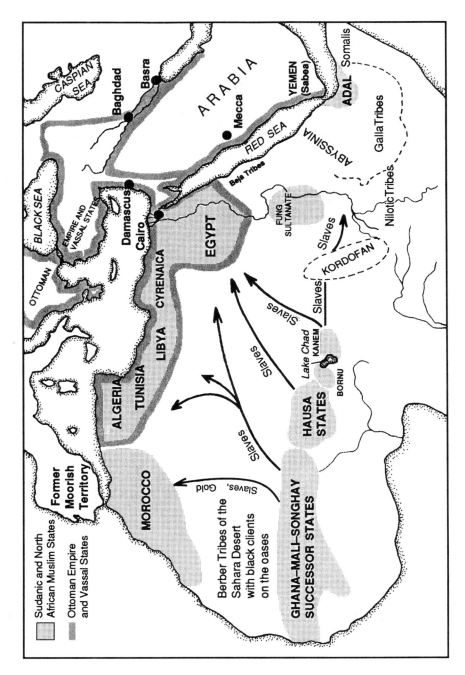

MAP 5. MUSLIM STATES IN AFRICA: 16TH CENTURY A.D.
Cartography based on a concept of the author.

During the eighth century B.C., the ancient Ethiopian kingdoms of the upper Nile Valley tried to resist Assyrian penetration of northern Africa, then withdrew from the power struggles of the Middle East. A few black Egyptian rulers and many Nubian soldiers subsequently fought against Turkish military encroachment but lost. By the beginning of the twentieth century, Ottoman Turkish power extended up the Nile as far as the borders of what is now Uganda.

There is no evidence that the black rulers of the savannah and sahel ever thought of mobilizing to challenge the relentless movement of the Turkish horsemen down from the Eurasian grasslands into the areas of the Middle East that had once been the imperial domain of the Egyptians—during the Eighteenth Dynasty, under the Twenty-Fifth Dynasty, under Ramesside kings, and from time to time under the Ptolemies. What the mahdi did in the late nineteenth century in opposition to British/Egyptian rule is conceivably something that might have occured earlier. Had it been supported from Kanem-Bornu, the outcome might have been different.

It is interesting to speculate on what the possiblities were for the black horsemen of the African savannah lands to erupt onto the stage where individual Blacks and small groups were involved in Islamic politics. To move northward across the Sahara and Libyan deserts was impossible. Only the Berbers on their camels could do that, and after installing the Fatimid Dynasty in the tenth century they never made another bid for power outside of western Africa and Muslim Spain. The black kingdoms of the grasslands might have taken their cavalry eastward to the edge of the Egyptian desert, but there were no corridors to enable them to break through into the broad fertile lands where Meroë once stood and where they might have assembled for a push northward. The logistics of a cavalry attack from such a staging ground near the confluence of the Blue and White Niles, designed to confront the Turks in Egypt or in the Middle East, would baffle the best tacticians. Black horsemen were fated to confine their prowess to western Africa. The Mahdi used camels to march on Khartoum in the 1890s.

STEREOTYPES OF BLACK PEOPLE IN ISLAM

Except for the lavish pilgrimages of Mansa Musa and Askia the Great, and trading expeditions, there was very little direct contact between the powerful black kingdoms of Africa and the larger Muslim world, particularly the cultural centers of the Central

Islamic Lands. Most of the Muslim intellectuals who wrote about Negroes between the ninth and sixteenth centuries had never seen Blacks living on their own soil, within their own cultures. For first-hand knowledge about Blacks, they had to rely on the reports of Africans living in the Diaspora, and these were usually slaves.

Although the early theology of Islam stressed the equality of all men, other elements in the tradition contained traces of color prejudice. These were not only the Bedouin component but also Jewish, Greek, Indian, and Persian ideas that were current in Baghdad at its cultural apogee. The stories about black cuckolds in *The Arabian Nights* were extremely pejorative. However, the favorite legend among the common folk was the story of Antar, the poet and warrior who wins the hand of an Arab woman with his courage. He was a mulatto hero.

Although Blacks were usually slaves in Muslim lands, that simple fact was less influential in attitude formation than the specific occupations Negroes pursued as slaves. Also, color prejudice was aimed at Negroes, rather than at all dark-skinned people. It was basically an expression of erotic and esthetic evaluations, and these were of secondary importance in forming the stereotyped conceptions of ability and temperament that determined status allocation.

Struggles for power—military and political—as we have described them in this chapter had a tendency to dissolve and recast stereotypes and to render self-fulfilling prophecies false. They brought people into contact over vast distances. Scholarly theories about black characteristics were available for ideological rationalizations by contestants. Conflict was a crucible that also put them to the test. But stereotypes persisted, nevertheless.

Scholarly Theories About Racial and Ethnic Differences

Before the rise of Islam, local origin myths had been replaced in much of the Middle East by Hebrew stories that became part of the Christian Bible. In the Arabian peninsula, variations on these stories were blended with Midrashic legends and other Semitic lore. In the Hedjaz, for instance, racial diversity was explained by the myth that God (i.e., El or Allah) had used several different colors of mud when he was creating mankind, not just "dust of the earth," as the Hebrews asserted. It is unclear whether Mohammed, in the Koran, was the first to say that only black mud had been used, or whether this variation had appeared among Arabs earlier.

Both Abraham and Noah appear in its pages, but the Koran says little about Nimrod or Cush, who loom large in Jewish folklore. However, commentators display familiarity with some of the rabbinic material. They knew a number of stories about Ham, who is not mentioned in the Koran.

Mohammed does not seem to have known the legend that descendants of Ham were cursed through his son Canaan to be servants of descendants of Shem and Japheth, the story that Hebrews found so useful in justifying their territorial battles with Canaanites. However, by the tenth century A.D., this story was known to intellectuals writing in Arabic and perhaps to a wider circle.[183] The rabbinic and Midrash stories that interpret black skin as a curse were apparently not part of early Arab oral traditions. However, they, too, became known, after the seventh-century Arab conquests, among scholars in Mesopotamia who were developing Islamic religious thought. By the eleventh century the black-skin-as-curse story was widely known, and in the fourteenth century, Ibn Khaldun, the North African scholar, ridiculed the belief.[184]

The scholars who assembled near the Abbasid court in Baghdad during the tenth and eleventh centuries—some Arab, mostly Perisan—assumed the task of translating the works of Greek and Hellenistic philosophers, scientists, and physicians into Arabic. Upon the basis of these works they began to develop their own critical analyses and unique intellectual contributions. This group of scholars must have been influenced, too, by Persian thought that stressed the Manichaean contrast between Light and Darkness.

As the Islamic jihad brought many cultures into the fold, other sources than the Koran came to have a strong influence on scholarly thought. By the tenth and eleventh centuries, translations of the works of some Greek and Hellenistic philosophers, scientists and physicians were under way. Aristotle's philosophy, and his work, *Physiognomy*, became very influential. However, the social ethic of the Stoics, with an anti-slavery bias that had strongly attracted early Christians, had little influence on Islam. Persian thought, including Manichaean contrasts between Light and Darkness, was strongly represented.

In addition to the foundation of Jewish and Koranic teaching, Islamic scholars now became aware of two Greek "scientific" theories about Negroes that did not seem to be necessarily incompatible. One was the old Greco-Roman belief that climatic conditions in the native lands of black people were not conducive to physical or mental health—as defined by people living in the Mediterranean area. The other was Galen's view, idiosyncratic among the Greeks, that Blacks were born with defective brains.

The work of one very popular Baghdad physician of the tenth century was destined to have a lasting effect on his peers. Persian by birth, Ibn Sina was largely responsible for embedding Manichaean contrasts in Muslim philosophy and theology. His works were translated into Latin by Constantinus Africanus of Sicily, and he thereby influenced the practice of medicine in Europe, where he was known as Avicenna.

Ibn Sina's cardinal principle was that climate had "a major effect" upon the human being, giving the inhabitants of various regions "a temperament appropriate for the conditions of the particular climate."[185] He and his followers introduced the widespread belief that Negroes in their original habitat had certain traits that made them metaphorically "hot." It was, to some extent, an argument by analogy: The people were like the exuberant tropical fauna and flora and the constant sunshine. From the tenth through fifteenth centuries, educated people throughout the Muslim world believed that, in his homeland, "the black is frivolous and light-hearted," to use Arabist Bernard Lewis's phrase. Lewis states that scholars also held favorable stereotypes that "show the black as brave, generous, musical, and with a strong feeling for rhythm." They also were said to have had "a gay and happy disposition."[186]

This characteristic "Negro temperament" was supposedly generated by the heat of the tropics. Scholarly writings were supported in this area by religious tradition, which taught that the word "Ham" meant "hot." Some legends suggest that Negroes were sons of Ham who did not develop dark skin color until they moved to the tropics after the Tower of Babel episode. In some accounts, the excessive heat gave sons of Ham both an offensive odor and instability of character.[187]

As we see, there were both positive and negative aspects of this Arab and Persian view of Blacks, elements that could be emphasized according to socioeconomic interests or political purposes. Ibn Sina did not state clearly what he thought the effects were of moving to zones other than the one where a person was born. Nor did he discuss the effects of miscegenation between people born in different climate zones.

It is important to note that these environmental theories assigned equally undesirable traits to Europeans born in the inhospitable northern cold. Some Middle Eastern scholars carried this thinking to an ethnocentric extreme that revealed esthetic preferences. For instance Ibn al-Faqui al-Hamadani wrote that Iraqis were not like either the despised Slavs to the North, who have a "blond, buff, blanched and leprous coloring" or the Zanj and Ethiopians who are black and "stinking, wooly-haired, with uneven limbs, deficient mind and depraved passions."[188] Thus in Iraq, where slaves were acquired from a pool that included white and African barbarians, the skin color of both was denigrated by this intellectual, who also linked physical traits with mental and emotional characteristics.

An Arab living in Spain in the eleventh century expressed the prevalent view about the effect of geographic differences on Europeans as well as Africans:

> For those who live furthest to the north between the last of the seven climates and the limits of the inhabited world, the excessive distance of the sun in relation to the zenith line makes the air cold and the atmosphere thick. *Their temperaments are therefore frigid, their humors raw, their bellies gross, their color pale, their hair long and lank. Thus, they lack keenness of understanding and clarity of intelligence, and are overcome by ignorance and dullness, lack of discernment, and stupidity.* Such are the Slavs, the Bulgars, and their neighbors. For those peoples on the other hand who live near and beyond the equinoctial line to the limit of the inhabited world in the south, the long presence of the sun at the zenith makes the air hot and the atmosphere thin. Because of this, their temperaments become hot and their humors fiery, their color black and their hair wooly. *Thus they lack self-control and steadiness of mind and are overcome by fickleness, foolishness and ignorance. Such are the blacks,* who live at the extremity of the land of Ethiopia, the Nubians, the Zanj and the like [italics added].[189]

Ibn Sina utilized the concept of "humors" or "natural dispositions" resulting from various combinations of earth, air, fire, and water. This Aristotelian idea dominated mainstream Muslim philosophy, fitting well with the idea of seven climatic zones affecting "humors," which was taught by Persian and Arab geographers.[190]

Another theory explaining Negro characteristics was not so widely accepted as Ibn Sina's geographic determinism. It involved biological determinism. Mas'udi, who died in A.D. 956, is the earliest Muslim authority who makes reference to Galen's "ten specific attributes of the black man which are found in him and in no other," attributes we discussed in Chapter 4. It is not clear, however, whether Mas'udi accepted the Greek physician/philosopher's view that Blacks had defective brains.

Other biological theories were occasionally advanced that seem to have attained some popularity among literates in the Muslim world. By the tenth century A.D., intellectuals writing in Arabic were developing what they considered the "science" of physiognomy, probably influenced by Aristotle's work. Indian philosophers may also have had an impact.[191]

Theories of physiognomy made the claim that mental and emotional traits were revealed by the shape, texture, color, and harmony, or lack of it, of various parts of the body. The analysis was applied within racial and ethnic groups as well as between them. Physiognomy was adopted by some individuals as a guide in the buying of slaves. For instance, Kai Kaus, a ruler in the Black Sea area who wrote an essay on "The Purchase of Slaves," was sure that

> Human beings cannot be known except by the science of physiognomy and by experience, and the science of physiognomy in its entirety is a branch of prophecy that is not acquired to perfection except by the divinely directed apostle. The reason is that by physiognomy the inward goodness or wickedness of men can be ascertained.[192]

He then put forward some esthetic principles that applied to the assessment of a head and face regardless of the race of the slave:

> Now let me describe to the best of my ability what is essential in the purchasing of slaves, both white and black. . . . Whoever it may be that inspects the slave must first look at the face, which is always open to view, whereas the body can only be seen as occasion offers. . . . God placed the beauty of human beings in the eyes and eyebrows, delicacy in the nose, sweetness in the lips and teeth, and freshness in the skin. To all these the hair of the head has been made to lend adornment.[193]

Although an acceptable purchase could be made by inspection of the head and face alone, plus shrewd questioning, one should, he thought, try to examine the entire body.

A generalization by Kai Kaus that did not seem to have a racial or ethnic reference suggested that:

> the mark of the slave who is clever and may be expected to improve is this: he must be of erect stature, medium of hair and in flesh, broad of hand and with the middle of the finger lengthy, in complexion dark though ruddy, dark-eyed, open-faced and smiling. A slave of this kind would be competent to acquire learning, to act as treasurer or for any other such employment.[194]

Some degree of blondness was thought to indicate a proclivity for "domestic service and cookery," the ideal slave for these pursuits being "clean in face and body, round-faced, with hands and feet slender, his eyes dark inclining to blue, sound in body, silent, the hair of his head wine-coloured and falling forward limply." Negroidness was definitely not preferred for this pursuit. There were no racial or ethnic preferences stated in describing the physical traits desired in soldiers or in the "slave suited to play musical instruments." But in another case, racial preference seems to be indicated:

> The mark of the slave suited for employment in the women's apartments is that he should be dark-skinned and sour visaged and have withered limbs, scanty hair, a shrill voice, little slender feet, thick lips, a flat nose, stubby fingers, a bowed figure, and a thick neck . . . He must not have a white skin nor a fair complexion; and beware of a ruddy-complexioned man, particularly if his hair is limp. His eyes, further, should not be languorous or moist; a man having such qualities is either over-fond of women or prone to act as a go-between.[195]

This seems to be a statement of preference for a Negro male, albeit a deformed, stereotyped one. Traits of individual personality as well as group membership enter into the specification, however. Kai Kaus goes on to say that he definitely does not mean an Indian male because such men have the habit of molesting the female servants. Of all Blacks, "The Nubian and the Abyssinian are freer of faults and the Abyssinian is better than the Nubian because many things were said by the Prophet in praise of the former."[196] Here theology is used to reinforce physiognomy in discrimination between various types of dark-skinned males.

Another "science"—an old Mesopotamian one—was also popular in classifying and assessing the traits of human groups. The astrological interpretation of ethnic and racial differences was sometimes at variance with environmentally-based views. According to the latter, Blacks had a "hot" temperament, but as Mas'udi pointed out, a contemporary poet and astronomer had written of the planets that:

> The doyen is the sublime Saturn, majestic elder, powerful monarch. His temperament is black and cold, black as the soul when a prey to despair. His influence is exercised on the Zanj and the black slaves, and on lead and iron.[197]

This opinion was said to be shared by many, "ancient and modern," who had discussed the influence of the celestial bodies on the character of Blacks. Saturn also symbolized sagacity and wisdom. At least one scholar argued that the heat of the tropics attracted the "humors" of the Zanj to the head and thus, "the soul could not exercise upon them its complete action, so discernment was altered and the intelligent action diminished."[198] Saturn's favorable celestial influence was offset by the terrestrial heat. How widespread these astrological beliefs were, we do not know.

Individuals who accepted Galen's biological determinism adopted an attitude toward black people that was close to modern racism. There was also a high potential for environmental theory to become racist. The brilliant fourteenth-century Tunisian scholar, Ibn Khaldun, was scornful of both physiognomy and astrology as theories to account for differences between groups, although the latter might have some value in explaining individual behavior. He thought inborn biological differences between human beings played a minor role. His reinterpretation of environmental theories tended to reduce their racist potential by making geographically determined differences subordinate to culture under some conditions.

Ibn Khaldun produced the work that Western scholars consider the first serious attempt to develop a sociological point of view, his *Discourse on Universal History*. The Berber scholar defines the basic dynamic of history as the interaction between urbanized people who had developed and conserved "civilization" and "Bedouins"—all nomadic and wandering peoples—who developed values and life styles different from those of settled people. The conflict between the two, and the ensuing acculturation, produces something close to what later scholars would call "Progress."

This drama, as Ibn Khaldun depicts it, unfolds within each of the seven climatic zones that had been regarded as determinants of temperament.[199] Ibn Khaldun spoke of both "the remotest Slavs" and "the remotest Blacks" as being "almost subhuman" because "they have no civilization." Both Slavs and Sudanese Blacks were said to have some traits in common because they lived at the climatic extremes. Other traits were due to the cold or the heat. Because they live in the hottest zone on earth, Ibn Khaldun said of the people south of Egypt and North Africa:

> The blacks of the Sudan are generally characterized by levity, excitability, and great emotionality. They are eager to dance whenever they hear a melody and they are everywhere described as stupid.[200]

Ibn Khaldun was aware of the fact that he might be criticized for discussing "uncivilized" Europeans as members of specific tribal groups while lumping the Africans together under a general term, "Blacks," making only three broad distinctions, Sudanese, Abyssinian, and "Zanj." He stated that it had become the custom to do so partly because "white" people were so similar to the Arabs in physical form that they didn't seem strange, and partly because their cultures and systems of social organization were better known.[201]

One original idea of Ibn Khaldun was that disabilities resulting from an inhospitable climate could be offset by cultural change, including conversion to a new religion.[202] Barbarian Europeans and Africans, he said, cannot be treated as equals unless they either become Christianized, as many of the northern barbarians had, or Islamized, as some Africans had.[203] Thus, he adopted the ancient Greek practice of distinguishing between themselves and "barbarians."

Ibn Khaldun opposed both racist thinking and theological determinism when he rejected the black-skin-as-curse tradition as a fable and dismissed Galen's views as "inconclusive and unproven." However, like Thomas Jefferson, he seems to have had some doubts about Blacks' capacity for *outstanding* achievement. Jefferson grounded his doubts, in part, upon what he considered to be the fact that the black race had never produced a Euclid.

Jefferson might be excused for not being familiar with Arabic works that explicitly described noted scholars and artists as being black. Ibn Khaldun cannot be so excused. The Tunisian had access to a record of black participation in the Middle Eastern, North African, and Andalusian Diaspora covering a period of almost a millennium. He mentions only four of the distinguished black individuals whose racial and ethnic backgrounds are provided in Ibn Khallikan's standard biographical work, a book Ibn Khaldun cites in another context.

These include Loqman, the sage honored by Mohammed, whose work, according to Ibn Khaldun, influenced Socrates and thereby Plato and Aristotle. (He is referring, of course, to Aesop.) He calls Loqman a dwarf but doesn't mention his Negroidness.[204] Ibn Khaldun casually mentions Antar in a discussion of poets, but doesn't refer to the "Romance of Antar," which mentions his difficulties as a mulatto in Bedouin society. Ziryab is credited as the greatest of early Andalusian musicians, but he is described as a "page," not as a black slave. Finally, al-Jahiz is presented as the founder of Arabic literary criticism, a master of Arabic semantics and linguistics, and one of the four great models who originally set the standards in Arab literature. But no mention is made of his Negro ancestry or of his work, *The Boast of the Blacks.* Ibn Khaldun does not mention Bilal at all![205]

Perhaps too much should not be made of these omissions. He may have assumed that all literate Muslims knew that these men were Negro in whole or in part. However, his general approach to the problem of "blackness"—of people and cultures—in the Islamic world leads to the suspicion that he exhibits some personal prejudices against Negroidness.

Ibn Khaldun evidently shared the general educated Muslim attitude of contempt for pagan black cultures. In speaking of uncivilized Blacks—Zanj and Lem Lem—he notes that they "brand their faces and their temples, go naked and have attributes that are quite similar to those of dumb animals." He specified cannibalism, incestuous promiscuity, and foraging for food.[206] He described "civilized" Blacks in a chapter on "Rois des Peuples Nègres" in his *History of the Berbers.* The kings of Mali were praised for having adopted Islam. He writes of both Berber and black kingdoms enslaving pagan Blacks. Although he mentions both black and white slaves acquired as "prisoners of war," his attention is focused on the Blacks. Black pagans seem more repugnant to him than white pagans, an attitude that is noticeable among Arab intellectuals and may be related to a somatic norm image that is contrasted unfavorably with Negroes.[207]

Ibn Khaldun does not refer to undesirable traits as being universal "uncivilized" traits when censuring the Blacks for possessing them. His failure to do so raises the suspicion that he shared the traditional Berber prejudices against Blacks in the oases and the savannah lands, although he made an effort to overcome them. But he also may have used a definition of "Blacks" that was narrow and excluded many Berber-Negro and Arab-Negro individuals who lived as Muslims outside of the area inhabited by "the black nations." He may have considered Islamized, assimilated Blacks in the North African Diaspora to be either Berbers or Arabs and therefore, despite their physiognomy, no longer sharing the traits of the people in their homelands of whom he disapproved.

Blacks in Muslim Literature and Folklore

Scholarly speculation about racial differences was an aspect of the culture of the intellectual elite throughout the Islamic world, the so-called "high culture." Some of these ideas may have filtered down to the unlettered, but folklore is a more reliable indicator of their conceptions of race and ethnicity. The problem here is that we can only assess the folklore through stories written down by literates. These accounts may reflect attitudes among this more sophisticated stratum, rather than the views of the humble folk.

Despite the failure of the Abbasid caliphate to unify the entire Muslim world politically, the spread of Islam resulted in an integrated cultural nexus that included a relatively uniform body of "classical" literature, available to all who could read the Arabic language. While the views of Blacks held by ordinary people need not necessarily be the same stereotyped conceptions found in the classical Arabic literature, the spread of literacy throughout the Muslim world widened the circle of people familiar with what literate elites had to say about black people. An antiblack tradition within the Arabic literary inheritance has not yet been subjected to the type of deliberate critical analysis by Islamic scholars that Western scholars have given to a similar phenomenon in their own literatures. It is ironic that black males appear in the classical literature in strongly contrasting roles—as brave soldiers, as trusted eunuchs, or as servants cuckolding their masters. Psychoanalytic as well as sociological explanations are needed for understanding the choice of themes and occupational types as well as the popularity of these stories among readers.

Pre-Islamic literature, like ancient Greek and Roman literature, reveals a lively general interest in color, and a considerably greater interest in the application of color terms to people. Lewis notes that human beings were described as black, white, red, green, yellow, and two shades of brown! Far northern people were usually referred to as white or pale, or as being various shades of red. The term *black* covered a wide range of actual human colors. When comparing themselves to Persians, Arabs sometimes refer to their own complexion as "black," but when comparing themselves with Greeks, they refer to their own color as "red."[208]

Sophisticated Arabs separated meanings of black and white associated with people from more abstract connotations of the two colors. There is the case of Arab emissaries who were discussing abstract values associated with the colors black and white with an unlettered Berber ruler in Spain. They were astonished to learn that he thought they were indirectly asking him whether he wanted white or black women as his bedmates! The emissaries patiently explained the difference between use of colors as metaphor and their use to designate persons, places or things.

Obviously, there was some ambiguity about the interpretation of color in the Muslim world. The poet Ibn Hazm of Cordova, for instance, wrote a long treatise on love that included a rather extreme reaction to criticisms of his own widely discussed preference for blonde women. In doing so he expressed symbolic equivalents in a derogatory way, linking mourning cloth, human skin-color, the flag of the Almohade invaders from North Africa, and the devils in Hell in a rare literary expression of such linkages:

> The farthest removed of God's creation from every wisdom
> Is he who prefers a body dark in color, blackened:
> In black are described the colors of Gehannam [Hell],
> And the clothing of those who weep, have lost a child and
>   are in mourning;
> And since the black flags have appeared the souls of men
> Became certain that there is no way to Right![209]

However, even when the metaphorical black/white contrast was applied to people, it was not always with derogatory reference to "blackness." According to Ignac Goldziher, an outstanding authority on ancient Semitic cultures, as "blackness" and "night" came to be equivalents in the Arabic language over a long span of time, the emotions associated with night were positive, not negative. The blackness of night was appreciated because the temperature was cool; the starry sky was beautiful, and it reflected the handiwork of the Creator.[210]

In the older Arab literature, as opposed to Persian-influenced writing, "complementarity" rather than Manichaean contrast is sometimes intended when white and black are used to define skin color. The same principle can be detected occasionally in Muslim Spain, as in this passage by Ibn Quzman, who, referring to a brown-skinned woman, wrote:

> Nature is composite . . . Its whiteness with its blackness is some-
> thing like a bright morning—tinged with a little darkness of the
> dawn.[211]

The Romance of 'Antar, a legend of pre-Islamic Arabia which we discussed earlier, became *the* great love story cherished by the Middle Eastern masses. The popularity of 'Antar as a hero reveals the deep identification of those masses with a defiant low-status individual. That he was part African apparently did not repel them. The popularity of the 'Antar story suggests that although negative color prejudice against the virile black male existed in Muslim cultures, it was probably more pronounced among the elites than among the masses. *The Arabian Nights* kept the negative image alive in the Arabic-speaking Muslim world through the medium of story tellers in cafes and other public places.[212]

The Arabian Nights, or *A Thousand and One Nights*, is a massive compendium of fascinating tales, many of them set in the Baghdad court of the eighth century. It had taken its more or less final form by A.D. 1100, when the Crusaders were filtering into the Middle East. In the fantasy world of *The Arabian Nights*, black males are presented as physically loathsome but sexually attractive neverthe-less, inspiring an insatiable desire in the Arab and Persian women who were their lovers. These black men have unusual sexual power, and they are arrogant in expressing their scorn for the white man being cuckolded and sadism toward the women whose favors they accept.

The striking thing about some of the tales is the extent to which white males are presented as persons who appear insecure about their own sexual adequacy and who define their own women, as well as the black males, as "oversexed." The very rationale for the work involves this theme, for the book begins with the story of a king who discovers his wife copulating with a black slave. He kills them both and then goes to visit his brother, also a king. He finds that his brother is away on a journey and, while watching the courtyard through a window, he observes a scene that shocks and depresses him and further confirms his view that women cannot be trusted. In one English translation, ten white mameluke slaves and ten female white slaves (who came disguised as males) fornicated in a fountain, "all paired off with each." In another translation the males were black. The queen, who was watching, cried loudly, "Come to me, O my lord Saeed," and

> then sprang with a dropleap from one of the trees a big blackamoor with rolling eyes which showed the whites, a truly hideous sight. He walked boldly up to her and threw his arms around her neck while she embraced him as warmly; then he bussed her and winding his legs around hers, as a button loop clasps a button, he threw her and enjoyed her.[213]

The horrified brother-in-law of the queen, witnessing this scene, remarked, "My brother is a greater king among kings than I am yet this infamy goes on in his very palace, and his wife is in love with that filthiest of filthy slaves. But this only shows that they all do it and that there is no woman but who cuckoldeth her husband." The basic prejudice expressed here is sexist, not racist.[214]

There are other stories, too, in which women of high status are involved with very lowly Blacks.[215] In one case, the queen is found by a king, "asleep on his own carpet bed, embracing with both arms a black cook of loathsome aspect and foul with kitchen grease and grime." He cuts the two into four pieces with his scimitar.[216] Another husband refers to his wife as a whore who has as a lover a "hideous negro slave with his upper lip like the cover of a pot, and lower like an open pot. . . . He was to boot a leper and a paralytic." She kissed the ground in front of her black lover, who reprimanded her for being late, saying, "What call had thou to stay away all this time? Here have been with me sundry of the black brethren who drank their wine and each had his young lady, and I was not content to drink because of thine absence." In reply, she called him "my heart's love." Her husband, watching all of this, heard the slave call her a liar and say,

> Now I swear an oath by the valour and honour of blackamoor men (and deem not our manliness to be the poor manliness of white men) from today forth, if thou stay away until this hour I will not keep company with thee nor will I glue my body with thy body. Dost play fast and loose with us, thou cracked pot, that we may satisfy thy dirty lusts, O vilest of the vile whites?"[217]

This tale is inconceivable as arising or being transmitted within the color-caste system of the American South. In another case a huge black jinni has captured a white girl on her wedding night. She outwits him by allowing two Arabs to have intercourse with her while he sleeps.

Black women appear only rarely in *The Arabian Nights* and still more rarely are they described as beautiful. An exception is the tale of "Judar and His Brethren."[218] After a palace had been built for Judar by magic, the jinns were ordered to "fetch him forty handsome white maids and forty black damsels and as many Mamelukes and negro slaves." So they "snatched up every beautiful girl and boy they saw . . . fetched comely black girls" and "brought male chattels." The jinns presented the most beautiful white women to the others saying "This is your mistress, kiss her hands and cross her not, but serve her, white and black."[219]

The well-stocked harem of the period was described as including beauties from many strange and far-off places, but at its center was the most beautiful of all women, an Iraqi or Iranian type with "seven tresses hung down to her anklets like horses tails . . . Nutre-kohled, ruddy . . . brow flower-white."[220]

Although these stories have become popular throughout the Islamic world, scholars agree that the basic core of tales is Persian and Indian, not Arab.[221] *The Arabian Nights* was apparently written within a highly cultivated stratum of the cosmopolitan society of the Abbasid Caliphate. It fused very old literary traditions, blending a touch of cynicism and hedonism with devout protestations of adherence to the faith of the Prophet.

No research has been published about which social strata liked which stories, or whether women in the harems told them, as well as men in the bazaars and coffee houses. Nor do we know whether they were as popular in Islamic Africa as in other areas. Also unclear is how early in Arab, Iranian, and Iraqi history some males accepted the belief in superior black male potency. By the eleventh century, however, various writers were contributing elaborations of the theme. It is even possible that this became a popular myth only after the tales of *The Arabian Nights* gained currency when recounted in the bazaars and bath houses, but we have no way of knowing.

CHART 7. Traits Associated with the Black
Stereotype in Muslim Lands

NEGATIVE ASPECTS	POSITIVE ASPECTS
ugly faces	cheerful
distorted bodies	exuberant
foul body odor	generous behavior
bad digestion	musically gifted
males lack sexual restraint	possess rhythm
vicious	exhibit piety
dishonest	fine footsoldiers
dirty	faithful as eunuchs
no intellectual interest or ability	happy disposition

Stereotyping: A Source of Racial Attitudes

An analysis of scholarly speculation about race, and of the literature and folklore of the Muslim world, suggests that relations between Negroes and non-Negroes are best understood without attempting to impose on the data those *structural* concepts that are used in analyzing race relations in the Western Hemisphere—color caste, ethnic caste, racial caste, or even *color-class* of the type found in Latin America, where the situation, in some respects, closely resembles the Muslim world.

A concept developed by American social psychologists during the 1920s seems more useful: the concept of stereotypes, those "pictures in the head" that an individual holds of people of various ethnic groups, pictures that do not always have a "close fit" with reality at a given time. Bernard Lewis makes effective use of this concept in *Race and Color in Islam*. Stereotypes, learned as part of a culture, provide cues for acting but they do not absolutely determine social interaction. They help to structure attitudes toward stereotyped people. They *predispose* to action, and are one element in negative prejudices formed against individuals, as well as in discrimination. Positive stereotypes help to generate positive attitudes and to give cues for favorable action.

By the eleventh century A.D., a generalized stereotype of Blacks based upon assumed traits of one specific ethnic category, the Zanj, had become prevalent among Muslim intellectuals. This stereotype appears later in the works of Ibn Khaldun, used in a more restricted critical manner. Mas'udi, before him, had used the term Zanj without pejorative implications. Lewis summarizes the traits of the stereotypes associated with Blacks in chart 7.[222] As always, the generalized stereotype includes positive and negative aspects, some of which may contradict others. Individuals may combine both positive and negative aspects of the stereotype, even contradictory ones.

It is important to remember that stereotypes about racial and ethnic groups, as well as prejudices directed against them and invidious discrimination, are socially conditioned, not inborn. They originate within specific cultures, not within individual minds uninfluenced by culture. In the Muslim world, stereotypes of color groups have not usually been institutionalized as aspects of roles in social systems, as indicating positions to be "properly" occupied by individuals of a specific ethnic group or race, or from which some are barred. The exceptions are important: the military's lower ranks and the harem eunuch, for instance, wherein Blacks had a special place.

Lewis, in *Race and Color in Islam*, emphasizes the prevalence of the negative aspects of the stereotypes on this list as having important implications for the fate of Negro individuals. *Stereotypes built up by daily contact with black people, or from believing myths and legends about them, were probably more important as cues for action among ordinary people than any stereotypes found in literary works.*

Stereotypes have arisen from two main sources. First, there are the natural reactions on initial contact to striking differences in somatic type and the tendency to invest outsiders differing in this way with an exotic aura tinged with eroticism as well as with mystical and magical qualities. Second, and of great importance in stereotyping, is the operation of the basic principle of hierarchical social organization that existed everywhere in the pre-capitalist feudal societies of the Muslim world. Sociologist Herbert Blumer has stressed the manner in which high-status groups with power contribute toward creation of prejudices against subordinate groups. (See volume 1, pp. 87-90.)

The Religious/Mystical Domain

Lewis states that "one of the most common favourable stereotypes of blacks is that of simple piety. There are many anecdotes of a well-known religious type in which the black appears as the simple pious man contrasted with the clever but wicked."[223] No anecdotes are recounted and the sole reference is to a Syrian source. There is a need for comparative study of such anecdotes. It is likely that differences will be found between Mesopotamia, Egypt, North Africa, West Africa, and Muslim Spain. In all areas the simplest expression of piety is praying five times a day while facing toward Mecca, after the requisite "ablutions" with water or sand.[224]

In much of West Africa and North Africa pilgrimages to the shrines of "holy men" or *marabouts* are an essential part of the behavior of the pious in addition to the daily ritual. There are no icons in Islam of Mohammed, Fatima, Bilal and other founders of the faith, nor are there any equivalents of images of Christian saints. So certain aspects of devotion familiar to Christendom are not present in Muslim lands. Veneration of *marabouts* seems to meet similar needs of unlettered worshippers among Berbers and to a lesser extent among West African ethnic groups. The most orthodox of Muslims deplore these manifestations as do most Protestants among Christians.

One tendency in Islam has become widespread throughout northern Africa and parts of the Middle East, Sufism—mystical and contemplative—and sometimes involving trance states. Arabist H. A. R. Gibb notes that "the function of Sufism was to restore to the religious life of Islam the element of personal communion with God which orthodox theology was squeezing out."[225]

In some areas of West Africa, the wearing of amulets—words from the Koran encased in leather—is both an act of piety and a charm to ward off evil spirits. The most orthodox of Muslims consider this a debasement of the faith and not an act of piety.[226]

For many making the pilgrimage to Mecca is expected of a pious person. Black African pilgrims have acquired a reputation for making the pilgrimage to Medina as well as Mecca, and of being hard-working in addition to being devout. Occasionally within the cultural ethos of African societies *mahdis* have appeared and won a wide following. Since Islamic communities in Western Africa retained traditional practices of curing, assuring good luck, and venerating ancestors, several reform movements have arisen, the most notable of which occurred among the Fulani, some of whose leaders declared a jihad against tribes that were considered lax Muslims or outright "pagans."

The acculturation process in Africa, as well as contact with Africans in the Diaspora, has given rise to a reputation of African cultures for producing individuals who are adept at sorcery as well as in the field of benign magic. Several stories in *The Arabian Nights* present Blacks as sorcerers.[227] A careful comparative examination of folklore is needed to describe the variety of forms this specific stereotype of Blacks takes in various parts of the Muslim World.

The Esthetic Domain

The concept of somatic norm image, as elaborated by Caribbeanist H. Hoetink, is valuable for understanding the esthetic dimension of the Black Experience in the Muslim world.[228] As this sociologist uses the concept, it involves two generalizations: (1) that all people in isolated homogeneous societies share a concept of an ideal body image similar to their own physical type, and (2) that in a heterogeneous society where people of one physical type are dominant with respect to economic and political power and social prestige, there will be a tendency among people in subordinated groups to prize the somatic norm image of the dominant group and to deprecate their own.

Muslim literature and folklore reveal many different norms of beauty in different lands, in what anthropologist Robert Redfield called "the little traditions," as well as a more uniform esthetic standard in the "great tradition" shared by all who were literate in Arabic. These standards were created by the classical writers of the common "high culture." The Negro was contrasted with that somatic norm image as the "ugly" Other. Although some evidence of this practice shows up in the pre-Islamic world, the first explicit, systematic derogation of the Negro physical type emerged after Persians replaced Arabs as dominant in the Abbasid caliphate. The very pejorative Zanj stereotype existed side-by-side with the benign Abyssinian image. Other images of African females existed, too. The Zanj stereotype incorporated most of the negative traits on the Lewis list, and the Abyssinian and Sudanese some of the others.

The Arabian Nights, which is so derogatory of black males, synthesizes Arab and Persian esthetic values in this portrait of the handsome male:

> a young man fair of face and neat of dress and of favour like the moon raining light, with eyes black and bright, and brow flower-white, and cheeks red as a rose and young down where the beard grows and a mole like a grain of ambergris [i.e., a small black beauty spot].[229]

This excludes all black males.

Kai Kaus, who was previously introduced as a practitioner of the "science" of physiognomy, also made an attempt to set objective standards for esthetic evaluation. He noted that "Turks are not all of one race, and each has his own nature and essential character," but "it is a fact well known to all that beauty or ugliness in Turks is the opposite of that in the Indians," and he proceeded to detail the specifics:

> If you observe the Turk feature by feature he has a large head, a broad face, narrow eyes, a flat nose, and unpleasing lips and teeth. Regarded individually the features are not handsome, yet the whole is handsome. The Indian's face is the opposite of this; each individual feature regarded by itself appears handsome, yet looked at as a whole the face does not create the same impression as that of a Turk. To begin with the Turk has a personal freshness and clearness of complexion not possessed by the Indian; indeed the Turks win for freshness against all other races.[230]

The standard of "freshness and clearness of complexion" rules out a very dark brown skin. However, the statement of preference for the

Turkish over the Indian somatic norm image by this Middle Eastern aristocrat did not mean that all persons of his social level in the Muslim world considered dark brown skin ugly per se. Indeed an examination of Arab, Persian and Andalusian literature reveals that it was not black skin color itself that was considered "ugly," but rather the combination of features that constituted Negroidness. Thus blackness, with the "proper" facial features, might be acceptable. In fact, according to some legends, both Abraham and Moses were very dark, and the mahdi or messiah awaited by the Shiites was described as a dark man.[231]

As "harmoniousness of features" so often outweighs individual characteristics, one must ask: Is it not true that some combinations of flat noses, thick lips, kinky hair and black skin are actually considered esthetically pleasing, perhaps even beautiful, while others are not? Were not some Negroes considered handsome? And a related question calls for research: Do the norms for what are esthetically pleasing and esthetically repulsive varieties of Negroidness differ from place to place within the Muslim world, and between Negro and non-Negro Islamic cultures generally?

No data exist to answer either of these questions precisely, but some hints can be found about the first. North African, Andalusian, and Arab intellectuals seemed to have a greater propensity for seeing beauty among some types of Negroes than did their counterparts in Mesopotamia and Persia. Abyssinians and East Indians, though dark-skinned, have other features similar to the Arab somatic norm image. So, too, do some mulattoes and quadroons. Consequently, Arab writers considered them "more attractive" than people living south of the Sahara in Bilad al-Sudan.

One specific group of Negroes—the so-called Zanj—became the basis for a stereotype of all "Blacks" that ignored deviations within that group. Negative evaluations of Negro physical features were associated with allegations of offensive body odors and bizarre bodily mutilations. Fastidiousness reinforced narcissism in the making of the Zanj stereotype, with both men and women being subjected to a negative esthetic appraisal.

The Muslims placed a high value on cleanliness. The public bath was a ubiquitous institution utilized by all classes and frequently spoken of in folk tales. Good grooming was also part of the social norm cherished by males in the upper strata of the Muslim world. The ethos of the male subculture verged on fastidiousness. The Prophet himself was held up as an example of a man who took great care of his personal appearance, who liked sweet-smelling ointments and was proud of his attractiveness to women.[232] Negroes in the Middle Eastern Diaspora who became acculturated and adopted these values could offset whatever handicaps their physiognomy presented.

But when Mesopotamians used the pejorative term Zanj, they described more than physical traits. For instance, the geographer Maqdisi said, "As for the Zanj, they are people of black color, flat noses, kinky hair, *and little understanding or intelligence*" [italics added]. A Persian writing in the tenth century also made a connection between "Negroidness" and other traits when he said of the Zanj: "Their nature is that of wild animals. They are extremely black." There is a suggestion in these remarks that black skin equals bestiality and Negroidness equals stupidity.[233] The association of Negro appearance with undesirable mental and emotional traits fused esthetic evaluations with appraisals of moral and intellectual worth.

An esthetic evaluation of a person or a group can imply more than a judgment about the somatic norm image. For instance, the Afro-American slogan, "Black is Beautiful," refers to behavior and attitudes as well as appearance. The definition of the Zanj as ugly referred to their culture and behavior as well as to their unmodified physique, and it was based in part upon reactions to what was believed to be their primitive and "pagan" state before they were brought out of Africa into Mesopotamia.[234]

Muslim writers spoke of these Zanj as people who sometimes had tribal scars and filed teeth, who had savage customs such as nudity, incest, and possibly cannibalism. "Civilized" Africans from Egypt and Ethiopia were not despised and denigrated even when they were slaves and Negroid in physique. Type of culture was a variable that was usually evaluated as more important than physical type within the Islamic world.

The reaction to Zanj was, in part, a reaction to their living conditions, which in Mesopotamian slavery were squalid. The Zanj stereotype, as spread widely by tenth- and eleventh-century scholarly writing in Arabic, contained a "kernel of truth." It constituted what social psychologist Gordon W. Allport calls a "well-deserved reputation" about most of the Blacks in Mesopotamia. They were slaves held under conditions that created a large population of Blacks who were unkempt and may have actually been foul-smelling, as so frequently charged. However, stereotypes have a way of persisting after the basis for a well-deserved reputation has ceased to exist.[235]

Many individuals within groups designated as Zanj were indistinguishable from Abyssinians and Nubians in any skin-hair-features test, assuming that all were bathed and dressed in clean clothes. However, the proximity to Baghdad of Mesopotamian Africans who had a different culture, and who were confined as slaves to menial and dirty occupations, fixed the Zanj stereotype in the minds of observers, who sometimes generalized about all Negroes on this basis.

In the same way that the term "Negro," as used in the United States, always includes a wide range of features and colors, the term "Zanj," covered a highly variable population in terms of physical characteristics. "Black," which once had connotations in the United States similar to Zanj in Mesopotamia, underwent a revalorization in the United States during the 1960s. Such a revalorization has not occurred in the Central Islamic Lands or North Africa; few Negroid individuals achieve prominence there, even in Egypt.

Bernard Lewis points out that derogation of black appearance was not universal in the Muslim world. He notes that a fourteenth-century Egyptian writer who believed that White was good and Black was bad went on to remark with disapproval that many people "nevertheless have begun to find beauty in the Blacks and to incline toward them."[236] How many and of what status levels are not specified. Moreover, Lewis notes that, although Muslim writers were prone to carelessly stereotype all black ethnic groups with the term Zanj they applied to those they considered most ugly and revolting,[237] virtually all who spoke in this fashion at times drew distinctions between various groups of Negroes.

However, even those Blacks whose social class and achievements distanced them from the Zanj stereotype occasionally were faced with another evidence of color prejudice in Islamic society. It can be found in the use of blackness or Negroid physical traits in insults.

Arabic literature is replete with insults used to deride enemies or rivals. The targeting of Blacks was a special instance. A case from twelfth-century Alexandria reveals this habit of using references to black skin color, where that trait was available, to express hostility. Al-Kadi ar-Rashid Abu'l Husain was a government official and poet, "black in color," according to biographer Ibn Khallikan, and a Yemenite "from a once honourable and influential family." A rival attacked him in a poem that contained ambivalent references to "blackness":

> O thou who resemblest Lokman [i.e., the sage]
> But not in wisdom;
> Thou who hast lost thy learning
> And not preserved it;
> Thou hast stolen everyone's verses
> And might be called The Black Thief.

Here the poet's skin color was invoked to emphasize his wickedness: To be a thief was bad; to be a *black* thief was worse. Yet, the same verse contains a reference to a black man who was neither witless nor wicked.

Even the most illustrious black members of the Muslim world faced attacks at this level.[238] The eminent author, al-Jahiz, was known as "The Goggle-Eyed." Abu'l-Misk Kafur, the black soldier and eunuch who came to rule Egypt, was ridiculed by his enemies because of his skin color, his Negroid features and ungainly walk. He was nicknamed "Musky Camphor." A famous poet ridiculed him as a "mutilated Negro." Black poets were called "crows" and worse. Al-Jahiz tells of a white poet who referred to a black colleague as looking like the penis of a donkey wrapped up in a white cloth. The black man answered with a poem. "Though my hair is wooly and my skin is black as coal, I am generous and my color shines. My color does not prevent my being valiant."[239]

In Sura XLIX, verse 11 of the Koran, Mohammed rebukes those who "mock" with name-calling people "who may be better than they are." According to legend, the Prophet's lesson was inspired when he heard a man insulting Omar, the second caliph, by referring to him as "son of a black woman." The persistence of the legend, regardless of its truth, is testimony to the fact that mocking individuals by referring to their Negroidness was a feature of the cultures of the Central Islamic Lands, even if it was considered un-Islamic. However, expressions of color prejudice used in individual verbal abuse should not be mistaken for evidence of ideological or institutional racism in the culture of the period. Also, though Kafur might be subject to ridicule for his blackness, he had power.[240]

There can be no doubt that the same kind of attitudes emerged, at times, in the ancient Islamic world, which brought into being the "Black is Beautiful" movement among North American youth in the 1960s as a counterattack to derogation. Not all Blacks were apologetic with regard to their color and physique. Al Jahiz's *The Boast of the Blacks* indicates what some psychologists would consider a healthy response by an individual. A black man is quoted by al-Jahiz as saying:

> God did not make us black in order that we should be ugly; our color comes from the sun. . . . If a black skin is thought unsightly what then must be said of the French, the Greeks, and the Slavs with their thin, red straight hair and beard? The paleness of their eyelids and their lips appear to us Negroes very ugly.[241]

Not all Blacks could so neatly turn color prejudice back against those who invoked it. Scorn and ridicule experienced because of skin color, or because of esthetic standards that defined Negroid appearance as ugly, no doubt caused personality damage. It is hazardous to "guess backward" in history about matters such as these, but the behavior of the poets called "the crows," who were culturally Arab but had some Negro ancestry, indicates the existence of what seems to have been an "unhealthy" devaluation of blackness on their part.

What are we to say, for instance, of the poet Nusayb, father of a young man who wanted to marry an Arab girl. Her uncle did not oppose the union. Yet, Nusayb not only objected but according to Lewis, "had his son beaten for aspiring to such a marriage which he regarded as improper, and advised the girl's guardian to find her a true Arab husband." He lamented over the fate of his own daughters, dark-skinned like himself, who never married, saying, "My color has rubbed off on to them and they are left on my hands. I don't want blacks for them and whites don't want them." Could his animus toward his son marrying a "white" girl have been resentment over the fact that "white" men (i.e., Arabs) were reluctant to marry black women?[242]

The Erotic Domain

The erotic component in stereotyping is closely associated with the esthetic component, especially when choices for mating or marriage are under consideration. Muslim male-dominated societies inevitably placed these two types of evaluation near the top of the scale in evaluating women, second only to considerations of potential dowry size among the propertied classes or in tribal societies. Beauty was a value that often ranked higher in buying concubines or choosing female companions for extramarital relations than in espousal and marriage. The prevalence of black concubines in harems and of black prostitutes indicates little discrimination on the basis of race in these contexts.

We have no way to tell how ordinary folk made erotic decisions. Systematic stereotyped denigration of Negroes seems to have been a class-linked type of behavior, but a small segment of the Islamic world made these derogatory images familiar through their writings. Folktales and folksongs that might reveal thoughts of humbler folk were not usually recorded. But some conceptions in the popular folklore ran counter to the elitest tendencies that confined black women to the role of second-class concubines. For instance, as the 'Antar story was elaborated over the years, his mother, a slave in Arabia, was originally a Sudanese queen, whom 'Antar sought in her African homeland. An element of status, as well as of esthetic and erotic taste, is revealed in the saga.

In evaluations of men, handsomeness was mainly relevant to their appearance in armed combat or public spectacles. There was widespread preoccupation with personal appearance that had erotic implications, even though they usually remain unstated in folklore and literature.

In the Arabic world, as among the ancient Greeks, dark skin color for males was a symbol of manliness, a trait of the warrior.[243] This does not seem to have been so among the Persian converts, however, but was the male esthetic norm at some periods in Muslim Spain. Sexual prowess was attributed to all black males without regard to their ethnicity—except those who had been subjected to the most severe form of castration when being made into eunuchs.

As prisoners of war, as slaves, and as concubines, black women were evaluated as objects of sexual pleasure. Connoisseurs of women set the tone of much of the discussion about skin-color values in medieval Islamic Arabic literature, and this tended to merge with discussions of prices in the slave market.[244] For instance, Ibn Butlan, writing from the perspective of the upper classes in the capital city of Baghdad, set up a model that glorified a non-Negro African type:

> The ideal slave is a Berber girl who is exported out of her country at the age of nine, who spends three years at Medina and three at Mecca and at sixteen comes to Mesopotamia to be trained in elegant accomplishments. And, thus, when sold at twenty-five, she unites, *with her fine racial excellencies,* the coquetry of the Medinese, the delicacy of the Meccan, and the culture of the Mesopotamian woman [italics added].[245]

Other women, too, were also described as highly desirable:

> Fair-skinned, the Turkish women are full of grace and animation. Their eyes are small but enticing. They are thick-set and are inclined to be of short stature. There are very few tall women among them. They are prolific in breeding and their offspring are rarely ugly. They are never bad riders. They are generous; they are clean in their habits; they cook well, but they are unreliable.[246]

Ibn Butlan did not reject all black women. He stated a preference among them for those from Nubia (south of Egypt), claiming that they were "the most adaptable and cheerful." Abyssinian women (i.e., those from modern Ethiopia) were praised for sophistication as well as their beauty by him as well as other writers. That Ibn Butlan spoke with favor of Nubian as well as Abyssinian women indicated that Negroid features and hair did not place a woman beyond the bounds of erotic desirability, even if they were not considered beautiful.

But there were *some* cultural norms that excluded *some* Negro women—the Zanj of Mesopotamia being explicitly mentioned as undesirable by writers during the Abbasid Caliphate.[247] Of these women, Ibn Butlan says: "They can endure hard work . . . but there is no pleasure to be got from them, because of the smell of their armpits and the coarseness of their bodies."[248]

It is significant that similar pejorative statements are not made by travelers in the western Sudan about women of the Negro kingdoms there. However, in praising the beauty of the women of Ghana, Mali, and Songhay, "white" women are sometimes specified, suggesting that the travelers preferred Berbers, Fulanis, Jews, mulattoes, quadroons, or octoroons. However, the Negro women are not referred to as repulsive or ugly.[249] Some elements of the Zanj stereotype do appear in second-hand accounts of women further south—the so-called Lem-Lem. Some Arab writers could not conceive of these women as sexual partners. For instance, Fazil, writing centuries later than Ibn Butlan, observed that the black girl "is not worthy of the bed but is right for the kitchen."[250] Not all agreed. The poet Farazdaq, writing before the period of Abbasid Caliphate literary dominance and known as a connoisseur of women, said: "How many a tender daughter of the Zanj walks about with a hotly burning oven as broad as a drinking bowl."[251] Reflecting on comments of this type, Lewis notes that "much Arabic poetry shows the same kind of prurient interest in the Negress as one finds in European anti-Semitic writing about the Jewess," what he calls "a simultaneous interest in the

repulsive ugliness and incandescent sexuality which they ascribe to
the black woman."[252] Exactly that kind of interest, but in black men,
is displayed in *The Arabian Nights*.

Despite the assertion of a few intellectuals that black, too, could
be beautiful, Negro women, even Abyssinians, who were prized as
concubines and prostitutes, were largely excluded from the cult of
romantic love as it found expression in poetry and story telling. This
is true even in Spain and North Africa, where Negro women were
sometimes cherished as wives, rather than concubines. A. R. Nykl's
Hispanic Arabic Poetry emphasizes the vogue, in this peripheral
area, of poetry written to and about lovers. Of verses by over 250
poets (all male except two) one man spoke of a beautiful *black*
woman. Two extolled *brown* beauty. Both of these poets wrote about
colored men they loved as well as women. Thus, Abu Hayyan, a
citizen of Granada who became famous mainly as a grammarian and
a commentator on the Koran, wrote: "I fell in love with one whose
face is dark;/ The only white therein are his teeth like pearls;/ Out of
the pupil's darkness his Creator shaped him,/ So all eyes are fixing on
him their glances." Of his teeth he wrote "Between those pearls and
red lips there is a wine which inebriates the one who tastes it."

Ibn Quzman, a famous Cordovan poet well-known for his love of
wine and women wrote: "I am in love with a pretty one who eschews
me—/ A graceful one with curly hair,/ A graceful one with curly
hair,/ My boy, the union with you is a joy, and what a joy!" The
subject of one of his poems was, apparently, a mulatto to whom he
wrote, "I want to tell you the news,/ In these brown faces there is
prettiness,/ What a fine and beautiful color—/ Its nature is compos-
ite . . . Its whiteness with its blackness/ Is something like a bright
morning/ Tinged with a little darkness of the dawn." *Complementarity*, not a Manichaean contrast, characterizes this esthetic
evaluation.

Morena women—those "tinged with a little darkness of the
dawn"—were considered very attractive in Muslim Spain as well as
in Christian Spain and Portugal. Some poets, however, wished to
enjoy both worlds. Ibn Zaidun of Cordova, representative of purest
traditional classical Arabic style, was in love with Wallada with her
"blond or rather, red hair, and white skin." She, too, was a gifted blue-
eyed poet who kept a famous salon in Cordova. She had "a black
maid who was an excellent singer." Ibn Zaidun, according to Nykl,
"liked her." When Wallada became aware that her lover's interest
was drawn to maid as well as mistress, she became furious. She wrote
a verse to him castigating him for "leaving aside the bough that

produced beauty's fruit" and "inclining toward a bough that no such fruit does show." Ibn Zaidun apologized abjectly in numerous poems but to no avail. Wallada spurned his pleas for forgiveness and married a wealthy government official.[253]

Neither beauty nor erotic desirability could assure a woman of any race or ethnic group of being accepted as a wife instead of being a concubine. Marriage is in the status-allocating domain and that involves values associated with the kinship system and, for some individuals, the economic and political systems as well. Muslim Spain seems to have been the only area in non-African Muslim lands where black women were sometimes "prized" as wives during the eighth and ninth centuries. Their usual status, however, was that of concubine. Men of very high status tried to find French and Circassian women for wives. Their blondness was the attraction, color here having a status-allocating significance as well as esthetic significance.[254] A reliable British observer reported of Arabia that "Abyssinian female slaves are kept by many men of the middle and higher classes . . . often instead of wives as requiring less expense and being more subservient." In his view many of the Abyssinian women were "very beautiful," but as to "Negro" women, "since few have any considerable personal attractions [they] are usually employed only in cooking and other menial offices."[255]

The ranking of Blacks was part of a more comprehensive ranking of all ethnics, initiated by the conquering Arabs in the early days of jihad. A major element of this hierarchical organization is the almost universal presence in Islamic societies of sexism or male chauvinism. The Koran explicitly states that men are superior to women.[256] Males of dominant ethnic groups defined the roles and rights of women in all ethnic groups. They defined concubinage as the proper "place" for black women with Negro features and hair.

Extensive use of black women as concubines and black men as eunuchs inevitably associated them with sexuality, and may have limited their access to roles not linked to sexual concerns.

Status and Role Allocation

Two categories, slave and free, constituted the fundamental social divisions in all Muslim societies prior to the twentieth century, and, initially, slavery had occupational implications that varied from society to society. "Blackness" and "whiteness" were separate variables. In Arabia, slaves were sometimes whites or Asians. In southern Arabia, Blacks were sometimes the masters, with Arabs, Jews, and other Blacks being slaves.

Neither Bedouin color prejudice nor the Prophet's pronouncements against it played a decisive role in determining the initial point of entry of a black slave into any of the social systems of the far-flung Muslim world after the first century of expansion. Roles to be filled determined that, along with prevailing ethnic and racial stereotypes. Insofar as Negroidness was a symbol of low status in the Muslim world, this was only one dimension of status-allocation, but a crucial one. Von Grunebaum, in his study of medieval Islam, sums the matter up:

> History brought equality of Persian and Arab and of Turk and Arab, but it did not help the Muslim Negro to vindicate his birth-right. . . . The [Kharijites] declared that *even* "an Abyssinian slave" was eligible for the caliphate, thus showing that such a person was considered at the very bottom of the social order. . . . *The offspring of a Negro mother and a white father was admitted to full equality; the full-blooded Negro generally remained an outsider.* The barrier was not, however, sufficiently strong to exclude Negroes from high office. From 946 to 968, Egypt was governed by Kafur, a Negro born in slavery [italics added].[257]

It was inevitable that "Negroidness," coinciding with evaluations of ethnicity, should enter into traditions about who should play what roles, high and low. When role recruitment and status alloca-tion are influenced by sexual, ethnic, or racial stereotypes over a long span of time, some groups will be less well-represented in some occupational categories and status positions than in others. In this regard, the experience of Blacks has been similar to the experience of women.

Environmental theories about racial origins often emphasized concepts of ethnic specialization, which also contributed to assess-ment of status. Along with Turkish and Persian insistence upon political and intellectual dominance, such concepts may have caused what Bernard Lewis describes as the closing off of avenues of self-expression to talented Blacks in the ninth and tenth centuries.

An example of ethnic specialization theory is provided by Abu'l Qasim Sa'id ibn Ahmad, an eleventh-century judge in Muslim Spain, who wrote *Tabaqat al-Umam* (The Categories of Nations). He grouped the following peoples as those who did not interest them-selves in science, probably because of their unfavorable climate: Turks, Khazars, Slavs, Russians, Berbers, Sudanese, and Negroes. Ethnic membership not color is the criterion of his assessment. Significantly, he distinguished Sudanese from other Blacks. Even more significantly, he included Egyptians among those peoples who had an intellectual bent. Many Egyptians, of course, *were* black, although Abu'l ibn Ahmad may not have recognized that fact. On the face of it this is ethnic stereotyping.

However, the author expresses some color prejudice when he says of India: "*In spite of the fact that its people were nearly black* they were devoted to science, mathematics, geometry, astronomy, virtuous conduct, and perfect government [italics added]."[258] Mas'udi also believed that Indians were "different from all the black races" in their intelligence, political principles, sagacity, and their robust constitution as well as their "purity of complexion."[259] Negroidness, not blackness, per se, was the object of his derogation.

Beliefs about ethnic specialization operated to create the idea of a "proper" place for Blacks and other ethnic groups. Even positive stereotypes based on geographical determinism might have had undesirable effects, if caliphs or emirs filling posts allowed their decisions to be guided by these stereotyped characteristics. Blacks themselves may have internalized these ideas.

Throughout North Africa, for centuries, Negroes have had a prominent role in the streets and markets as *griots* (entertainers who recite verses and sing) and as diviners or sellers of good luck charms. The "frivolity" of the black stereotype may have been an attribute that endeared them to their audiences. However, in so far as it reinforced that specific aspect of the stereotype, it may have limited the easy access of Negroes to other roles.

As we have seen, Negroidness was strongly associated with negative attitudes toward slavery in the Bedouin society that was the first home of Islam. In Yemen, however, the image of the Negro as the enslaved stranger was offset by occasional contact with Abyssinian Blacks as conquerors. In the Ottoman Turkish empire black slaves as well as white had high status at court. The extremely derogatory image of Mesopotamia's Zanj agricultural workers does not seem to have existed anywhere else in the Muslim world because there were no masses of depressed black agricultural laborers elsewhere.

Most Arab and non-Arab Muslims were not, of course, status-conscious intellectuals or lineage-conscious Bedouins. However, we should not conclude that confronting Blacks as slaves necessarily excited contempt, dislike, or aversion. Connection with black "pagan" cultures was more demeaning than being a slave.

It is unlikely that an increase in the volume of black slaves, as compared to other slaves, would alone have resulted in the derogation of black people. In fact, slavery in the Islamic world did not necessarily carry implications of intellectual inferiority and undesirable traits of personality and character. In the Ottoman Turkish Empire a point was reached where nearly every post was filled by a slave. The influential eunuchs in charge of the sultan's harem were Negroes. A contemporary scholar notes that

> The people despised and loathed the eunuchs, but high society was fond of them and paid exorbitant prices for them. In fact, together with well-trained singers they were among the most expensive slaves. . . . [But] it cannot be overlooked how, at the barrier between bond and free, interest in the feelings of the fellow-human and awareness of his dignity are silenced only too frequently. Muslim society harbored a considerable number of slaves, but it was not wholly dependent on slave labor. In most places free, or freed, labor served its needs equally well. Therefore, the humane tendencies toward amelioration of the slave's lot which are embodied in both Koran and Tradition were never actively opposed. . . .
> To this day, slavery continues in one form or another in certain parts of the Muslim world. Travelers, almost unanimously, report favorably on the lot of the unfree. Be this as it may, the only redeeming feature—and this of not too much saving force—is the absence of that self-righteous rationalization of slavery with all the cheap flattery it affords the masters and the equally cheap contempt it piles on the slaves that was developed in Christian lands in order to justify what conscience knew could not be justified. As the Koran took the institution for granted, its continuance did not warp too badly the souls of those who upheld it . . . The institute of the slave army that gains control of the state and whose members, theoretically at least, combine supreme political power with extreme social and legal disabilities is perhaps the strangest paradox with which medieval Islam confronts us.[260]

The extent to which stereotypes and prejudices entered into status allocation in specific situations throughout the Muslim world has not been thoroughly studied by any scholars, Muslim or non-Muslim. Research on the subject is impeded by the unconscious denial by most Muslim scholars that ethnic stereotypes and prejudices play any part in limiting upward mobility, and by the conscious "talking away" of evidence that presents an embarrassing inconsistency between actual behavior and ideals of Islamic universalism in modern Muslim states in North Africa and the Near East.

Summary

Mohammed proclaimed the equality of all believers and called for justice and compassion for the weak and the poor, as well as the abolition of some onerous religious and social customs. However, many of those who brought his message to others were members of Bedouin tribal groups whose anti-Negro prejudices were reinforced by biases already existing in conquered lands.

Divisions of race, color, class, and ethnicity were temporarily dissolved in the euphoria of the initial jihad, but as time went on the so-called Companions and Followers of Mohammed themselves became an upper class, and one that was largely Arab. Reform movements arose, as some questioned the righteousness of Arabs who used the jihad as a means to enrich themselves. As Blacks increasingly came under the influence of these radical Islamic sects, the caliphs in Baghdad turned toward the plains of southern Europe and Asia for "Turkish" cavalrymen to balance their large units of black soldiers.

The involvement of Blacks in the political struggles of the Muslim world cannot be ignored as a factor in depressing the status of Negroes in the newly organized societies. Certainly the connection of Blacks to the Fatimid dynasty brought some power, but the decline of that dynasty resulted in a decline in black political influence in Egypt. The revolt of the Zanj agricultural workers, a rebellion that persisted for fifteen years and at one point threatened Baghdad itself, was one factor in the entrenchment of Turks in the army, and their eventual rise to political as well as military power.

The development of antiblack ideology in elite circles was no doubt accelerated by the definition of Negroes as "subversive troublemakers" challenging Baghdad's power. Also of great importance in stereotyping was the impact of contact with Blacks whose cultures appeared "uncivilized" and "pagan" to Arabs and Persians, as well as an increasing tendency to import masses of such Africans into the Middle East and Mesopotamia as slaves.[261] A pejorative description of agricultural slaves, vilified under the generic term of Zanj, expanded from reaction to physical attributes to assessment of personal habits and mental and moral worth. This image strongly resembles the unsavory collective impression left by the male menials in *The Arabian Nights*.

These stereotypes were supported by "scientific" theories that linked the climate of the native land not only to physical characteristics but to personality traits and intelligence. Even Ibn Khaldun, who mitigated the deterministic element in the theory by suggesting that conversion to Islam could overcome such disabilities, neverthe-less was very derogatory in assessing Negro cultures. Interestingly, all this speculation occurred in the absence of much direct knowl-edge about sub-Saharan Africa, the area to which most of these slaves traced their ancestry.

Prejudice against black people in Arabia and in other parts of the Islamic world had its roots in social relations, not in ideas about "blackness" as a color that "carried over" to black people. The data presented in this chapter indicate how difficult it is in the Muslim world, as elsewhere, to determine the extent to which attributions of value to *black* and *white* in literary allusions carry over to social relations. They may be expressions reflecting what is possible in the culture where Manichaean contrasts exist alongside some racial prejudices, rather than indicative of the actual behavior of most people. With social relations constantly changing in response to political and social changes, stereotypes as well as values attached to "blackness" change over time, too.

Comparative studies make increasingly clear that *the meanings associated with the black-white contrast may vary greatly within a single culture, and that tendencies toward extending meaning to human relations are not uniformly present.*

It is significant that whatever abstract color symbolism may have originally existed among the Arabs, it had nothing to do with the allocation of a subordinate role to black people. This occurred not because they were black, but because they were bought or captured as slaves in East Africa, conveniently nearby. The most pervasive discriminatory behavior patterns were associated with the institu-tion of slavery. Among the Bedouin Arabs, who had known African Blacks mostly as slaves, Negroidness was a sign of that low status.

Even though "slave" was a basic element in the stereotype, Negro, the extent to which being Negroid was viewed in a derogatory manner in a specific situation was probably related not so much to the actual number of Negro slaves as it was to: (1) the extent to which Africans with traits considered very repulsive were present, that is, those associated with the Zanj stereotype; (2) the extent to which Blacks as soldiers or rebels were involved in power struggles in such a way as to excite popular hostility toward them, and (3) the extent to which Blacks were used for the most undesirable kinds of labor.

In our study of esthetic attitudes, we examined the Zanj stereotype, and noted how the conditions of their work in Mesopotamia contributed to an unfavorable image. The division of responsiblity between two groups of slaves—white soldiers and black eunuchs at the Ottoman court—reveals a distinction that was prejudicial to Blacks and may reflect beliefs about inherent racial traits. The fact that Islamic sultans and caliphs were willing to place Negroes in positions of power does not necessarily mean that the populace shared their view. The idea that Blacks were "vicious" or "dishonest" may have arisen in those areas where black eunuchs were frequently invested with power.

Such individuals may have been tolerated and even honored in elite circles, but there is evidence from Egypt that they were sometimes despised by the masses of the people. The term "mutilated Negro" became an expression of contempt in Egypt, and referred to the prevalence of black eunuchs at the Cairo court. It is likely that similar attitudes were to be found in Baghdad. Soldiers, black or white, were often the targets of hostility when they were used to keep order. In Egypt and parts of Muslim Spain, there is evidence that the hostility to palace guards occasionally took on a racial aspect. However, cruelty is not among the negative attributes in the Negro stereotype. There were too many soldiers of too many racial and ethnic groups, all assigned to carry out the will of rulers, for Blacks to be allotted a monopoly on cruelty.

The stereotypes that emerged from the operation of all these factors provided cues for esthetic and erotic judgments, as well as the allocation of roles and status. Their influence was strongest in the esthetic/erotic area. Even illustrious and powerful black men faced ridicule over their appearance, and black women were accepted as concubines rather than as wives or subjects of romantic poems. Yet, tradition and paternal pride in the talent and skill of sons by Negro concubines prevented an absolute taboo on intermarriages and accession to power in some Muslim lands. Although "son of a Negress" remained a customary pejorative epithet, prejudice could be overcome, as the legendary Antar and other poets and soldiers proved. Any number of episodes in this chapter can be used to illustrate that persistence of color prejudice was not decisive in actually determining who would exert leadership, particularly in lands like Morocco, India, and Andalusia, far from the Central Islamic Lands, or in Egypt, where there was a long tradition of black political participation.

During the same millennium that Blacks were omnipresent in the Muslim world, and in a variety of roles, Blacks were seldom seen in medieval Europe north of the Pyrenees and the Alps. Images of Blacks existed there, too, stereotypes that had no connection to slavery, stereotypes that were largely favorable. Ironically, this Christian world would create a Diaspora for black slaves of far greater cruelty than any suffered in the Islamic world.

Although there was certainly color prejudice in Muslim lands, it was nowhere reinforced by a system of *racial* slavery such as the one that would emerge in the New World.[262] When Muslims went so far as to justify the enslavement of fellow Muslims—usually Negroes who had recently converted to Islam—the authority of Islamic law could be invoked against this breach of values. The liberality of Islamic law toward slaves operated to the advantage of Blacks as it did to others who were enslaved, the theory being that, ideally, all men should be free and that emancipating slaves was a meritorious act. Several centuries would elapse before the nations of the West would adopt a similar ideal. But two groups of settlers in the Diaspora—the Spanish and the Portuguese—carried cultures that had absorbed liberal Islamic values concerning slaves and slavery, as well as familiarity with black men occupying high status positions, and the Mediterranean custom of evaluating customary behavior as more important than skin color.

6. THE BLACK EXPERIENCE IN MEDIEVAL EUROPEAN CHRISTENDOM

About 1525, Cardinal Albrecht of Brandenburg, archbishop of Mains and Magdeburg, administrator of the bishopric of Halberstadt, and imperial chancellor, commissioned Matthias Grünewald to prepare a painting of St. Maurice for the cathedral at Halle-on-Saale. This early thirteenth-century Dominican church was being renovated at considerable cost before its consecration as a shrine cathedral of St. Maurice.

There is some indication that the Cardinal was trying to co-opt a popular local symbol, St. Maurice, who was a patron saint of several cities in the Hanseatic League, including Halle. He was also patron of several guilds of artisans and merchants that had been resisting the church's attempts to assert its authority over the town.[1]

Although St. Maurice had lived and died for his faith in Roman times, Grünewald portrayed him wearing medieval armor, as he had been depicted in a stone statue for the Magdeburg cathedral a couple of centuries earlier (see plate 6). Hans-Joachim Kunst, author of *The African in European Art*, describes that statue, part of a grouping of several knights, in this way:

> The face, enclosed in a helmet of mail, is that of an African—thick lips, flat nose and widely arched forehead. . . . Here we see an African placed on an equal footing with the European; indeed he expresses the same knightly ideal as the equestrian statue of the Emperor Otto.[2]

At the time, there was nothing noteworthy about the popularity of an African saint among the German people, or in his depiction as an equal of a white European soldier. Indeed, Otto, King of Saxony, was the first of several Holy Roman emperors who made St. Maurice a symbol of their hopes and ambitions. Charles V, the German king who led the Holy Roman Empire at the time the Halle cathedral was being dedicated to St. Maurice, had already decorated a statue of the saint with the Order of the Golden Fleece.

Charles V, who was the last of the Holy Roman emperors to be crowned by the Pope, spent more than half of his forty-year rule fighting to stop the thrust of the Ottoman Turks westward into Europe and North Africa. St. Maurice was a fitting symbol of Charles' ambition to maintain Catholic sovereignty over much of Europe. When he abdicated in 1555, that dream, and his more ambitious dream of universal rule, was dead.[3]

Unlike his predecessors, Charles V was the king of Spain as well as Germany. When dreams of a European empire died, Spain's "Catholic kings" turned to the promise of a new empire in the Western Hemisphere, consolidating lands there under Castilian rule, to be worked by Indian serfs and African slaves. While a very Negroid saint was being honored at one end of Charles' empire, Africans were doomed to a degrading form of chattel slavery at the other end. A new form of slavery was just beginning to appear in human history, *racial* slavery.

There is a tantalizing irony in the tension between these opposite images of the proper roles for black people as the sixteenth century began; the century would mark the end of an epoch in black history. White Racism was replacing less severe forms of European color prejudice. Racial slavery and colonial imperialism became the dominant forms of ethnic and racial interaction until very recent times.

During the thousand years that preceded this turning point in black history, the Black Experience in Western Europe was far different from what we have seen in the Muslim world. There were very few people of African descent living within the boundaries of European Christendom, as compared with the Central Islamic Lands. As a result, there was little color consciousness of the kind that resulted from sustained contact between large numbers of Negroes and non-Negroes in the Muslim world, leading to constant esthetic comparisons and manipulation of color consciousness for individual and social objectives.

Derogation of "Negroidness" in Muslim lands occurred to an extent unknown in Western Christendom during the pre-medieval and medieval era. Such pejorative verbalization was by no means decisive in determining the status of Negroes in Muslim cultures, but it was nevertheless demeaning. Western European cultures would not embody such a practice until they became involved in the massive enslavement of Africans during the sixteenth century.

Except for Spain, Portugal, and some parts of Italy and southern France, there were also no concentrations of black people living as slaves in Western Europe. In the Central Islamic Lands, Blacks were numerous and most of them were slaves. Many slaves were white, however, and slavery was not viewed as a social condition uniquely appropriate for Blacks. Also, access to positions of power was possible for Negroes in the Muslim world to an extent unknown in European Christendom during this period. The absence of competition for power and of the need to maintain a position of dominance over black people—as well as their rarity—made for a far different situation than in Muslim lands.

Black people were the folk of legend and mythology in Western Europe in the millenium before the opening of the New World to colonization. They were referred to in the Bible and folklore, but were rarely seen in the flesh. As the Crusades moved forward in the eleventh and twelfth centuries, stories of "Ethiopians" functioning as Christian monks and Saracen soldiers were brought home from the Holy Land. Also, increasing numbers of sub-Saharan Blacks appeared in the slave markets of the Mediterranean islands and in menial pursuits in Italian cities.[4]

During the medieval period, the church encouraged veneration of the Virgin Mary portrayed as a dark-skinned woman, and several German monarchs made St. Maurice their patron saint and symbol of their political ambitions. The windows of cathedrals included depictions of a black Wise Man among the three, and, in one case, a black Queen of Sheba. The black image that emerged in the fourteenth and fifteenth centuries, on the eve of New World exploration, was highly favorable and, according to Henri Baudet, a French scholar, was well-attuned to the psychological needs of a troubled era.[5]

The historian W. H. McNeill, commenting on "the waning of the Middle Ages," has stated that

the period from the end of the thirteenth century to the beginning of the sixteenth was one of general confusion in Europe. . . . At the beginning of the fourteenth century the papal hope of establishing a universal rule throughout Latin Christendom was quite decisively destroyed . . . a long struggle between France and England began. . . . In the older urban centers the fourteenth and fifteenth centuries saw the differentiation of classes and the development of a sizeable proletariat often sunk into serious poverty.[6]

In this tumultuous atmosphere of change and popular fears, belief in the imminent end of the world was widespread, as was the idea of a black Emperor-Redeemer who would inaugurate a New Age.[7]

We shall first look at color symbolism and secular portrayals of black people in Western Europe, before and during the medieval period and the early Renaissance. Then, we will sharpen our focus on the image of blackness and black people presented by the Roman Catholic Church, which was the dominating integrating force in Europe in the centuries before the birth of Protestantism. Although the legacy from early church theologians included ideas of what one classicist calls "spiritual" whiteness and blackness that denigrated Negroes, a wide range of alternative images emerged in medieval Europe.[8] While the Devil and demons in general were sometimes portrayed as black, the preponderance of images in Catholic iconography were positive, including Black Madonnas as well as the black warrior-saint we have already met. This was the context in which the concept of a black Emperor-Redeemer could arise and win acceptance.

BLACKNESS IN WESTERN EUROPE: PRE-MEDIEVAL AND MEDIEVAL

When the Arab and Berber Muslims crossed from Africa into Spain in A.D. 711, the king of the Franks—Catholic and loyal to the Bishop of Rome—was engaged in the work that had busied his ancestors for two centuries: making forcible conversions among the pagan tribes who lived north and east of his kingdom. Fifty-seven years after the Islamic invasion, Charlemagne was continuing this holy war, while simultaneously trying to confine the Muslims to the other side of the Frankish border with Spain, and if possible, to carry the battle into that land of the Infidel.

Three centuries after the Carolingian dynasty had passed away, the kingdom of the Franks was consolidated alongside a number of German and Italian states that formed the Holy Roman Empire, ruled by several dynasties of German kings who were crowned by the Pope in Rome (see map 6). Although the "civilizing mission" of the Christian church was scoring impressive victories over the resident white pagans of Europe, Islam still remained a challenge in the Near East. Five Crusades against the Saracens in the Holy Land, beginning in the eleventh century, generated a sense of Christian identity vis à vis the Infidel "Other." This Western European "Christendom" would persist until the Protestant Reformation destroyed the Catholic consensus in the sixteenth century and unleashed latent nationalist and class struggles.

Attitudes toward blackness and the status of black people throughout the early years of Western European Christendom can only be

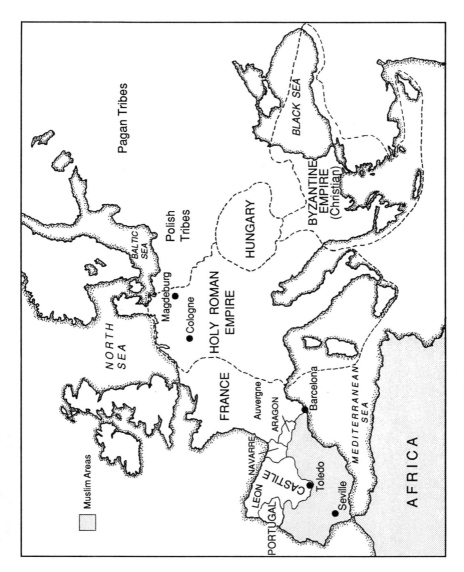

MAP 6. Europe During the 11th Century a.d.
Cartography based on a concept of the author.

understood in relation to the political and cultural situation described by historian W. H. McNeill in *The Rise of the West*:

> Not until the end of the fifth century did Clovis, king of the Franks, accept the orthodox form of Christianity and compel his principal followers and lieutenants to do the same (496); . . . However superficial the initial conversion of German princes and kings to Christianity may have been, baptism nevertheless brought in its train not only churches and monasteries, but literacy and a general initiation into the traditions of Roman and Christian civilization. . . . By Clovis' time, therefore, the Rhine was no longer a terminus, but was becoming the axis of a German-Roman cultural amalgam from which Western civilization later developed.[9]

Before the Eastern church and the Roman Church had split—before the Holy Roman Empire had been established as the counterpart of the Byzantine Christian Empire that had its capital in Constantinople—Eastern influences were strong in Western Europe. Cologne, near the mouth of the Rhine, became a center where important Eastern ideas penetrated the "German-Roman cultural amalgam." In the East, dark skin was traditional in depicting Madonna and Child, though not with black color or Negroid features. A Negroid king, the so-called "Black Magus," was believed to have been among the Three Wise Men.[10]

Attitudes Toward the Color Black

Some pagan religious beliefs and rites in Europe were gradually transformed and absorbed by Christianity. The synthesis found expression in art, literature, folklore, dress styles, and drama. It is clear that the tribal peoples of pre-Christian Europe assigned symbolic meanings to various colors, but what those meanings were can only be inferred from folklore that was written down by Christian clergy, from Roman sources, and from a few surviving traditions.

Among the Celts, a systematic color code was used by the ancient Druid priesthood. Faber Birren, who has made a detailed analysis of color symbolism in various cultures and in historical perspective, notes that "to the Druids green represented wisdom, blue represented truth, white was the supreme emblem of purity." Black was not defined as the opposite of white. These colors were used for the robes of the three ascending orders in the priestly hierarchy—Ovate (Green), Bard (Blue), and Arch-Druid (White). While Druid usage reinforced the Christian use of white as a master symbol of purity, chastity, and innocence, it did not contrast white to blackness.[11]

In pre-Christian times white, along with black, sometimes had a neutral rather than a highly charged symbolic character. In parts of Ireland, for instance, black stood for North, white for South, purple for East and dun for West. No virtues or vices were attributed to the colors in this context.[12]

Among the beliefs about magic subscribed to by ordinary people in pre-Christian Europe, there was little consistency in the attributes attached to colors, and black was not invariably associated with impurity, evil, or ill-luck. For instance, Yorkshire fishermen dreaded white, while their Northumberland neighbors dreaded black. In Spain, seeing a black cat and a white insect together meant good luck. However, at some undetermined period, "good" magic became "white magic" and "bad" magic became "black magic."[13]

Defining black as the Manichaean contrast of white was not part of the pagan culture of Western Europe. Since the Roman Catholic Church was the dominant institution affecting basic values throughout the Middle Ages, the meanings that its priests were taught to assign to colors were no doubt strongly influential. All learned priests were familiar with a basic symbolic triad of colors. God the Father, Son and Holy Ghost were represented by blue, yellow and red, respectively. The same three colors symbolized Heaven, Earth and Hell, in that order, and Spirit, Mind and Body.[14] There is no evidence that black became the major polar opposite to white in medieval religious symbolism, although it was in early North African Christianity. Black was traditionally associated with mourning and death, although white mourning garments were sometimes worn—and the shroud, of course, was white. We have described in Chapter 4 how, in the allegorical writing of early Church Fathers, black served as the symbol of sin and impurity and sometimes "carried over" to people; but medieval Christianity did not emphasize a black/white contrast that applied to people.[15]

Near the middle of the fifteenth century, according to a twentieth century Dutch scholar, Johan Huizinga, a clear distinction was being made between esthetic and symbolic evaluations of color. Symbolic evaluations were further divided according to erotic and religious/ mystical domains. In his book, *The Waning of the Middle Ages*, Huizinga talked of esthetic preferences:

> To determine the taste in colours characteristic of the epoch would require a comprehensive and statistical research, embracing the

chromatic scale of painting as well as the colours of costume and decorative art. Perhaps costume would be the best clue to the nature of the taste for colour, because there it exhibits itself most spontaneously.[16]

Using the data on clothing available for the fifteenth century, mostly relating to "garments of state and luxury, differing as to color from ordinary costume but showing the esthetic sense more freely," Huizinga notes that "the quiet colours, grey, black and violet, occupy a large place" in the ordinary daily wardrobe,[17] while red, and then white, were popular for festive garments.

> Black was already a favourite colour, even in state apparel, especially in velvets. Philip the Good, in his later years, constantly dresses in black, and had his suite and horses arrayed in the same colour. King Rene who was always in quest of what was refined and distinguished, combined grey and white with black. Together with grey and violet, black was far more in vogue than blue and green, whereas yellow and brown are as yet almost completely wanting.[18]

In the symbolic area, Huizinga connects the "waning" of the Middle Ages to a secularization of color symbols. Yellow had begun to mean "hostility" as well as the "power and glory of the Son of God." Blue had come to mean marital infidelity, while green denoted amorous passion as well as religious faith. There was no fixed relationship between color and meaning.[19]

After the middle of the fifteenth century, neutral and favorable connotations of "blackness" were gradually overshadowed, and black became a master symbol for undesirable moods, character traits, and people. Symbolism contrasting white and black to the disadvantage of the latter was thus available to function as one factor in the development of an ideology sanctioning the exclusive use of Negroes as slaves, and justifying their subordination to white masters. We say "available" for an ideological use involving "carry-over" of a color symbolism to people because there is no *necessary* "carry-over."

Portrayals of Black People

Short periods of contact with Negro individuals may have occurred in Europe prior to the eighth century, when black Africans were present in substantial numbers among the invading armies of Islam. There are some legends referring to black settlers in Wales, Scotland and England, prior to the coming of Christianity. They do not speak of "Blacks" as either sinister or inferior. Whether these are references to very dark Caucasians, to Arabs, or to Negroes is not clear.[20] A few Negroes were in the Roman armies that invaded Britain,[21] but legends about a Black Knight connected with King Arthur's Round-table may not have arisen until European contact with the Moors began in Spain and Portugal.[22]

The eighth century marked the beginning of extensive contact between Europeans and Negroes on the Iberian peninsula. Upon their initial contact with the armies of Islam, the Franks defined the Muslims—Moors, Arabs and Berbers—as Infidel enemies to be eliminated. Once a border was stabilized between the Christian states and Andalusia, the relationship often resembled what William Graham Sumner described in *Folkways* as "antagonistic-coopera-tion."[23] Both sides captured slaves and made concubines and wives of female prisoners of war. Shifting alliances between Christian and Muslim city-states were frequent. Ethnic consciousness in Franco-Spanish border areas was high, but color prejudice seems to have been minimal except as an occasional vehicle for expressing religious antagonisms. Skin color then became a marker used by the Christians to identify—and vilify—the Infidel.

Before the Crusades began in the eleventh century, there was little to excite antagonism toward black people in most of Europe. The Franco-Iberian border was a localized exception. Skin-color differ-ences within other local areas were rarely pronounced enough to provide a basis for ethnic classification, or for institutionalizing prejudice and discrimination based upon physical traits. The major "enemies" were white—Goths and Norsemen. Tribal ethnocentrism was common but any existing skin-color prejudice prior to the Muslim invasions seems not to have been socially salient. The Augustinian Christianity that the West valued so highly stressed belief in the descent of all human beings from common ancestors, Adam and Eve, and taught that Adam had been created from "the dust of the earth." This dogma and its associated myth was a counter-weight to ethnic and racial particularisms. However, Augustine's attitude toward Ethiopians made their skin color a symbol of sin that only baptism could "wash" away.

After the eleventh century, some legends that became well-known throughout Western Europe have special significance in the study of attitudes toward black people.

The Black Presence in the Song of Roland

When William of Normandy crossed the English Channel in 1066 to begin the conquest of the Anglo-Saxons in England, the ballad singer Taliafero reputedly rode through the surf at Dover beside him, chanting *The Song of Roland*. Legends of heroic deeds performed by Charlemagne and his followers, including Roland, had been preserved in the oral tradition of France for two hundred years.[24]

No one knows what is fact and what is fancy in these tales of eighth- and ninth-century conflicts with Muslims in southern France and northern Spain. Although it may have taken form as a long unwritten poem by the eleventh century, *The Song of Roland* appeared in manuscript for the first time in the thirteenth century. By then all of Europe had been affected by the Crusades. Negative attitudes toward brown and black foes that developed in these later struggles between Christians and Saracens may have been "read back" into the legends. On the other hand, they may actually have arisen during the eighth- and ninth-century conflicts.

The Roland epic includes ancient legends about the military and amorous encounters of the Christian warriors. Ambivalence toward the Muslim foe is expressed: there is hostility, but also admiration for the skill and appearance of some soldiers and for the character of individual knights. Appreciation was expressed for the beauty of Saracen women, along with intense hatred of the Infidel religion. The terms "Moor" and "Saracen" seem to refer to a non-Negro North African or Middle Easterner, with "Black," "Ethiopian," and "Nubian" being used to refer to sub-Saharan Negroes.

The poem describes how, at one crucial point in the battle between Charlemagne and the Saracens, many racial and ethnic groups had been assembled by both sides. In one version, an enemy leader—Morganice, who ruled Ethiopia, "an accursed land"—is described as one who "has the black people under his command." European esthetic biases are mobilized to stigmatize the Blacks: "their noses are big and their ears broad, and together they number more than fifty thousand." Roland is discouraged when he sees them because they "ride fiercely and furiously," these "accursed people who are blacker than ink and whose teeth alone are white."

There are also uncomplimentary remarks about other foes, whose color difference is not a ready trait to seize upon for vilification. There are references to "the large-headed men from Misnes" who had spines along the lengths of their backs like bristles, and to the "ugly Cananeans"; and to one group whose skins were "as tough as iron" and "who do not serve the Lord God."[25] Physical traits were convenient indicators of out-group membership.

The general impact of the thirteenth-century French versions of *The Song of Roland* is to contrast the masses of Nubian foot soldiers who fought Charlemagne unfavorably with the individual Saracen knights who fought single-handed combats with their Frankish counterparts. We have no way of knowing whether or not these images were confined to the upper classes whose troubadours sang these versions of the legend. Did serfs and villeins share them?

Although the thirteenth-century French version of *The Song of Roland* preserved in manuscript form presents only a negative image of Blacks, some sixteenth-century Italian versions present both positive and negative images of "Ethiopians." Between the thirteenth and the sixteenth centuries, *The Song of Roland* and the legends of the knights of King Arthur's Round Table were being recast in Italy and France to reflect the intense conflict between Muslims and Christians that had been unleashed by the Crusades. The Crusaders came in contact with Ethiopian churchmen in Palestine as well as Ethiopian mercenary soldiers fighting for the Turks.[26] Hope was aroused in some quarters that the Christians of Ethiopia might strike the Saracens on their flank south of Egypt, and stories of past cooperation between European Christians and Ethiopians encouraged those hopes. Therefore, some recastings of old legends portrayed Blacks in a favorable way. The legend of Senapo is a case in point. It presents a counter-image to that of Morganice.

The Story of Senapo

During the fifteenth century, two seemingly contradictory attitudes toward "Ethiopians" can be discerned within European Christendom. Among those who fought black people in the Crusades, expressions of hostility and even contempt sometimes appear in the literature. But at another level—the level of myth—interest grew in the story of Senapo, the "good" Ethiopian king who was believed to have helped Charlemagne. Senapo is also called Prester John.

The legend is told by the Italians Ariosto, Palci, and Boidardo, who codified, edited and rewrote a mass of legends, including the *Roland* epic, during the sixteenth century. They tell how Astolfo, one of Charlemagne's twelve peers or paladins, journeyed to Abyssinia to seek help from its king, Senapo. Riding a hippogriff, a mythical animal with the head and claws of an eagle and the body of a winged horse, Astolfo set out for Abyssinia, which was believed to be at the headwaters of the Nile in the east African highlands.

En route, Astolfo pursued a flock of harpies who had been harassing the king, and drove the mythical birds into a cave at the bottom of a mountain, where the entrance to hell stood. Blocking the mouth of the cave with stones, Astolfo flew to the mountain top, where he found a "Terrestrial Paradise." There, the Apostle John gave him a charm to cure the blindness of Senapo. In return for his sight, Senapo agreed to aid Charlemagne, who was then locked in battle with the Saracens. According to the legend, the Ethiopian king not only granted him a hundred thousand men but offered to lead them himself. The Abyssinians crossed without difficulty the vast fields of sand which separate their land from the kingdoms of Northern Africa. When they reached the sea, Senapo was distressed because he had only elephants and camels, but no horses. Using knowledge imparted by St. John, Astolfo turned great stones into horses— complete with saddles and bridles. With eighty thousand cavalrymen thus equipped, Astolfo "reduced all the country to subjection," and besieged the North African city of Biserta, thus diverting Saracen forces that would have otherwise joined the attack on Charlemagne.[27] How old this story of Ethiopians helping Charlemagne is we do not know, but it spread widely among literates after the fourteenth century.

The Legend of the Black Knight

Nowhere in Christendom was there an epic or a saga with a black folk hero who captured the imagination of the masses as 'Antar did throughout Central Islamic Lands. However, the story of the Black Knight may have achieved some popularity in parts of France between the thirteenth and sixteenth centuries. Another black military hero was added to St. Maurice and Senapo. The adventures of the Black Knight were sung as part of the saga of Lancelot, Percival, and Gawain and their quest for the Holy Grail. This was a French appropriation and elaboration of British stories about King Arthur's Round Table, but no manuscript of the troubadours' songs survives in either English or French. Translations into German and Dutch have preserved the story of Morien, who chanced upon Lancelot and Gawain when he was on his own personal quest, a search for his father.

In the version we have, the father of the Black Knight is Sir Agloval, brother of Percival. In another version it was Percival himself who was the father! The Black Knight had sworn to fight every knight he met until he was guided to his long-lost father. Lancelot and Gawain were in France searching for Percival, who also was lost, when

> there came riding towards them a knight on a goodly steed, and well armed withal. He was all black, even as I tell ye: his head, his body,

and his hands were all black, saving only his teeth. His shield and his armor were even those of a Moor, and black as a raven. He rode his steed at full gallop with many a forward bound. When he beheld the knights, and drew nigh to them, and the one had greeted the other, he cried aloud to Sir Lancelot: "Knight, now give me to wit of one thing which I desire or guard ye against my spear. The truth will I know."[28]

We do not know whether the original French story expressed the same consternation at seeing a black knight that this Dutch translation does:

Therefore stood Sir Gawain still, as one who had no mind to fight, nor to break the laws of courtesy. Nevertheless he deemed that this was a devil rather than a man whom they had come upon! Had they not heard him call upon God no man had dared to face him, seeming that he was the devil or one of his fellows out of hell, for that his steed was so great, and he was taller even than Sir Lancelot, and black withal as I said before.[29]

The Moor and Sir Lancelot fought furiously, first with the lance, then with the sword. Eventually, Sir Gawain intervened, persuading both men to agree to a truce and saying to the Moor, "Tell me what ye seek and I will give ye good counsel withal." The Moor answered:

Ye say well. Now I pray ye by all who own the laws of knighthood, and by Sir Gawain afore all, since he is reckoned the best, he and Sir Lancelot, wherever it may be, far and wide throughout the world, of all men are these twain most praised. . . . Know ye aught of Sir Agloval, brother to Sir Percival of Wales? Of him have I asked many this long time past.[30]

Sir Gawain asked the Moorish knight to tell him why he was seeking Sir Percival's brother, and the answer reflects the values of a code of knighthood that cuts across boundaries of race and religion:

So will I tell ye all. Sir Agloval is my father, 'twas he begat me. And more will I tell ye; it chanced aforetime as ye may now learn, when he came into the land of the Moors; there, through his valiant deeds he won the heart of a maiden, she was my mother, by my troth. So far went the matter between them through their words and through his courtesy, and because he was so fair to look upon, that she gave him all his will—the which brought her small reward and great sorrow.[31]

The knight then told how his father and many other knights of Arthur's court were searching for Sir Lancelot and had sworn not to tarry any place more than a day or two. Therefore, Agloval had to leave before he wished. Having fallen in love,

> Each plighted their troth to the other ere she granted him her favours. Therein was she ill counselled, for he forsook her there-after. . . . But ere he departed he sware to her that he would return when he had achieved his quest but he kept not his oath. Thus have I sought him in many a court.[32]

Now, after fourteen years The Black Knight was searching for Agloval because being fatherless, he could not receive his inheritance. "Little good hath it done me that he be my father, and that he sware to my mother, ere he departed, that for her honour, and for her profit, he would return to her without fail." As to Sir Gawain and Sir Lancelot, "the tears fell from their eyes when they heard the knight's tale."[33] Here the translation presents an interesting skin-color contrast:

> Such pity had they for him, they waxed pale and red. . . . Then was the black knight blithe and drew near to Sir Lancelot, and bared his head which was black as pitch; that was the fashion of the land— Moors are black as burnt brands. But in all that men would praise in a knight was he fair, after his kind. Though he were black, what was he the worse: He was taller by half a foot than any knight that stood beside him, and as yet he was scarce more than a child.[34]

After Gawain and Lancelot promise to bring Morien to King Arthur's court and to help him find his father, the text returns to its preoccupation with his physical appearance: "When the Moor heard these words he laughed with heart and mouth (his teeth were white as chalk, otherwise he was altogether black)."[35] As he proceeded toward the Channel en route to England, "all who saw him fled from him."[36] But in England at Arthur's court he was well received. When Lancelot, Percival, Gawain, and Agloval arrived, "Sir Gawain told the king all the matter of Morien and of his father and of the chance that had parted them. All this did he tell afore the folk, wherefore was Morien much gazed upon." But no mention is made of his color in this context. Whether the previous comments about the Moor's "blackness" are glosses made by the translator for the benefit of Dutch readers or appeared in the French source is not known. One curious feature of another northern European translation, however, is that the Moor is referred to as being white spotted with black, not all black! In any event the total impact of the account is favorable to the Moor. It is recorded that

> when the strife was ended, and Arthur's land once more at peace, Morien bethought him that he would make his father be wedded to

the lady his mother; and he prayed his uncle to journey with him if he would, and Sir Percival was right willing thereto. Further said Sir Gawain and Sir Lancelot that they twain would ride with them for honour and for good fellowship. For this did Morien thank them much.[37]

And so the story ends with Sir Percival telling his brother Sir Agloval that "Your son is so good a knight, and stout a warrior, that ye may well thank heaven that ye begat him . . . Sir Gawain and Sir Lancelot be come hither in faith and good fellowship, and with us will they journey to the Moorish land."[38] The story has a fairy tale ending with a great wedding feast and the delivery of her inheritance to Morien's mother: "When this was done, and they had proclaimed her queen over all the kingdom of the Moors . . . there was bliss and great rejoicing fourteen days. . . . there was feasting and great merriment; they were all well-served with everything on earth that they might desire."[39]

Sir Gawain, Lancelot, and Percival returned to King Arthur's court when the feast was ended for "'twas nigh to Pentecost" and Lancelot's son Galahad was to be knighted and proceed on the quest of the Holy Grail. The three knights reported to the Round Table on the marriage of Agloval to his Moorish wife and "then were king and queen alike glad at heart."[40]

Here is a positive image of Moors in their native land and of esteem for a black woman on the part of the natives and the knights. Some somatic norm shock on initial contact soon wears off as skill and character prevail in evaluating the Black Knight as a fellow human being.

Esthetic and Erotic Evaluations of Blacks

Esthetic elements are clearly present in the initial reactions to the Black Knight, and erotic evaluations are implicit in judgments about the relationship between his mother and Sir Agloval. These considerations are also relevant in other works.

Ariosto's long poem called *Orlando Furioso* not only contained the favorable verses about Senapo that we have just discussed but also some very unfavorable ones about a stereotyped unnamed Ethiopian. The contrasting images of "le bon éthiopien" and the "bad nigger" may or may not have a longer history in the European folk mind, but they made several appearances beginning in the fifteenth century. As the derogatory images of black men in *The Arabian Nights* were counterposed to the heroic Antar and Bilal, so a repulsive black image became the counterpart of Prester John in this most popular Renaissance romance of the sixteenth century. It should be noted that its popularity among the literate upper classes may or may not have extended to a wider audience.

The unnamed Ethiopian appears in a subplot within a long tale involving multiple adulteries and murder by enraged spouses and lovers. The main character, an Italian judge named Anselmo, agrees to commit sodomy with the Negro—the black man being the active partner.[41] The Negro promises the judge a fine estate in return for the single night of sexual pleasure. The judge's wife previously cohabited for a year with the owner of a performing dog she wanted to obtain. Both husband and wife, therefore, are swept away by desire for things that, in the Christian scale of values, should surely not be secured at the price of fidelity or chastity.

In any case, the wife catches the husband and the Negro *in flagrante delicto*. Anselmo, who had threated to have his wife murdered for her infidelity, suggests they forgive each other. As they are reconciled, she reminds him that at least she was swept off her feet by a *handsome* man and asks, "What punishment in justice could approach the sin which with this monster you commit?" He had compounded his sin of sodomy by committing it with an *ugly* person. A distinctive Italian Renaissance approach.

Negroidness is presented as the acme of ugliness, and Ariosto's portrayal of the repulsive black male in *Orlando Furioso* is reminiscent of *The Arabian Nights*. As Anselmo approaches the mansion:

> Before the gate he sees an Ethiop
> Broadnosed, thick-lipped; the judge
>   would roundly swear
> This of all ugly faces is the top.
> Comparison with Aesop he would bear.
> The music of the spheres would surely stop
>   if this monstrosity in heaven were.
> Greasy and dirty like a beggar dressed
> Still only half his squalor is expressed.[42]

Why Negro physiognomy is singled out as the acme of ugliness is a matter that merits some study, especially since mulatto coloring and facial configuration were not normally vilified. Indeed, portraits of prominent Italian families, including the Medici, occasionally show dark skin color and Negroid features.[43] Significantly, Ariosto compares the Negro's looks to Aesop, and thus apparently accepts that Negroidness carries with it no necessary cognitive deficit.

Whatever the deeper psychological and semiotic implications may be, to explain Ariosto's depiction of the Negro's physical ugliness and distasteful sexual orientation, the most important element from our vantage is that the same work provides the positive and even heroic image of the good King Senapo.

"It is true that the dark skin of Africans was generally perceived as unsightly during the European Middle Ages," says Paul H. D. Kaplan, in a generalization for which it would be difficult to assemble conclusive evidence. A stained glass window of a black Queen of Sheba, which he presents in his book, contradicts his own generalization. His statement also leaves ambiguous whether "dark skin" is separate from "Negroidness"; nor does he say who was doing the perceiving. Even if it was the *general* perception, it was certainly not the *universal* one, as his own research shows.

When troubadours sang of the Black Knight, they assumed that French peasants and artisans would not be repelled by the idea of Percival's brother falling in love with a Moorish woman—knights did not make love to "unsightly" women[44]—or to his having the Black Knight as a son, and eventually marrying the dark-skinned mother. Yet French troubadours did not sing elsewhere about white knights enamored of dark ladies.

Except in Spain and Portugal, poets and troubadours did not make black women objects of romantic love, nor did artists depict them as such. Luís Vaz de Camões, a Portuguese poet, was heir to the Andalusian tradition of the *morena* as a model of beauty: "Her brown skin so apt for love would have aroused the envy even of the snow."[45] Most European males—even those who had been on Crusades—did not share his unique experience as a soldier in India and Africa. Some in the upper and middle classes may have had black concubines or mistresses,[46] but their openly expressed, conventional view of feminine beauty, especially in France, follows the description in this medieval poem:

> Fair hair, curving eye lashes,
> Large space between the eyes, pretty looks . . .
> That fine straight nose, neither large nor small,
> The dimpled chin, well shaped bright face.[47]

Throughout the Middle Ages, appraisals of "the Negro" tended to concentrate on good versus bad, rather than beautiful versus ugly. With the advent of the Renaissance, esthetic and erotic elements, sometimes intertwined, become more frequent and explicit in literature and painting. During this great flowering of the arts in the fourteenth and fifteenth centuries, artists in the Netherlands, significantly, were more interested in Blacks than artists in the Italian city-states where the Renaissance began. Negroes were present in some numbers in both places, but in the Italian cities, they were mostly slaves. In the northern cities, Blacks were seamen and dock workers, presumably free or apprentices. Black males were often used as models.

The great Italian painters used Blacks only in depictions of the Magi, but not the Dutch. Kunst notes that "Hieronymous Bosch (1450-1516) has incorporated Africans into the dreamworld depicted in the centre-piece of his Madrid triptych, a garden of desire populated by naked figures, terrifying animals, sexual symbols and figures of pure fantasy." In one detail of Bosch's "Garden of Desire," a lithe, naked black woman stands out in stark contrast to the ivory bodies of several nude white women. Commenting further, Kunst interprets the Bosch painting:

> Indeed, the triptych does seem to portray a world of dreams: a world inhabited by naked figures in a state of sexual abandonment, a world in which suppressed wishes are symbolized by fantastic construc-tions. . . . Among the naked mother of pearl bodies there are many dark-skinned personages of slender stature.[48]

Some are markedly Negroid as well as dark-skinned. Kunst empha-sizes the esthetic rather than the erotic aspect of these images when he writes, "they form groups in the foreground and make an attrac-tive contrast with the fair bodies of the others." But he imputes sexual symbolism, too:

> African women bathe in fountains of youth, around which young men ride on horses, donkeys, bulls, boars, panthers, lions, and many other beasts. Flowering creepers cling to the women's thighs and breasts, and from them hang grapes and cherries, fruits which as dream books of the time tell us, are nothing but symbols of sexual desire. Enormous dark cherries crown their heads.[49]

While no other Dutch artist handled black female subjects in a fashion as frankly seductive, there were erotic undertones to other presentations. Cornelius van Haarlem, a Dutch Mannerist of the late Renaissance period, used an attractive black woman in his portrait of "Bathsheba in Her Bath." Kunst's comment that "the dark-skinned servant balances the white-skinned one" ignores the erotic impact of the painting. No black or brown women are presented as "ladies" in European contexts or even as high-status women on African soil.

Nor can critics point to examples in medieval or Renaissance art of dark-skinned women as love objects.

The Dutch painters were intrigued by the color and physiognomy of Negro men. Kunst refers to artists who used black men as models for portraits or in group scenes: Albert Eeckhour (1621-1674), Rembrandt (1609-1669), and Rubens (1577-1640). Of these, Kunst says, "Later artists have never produced anything better in the way of Negro portraits than these of Dutch and Flemish artists."[50] He might have mentioned another European artist of an earlier period, the German, Dürer (1471-1528). Some paintings of Blacks by Dürer have esthetic appeal from an artist's point of view but would not have struck Europeans as pictures of beautiful women or handsome men, though they may have been viewed as sexually attractive. We have few paintings or drawings of scenes in which ordinary folk of both races may have participated: pilgrimages and carnivals, public houses and taverns.

Kunst remarks on an interesting contrast between medieval and Renaissance depictions of Negroes as subjects in paintings.

> It is revealing for the attitude of the European to the African that from the renaissance [sic] onwards the black people have figured in art as servants. Whereas in the Adoration of the Magi the representatives of all three parts of the earth bow down before the dominion of the son of God, profane art portrays the African as his brother's servant, to use the words of the Bible.[51]

The Adoration paintings continue a tradition of presenting Blacks in dignified roles.[52]

BLACKNESS AND BLACK PEOPLE IN THE CHRISTIAN CHURCH

Medieval scholars inherited from the early Church Fathers a traditional interpretation of the skin color of Ethiopians as a symbol of sin. A Manichaean contrast between black and white was viewed as a metaphor for impurity versus purity. Ethiopians were also considered a special missionary target. Only a detailed content analysis of medieval homilies and commentaries will reveal how pervasive the Manichaean intellectual legacy was, compared to more favorable views of Ethiopians derived from Old Testament references, or from friendly contacts. Neither the Black Knight or Senapo are symbols of sin.

Along with the Manichaean black/white dichotomy, the early Christian tradition transmitted the idea that Christianity could "wash an Ethiop white." The crucial question was not whether a person was white or black, but whether he was Christian, Jew, pagan or infidel. In the world of the supernatural, as in the earthly domain, there were "good" Blacks and "bad" Blacks. Black Madonnas were worshipped here and there across Europe; some black saints were venerated, and one black king among the three Magi stood out vividly as a symbol of the multiracial character of the Christian community. On the negative side, however, devils and imps were sometimes described as black, although red was the most prevalent color assigned to them before the late Renaissance.

Blackness in Christian Demonology

Ambrose, Origen, and Augustine, among the early Church Fathers, considered the color black to be a symbol of sin. Some of the early Christian ascetics envisioned devils as black, but there is no evidence that they developed a consistent demonology featuring black devils. However, other theologians and illustrators of manuscripts, coming later, did so.

One scholar, Hannes Vatter, has defined six types of devils that have always been present in the dreams, visions, hallucinations, and fantasies of English Christians: (1) the Emperor of Hell, (2) the Fallen Angel, (3) the Tempter, (4) the Angel of Death, (5) the *instrumentum dei* or Angel of God, and (6) the Comic Devil.[53] The same types were said to be present on the continent.

Red seems to have been the favorite color used in depicting the Emperor of Hell. Devils who tempted monks and nuns in late medieval times have been described in some detail. They were often black. In pre-medieval times, St. Anthony of Egypt had confrontations with the Devil in many forms and colors, and in one meeting, the Prince of Demons was gigantic and black.[54]

Black "angels of death" occur in British folklore. The expression "black as devils" was sometimes used in England, apparently related to the idea that demons of the lower rank—small black ones—were assigned the task of carrying off condemned souls to hell.[55]

Lucifer, the Fallen Angel, does not seem to have been depicted as black in pre-medieval times. When Dante presented him later, his head bore three faces: black on the left, whitish yellow on the right, and red in the center.[56] *The History of the Damnable Life and Deserved Death of Dr. John Faustus* described Lucifer as "all hairy, but of browne colour like a squirrel."[57]

R. E. L. Masters, in *Eros and Evil,* talks of the extent to which black male demons reportedly seduced women during the Middle Ages and quotes the famous exorcist Brognoli as saying, "the demon would appear in the form of a small black shaggy man with a huge phallus." Intercourse with him was usually described as very unpleasant. Masters notes that when the "witch epidemic" swept Europe, the devil appeared most often as a black man, although "virtually never does anyone report black female succubi [attractive seducing witches]."[58]

These myths arose in the monastic tradition of Catholicism, which emphasizes asceticism and sexual repression. Arturo Graf reports that "black appears as the native color of the demons from the very earliest centuries of Christianity." This, he says, is because the pagans living south of Egypt were black. Jean Devisse has assessed the impact of this ancient tradition on medieval Christians. An older classical tradition in which sexual relations involve pleasure often casts Satyr-Pan as Negroid. This tradition is evident in some of the medieval gargoyles and merges with the concept of the Comic Devil in religious folk drama. In English Morality Plays, the Comic Devil came to prevail over other types, and he was sometimes black. Vatter notes that "the loose talk and obscene gestures of Old Nick on the stage go back to the impish spirit of joyful nature worship." A black Comic Devil was not, therefore, necessarily a demeaning symbol. He might be, rather, a symbol of pleasant experiences to ordinary people. Whatever the reactions were to any of the types of devils presented to the ordinary people in Europe and Britain as black, all devils were never portrayed as black and all Blacks were not cast in the role of devils.[59]

Tendencies to equate "Negroidness" with the demonic, and for the demonic, itself, to have meanings that vary from time to time and place to place, can be explained by the anthropologist's concepts of diffusion and acculturation. They do not require a psychoanalytical explanation such as Carl Jung's suggestion that the presence of black people in dreams is somehow "primordial."[60] Neither Jungian archetypes nor the writings of the early Christian Fathers are needed to account for the tendency in Europe after the ninth century occasionally to make black people demonic symbols. Just as the proximity of Negro pagans influenced the attitude of North African Christians toward Negroes, so did the prolonged conflict with brown and black Muslims after the eighth century. Arabs, Berbers, Moors, Saracens, and Negroes—in the role of Infidels—may have embedded "demonic" images of "black" people in some medieval minds. At times Mohammed himself was called the Devil.

Veneration of the Black Madonna

Standing in sharpest contrast to negative images of blackness and black demons were the Black Madonnas of Western Europe, worshipped not just in the Middle Ages but through to contemporary times. In 1945, over 250 shrines to Black Madonnas existed in Europe; some still attract thousands of pilgrims and thus remain a vital part of contemporary European Catholicism.[61]

There is evidence to indicate that during the period of the first and second Crusades, a popular cult may have flourished in central France that contemporary scholars refer to as the cult of *la vierge noire*. In the early eleventh century, Bernard d'Angers reported his astonishment at what he called the "idolatry" that he witnessed in the upper Loire Valley, which included the Auvergne, Ronergue, and Toulousan, where by ancient custom each church had a statue of its patron on the altar. Apparently these "idols" were small images of the Virgin Mary. There is documentary evidence of a procession in 1255 that included the image of the Holy Virgin from the Puy cathedral. Another text reveals the existence in 1096 of a statue in that cathedral, although no reference was made to its color.[62] The first statue of the Puy Cathedral group that can be definitely characterized as black is documented from manuscript paintings around the year 1601.

We will begin with a look at the history of this veneration, examine some theories that may account for the blackness of certain Madonnas, and finally look at how the cult has survived in modern times.

Vassivière: A Look into the Past

An illustrated travelogue by J. Ajalbert, published as this century began under the title *L'Auvergne*, described the unusual geography of this region in the French Alps, noted for its numerous small extinct volcanic peaks (puys). The author tried to wrap the entire area in a bit of mystery. One chapter was devoted to a discussion of "les vierges noires" with special emphasis upon "Notre Dame de Vassivière."

Ajalbert found that the cult of *la vierge noire* was flourishing in the sixteenth century when the Reformation first came to the Auvergne. The earliest document cited by Ajalbert comes from that period. For reasons that are not clear, the custom of venerating the

Black Virgin was soon "eclipsed" and "abandoned," except in the mountain church at Vassivière. Tales of miracles that were alleged to have occurred there spread, and in 1547 it was said that a local priest was cured when he invoked the Virgin. A sergeant who tried to steal some money left by pilgrims was struck with blindness during the same year. Another sergeant, sent by regional authorities to investigate the reputed miracles, reported that pilgrims were even climbing on their knees up the hill "into the pure air" of the mountain to seek favors. A stillborn baby was revived. Some buried treasure was found. A person struck by lightning was healed. And there was "a peasant, barefoot," who gave thanks to the Black Virgin for rescuing his three-year-old son. A wolf had dropped the boy when his father cried out, "Virgin Mary of Vassivière, save my child!" Someone who scoffed at a procession winding its way up toward the shrine was suddenly crippled in all his limbs.

Such stories impressed the authorities in the administrative city of Besse, and they decided that such a wonder-working image should not be left in a hard-to-reach mountain church. They brought the statue to their city with great pomp and ceremony and installed it in the cathedral. The next morning it was gone. They found the statue back in the shrine at Vassivière. Three more times they brought it down, and three more times it "miraculously" went back.[63]

The authorities in the cathedral town concluded that the Virgin considered her proper place to be a shrine on the solitary high plateau guarding the lowlands. There the image remained, and more "miracles" were noted. An "inexhaustible fountain" that provided drinks for pilgrims dried up when some people tried to defile it by using it for washing. A heretic once tried to drink from it and the water turned foul in the cup, before it touched his lips.[64]

Records of elaborate ceremonies that took place in 1601, and again in 1608 and 1609 tell how pilgrims from throughout the Auvergne, led by religious and secular dignitaries, marched to the shrine amid colorful pageantry. Six thousand people bearing silver crosses, incense burners, tapers, and torches wound their way up the hill. Barefoot girls in white linen led the procession, followed by dignitaries in gold-embroidered satin, velour, and damask, chanting songs and hymns. Children in white robes carried a red and blue banner with an image of the Black Virgin on one side and of St. John the Baptist on the other. Young boys with torches were clad in colorful costumes and crowned with roses.[65]

Within sixty years all of the pomp and ceremony surrounding the Virgin of Vassivière was gone. By 1699, thieves had stolen the lamps, chalices and chasubles, sacred vases, and golden chains from the shrine. The black virgin who had blinded the sergeant who was guilty of larceny now let the plunderers have their way.

Ajalbert does not tell us why. He is more curious about why, in a region noted for the beautiful, blonde women he repeatedly describes in his book, a black Virgin Mary image was so prevalent.

Why Are They Black?

A naive but popular belief is that the Black Madonnas are accurate depictions of the historical mother of Jesus. The distinguished French writer, Romain Rolland, was inclined to think that Christ's mother may have actually been a black woman. As J. A. Rogers quotes him in an article, Rolland wrote:

> Why are the majority of the Virgins that are revered in the celebrated pilgrimages black? At Boulogne-sur-mer, the sailors still carry a Black Virgin in the procession. . . . The famous Virgin of Oropa in the Piedmont is still a Negro woman, as well as the not less legendary one at Montserrat in Catalonia, which receives 60,000 visitors a year. I have been able to trace the history of this one to 718 A.D., and it was always black. Tradition says that it was St. Luke who knew personally the Mother of Christ and carved with his own hand the majority of these Black Virgins. It is interesting to know, therefore, that if the Mother of Christ was not a Negro woman, how it happens that she is a black in France, Switzerland, Italy, and Spain.[66]

Romain Rolland was a novelist, not an anthropologist; he could not be expected to elaborate tests for his hypothesis.

Another possible explanation with biblical ties is suggested by Ajalbert, who begins his chapter on the Black Madonnas with a discussion of the "I am black but beautiful" passage in the Song of Solomon. According to him, the black color is not viewed as racial/ ethnic; instead, he cites the scholars' view of blackness as a symbol of the suffering and the emotional turmoil of both the Shulamite girl who loved Solomon and the Mother of God—the "dark night of the soul" due to disappointment.[67]

Prototypes of the Holy Virgin may have incorporated legends about the black Queen of Sheba and about the Shulamite girl. An erotic aura about them would not have prevented their veneration, for the concept of "Our Lady" in certain areas of feudal Europe referred both to the Virgin Mary and to the knight's beloved (often someone else's wife) when he fought in a tournament. Most students of the subject do not believe that Black Madonnas were ever invested with this erotic quality.

There is one eloquent exception. Olivia Bitton-Jackson, in her book *Madonna or Courtesan*, presents a detailed case for viewing the dark-skinned woman in the Song of Solomon as the prototype for the European Black Madonnas. She writes:

> Young Abishag the Shulamite lives in collective memory as the nubile young woman whose warm flesh comforted the aging king, while Shulamite of the vineyard is remembered as the one who set Solomon, the young king, aflame. As the heroine of the Song of Songs, she is the romantic-erotic element of classical Hebrew poetry.
>
> In Christian art and literature Shulamite is a mystical figure. In early Byzantine miniatures she symbolizes the Church in a dual image. She is either the bride of Jesus or the Virgin Mary. In a series of medieval interpretive illustrations to the Song of Songs called "Hortus Deliciarum," the Jewish maiden Shulamite is depicted as the Virgin flanked by monks on both sides while the daughters of Zion sprawl at her feet. The Church continued this extraordinary identification of Shulamite with the Virgin. For instance, in the sixteenth-century tapestry "Story of the Virgin" in Rheims Cathedral the identification is complete but with the roles reversed: it is Mary who is depicted as Shulamite. Medieval French and Spanish portraits of the Virgin with dark complexion, the celebrated "black madonnas," are in fact representations of the Shulamite described in the Song of Songs as "black but comely." Biblical metaphors for Shulamite, the "Rose of Sharon," the "Garden-dweller," and the "Fountain of the Gardens," were also interpreted by Christian theologians as references to the Virgin Mary. These interpretations must have provided the initial rationale for the association between the erotic Jewess of the vineyard and the Holy Virgin of the Church.
>
> Christian liturgical music also capitalized on the Shulamite theme in celebrations of the Virgin Madonna. English composers of the fifteenth and sixteenth centuries vied with their Dutch and Italian counterparts in providing musical background for verses from the Song of Songs. Some are delectable lyrics of love, others outpourings of passion singing the praises of both the Shulamite and the Madonna. *Monteverdi's choral "Nigra sum" and "Pulchra es" were popular Marian hymns of the seventeenth century*. Cantatas, oratorios and symphonic poems picked up where liturgical music left off, and the phenomenon of the Shulamite-Madonna entered Christian consciousness [italics added].[68]

Ajalbert, too, thought that European interest in the Shulamite woman and in the Queen of Sheba might have led to the cult of the

Black Madonna. Current scholarly opinion does not support this view. Others deny that linkage, but hold that the skin color has symbolic value: expressing mourning or the process of initiation or various occult meanings.

The Puy Madonnas

Other possible explanations for the color of the Black Madonnas have been put forward in a definitive monograph on the French Black Madonnas, and in particular about the Puy Cathedral group. The monograph was published in 1983 as the catalog for an exposition of the Madonnas, presented by Madame Frédérique Vialet, conservator of antiquities and objects of art of the Department of Haute-Loire in France. *Iconographie de la Vierge Noire du Puy* is well documented, with attractive illustrations.[69] A preface by M. Pomarat, president of the Société Académique du Puy, congratulates Madame Vialet and her associates for their meticulous research. He pointed out that "les statues de Vierges Noires" were numerous in France but that their origins were shrouded in legend and mystery.

The history of the Black Madonna in the cathedral at Puy has substantial documentation since the fifteenth century. It has numbered among its visitors not only thousands of pilgrims but also nine kings of France and four popes. She is referred to as "A Virgin in Majesty" because of the regal way in which she sits and holds her child and is clothed and adorned. Madame Vialet, an art historian, defines this as a type that can be compared with Black Madonnas in other parts of France.

By comparing changes in posture of mother and child, type of clothing and adornments placed on the Madonna, presence or absence of a crown and mantle on the mother, and objects held in the baby's hands, Vialet concludes that before the fifteenth century, two types of images were probably venerated in the cathedral at Puy. One of these, the "Roman Majesty" type, is distributed throughout France. In Vialet's opinion a simpler archaic image became merged with some "Roman Majesty" characteristics in the "Puy Cathedral" type, which is found only in towns and monasteries of the central French plateau.[70] A picture of this style that was painted in 1622 by Hieronymous Dumonteilh (see plate 7) is highly relevant to our discussion. Not only is this seventeenth-century Virgin a Dark Madonna—she is a *Negro* Madonna. The Child Jesus is Negro, too. This painting should be contrasted with plate 8. Non-negroid Black Madonnas were more prevalent.

During the twentieth century, Vialet relates, historians have tended to explain the "blackness" of the statue in the Puy cathedral in one of three ways. Some believe that a statue of Isis was brought from the East and placed upon the altar at an unspecified early date. When the clergy substituted a "white Christian statue," indignant and dissatisfied worshipers blackened it to make it look more like the original Isis.[71] A similar theory holds that an Isis-Horus concept was merged with a so-called "Roman Majesty" concept of the Madonna to produce the Puy type. Finally, some believe that an ancient "Roman Majesty" reliquary statuette was gradually blackened, beginning in the eleventh or twelfth century, to mimic the fashion of Oriental icons with a bronze tint, which were brought home by returning Crusaders. A gradual blackening due to other causes followed, reaching its peak at the end of the Middle Ages.

Vialet finds no convincing evidence to support any of the theories connecting the Black Madonna of Puy with the Isis-Horus concept. However, she does not rule out the likelihood that the popularizing of Middle Eastern myths brought back by Crusaders—including a belief that the Prophet Jeremiah had carved a Madonna and Child out of a Palestinian wood—made a dark-skinned Madonna acceptable. This myth may have influenced the "blackening" process in its early stages.

In presenting her own theory, Vialet notes that in the sixteenth century, the color of the statue was being referred to as "machares" or "bruns." During the seventeenth century, it was described as "noir," like "l'Ethiopien et le More"; while in the eighteenth it was said to "look like polished ebony."[72] Vialet is convinced that these descriptions reflect a process of progressive "blackening" of the statue itself and of the Virgin and Child in the minds of the devotees.

She believes that prior to the sixteenth century the statue was accidentally blackened due to smoke from the candles burning constantly beside it. In fact the word "machares" was a local vernacular term that meant "darkened by soot." During the seventeenth and eighteenth centuries, when it became fashionable to think of this particular Virgin as black, paint of that color was deliberately applied. Numerous paintings of the image show an elaborately dressed and bejewelled very black Madonna. In the eighteenth and nineteenth centuries an esthetic style rather than religious mysticism may have been involved in the increased blackening of the image. In any event "black" had positive associations.

The theories that Vialet puts forward echo or include elements of those presented elsewhere to account for Black Madonnas throughout Europe.[73] Some modern scholars argue that age—or candle smoke—darkened images that were once white. Another theory holds that they were exotic items brought home by Crusaders from the Middle East. Ajalbert suggested that, in some places, the Egyptian goddess Isis with the infant Horus on her lap had been transformed into the Virgin Mary holding Jesus, and so the tradition of a black Mother of Christ was handed down. Another possibility was that Black Madonnas were ancient idols of old indigenous European cults, effigies that Christianity co-opted just as its priests utilized old sites where ancient divinities were worshipped.[74]

The French anthropologist, Roger Bastide, attributes the popularity of the Black Madonnas to the assumed fact that ordinary people conceived of her as "a sorceress," not as the "pure Mother of God," that role being reserved for the white Madonnas.[75] We know from other Bastide writings that his devotion to Freudian interpretations leads him to think that black people are id symbols for Europeans, incorporating attitudes connected with repressed sexuality. We can assume that he combines this idea with a prevalent theory that Christianity suppressed some ancient, female-dominated religious cults that subsequently emerged in the Middle Ages as "witchcraft." Bastide presents no empirical evidence to support his view of Black Madonnas, although serious anthropological field work might conceivably turn up such data. In fact, evidence from two existing shrines indicates that the Black Virgin is not viewed as a sorceress, but has functioned much as White Virgins do at their shrines.

Black Madonnas Today

An American anthropologist studying the Black Madonna of the Montserrat monastery in Spain during the mid 1980s provided some data for checking Bastide's generalization.[76] Over 50,000 pilgrims a year come to this Benedictine monastery nearly 3,000 feet up the side of a mountain near Barcelona. The *Encyclopedia Britannica* describes this Nuestra Señora de Montserrat, Patrona de Catalonia, as "one of the most celebrated images in Spain. . . . small, black, and carved of wood, but possesses magnificent robes and jewels."[77] The anthropologist conducted numerous interviews with pilgrims and residents of surrounding villages. He also took photographs of the shrine and statue and examined all the available documentary material.

The present statue, replacing one that was destroyed by fire early in this century, is carved of white wood and painted very black. The features of the woman are aquiline, not Negroid. The unsophisticated still believe that the original was carved by St. Luke and brought to Barcelona by St. Peter. When the Muslims landed, the statue was hidden in a cave near Montserrat. According to the legend, Gondemar, the bishop of Vich in the time of Charlemagne, heard sweet sounds and smelled pleasing odors coming from a cave, and found the statue there.[78] When he tried to take the statue back to town, it grew so heavy that he put it down and erected a chapel on the spot.

Contemporary devotees do not think of the Black Madonna as Negroid, Moorish, mulatto, or morena despite her color, the anthropologist found. No mystical or magical significance is attributed to her blackness, but being black does not detract from her holiness or miraculous powers. A study of the offerings and requests for aid over the years at Montserrat reveal no evidence that she was ever conceived of as a "sorcerer," to use Bastide's term. Today Our Lady of Montserrat is asked to cure physical ailments, assist in passing examinations and to provide good luck in ventures ranging from fishing and farming to wooing fair ladies. In the villages of Catalonia, young people view the Virgin as a symbol of Catalan nationalism, not at all troubled that she does not fit the somatic norm of the area.

The much-publicized Black Madonna of Czestochowa also functions as a symbol of national unity to the Polish public, according to two Polish anthropologists who have studied that shrine.[79] Although not as dark as the Virgin of Montserrat, she is far from the Polish somatic norm image. But esthetic and erotic evaluations seem irrelevant in both cases. The mystical/religious domain is the sole concern: she preserves the nation and cares for individuals.

The Polish people do not view her as black in an ethnic or racial sense, the anthropologists tell us. The word they use for her, *czarna*, means black, but there is a different word for "mulatto woman" or "Negress."[80] The legend surrounding Our Lady of Czestochowa also links St. Luke with its fabrication.

It is unlikely that we will ever know precisely why the Black Madonnas were fabricated, or even if the same explanation covers all. What is clear from both historical and contemporary accounts is that their blackness is no deterrent to their veneration by ordinary people. This provides a crucial test of the Degler-Gergen theory that all people share negative attitudes toward blackness.

The Cult of St. Maurice

An interesting ecological fact is that shrines to the Black Madonna are concentrated in certain parts of Latin Europe while the cult of the Black Warrior, Maurice, was concentrated in Germanic Europe (see map 7). There is seemingly only one point of overlap: the area around Zurich, Switzerland, where the Benedictine monastery at Einsiedeln included a shrine to the local Black Madonna at a time when relics of St. Maurice from the same monastery were being taken away to cathedrals in Cologne and Prague. Here both male and female black sacred symbols were venerated.[81]

There are strong similarities in the devotion to both figures, and their study leads us to the same conclusion about the positive image black people enjoyed in Western Europe at the dawn of an age dominated by White Racism. We will begin with the historic St. Maurice, and then examine how German emperors used him as a political symbol.

The Theban Martyrs

In A.D. 287, a legion of African soldiers was sent to suppress an uprising of slaves in Gaul. According to one tradition, their *leader primicerius* was Maurice, an African from Thebes in upper Egypt. Arriving at Aganaum in what is now the Swiss Rhone valley, Maurice learned that these rebels were Christians, like him and his legion. According to one source, he refused to march further. The legion agreed to send a message to the emperor that they would not fight fellow Christians.

Maximian, then reigning with Diocletian, rushed to Aganaum with soldiers. He first demanded that Maurice and his men make a sacrifice to pagan gods. They refused. Tradition attributes heroic words to Maurice:

> Sire, we are soldiers but we are also Servitors of Christ, a fact that we proudly confess. To you we owe military service; to Him, the homage of a pure and innocent life. From you we receive our pay; from Him, we hold the benefit of life. That is why, sire, we cannot obey you without denying God, the Creator of all things, our Master as well as yours, whether you acknowledge it or not.

The emperor, enraged, ordered his soldiers to decimate the legion of six hundred men. As every tenth person stepped forward, he was promised wealth and promotion if he would repudiate Maurice's stand. As each refused, he was put to death by the sword.

The remaining soldiers were ordered again to sacrifice. Again, they refused, "bidding one another to be courageous in the name of Christ." Another decimation was carried out, and a third. Finally Maurice spoke:

> We have seen our companions fall under the sword. We have been spattered with their blood. We do not grieve for them. We rather

envy them the privilege of dying for the one who died on the cross for us. Do what you will. No terror or torture can frighten us. We are ready to die. We boldly confess that we are Christians and that we cannot attack fellow Christians.

Emperor Maximian then ordered the remaining troops, including Maurice, their commander, put to death.

The story of these "Theban Martyrs" spread as the scope and vigor of persecution of Christians increased under the Roman Empire. Eucherius, bishop of Lyon, later built a church where the marytrdom occurred. Eventually their leader was canonized. J. A. Rogers calls Maurice "the principal saint of central and southern Germany, and parts of France, Switzerland, Spain and Italy" and patron of Cracow, Coburg, Lauenberg, and Savoy, as well as "of dyers, clothmakers, and swordsmiths."[82]

A Symbol of the Empire

During the late ninth and early tenth centuries, power in Western Europe shifted from the Franks to the Saxons, who were expanding in an area occupied by pagan Slavs and functioning as a bulwark against Hungarian invasions. The early rulers of what has been called the Saxon Dynasty cemented relationships between the Crown and the Roman Catholic Church.

Otto I of Saxony made St. Maurice a symbol in one of Christendom's largest cooperative armed ventures, which smashed the Hungarian threat at Augsburg in A.D. 955. Afterward, he founded and endowed an archbishopric at Magdeburg, establishing a cathedral there that was to be the spiritual center of a large missionary province devoted to converting the pagan Slavs of Poland to the east. St. Maurice was also a key symbol of this project.

When Pope John XII anointed Otto as head of the Holy Roman Empire in A.D. 962, the coronation probably took place at the altar to St. Maurice that already existed in St. Peter's.[83] The following year Otto accepted the surrender of Mieszko I, prince of Poland, who eventually accepted Christianity as well as Otto's sovereignty. In this victory over the Poles, Otto marched under the banner of Maurice, and the banner of Saxony bears the black saint's insignia to this day. Kunst tells us that Otto carried into battle a lance that tradition said belonged to Maurice. Otto believed that the lance gave him victory over the heathens of Europe. The lance

was henceforth looked upon as a symbol of German kingship and can be seen even today among the imperial insignia in the treasury

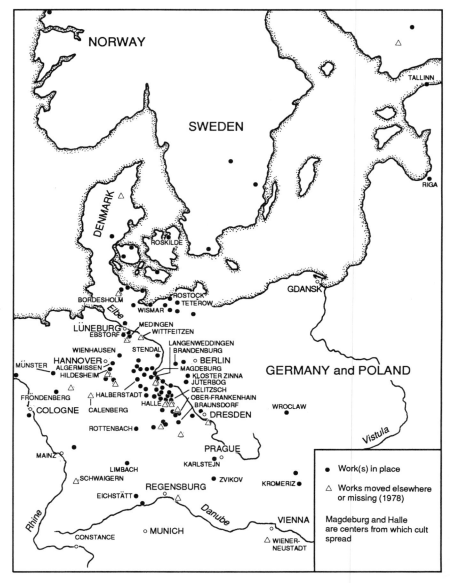

MAP 7. Saint Maurice: Diffusion of the Cult since a.d. 1200
Adapted from Jean Devisse, *The Image of the Black in Western Art*,
vol. 2, pt. 1, p. 270.   Menil Foundation, Houston

of the Vienna Hofburg. The veneration of St. Maurice quickly spread from Magdeburg to other parts of eastern Germany.[84]

In the thirteenth century, Maurice became a symbol used by German kings in their effort to give meaning to what had been considered an empty title: Emperor of the Holy Roman Empire. Frederick II of the Hohenstaufen Dynasty, which used Negroes on its coat of arms, became King of Sicily and Jerusalem as well as of Germany. Frederick turned St. Maurice into a highly visible symbol of something the early Church Fathers had spoken of, Christian Ethiopia as precursor of the triumph of the Universal Church.

But Frederick was also a lover of the dramatic and the exotic, and he realized the value of pageantry in popularizing the aims of his dynasty and publicizing himself. Having made Sicily a part of the Holy Roman Empire, he proceeded to exploit the black presence that had long been a part of the island ethos. Frederick took black Moors into his entourage and introduced Germans to Moors—in the flesh. They no longer knew Blacks only in mythology and legend. Kaplan writes of this king as follows:

> Among the Moslems who remained in Sicily after its return to Christian rule in the eleventh century there were many blacks. . . . In 1224-1225 Henry's son the Holy Roman Emperor Frederick II moved many of the remaining Sicilian Moslems to Lucera in Apulia, and bound them directly to his personal service. The Moslem enclave functioned as a repository for camels and other exotic beasts used by Frederick to impress the populace while on the march across Italy and Germany during the 1230s, and black Lucerans accompanied the animals on these processions ["Ethiopians having knowledge of rare skills accompanying apes and leopards and serving as guards"]. . . . Frederick also kept several young black musicians in his retinue and by 1240 his personal chamberlain was a black African by the name of Johannes Maurus, who later became the governor of Lucera itself. The proclivity for blacks at Frederick's court was not merely a capricious idiosyncrasy, but a means of suggesting the Hohenstaufen's claim to a universal imperial sovereignty that might include "the two Ethiopias, the country of the black Moors, the country of the Parthians, Syria, Persia . . . Arabia, Chaldea, and even Egypt." Given Frederick's personal preferences and propaganda needs, *it can scarcely be an accident that St. Maurice is first depicted as a black man in a work from the imperial city of Magdeburg executed during the 1240s.* So particularly was Frederick associated with African retainers that an imposter who appeared in Germany in 1283 (long after Frederick's death) used three black

servants and a black chamberlain dispensing treasure as proofs of his imperial identity [italics added].[85]

A third period of intense preoccupation with black symbols occurred during the reign of Charles IV (1347-1378). Through the influence of Pope Clement VI, Charles, hereditary king of Bohemia, was elected king of Germany. To establish his continuity with the Saxon kings, he immediately began to emphasize his devotion to the cult of St. Maurice. In 1354, he journeyed to the monastery of Einsiedeln near Zurich to secure a portion of the alleged relic of St. Maurice's arm that had been kept there since the reign of Otto. Artists and makers of stained glass windows took their cues from the Emperor's emphasis on Maurice, and the image of the black saint began to appear at churches and chapels throughout the empire. Kaplan, mentioning some of these, comments that

> Representations of St. Maurice executed under Charles and his successors usually show him as black. The first and most important such image was painted just before 1367 in the Chapel of the Holy Cross at Karlstejn by the great master Theodoric. One of 127 separate images, mostly of saints whose relics were to be found in the chapel, this is a moving depiction of an African black as a god-fearing and soldierly saint.[86]

St. Maurice served several political ends for Charles IV. This sophisticated scholarly man spoke Latin, Greek, French, German, and Italian; he founded Charles University in Prague, the capital of Bohemia. But he also had to be a soldier and statesman. When he was crowned king of Burgundy and wished to emphasize the separateness of that area from France, he chose St. Sigismund as a symbol. According to one tradition, this sixth-century ruler of pre-Frankish Burgundy had discovered the relics of St. Maurice and the Theban Martyrs and instituted the custom of venerating them.

At his coronation, Charles was welcomed by Count Amadeus VI with a banner bearing the white and red arms of St. Maurice. The two of them later journeyed to St. Maurice-en-Valais to venerate relics of Sigismund and Maurice there and to negotiate release of a portion of Sigismund's skull and Maurice's battle axe. Charles IV named his new son Sigismund. When he in turn became King of Germany, Sigismund, like his father, journeyed to St. Maurice-en-Valais. Meanwhile two churches had been dedicated to the black saint in Prague.[87]

St. Maurice thus provided a unifying symbol for Germans, Bohemians, and Burgundians. Charles had a broader, old historic objective.

Kaplan suggests that "The closely woven blend of religious and secular acts and imagery, which the cults of Sigismund and Maurice exemplify, is of course typical of fourteenth century culture." Charles, like Frederick II, saw himself as destined to make the Holy Roman Empire universal and this included bringing all of "Ethiopia" within the orbit of Christianity. "Frequently the ideas of Frederick II are alluded to, although without the antipapal and cosmically arrogant tone which the Hohenstaufen emperor had favored."[88]

At the very beginning of the reign, one of Charles' apologists was already speaking of his sovereign's right to rule all nations. Kaplan refers to "the political iconography which he and his advisors fostered." Charles IV likened himself to the biblical priest-king Melchizedek. Kaplan suggests a parallel with "the African priest-king Prester John," to whom considerable attention was being given at the time. He states further that

> In the art of this place and period [Prague] black Africans frequently serve as representatives of the immense variety of human peoples, all of whom are offered spiritual salvation. Charles, attempting to merge the spiritual with the material world, also offers these varied peoples the benefit of a just rule on earth.[89]

A complicated mural in the Emmaus monastery of Prague is viewed by Kaplan as an extreme example of Charles portraying himself in the role of priest-king, feeding the hungry multitudes in both a literal and figurative sense. Several Blacks appear mixed in with crowds of whites. In Kaplan's view,

> In the broadest sense the group of images in which blacks appear is a universalist statement which can be interpreted in either secular or ecclesiastical terms: all people shall be nourished by Christianity. . . . Secular overtones are inescapably present . . . the entire spectrum of humanity is depicted in these scenes, with the black component most forthrightly expressing the central universalist notion. . . . Charles while skirting outright blasphemy makes an attempt in his official propaganda to liken his person to Christ himself.[90]

Maurice remained a symbol of the Holy Roman Empire through its conclusion under Charles V, who went on to rule an empire in the New World.

When the German core of the Holy Roman Empire, along with Bohemia and Moravia, became the center of the Protestant Reformation, Maurice, associated as he was with practices and regimes ridiculed and denounced as "corrupt," must have suffered a loss in prestige among the masses throughout Germany and other Protestant lands. His name remains attached to a few cities in Alpine areas where the legend of the Theban Martyrs also began, but they stir no deep emotion-laden memories.

As with cases involving Black Madonnas, some contemporary scholars attempt to "talk away" the blackness of St. Maurice. One scholar, writing in the *Encyclopedia Britannica*, claims that the legend is a garbled version of a story about an *Asian* martyr. Kaplan, who has studied the growth of the Maurice cult carefully, is convinced that as late as A.D. 1070, Maurice was not thought of as black. However, lack of references to his color should not be taken as conclusive. It is likely that Otto, as well as those who treasured the story of the Theban martyrs for centuries before him, considered him black because of his name. Both the name Maurice and Thebes have onomastic value in placing the saint as an African.

In any case, paintings and statues of the thirteenth and fourteenth centuries clearly show that St. Maurice was believed to be a black man during the height of his celebrity as a symbol of the Holy Roman Empire. This, more than the historical actuality of his origin, is crucial to our inquiry. It provides another important case refuting the Degler-Gergen proposition about the universal denigration of blackness. It also points up the extent to which attitudes toward "Negroidness" have been conditioned by struggles for power among non-Negroid groups who co-opt "blackness" for their ends.

In a monumental contribution in the study of European religious iconography, *The Rise of the Black Magus in Western Art* (1983), Dr. Paul H. D. Kaplan argues that the cult surrounding St. Maurice was reinforced, under certain conditions in the thirteenth and fourteenth centuries, by Europe's fascination with the concept of "the black king."[91] One source was legends about a black Wise Man among the three Magi who "came from the East" to adore the infant Jesus. The other source was legends about the great Christian king of color, Prester John.[92]

Although the Black Magus was rarely in the central role, he was used routinely in artistic and liturgical depictions of the Adoration of the Magi, and not necessarily in a subordinate position.[93] We shall now examine the origins of the Prester John legends and how they became a focus of hope among distraught Europeans on the eve of the overseas expansion that led to the New World.

"Le Bon Ethiopien" and Prester John

Throughout the Middle Ages, legends of the king Senapo, whom

we previously discussed, grew and were transformed. Ariosto's
Orlando Furioso gives this version:

> The Emperor Senapo [Prester John]
> Rules Ethiopia, and in his hand
> He wields no scepter but the cross alone.
> The Red Sea is the border of his land
> Where cities teem and golden bullion abounds . . .
> Inlaid on walls, on roof-tops, and on floors,
>   are rarest pearls and other precious gems. . . .
> And the Egyptian Sultan, it is said,
> Pays tribute and is subject to the King.
> Senapo by his subjects he is named,
> And Prester John among us he is famed. . . .
> Of all the many kings of this domain
> None could compare with him in wealth and
> might.[94]

Out of the story of African military aid for Charlemagne grew the
myth of a great Christian king living somewhere in the East, either
in Asia or Africa. As the struggle between Saracen and Christian
became almost institutionalized after the first Crusade, Prester John
was considered a possible ally of Western Christians struggling
against the Muslims.[95]

Henri Baudet, a European scholar who stresses the importance of
the medieval concept of *le bon éthiopien*, notes that during the
period after the last Crusade, a consensus emerged that Prester John's
kingdom was in Africa. In 1440 an Ethiopian diplomatic mission
visited the Vatican. By then there was no doubt about where
Ethiopia was located or about the color and features of its people.[96] It
seemed logical to the medieval mind to assume that Prester John
would be found in Africa, the home of the delegation, and that he
would look like the well-known St. Maurice was thought to have
looked.

> The idea gathered momentum that the old Christian kingdom of
> Ethiopia might perhaps prove to be an ally on the other side of the
> hostile world of Islam. . . . All sorts of detailed accounts of Ethiopia
> now reached the West and caused hitherto nebulous ideas to take
> clear and expressive shape, crystallizing Europe's image of Ethiopia
> in a highly positive way. They revived memories of old legends that
> suggested the existence of traditional and natural ties between
> Ethiopian and Latin Christianity.[97]

Baudet has suggested that, with the rise of Islam as a threat to Christendom, the status of Blacks tended to rise in the eyes of the literate classes. The concept of *le bon éthiopien* was related to this phenomenon of increased contact. Referring to the Crusades, Baudet notes that "large scale sorties from the beleaguered Western fortress in the twelfth and thirteenth centuries revealed new horizons and created a new outlook."[98] People from all over Europe saw Saracens (i.e., eastern Muslims) living on their own soil—black, brown, yellow, and white—and were impressed by what they saw. They fantasized about India and China, too, as travelers explored these lands and brought back tales of wealth and splendor. The myth of Prester John grew.

By the end of the fifteenth century, Prester John was more than the object of hopeful fantasy. He had become the object of an actual search in Africa by the Portuguese. Finding Prester John and his fabled land provided some of the impetus for their exploration of Africa. Baudet continues:

> Pierre d'Ailly, whose famous work *Imaga Mundi*, written at the beginning of the fifteenth century, contained all of the geographical knowledge of his day and had such a profound effect on Columbus, provided a full account of the theories put forward over the years concerning both Ethiopia itself and the nature of its inhabitants. He thus expressed the pronounced interest which the late Middle Ages took in the Ethiopian question. . . . Vasco de Gama [sic] carried letters for Prester John as Columbus was to do later for the Great Khan.[99]

The burning of John Huss at the stake in 1415 had unleashed Utopian currents and anticipation of a New Age. Especially after 1456, when the first Bible came off Guttenberg's press, peasant revolts were sometimes clothed in millenarian ideology and imagery. Armed conflicts within Europe were not only frequent but prolonged, as witness the Thirty Years War and the Hundred Years War.[100] Among ordinary people during these troubled years the belief that the end of the world was near became very widespread, and the many trials and tribulations were interpreted as "signs of the times."

There was a widespread belief in the coming of an "Emperor-Redeemer" who would also be "The Great Prince of Peace." His arrival would signal the final battle between the forces of Light and the forces of Antichrist. Baudet contends that

> Europe now became aware of a connection between the expectation and the almost celestial ruler of blessed Ethiopia. . . . So Prester

John came to be seen in many perspectives, being linked with Caspar [the Wise Man], with Queen Bilkis of Sheba, whose dominions Josephus had localized on the Nile, and with the myths relating to an earthly Paradise. . . . *the Negro thus appeared "canonized" in our culture before the Indian was discovered* [italics added].[101]

It is significant that Europeans in the Middle Ages did not see anything incongruous in the idea of a black Priest-King leading the forces of Light to victory in the struggle against the Antichrist (i.e., "Prince of Darkness" in Christian symbolism). This only poses a problem for those interpreters of symbols who have been conditioned within our own post-medieval racist cultures, and who think that Manichaean verbal symbolism must necessarily transfer to social relations.

Summary

While there were some negative attitudes in Europe toward the color black and toward black people prior to the sixteenth century, most of the images presented in Church art, and in some of the legends, were positive.

Historical research suggests a high positive evaluation of the color white during the Middle Ages and considerable ambivalence about black, but little carry-over of any negative associations to people. Neither black as a color or as a skin pigmentation was evaluated as being completely negative until the transatlantic African slave trade became a lucrative international enterprise during the sixteenth century. This required a conscious or unconscious suppression—or perhaps sheer neglect—of favorable Negro images in the cultural lore of Europe and in its religious iconography.

The images of Blacks in the popular literature of the troubadours were mixed. There was hostility toward non-Christian religions to which most Blacks adhered, and some initial shock at the black appearance, but these were portrayed as overcome by displays of courage and good will, as the Black Knight and the portrayals of St. Maurice and Prester John show.

Real black people were seldom seen outside of the Iberian peninsula and the Italian city states. Elsewhere, well-defined socially transmitted stereotypes about Negro behavior and temperament (esthetic, erotic, status-allocating, and mystical/religious) did not exist within European Christendom prior to the sixteenth century. However, a very favorable image of mythological Blacks was widespread during the thirteenth and fourteenth centuries. Of importance is the fact that the Blacks who were favorably portrayed as sacred figures or legendary heroes among the European Christians were not slaves or the descendants of slaves, like Bilal and Antar in the Muslim world. They were figures of considerable status.

Maurice entered European history as a soldier martyred for refusing to repudiate Christianity. Otto I made him a symbol of his fight against white pagans, adding Slavic lands to his expanding Saxon kingdom in the process. Maurice was later adopted as a symbol of the "universal" pretensions of the Hohenstaufen emperors and became the most cherished among a number of black symbols during the rule of Charles IV. The final use of Maurice as a symbol of "the universal Holy Roman Empire" came under Charles V, but by then, Spain had embarked upon a policy of using African slaves in the newly discovered American lands. A very different image of "the Negro" was about to replace the images of medieval Christendom. Local shrines in Europe devoted to the Theban Martyrs continued to attract some pilgrims since Maurice was canonized, even though the concept of a Holy Roman Empire was dead, and the image of the black man as a born slave eventually supplanted the benign black images of medieval Christendom. St. Maurice as a hero was dysfunctional to the regimes based on White Racism in the Americas, and his cult was not introduced there.

Although Baudet asserted that the Negro was virtually "canonized" in European Christendom on the eve of the great overseas expansion, he did not mention that the Black Madonna—the black Virgin Mary—was the object of veneration at numerous European shrines. These remain a feature of contemporary European Catholicism. Whatever way they became so colored, the Black Madonnas were esteemed, both for the woman they portrayed and for the miracles attributed to their invocation.

Even a relatively minor figure, the Queen of Sheba, is instructive. Kaplan believes that a shift toward conceiving the queen as black rather than white can be attributed to three individuals: Isidore of the seventh century, Hrabanus Maurus of the ninth, and Honorius Augustodunensis of the twelfth century. A cumulative study of their work led churchmen to accept the idea that Ethiopians were symbols and prototypes of the Gentiles who were to be eventually brought under the wing of the universal church. That idea was reactivated with some vigor by the Crusades.

There were negative images as well. On the abstract level, Manichaean symbolism of black and white tended to be reinforced at the "dark" pole by the cults of alchemy and witchcraft that existed within Catholicism, as the Black Mass shows. In the southern European countries where contact with Blacks was frequent, there was some color prejudice, though not nearly as strong as the religious prejudice that targeted Moors, Saracens and Jews.

There are differing opinions, too, about the meaning of black sacred symbols. Bastide, the French anthropologist who says the Black Madonna was viewed as a sorceress, insists that contemporary Blacks bear the burden of traditional derogatory images of blackness and Negroes that have very deep roots in Christianity. Bastide ignores St. Maurice and the Prester John myth and claims, without providing empirical evidence, to find unhealthy attitudes among the peasants and proletariat.[102]

A devoted Freudian, Bastide, in one article, interprets "the actual Black person or mulatto as an 'id symbol,'" representing sexuality, and therefore *evil*, to Christian scholars and laymen. Granted, for the sake of argument, that his interpretation is plausible, the fact remains that cultural patterning as well as Freudian mechanisms have played a role. It would seem that Bastide, in this instance though not always, overemphasizes the effects of abstract color systems on interpersonal relations and the influence of Freudian mechanisms on race relations.

Bastide ignores the economic sphere in which the sociocultural and psychological evaluations of blackness took place. As European explorers moved down the coast of Africa and across an ocean to the New World, Utopian conceptions of Africa and Africans began to give way to the imperatives of mercantile capitalism.

The Portuguese discovered the Kongo, but its ruler was pagan and some of its customs shocking. Zimbabwe's inhabitants were rich in minerals but "barbarian." Finally, they reached the land of "Prester John." Ethiopia was Christian but hostile to Roman Catholicism.[103] It became a military ally, but it was clearly no earthly "paradise." The English adventurers who followed made no pretense of looking for a Priest-King as they scrambled after gold and the land's other wealth.

Meanwhile, the discovery of the Americas shifted much of the Utopian expectation away from Africa. The location moved west: in his third letter home, "Columbus expressed the view that Paradise was situated south of the Equator, lying somewhere on top of a mountain in the land recently discovered."[104] Columbus also noted, on this first voyage, that the Caribbean people he had found were not only attractive and ripe for conversion, but "ready for productive labor."

A few Spanish conquistadores searched for Paradise; most, however, searched for mines of gold and silver, enslaved the Indians, and pillaged prosperous kingdoms where they found them. The British never searched for Paradise. After pirating the Spanish galleons, the British settled down to make a fortune from sugar grown on plantations by Africans they transported from the land of the fabled Prester John to a place that was the hoped-for American Eldorado only to white folk.[105]

Although some negative attitudes and emotions about blackness and black people existed in Mediterranean and European cultures, these concepts did not create the system of racial slavery or the ideology that sanctioned it, White Racism. That was accomplished by the capitalist system's need for a plentiful supply of low-cost labor.

7. THE EVOLUTION OF RACIAL SLAVERY

In 1786, one year before the American Constitution was adopted, John Jay made a significant statement about slavery. Congress was being pressured to urge the British to return black slaves who had run away and taken refuge with them during the Revolutionary War. Jay, who was secretary for foreign affairs under the Confederation, objected to making any such attempt:

> If a war should take place between France and Algiers, and in the course of it France should invite the American slaves there to run away from their masters, and actually receive and protect them in their camp, what would Congress and indeed the world think and say of France, if, in making peace with Algiers she should give up those American slaves to their former Algerian masters? Is there any difference between the two cases than this, viz., that the American slaves in Algiers are white people whereas the African slaves at New York were black people?[1]

As late as 1847, Senator Charles Sumner was lecturing on "White Slavery in the Barbary States," and "redemption societies" were still trying to rescue white Christian women from North African harems and white artisans from slavery. Incidentally, there were reports that captives were not always willing to exchange life as a slave in North Africa for life in the working-class slums of English cities.[2]

These events of the not too distant past remind us that while a brisk commerce in human bodies existed around the Mediterranean from antiquity through the eighteenth century, the merchandise was never exclusively black. War captives increased this pool of unfree labor.[3] Those who write popular histories have allowed the public to forget how recently white people were enslaved by other white people in Europe and by brown and black people in North Africa.

The textbooks inform us that serfdom replaced slavery in Europe, but fail to indicate that slavery still existed in some places on that continent when the Spaniards pushed out across the Atlantic in 1492. Contemporary scholars, using a voluminous body of well-researched literature on the transition from slavery in ancient

Greece and Rome, point out that slavery continued on a small scale as serfdom became the dominant social formation in Europe.[4]

European Christians objected to the enslavement of other Christians, just as Muslims objected to enslaving other Muslims.[5] However, this principle never endangered the maintenance of a slave sector. Slaves from the pagan lands of eastern Europe were marched through Germany and France, down the Rhone Valley to Mediterranean slave markets.[6] The word "slave" or "esclavus" gradually replaced the old Roman term, "servus." Thus, an ethnic name came to refer to a form of bondage: "Slavs" became "slaves." Why this occurred is outlined in the *Encyclopedia Britannica Dictionary* under the definition of slave: "originally a Slav because many Slavs were conquered and enslaved." The word is a reminder that black Africans have not been the only people in relatively modern times who have been bought and sold as slaves.

After the Crusades began, Muslim prisoners of war added merchandise of many colors to the slave market.[7] But for centuries, color was not a salient factor in describing slaves. It would become so. On November 17, 1450, less than half a century before Columbus sailed, Bertrand Cristels of Peripignan in France sold Jean Salvator, "un nègre de 20 ans," for the price of forty ducats. On July 5, 1451, he bought a Russian of the same age from a native of Barcelona for 84 ducats. The record does not say why the Russian brought over twice as much on the market, but from a black perspective the most significant point is that whites as well as Blacks were being sold as slaves.[8]

In fact, Jean Salvator, the twenty-year-old Negro, represented the minority color group among the slaves in southern France and the Iberian peninsula during the early fifteenth century.[9] Yet within a hundred years, black slaves would outnumber whites. In this fact lies the key to the ascendancy of derogatory images of Blacks.

The rise of the Turks, who captured Constantinople in 1453, caused pressures on Western Europe that brought an escalating demand for cheap agricultural labor at the same time that a steady flow of white slaves from the Black Sea area was diminishing. The Turks preferred to use the white slaves themselves, not to sell them. Portugal, on the other hand, was now able to provide a regular supply of slaves from the coasts of West Africa and Angola.

The transformation of slavery from a multiracial phenomenon into *racial* slavery involving Negroes exclusively has been traced in a masterful manner by the Belgian scholar, Charles Verlinden. He and his students have produced a definitive work in French on the history of slavery, supplemented by eleven essays published in English by the Cornell University Press in 1970. It is his conclusion that there is an *"uninterrupted succession from medieval slavery in Europe to the colonial slavery of the Italian possessions in the Levant and Atlantic Islands of the two Iberian states, and the transfer of the institutions to the New World"* [italics added].[10]

We shall begin our consideration of the evolution of *racial* slavery with an examination of how Turkish pressures in eastern Europe influenced both the sugar industry and the slave trade in a way that restructured social institutions. We shall see how the type of slavery changed as it was transported to the New World, and how White Racism emerged to support the new institution. There were very clear distinctions between attitudes and behavior toward black people in the various European nations that were the chief settlers of the Americas.

Most relevant were differences between the Iberian nations of Spain and Portugal, Catholic countries where black and brown people had filled various roles for centuries, and England, a Protestant nation that had little recent experience with Blacks or with slavery when that country began its colonial empire. Taking each country separately, we shall look at historical factors that shaped attitudes and behavior toward Blacks and slavery. Then, we shall make a closer study of these attitudes, noting how Blacks fared in these countries during the centuries when the institution of racial slavery was emerging in the New World. Finally, we shall see how sharply the situation in the "Mother Countries" differed from that in the overseas colonies where White Racism would become the dominant form of race relations for centuries, eventually "corrupting" the European continent as well.

THE SUGAR INDUSTRY AND THE SHIFT TO RACIAL SLAVERY

The first references to "Soudannise" slaves in southern Europe appear on bills of sale and wills after the twelfth century, distinguishing "strange" pagan Blacks from the more familiar Islamized Blacks—Sarrasins—and *ladinos* or Christian Negroes. During the thirteenth century, the color of captured Muslim slaves—"white Moor" or "black Moor"—is regularly included in various documents from the Christian Catalonia-Aragon area of Spain. The reason for specifying skin color is unclear. Professor Verlinden believes the references are used descriptively to identify individual slaves, and have no ethnic or racial import.

> A new element made its appearance in the documents of the 13th century, always qualifying the term "sarrasin." The captives could be white, brown, olive, etc. It is evident that these qualifications although very imprecise were introduced into the legal instruments because the buyers and sellers were emphasizing the diverse sources of the slaves.[11]

Conversions to Christianity began to reduce the supply of white slaves in Andalusia at the same time that the Christian Reconquest was diminishing the flow of Muslim prisoners of war. Yet, as one outstanding medievalist informs us, the slave trade actually became more active in southern Europe during the twelfth and thirteenth centuries, thanks to a new source of supply: black pagans from below the Sahara. Black slaves first appeared in large numbers on the Iberian peninsula in the last quarter of the thirteenth century, with distinctions being made between "sarrasin noir," "nègre baptisé," and just plain "noir." Obviously both race and religion were important to prospective buyers (see chart 8).

Color of slaves was also mentioned in the eastern Mediterranean during this period, as seen in records of slave sales at the Genoese colony of Caffa in Crimea from the thirteenth and early fourteenth centuries. Some Tartars and Mongols are described as brown. One Caucasian is described as white, but another is "brunetum" and a third "olivegna." The word "laurus" is used to describe some slaves. One scholar translates this word as "blone," the French word for a "blond" European or Arab. Another scholar, J. Segura, insists that "laurus" means a person of mixed black-white heritage.

Verlinden is convinced that in Crimea these distinctions were not merely descriptive, as they were in Spain, but reflected emerging social evaluations of skin color.[12] In the eastern Mediterranean, slaves were used in agricultural production as well as household service, and this status difference may have generated ethnic stereotypes with implications of "high" versus "low."

During the fourteenth and fifteenth centuries, prisoners of war, not individuals secured by purchase, continued to be the main source of slaves in Italy, Spain and the Mediterranean. By this time, both geographic and color designations were standard in record-keeping, according to Verlinden. Among the designations were: Grecs; Sardes; Russes; Caucasiens; Criméens; Asiatiques: Turcs and Arméniens; Balkaniques: Albanais, Bosniaques, Bulgares and

CHART 8. A Sampling of Slave Records from
the Iberian Peninsula (14th and 15th Centuries)

Ethnic Origin or Color Designation	Sales Price of the Slaves								Total	
	Under 100 sous	100-300 sous	Over 300 sous	Under 20 livres	20-30 livres	31-50 livres	Over 50 livres	Total	No.	%
Sarrasin noir (m. & f.)	–	–	1	–	1	12	7	21	45	21.7
Noir (m. & f.).........	1	2	–	–	1	15	5	24		
Laurus, laura	–	–	–	–	–	2	1	3		
Llor or llora	–	3	1	–	–	–	–	4	91	44.0
Tartar (m. & f.).......	–	–	–	1	10	22	14	47		
Sarrasin (m. & f.)	–	–	–	–	4	26	7	37		
Circassian (m. & f.)...	–	–	–	–	–	6	9	15		
Balkan (f. only).......	–	–	–	2	1	7	24	34		
Greek (m. & f.).......	3	1	1	–	2	–	–	7	60	29.0
Sarrasin blanc (m.)....	–	1	–	–	–	–	–	1		
Blanc (m. & f.)........	–	2	–	–	1	–	–	3		
Unspecified..........	–	–	–	2	1	4	4	11	11	5.3
Totals	**4**	**9**	**3**	**5**	**21**	**94**	**71**	**207**	**207**	**100.0**

*Laurus, laura, llor, llora mean "light colored"

Tabulated from a listing of data on bills of sale in
Verlinden, *L'Esclavage*, Vol. 1 pp. 440 – 449.

Summary

Black 45 (21.7)
Other colored 91 (44.0)
White 60 (29.0)
Unspecified 11 (5.3)

Valaques; Canariens; Nègres; and Maures. The Canariens were Berbers from the Canary Islands, and they were described as "Bestiales in moribus" and "idolatres." Enslaved "Ethiopiens" were not vilified in this way, and some were discussed favorably as wards of a monastery.[13]

Analysis of fourteenth-century deeds, wills, and sales documents throughout the Mediterranean suggests that color was assuming social salience along with religion, but the precise meaning of this usage is unclear. Such distinctions, of course, had a potential for becoming invidious; but at the time, there was no evidence of racial slavery confined exclusively to Blacks.

Sugar Cultivation Moves West

During the fifteenth century, a profitable sugar industry in the eastern Mediterranean, financed by Venetian and Genoese investors, was gradually relocated as the Ottoman Turks and the Islamic rulers of North Africa threatened to turn the whole Mediterranean into a Muslim lake (see map 8). Sugar operations were safer in the west.

The Crusaders had begun the cultivation of sugar in conquered parts of Syria and Palestine, using Arabian methods and slave labor. When the Crusaders were expelled from these lands after the twelfth century, they moved their sugar operations to Crete, Cyprus, and Sicily.[14] These plantation economies had no slave codes, such as those evolved from Roman law in some areas of southern Europe.

The Christian rulers of Cyprus used Syrian and Arab prisoners of war as slaves, along with many Slavs imported from the historic hunting ground for slaves, the Black Sea coast. Cyprus became the largest slave market in the Mediterranean, with slaves of all races bought and sold there, including a few Negroes.[15] Documents from the port of Famagusta in Cyprus show Greeks, Jews and a variety of other white slaves. A will dated December 21, 1300, made by a Genoese in Cyprus, left houses to three domestic slaves, two white and one "a Negress." She was to continue serving the dead man's wife for four years, and then she would be freed, as were her brother and her daughter.[16]

Commenting on this case and hundreds of others he documented, Professor Verlinden remarks that

> Cyprus, as we can see from the variety of ethnic origins of the slaves already mentioned, was a center of the slave trade. . . . The Cypriot merchants, themselves, especially the Famagustans, were playing an active part in this traffic. They would seize the inhabitants of the islands of the Aegean Sea as slaves and maintain constant traffic with Egypt.[17]

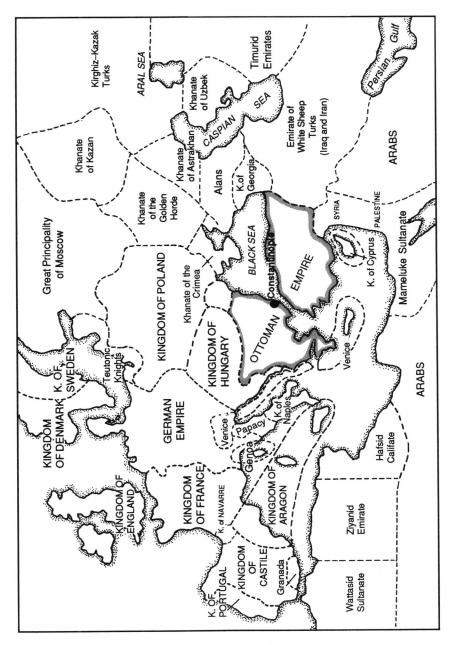

MAP 8. EUROPE AND THE MIDDLE EAST ON THE EVE OF THE FIRST TRANSATLANTIC CROSSING
Cartography based on a concept of the author.

As pressures from the invading Turks in the eastern Mediterranean increased, the sugar industry continued to move west, first to Spain and Portugal, where some sugar cultivation had been introduced earlier by the Muslim occupation, and then to newly discovered islands in the Atlantic off the coast of Africa. While slavery and blackness were still not equated in the minds of Mediterranean peoples, an increasing number of brown and black slaves appear on bills of sale as the "retreat" of sugar planting proceeded (see chart 9).

A Changing Labor Pool

The decisive event increasing the flow of sub-Saharan Blacks into the Mediterranean labor pool was the victory of the Ottoman Turks over the Byzantine Christian empire which included the seizure of Constantinople in 1453. With the flow of white slaves from Russia diminishing, the demand for sub-Saharan Blacks, as well as prisoners of war from all ethnic groups, increased sharply.[18] The gradual shift from a predominantly white group of enslaved sugar workers in Cyprus to a predominantly black slave labor force took a critical turn when investors moved the industry to the offshore islands of Madeira, the Canaries, Cape Verde, and then to Fernando Po and São Tomé off the coast of Nigeria.

The soil and climate were favorable to sugar on these islands discovered between 1420 and 1479. The Muslim-Christian conflict in the Mediterranean was a long, safe distance away. And of great importance, a plentiful labor supply was close at hand in sub-Saharan Africa. The industry prospered.

During the last quarter of the fifteenth century, the Canary Islands controlled by Spain developed a thriving sugar industry using black slaves and Italian capital. Portugal also relied on Italian investors for its plantation economy on the Cape Verde Islands. Of some importance in the increasingly mono-racial character of the enslaved labor pool was the fact that Portuguese settlers on the islands were under orders not to trade with Guinea for gold but only for the slaves needed to increase sugar production. The West African gold was to be reserved for Lisbon.

Seven years before Columbus sailed across the Atlantic, Spain sent its fleet to attack the Portuguese. Spain hoped to extract a twenty-percent "cut" on the Guinea slave trade, but it lost the battle. When Columbus delivered the Caribbean to Ferdinand and Isabella in 1492, however, such a "rip-off" became irrelevant. The Spanish were content to let Portugal keep the Guinea coast monopoly, for they

CHART 9. CHANGING PATTERNS IN RECRUITMENT
AND USE OF SLAVES IN EUROPE

8th and 9th c.	Slavery replaced by serfdom in almost all of Western Europe, but "pagan" Slavs are captured and marched through Germany and France for sale to Muslims in Spain. Anglo-Saxons, Irish, Welsh and Scots often enslaved for sale to caliphate of Córdoba in Spain.
10th and 11th c.	Marketing of Slavs in Spain decreases after Christians defeat the Córdoba caliphate; Christians now enslave Muslim prisoners of war. As Crusaders colonize parts of Syria and Palestine they begin growing sugar, along with other crops, using "white" slaves.
12th c.	Venetian and Genoese investors and colonists in eastern Mediterranean become involved in slave trade on a massive scale. Sugar being grown in Crete and Cyprus using slaves of all racial groups, but Blacks are in minority. Black Sea coast a heavy supplier.
13th c.	Continuation of Genoese and Venetian involvement in production using slaves, and in slave trade in eastern Mediterranean. Color terms being used to describe slaves on bills of sale as, e.g., "white," "brown," *brunetum, olivegna,* etc. Significance of this not clear.
14th and 15th c.	Italians importing slaves for sale to Mediterranean countries from Black Sea area and Balkans. Ethnic origins: Tartars, Russians, Circassians, etc. mentioned, as well as color, in descriptions. Proportion of Blacks increasing rapidly during 15th century, particularly after sugar production shifts to Madeira, Cape Verde Islands, and Canary Islands. "Guinean" and "Negro" being used to describe sub-Saharan Africans. (Slavery continues in Sicily until 1812, in Spain until 1820, and in Portugal until 1836, but center is in Caribbean and Brazil.)

had what seemed to be a grander prize; the whole Western Hemisphere allotted to them by a papal order. Portugal was given only Brazil in the Americas, but it was granted all of Africa.

With both Spain and Portugal laying claim to land in the Western Hemisphere, a transfer of sugar cultivation from the African offshore islands to the Caribbean inevitably took place.[19] In one integrated "package" were the techniques, the machinery, and what had by then become the custom of using black labor. The Cuban anthropologist Fernando Ortiz, writing in *Cuban Counterpoint: Tobacco and Sugar*, notes that the first sugar cane in the Western Hemisphere was planted by Columbus in December 1493 and that the first sugar was produced in the Caribbean in 1506, the year the first grinding mill was erected. This was five years before Spain granted permission for Africans to be imported into Hispaniola directly from Africa. The Amerindian labor pool had been almost wiped out before sugar planting began. Ortiz stresses the role of the Spanish crown in creating conditions under which the sugar industry could flourish:

> In those days the settler who wanted to raise sugar could ask the King for whatever he needed, aside from the audacity and enterprise supplied by himself; he could ask for land grants for plantations, money for mills, subsidies for bringing in expert workmen, tax exemptions, and above all, the privilege of importing Negro slaves.[20]

According to Ortiz, investment capital came from Genoa and Venice as well as Spain, and he stresses the presence of Jews among the early entrepreneurs. He refers several times to the role of experts from the Canary Islands, including Oviedo's account of the very first mill, built by Gonzalo de Velosa, who "brought out workmen from the Canary Islands, and ground cane and made sugar before anyone else."[21] Professor Verlinden sums up the whole transfer process in a few words:

> The methods invented in the Middle Ages in the Mediterranean zone made possible the expansion of sugar production across the Atlantic world. . . . There has been a gradual shift to the West, from the Palestinian sugar plantations in the twelfth century to those in Cuba in the eighteenth century.[22]

Blacks and Slavery in the New World

The native Indians of the Americas were the first to be enslaved by the white conquerors of the sixteenth century. But when death from disease and overwork rapidly depleted their ranks, there was a crisis. At first, by royal decree, the only Blacks permitted in Hispaniola were the *ladinos*, Africans who had been Christianized during their residence in Spain. Pagan Africans might interfere with the process of converting the Indians, it was feared. Jewish and Muslim slaves were barred from the New World for the same reason, and deported criminals were not a dependable labor supply.

Under pressure from settlers who wanted to expand sugar operations, and with advice from Father Las Casas who wanted to save the remaining Amerindians, the Spanish Crown relented and allowed the colonists to import Blacks directly from Africa, beginning in 1511. Hoetink suggests that some nonblack slaves were still used, because in 1530 the king reiterated his ban on Jews, Berbers and Moors as slaves. The same year that the king sanctioned import of black African slaves, he also approved shipment of "white Christian female slaves," according to Hoetink, so that "Spaniards could take them as wives" instead of marrying non-Spanish women or living outside of marriage with Indian women.[23] It is unclear whether these women passed on their slave status to any offspring, or whether servitude expired with the death of the wife. In any event, the practice was of short duration.

By mid-century, no white people were being held as slaves in the Spanish-American colonies, and it became the unalterable code that no people designated as "white" were to be held in slavery. In this way, New World slavery became a unique system: it was *racial* slavery, in which all of the slaves are of a different racial group from the master. The ideology supporting the system was reinforced by color prejudice against Blacks, but it also propagated the idea that no individuals from the masters' group should be slaves. This represented a radical break with the centuries-old Mediterranean tradition of multiracial slavery.[24]

Since the overseas explorations had given Spain no territory in Africa, that nation had to contract with other countries for its slaves. The so-called *asiento*, an agreement to supply 4,000 black bodies a year, became a much-sought-after prize that finally went to Britain in 1713.[25] Portugal, with its colonies in the Kongo and Angola, not only supplied its own New World plantations in Brazil but also sold to others.

The Europeans defended their slave trade in many ways, but one kind of justification contributed to the derogatory stereotyping of Africans south of the Sahara. It was argued that they were being rescued from two more horrible types of slavery: one that was native to Africa, and the other enslavement by the Arabs and other Muslim slave hunters. The argument was meretricious. Most slaves in Africa lived as "slaves of the house" under a mild type of what specialists call "domestic slavery." However, black conquest states in western and central Africa took captives in war, and while some of these were put to work at home, others were sold east into the Central Islamic Lands. With the appearance of Europeans on the Atlantic Coast, the African elites who trafficked in slaves secured a new market. More active raiding of inoffensive peoples was encouraged.

The transportation across the desert to the East may have been more cruel than the Middle Passage across the Atlantic, but the system of slavery at the end of the trek to Muslim lands was a more humane one than the chattel slavery of the Americas. The slaves who flowed to North Africa and the Middle East were fated to become porters and soldiers, domestic servants and entertainers, harem girls and concubines. Only rarely were they used to produce commodities for the market or even subsistence products for their masters.[26]

Those whose fate carried them West became part of large-scale capitalist agriculture—the plantation economy—of vital importance to investors and traders in Europe and Britain. A limited pattern of using black slaves in agriculture in southern Europe had become the dominant pattern in the colonies of the Western Hemisphere.

The slavery of the New World Diaspora also differed in another crucial aspect from the slavery practiced in southern Europe. Black slaves greatly outnumbered white planters and their families in the sugar-growing areas of the Caribbean. Slaves were not a minority of the national labor force as they always were in Europe on the eve of overseas exploration. A condition that sociologist Herbert Blumer defines as conducive to heightened race prejudice predominated in the sugar colonies—the fear of an ethnic minority dominating others that it might be overthrown by the majority it dominates. Slave revolts had been rare in the Mediterranean lands; they were endemic to the Americas. (See discussion of Blumer's ideas in volume 1 of *Black Folk Here and There*, pp. 87-90.)

Color and Slavery: Variations

As the Americas and the Caribbean islands were incorporated into European Christendom politically, the process of acculturation imposed European cultural patterns on both the native Indians and the imported African slaves. The process of acculturation was selective. Only those symbols that were compatible with a system of *racial* slavery were transmitted to the Americas. Black Madonnas and black warrior-saints were not welcome in the New World.[27]

Moreover, the actual status of Blacks and attitudes toward them were, of necessity, different in Europe and in the colonies of the Western Hemisphere. Lacking the imperative of the plantation economy, the European homelands provided, as a whole, a more favorable environment for black slaves. Moreover, freed Blacks were much commoner in the old world of Europe, and a range of opportunity was open to them that would have been inimical to the operation of societies based upon a slave economy. However, increasingly derogatory attitudes toward Blacks grew up in Europe as the institution of racial slavery took hold in the New World. These were generated by caricatures in the print media and tales told by visitors from America.

Benign stereotypes associated with Negro domestic servants and exotic entertainers began to give way to harsher stereotypes of crude plantation workers. Also, the African slave trade and New World systems of slavery accentuated contrasts between the characteristic Negro appearance and that of other races. It is important, however, to remember that physical differences did not result in the enslavement of Blacks. Rather, as enslavement became more commonplace, these differences assumed a salience they had not previously had among Europeans. "Black" became a master symbol of subordinate status and inferior culture, where previously it had merely stimulated esthetic, erotic, and mystical/religious evaluations. "Negro" was an even more pejorative concept in English-speaking areas.

The theory and practice of *racial* slavery, justified by the ideology of White Racism, became an integral part of Western Christendom. While slavery was not widespread in the European sector of Christendom as compared with the colonial periphery, it was not condemned by either Church or State. In 1488, Ferdinand, that most Catholic of kings, sent Pope Innocent VIII one hundred Moorish slaves for distribution among cardinals and other notables. All large monasteries had a contingent of slave labor. Both Catholic and Protestant clergy justified the slavery system on the grounds that it helped complete the process of Christianizing the "Ethiopians"[28] that was begun by the early Church Fathers.[29]

However, differences between Catholic and Protestant values and norms did have implications for race relations. Catholic males in the colonies, for example, accepted sexual relations with Negro and mulatto women as a pleasant way of "sinning." Progeny were not viewed with shame. There was a strong Puritan element among the Protestant English settlers of the New World, on the other hand. A strong sense of guilt surrounding interracial fornication led to elaborate systems of apartheid and color caste, as wished-for "shields against temptation." While both Catholic and Protestant systems enshrined the "pure" white woman, Protestant males in North America were more likely to use violence against black males to prevent miscegenation with white women than were males in Latin America. Significant variations within Protestant colonies did occur.[30]

Some scholars have been impressed by the differences between slavery in Spanish and Portuguese colonies, on the one hand—what Hoetink calls the "Iberian variant"—and in those controlled by "North European" colonists. Because of their experience with Muslim invaders and rulers, the Catholics of Spain and Portugal had had recent experience with black people in a wide range of roles from slave-soldier and menial slave to poet and ruler. They also came from cultures that took slavery for granted as a legitimate system for organizing some aspects of economic and social relations. The Iberian colonists had seen both whites and Blacks as slaves. In the colonies, although the settlers rejected the relatively liberal slave codes of their European homelands, they were familiar with a tradition that assigned legal rights to slaves and gave them some protection through Catholic church officials.[31]

Englishmen knew little about slavery and less about Negroes when they started their first colonies in the Americas in the early seventeenth century, almost one hundred years after Iberian settlements in the Americas had become well-established. British colonists had no slave codes from the past to accept or reject. As the colonies became established, they belatedly examined theories of racial differences that had been widely known in the Mediterranean lands for centuries, elaborating and distorting them.

Until recently there has been a tendency to accept a facile generalization that Spanish America and Brazil were "less prejudiced" against Negroes than were other areas and that slavery was "milder" in Latin America. A view much closer to the facts now prevails, and H. Hoetink, who has done much to establish it, has said:

> It may be that in comparable economic situations in Iberian society the relations between white master and black slave were friendlier and more supple than in a Northwest European Caribbean society, in the same way as, in general, the non-intimate social relationships between races in the Iberian variant were warmer.[32]

But Hoetink, as well as other scholars, insists that it would be an error to deny that skin-color prejudice existed in the Iberian systems whether in metropolis or periphery, and there is evidence that at similar stages of plantation economy, differences tended to disappear.[33] But the difference between Iberian systems and those in British areas was still significant.

An examination of race relations in sixteenth- and seventeenth-century Britain, Spain and Portugal, will throw some light upon the way these differences manifested themselves in the "mother countries," and the degree to which they provided models for institutions and behavior that evolved in the colonial context. Theoretical questions raised by Degler and Gergen as to the universality of prejudice against "blackness" and black people can be put to the test, and the paradigms about change in race relations advanced by Blumer and Cox examined, through such comparisons. (See *Black Folk Here and There*, volume 1, pp. 89-90.)

SKIN COLOR AND THE PORTUGUESE ETHOS

In their forays into Africa, and eventually in their establishment of the colony of Brazil in South America, the Portuguese revealed esthetic prejudices against the Negro physical type, but not against dark skin color as such. In Africa this did not prevent cordial cooperative working relations with Negro rulers. In Brazil where *racial* slavery was institutionalized, "Negroidness" became a symbol of the lowest social position in a complex stratification system. Nowhere was race or color a barrier against miscegenation, but marriage with Negroes was not encouraged in colonial areas where a slave hierarchy was crucial to the economy. However, it occurred frequently at home in Portugal without opposition.

Until recently it was the custom to refer to Brazil as a country where racial prejudice was virtually unknown, and to attribute this to the Portuguese ethos brought to South America by the same people who brought Africans as slaves. That idyllic view has been challenged by a number of scholars, even though they admit that Portuguese race relations are significantly different not only from Protestant Europe but also from Catholic Spain.[34]

Gilberto Freyre, in emphasizing what he considers the Brazilian lack of color prejudice, stresses favorable attitudes toward Moors that had developed in Portugal before exploration in Africa, America, and the Indies began:

> To the Portuguese, the Moors had been not only the efficient agricultural workers who knew how to transform arid land into

gardens as if by a miracle, but also a dark race who had not always been the serfs, but sometimes had been the masters of a large part of the Iberian peninsula. Portuguese of the purest Nordic blood had found in brown Moorish women, some of them princesses, the supreme revelation of feminine beauty . . . the Moorish brown girl is regarded as the supreme type of beauty and of sexual attractiveness, the Moors are considered superior and not inferior to the purely white Portuguese . . . most of the Portuguese who discovered and colonized Brazil knew that a brown people may be superior to a white people. . . . The Portuguese in Brazil retained many marks of Moorish influence in their not very strictly European or very strictly Christian moral and social behavior. This was especially true of the common men, though in general it applies to Portuguese of all classes.[35]

None of these benign attitudes, however, prevented the Portuguese from being drawn into a trading network in which Negroes from south of the Sahara became both a valuable commodity and a medium of exchange. Nor did approval of brown beauty indicate admiration of Negroidness.[36]

A Look at Portuguese History

Prior to the fourteenth century, Portugal had a different experience with Muslims from North Africa than did Spain. Northeastern Portugal was, at first, a part of the kingdom of Leon. It had not been occupied by the Moors and so served as the marshaling ground for the forces that led the Reconquest. The major battles occurred on Spanish soil. Much of the energy of Portuguese kings and queens and princes was expended in trying to secure independence from Leon and then to keep from being incorporated into Castile.

By the middle of the twelfth century, Portugal had pushed its borders southward toward an area that was occupied by Moors, while Leon and Castile were pursuing the Reconquest by capturing Moorish city states in Andalusia. Facing the Atlantic as it did, the kingdom of Portugal was able to provide ports where English, French, Flemish, and German knights and their followers could land en route to the Holy Land on their Crusades. Some of these fighters for the Faith assisted Portugal in expelling the Moors from their kingdom. While Castile and Aragon were still mobilizing forces to drive the Muslims into Morocco from Spain, members of the Portuguese royal family were planning to invade Morocco itself in order to make direct contact with the sources of gold in Africa south of the Sahara.

By 1415 members of the Portuguese royal family had succeeded in conquering an enclave in Africa and had established institutions there for training in maritime pursuits and research. Prince Henry the Navigator was sending forth his men to take the Azores, Madeira, and the Canary Islands while making plans to sail down the west coast of Africa. The few slaves brought back during the first exploratory voyages were an incidental by-product of the venture, captured by occasional raids on the African coast. When Portuguese invaders took Ceuta in Morocco, a town just across from Gibraltar, they turned it into a base for planning the maritime adventures that made Lagos in Portugal a major port of assembly and embarkation.

Attitudes Toward Blacks and Slavery

Gomes Eannes de Azurara, in *The Chronicle of the Discovery and Conquest of Guinea*, has left a vivid account of the adventures of the first Portuguese sailors who inched their way down the west coast of Africa to the mouth of the Senegal River between 1434 and 1446. They were ruthless in their hit and run attacks, taking hostages to carry back to Lagos and making deals with Berbers and "tawny Moors" who were anxious to buy their own freedom with gold or in the coinage of "black Moors."

Azurara reports the dramatic scene as a crowd in Lagos, Portugal, watched the first large group of captive African Blacks being divided up among their captors. His oft-quoted account reveals his hypocritical religiosity as well as the esthetic and symbolic meanings that "blackness" of skin color and "Negroidness" had to a Portuguese of his own station in life—and perhaps to some of the lower orders.

> O, Thou heavenly Father . . . I pray Thee that my tears may not wrong my conscience; for it is not their religion but their humanity that maketh mine to weep in pity for their sufferings . . . seeing before my eyes that miserable company and remembering they too are of the generation of the sons of Adam. . . . On the next day, which was the 8th of the month of August (1444), very early in the morning, by reason of the heat, the seamen began to make ready their boats, and to take out those captives, and carry them on shore. . . . And these, placed altogether in that field, were a marvellous sight; *for amongst them were some white enough, fair to look upon and well proportioned; others were less white like mulattoes; others again were as black as Ethiops, and so ugly, both in features and in body, as almost to appear (to those who saw them) the images of a lower hemisphere* . . . some kept their heads low and their faces

bathed in tears . . . others stood groaning . . . others struck their faces with the palms of their hands, throwing themselves at full length upon the ground; others made their lamentations in the manner of a dirge, after the custom of their country [italics added].[37]

Prince Henry was there to collect the "Royal Fifth" and watched as families were separated, for "in order to make an equal partition of the fifths it was needful to part fathers from sons, husbands from wives, brothers from brothers." The division was made by casting lots, and "No respect was shown either to friends or relations, but each fell where his lot took him." People who resisted the separation were beaten and dragged away. At one point the watching crowd "caused such a tumult as greatly to confuse those who directed partition." There was weeping among the Portuguese, whose employers had given them a holiday "for the sole purpose of beholding this novelty."

The Prince received forty-seven of the 235 individuals who were allotted that day, but Azurara hastens to say that it was not the profit that interested the prince, but only the prospect of their salvation. In his characteristically sanctimonious way, the chronicler proceeds:

And certainly his expectation was not in vain . . . as soon as they understood our language they turned Christians with very little ado; and I who put together this history into this volume, saw in the town of Lagos boys and girls (the children and grandchildren of those first captives, born in this land) as good and true Christians as if they had directly descended from the dispensation of Christ, from those who were first baptized.[38]

Throughout the chronicle Azurara waxes enthusiastic about the tactics of the raids that he says frankly were for "booty." He imputes no motives of saving souls to the ruffians who destroyed villages, pillaged crops, and captured as many Moors as they could, "tawny" and black. But he is impelled to justify the enslavement on the grounds that after arrival in Portugal, the Blacks were not only well-treated, but were accepted without any prejudice against their "Negroidness."

Azurara's *Chronicle of the Discovery and Conquest of Guinea* was written to justify the Portuguese intrusions into the west coast of Africa and the carrying off to Portugal of some of the inhabitants. The concepts of a "civilizing mission" and of a missionary obligation were constantly invoked. That this "cultural" imperialism was not the same as racism is evident in Azurara's discussion of the fate of the Africans landed at Lagos in 1446 and their descendants:

> But from this time forth they began to acquire some knowledge of our country; in which they found great abundance, and our men began to treat them with great favour. For as our people did not find them hardened in the belief of the other Moors; and saw how they came in unto the law of Christ with a good will; they made no difference between them and their free servants, born in our own country; but those whom they took while still young, they caused to be instructed in mechanical arts, and those whom they saw fitted for managing property; they set free and married to women who were natives of the land; making with them a division of their property, as if they had been bestowed on those who married them by the will of their own fathers, and for the merits of their service they were bound to act in a like manner. Yea, and some widows of good family who bought some of these female slaves, either adopted them or left them a portion of their estate by will; so that in the future they married right well [i.e., because they had a good dowry to offer in a marriage transaction]; treating them as entirely free. Suffice it that I never saw one of these slaves put in irons like other captives, and scarcely any one who did not turn Christian and was not very gently treated.
>
> And I have been asked by their lords to the baptisms and marriages of such; at which they, whose slaves they were before, made no less solemnity than if they had been their children or relations.
>
> And so their lot was now quite the contrary of what it had been; since before they had lived in perdition of soul and body; of their souls, in that they were yet pagans, without the clearness and the light of the holy faith; and of their bodies, in that they lived like beasts. . . .

Azurara states that this type of rapid acculturation was possible because Negroes from Guinea were less intractable than the Islamized captives from Morocco. Although he referred to Guineans as Moors he drew important distinctions between them and others:

> Now there were four things in these captives that were very different from the condition of the other Moors who were taken prisoners from this part. First, that after they had come to this land of Portugal, they never more tried to fly, but rather in time forgot all about their own country, as soon as they began to taste the good things of this one; secondly, that they were very loyal and obedient servants, without malice; thirdly, that they were not so inclined to lechery as the others; fourthly that after they began to use clothing they were for the most part very fond of display. . . .

While this is the beginning of stereotype formation—a benign one from the Portuguese point of view—it may have some elements of a "well-merited reputation." In any event, unlike Muslim stereotypes, "lechery" was not imputed to these sub-Saharan Blacks.

> And what was still better, as I have already said, they turned themselves with a good will into the path of the true faith; in the which after they had entered, they received true belief, and in this same they died. And now reflect what a guerdon should be that of the Infant [i.e., the Portuguese ruler] in the presence of the Lord God; for thus bringing to true salvation, not only those, but many others, whom you will find in this history later on.[39]

Elsewhere, Azurara refers to Negroidness in a garbled version of the biblical story of Noah's curse. His story combines the official Christian position of an inherent right to freedom with a biblical story purporting to explain how that right was abridged by sin. The belief in "a natural desire" for freedom is given an aristocratic twist. The context for Azurara's remarks is a recounting of negotiations between Portuguese and Moors for hostages the Portuguese had seized on the West African coast. The Portuguese recognize a status distinction for which "Negroidness" is the marker:

> naturally every prisoner desireth to be free, which desire is all the stronger in a man of higher reason or nobility whom fortune has condemned to live in subjection to another; so that the noble of whom we have already spoken . . . often asked Antam Goncalves to take him back to his country, where he declared he would give for himself five or six Black Moors. . . . And here you must note that these blacks were Moors like the others, though their slaves, in accordance with ancient custom, which I believe to have been because of the curse which, after the Deluge, Noah laid upon his son Cain (sic), cursing him in this way:—that his race should be subject to all the other races of the world.[40]

All Moors were sometimes contrasted in Portuguese records with all Guineans, the former being considered "civilized" and the latter "barbarian" or "pagan." This follows an old pattern we have seen in the Central Islamic Lands that distinguishes between Ethiopians and "Zanj," and an even earlier distinction in Greco-Roman writing between "savage" and "civilized" Ethiopians. The basis of the distinction was cultural, not biological; individuals in the two categories might be equally Negroid. Later, Africans who had accepted Christianity and Portuguese customs would become *ladinos*, i.e., civilized. The others were *bozales*.

As Azurara has described it, at least some of these Africans were accepted as social equals in Portugal. This was a kind of slavery Africans knew, a system in which prisoners of war, after a period of servitude, were freed to join the families of their captors through adoption or marriage. What the record does not make clear is whether or not there was discrimination in favor of those "fair to look upon and well proportioned" as against those who were "as black as Ethiops" and "ugly." The suggestion in Azurara is that "Negroidness" was disliked. This same attitude is evident in Brazil's system of color discrimination with *preto* (black) at the bottom, *branco* (white) at the top, and various kinds of mixed bloods categorized in between.

There is some evidence to suggest that the Moorish women of whom Gilberto Freyre wrote, the Moorish girls of Portuguese male dreams, were not *preto*, that is, black, but *moreno*, or brown, and this type of idealization carried over into Brazil. Early chronicles indicate that the Portuguese distinguished between what the British called "tawny" Moors and "blackamoors," although what kind of social discrimination followed these divisions, if any, or what other traits could override differences based upon skin color, we do not know.

In one of the passages quoted above, Azurara explains how ladinos were "integrated" into the Portuguese social system without mentioning whether any were handicapped by what the Portuguese considered their "ugliness." During the centuries of contact with Moors that had preceded this period, there is evidence that not all of the Portuguese dismissed Negroes as being ugly or, if they did make such an appraisal, other considerations weighed against this factor in choosing mates. These included talent, wealth, bravery, or erotic reputation.[41]

Africans in Portugal

During the two decades following the landing at Lagos, tens of thousands of Africans were brought to Portugal, many of whom were sold in the slave markets of Italian and Spanish cities. Others, however, were used as menial laborers in Lagos, Lisbon, Oporto, and other Portuguese cities. In southern Portugal, some were plantation hands. By 1500, over ten thousand Africans and their descendants were living in Lisbon, divided into two social groups with differing customs and subjected to differential treatment by the Portuguese.[42]

On the one hand there were ladinos, families of Africans and their descendants who had become Christianized and spoke Portuguese. Some of these were gradually absorbed into the general population through the process of intermarriage described by Azurara.[43] Others, by marrying each other, kept self-perpetuating communities of ladinos in existence. The acculturated Africans were considered acceptable as social equals by Portuguese with similar occupations and economic means, in contrast to treatment accorded *bozales* or individuals recently imported from Africa.[44] Many of these were used as plantation laborers in southern Portugal, in the Algarve, on the islands of the Azores, in the Canaries, and in Fernando Po, opposite the mouth of the Kongo.

E. W. Bovill, author of the *Golden Trade of the Moors*, describes the psychological and demographic consequences of Portugal's rapid fifteenth-century overseas expansion. These included not only a massive increase in the number of Africans living in the metropolis, but also a more benign cast to slavery in Portugal itself than it would have in Portuguese colonies:

> The great and rapidly acquired empire imposed a burden too great to be supported by a small country whose manhood had been sapped by centuries of fighting against Moors and Castilians. . . . The drain of these great possessions on the country's manpower continued. The garrisoning of the new settlements, the manning of the fleets and the recruitment of the colonial administrative services became increasingly difficult as more and more Portuguese left the mother country to seek fortunes in Brazil or lucrative sinecures in India. Of the many thousands of emigrants drawn mostly from the flower of the country's manhood, only one in ten ever returned. How grave for the country this was is clearly shown by the decline in the population from two million in 1500 to half that number before the close of the century. One of the worst consequences of this steady depopulation was the decay of agriculture. *To make good the shortage of peasants and labourers great numbers of negro slaves had been imported from Africa, especially into the south where the population had become predominantly black* [italics added].[45]

The demographic imbalance Bovill describes may also explain why marriages between Blacks and whites could be arranged. Eventually, most of the resident black population was absorbed by the Portuguese population. However, since slavery in that country was not abolished until the nineteenth century, a new infusion of African genes was constantly taking place.

This pattern of socially accepted amalgamation in fifteenth-century Portugal could not be transferred to either the sugar colony of Brazil or the colonial and semi-colonial situations in Africa. Such massive miscegenation would have disrupted structures considered essential to maintaining white political and economic dominance.

Portuguese in Africa

We have seen how Blacks fared in Africa both in the Egyptian kingdoms that influenced civilizations throughout the Mediterranean and Middle East, and in the great kingdoms of the West African heartland. Negroes held prominent positions in both. As we studied the condition of Blacks in the Muslim world, we saw how the coming of Islam affected West Africa. Before returning to our comparative look at Blacks in the Western European lands that generated New World colonies, we should pause to examine the impact of the white Portuguese on African societies. Here was the testing ground for Portuguese attitudes toward Negroes.

The black kingdom of the Kongo posed the first test for the "spirit of Lagos." But, here the issue was not whether there was a willingness to sanction intermarriage between Portuguese and Africans. Rather, it was whether there was a willingness to share economic and political power with native monarchs anxious for an egalitarian relationship that would benefit both parties. The Portuguese monarchs proved unwilling to deal on those terms with African monarchs, although some of the black kings addressed their European counterpart as "My Christian Brother."

The first Portuguese reached the Kongo in 1482, when the caravels of Diogo Caõ reached the mouth of a river called Nzadi (or Zaire) in West Central Africa and sailed inland to search for gold and Prester John. But the large influx of Portuguese came some time later, as the sociologist Georges Balandier informs us:

> In 1490, eight years after the discovery [of Kongo], a veritable missionary expedition was organized at the instigation of João II of Portugal. It . . . included missionaries—secular priests, Franciscan or Dominican monks, and canons of St. John the Evangelist—armed soldiers, peasants, artisans—masons and carpenters equipped with tools—and a few women. Its purpose was to reinforce a settlement which, although sparse, had been sufficient to convince the Portuguese that "trade with the people of the Kongo was very profitable," to quote Pigafetta [a Catholic priest who kept a record of events during this period]. Three vessels loaded with men, sacerdotal objects and ornaments, gifts, and even with building materials made up the fleet. Thus it was a microcosm of European society which was exported for the purpose of shaping Kongo society and civilization in its own image.[46]

The Portuguese, with their sense of a "civilizing mission," were not daunted by the culture they had come to "reshape": its people welcomed them, and the head of the welcoming delegation immediately submitted to baptism:

> Three thousand warriors, armed with bows and arrows, had gathered at the call of the tom-toms. Another group had been formed by the musicians who carried drums, ivory trumpets, and instruments resembling violas. They were naked to the waist and were painted with white and various colored paints, a symbol of great joy. On their heads they wore headdresses made of the feathers of parrots and other birds. The chief wore on his head a kind of night cap decorated with skillful embroidery representing a snake.[47]

An armed escort led the Portuguese on a twenty-day journey from port to the capital, where they presented luxurious gifts of expensive fabrics to the king. He was baptized immediately, taking the name João the First, after the Portuguese king. The queen followed suit some days later, taking the Portuguese queen's name, Eleanor.

The king soon put down a rebellion, thanking the Christian God and St. James for his victory. The Portuguese also aided João's efforts to retain the lands that were included in his title, some of whose rulers were defying his authority: "king of Kongo, of Loango, of Kakongo, and of Ngoyo, this side of and the other side of the Zaire, lord of Musuru, of Matamba, of Mulilu, of Musuku, and of the Anziko, etc., etc."

The Portuguese felt at ease with a monarch who was building an empire by incorporating other political units, some of them fiefs of lords and others the domain of rival monarchs. But their incentive to aid him was the rumor that gold and silver were to be found in abundance a short distance inland. Balandier notes that the Portuguese, "excited by the idea of planting the cross in the heart of the dark continent and the hope of a profitable trade, regarded [the Kongo] as an enlarged version of their own kingdom, a kind of negative that was to be subjected to that developing agent which was Christian and Lusitanian civilization."[48]

About the time Columbus was adding Caribbean islands to Spain's empire, the Portuguese experiment in Africa met its first failure. João had kept his influence strong by taking wives from various factions. The Catholic priests now assailed him for adultery. They also burned "superstitious objects and the huts of fetishes." Faced with the loss of his African supporters, whose loyalty depended upon matrimonial alliances, João forced the missionaries out of the capital. He sent them to the domain of his hand-picked successor, an act that was not unfriendly and that resulted in ties with the next king. Nevertheless, a Catholic priest wrote that "King John was Christian in name only . . . we know that he returned to his fetishes and his harem."[49]

His successor, Afonso I, was so devout that he was described as "The Apostle of the Kongo." He studied the Scriptures, attended Mass regularly and kept his affairs with women as discreet as the priests kept theirs. A modernizer who defied traditionalists, Afonso is the one king the Kongo people, through their folktales, have never forgotten. According to Balandier:

> Christianity and useful knowledge seemed inseparable. . . . Afonso I had, in a certain sense, an educational policy. He connected the consolidation of his power and of the state with the creation of a literate class and the establishment of a more bureaucratic government. By 1509 he had built school buildings for four hundred pupils. . . . In 1516 [the year Charles of Spain became Emperor of the Holy Roman Empire] Rui d'Aguiar, vicar of the kingdom of the Kongo, notes the presence in the capital [that had been named San Salvador] of a thousand students, "sons of noblemen," who were not only learning to read and write but were studying grammar and the humanities "as well as things of the faith." More surprisingly he alludes to the existence of a school for girls, directed by a sister of the king, a woman of some sixty years. . . . Alongside this education provided at home we must consider that which the cream of the elite acquired in Portugal. [One student returned as bishop of the Kongo.][50]

Yet when Afonso sought to trade with Portugal as an equal, even asking to purchase a ship, the Portuguese monarchy refused. He and his advisers also turned down a plea for technical and medical assistance, in addition to more missionaries. The Assembly of the Council of Portugal, in a memorandum to King Philip III in 1607, said of the Kongo sovereign, "Although he is not directly vassal to your Majesty he is however subject to the royal patronage," and they refused his request by saying "he should not be sent workmen; it is not proper that he should have in his kingdom some one who knows how to work with stone and lime or with steel because this would be an occasion for disobedience."[51]

There was a more serious problem, too. Early in the sixteenth century, one interest came to dominate all others among the Portuguese of the Kongo: the procuring of slaves for sale in the New

World, which needed labor for its plantations. Balandier has given us an eloquent statement of what this meant to the Kongo and neighboring Angola:

> The hunting down of men—justified in the name of economic necessity, sanctified, practised in one way or another by all the "foreigners" and their native agents, was one factor in the destruction of the old Kongo. It perverted social relations. It stimulated the *razzias* carried out with the aid of the Yaka, the enemies of the kingdom.[52]

The Yaka soldiers were cannibals based in Angola. The Portuguese came to prefer them, as allies, to the Christian and increasingly "civilized" leaders of Kongo.

In a letter to his "brother," João III, the king of Portugal, Afonso I complained of those who

> by their slave trade are ruining our kingdom and the Christianity which has been established here for so many years and which cost your predecessors so many sacrifices. . . . The lure of profit and greed leads the people of the land to rob their compatriots, including members of their own families and of ours, without considering whether they are Christians or not. They capture them, sell them, barter them.[53]

Balandier notes that

> . . . the clergy openly participated in the system of slavery. The bishops and missionaries in Kongo had slaves for their personal service and for their plantations [just as monasteries and priests had for centuries in Europe] But now . . . the clergy were involved not only directly . . . in the slave traffic, but also indirectly, by the pretences of conversion and spiritual protection that obscured the ignoble commerce. It baptized slaves without performing the necessary catechisms.[54]

Afonso I died in 1539, after an unsuccessful assassination attempt, apparently part of a plot by a "misguided monk" and a group of slave traders to seize the government. A struggle for power now broke out, and relations between Afonso's successors and the missionaries deteriorated. The Portuguese king, who took his profit from the slave trade, seemed increasingly inclined to make a colony out of the Kongo. By the middle of the sixteenth century, Portugal had shifted its base of operations to Luanda in Angola, and cooperated openly with the fierce Yaka warriors who invaded the Kongo in the 1560s.

PLATE 1. Negro Dancer on Apulian Askos (380–360 B.C.)
Courtesy Deutsches Archäologisches Institut, Rome

PLATE 2. Kantharos of Negro and White Heads (6th Century b.c.)
H.L. Pierce Fund
Courtesy Museum of Fine Arts, Boston

PLATE 3. Life-Size Bust of Ambassador or Hostage
Courtesy Deutsches Archäologisches Institut, Rome

PLATE 4. TWO GENTLEMEN PLAYING CHESS

Chessbook of Alfonso X (13th century A.D.), Escorial, Real Monasterio, Biblioteca

Reprinted by permission of El Patrimonio Nacional, Madrid Courtesy Menil Foundation/Hickey & Robertson, Houston

PLATE 5. PORTRAIT OF MALIK AMBAR
Ahmednagar, Mughal (A.D. 1610–1620), Ross-Coomaraswamy Collection
Courtesy Museum of Fine Arts, Boston

PLATE 6. STATUE OF ST. MAURICE (ca. A.D. 1240–50)
Cathedral of St. Maurice and St. Catherine, choir, Magdeburg, Germany
Courtesy Menil Foundation/Hickey & Robertson, Houston

PLATE 7. NOTRE DAME DU PUY BY DUMONTEILH
Courtesy P. Burger

PLATE 8. NON-NEGROID BLACK MADONNA AT PUY
Courtesy Musée Crozatier, Le Puy-en-Velay, France

However, the quixotic, crusading King Sebastian of Portugal sent six hundred well-trained soldiers and a group of "adventurers" to help King Alvaro, Afonso's successor, drive the Yaka invaders out of Kongo in 1569. This joint military venture was successful after four years of conflict.[55]

Yet the king of Kongo sided with the Dutch a century later when they tried to drive the Portuguese out of Angola in 1648. The Dutch were defeated, with help from Blacks brought over from Brazil to help the Portuguese who had enslaved them! The Portuguese proceeded immediately to demand that the Kongo king sign over to them all the mines in his country. When he refused, a war resulted and the defeated Kongo king was beheaded.

In the years that followed this defeat, the capital of San Salvador was abandoned and the kingdom became fragmented. Toward the end of the century the Portuguese formed an alliance with the Yaka. Balandier points out:

> when the political structure had dissolved and misery had become universal a series of movements combining mysticism with realism caused the awakening of the Kongo. A revealed religion was born at the same time that, under the impetus of its founders, the rebirth of political unity was being prepared.[56]

What some anthropologists call a "revitalization" movement was in the making.[57] Kongo now produced the equivalent of a Joan of Arc.

A 22-year-old Bukongo woman of aristocratic rank, named Kimpa Vita, became a priestess in a traditional African religious society. She also had a Christian name, Dona Beatriz. She now founded a syncretic cult. Balandier states that:

> She had been a priestess of the cult of Marinda before having the experiences that revealed her "saintliness" to her, before curiously repeating the adventure of Joan of Arc; like her she was called a heretic and undertook the mission of correcting the evils of the kingdom.[58]

Dona Beatriz claimed that when she was sick and at the point of death a monk dressed as a Capuchin brother appeared to her and said he was Anthony, patron saint of Portugal, "sent by God through her person . . . to preach to the people, hasten the restoration of the kingdom, and threaten all who tried to oppose it with severe punishments." She believed that, after her symbolic death, St. Anthony's soul entered her body. Then she arose, "called her parents, explained the divine commandment," and, "So as to do everything properly she began by distributing the few things she possessed, renouncing the things of this world." She withdrew to a mountain for prayer and meditation and lived as a hermit.[59]

In less than three years, Dona Beatriz attracted a sizeable band of followers for a movement that was complete with mythology and a creed. She became the spokesman of a remodeled African Christianity. Blacks and whites were essentially different, she said, Blacks made from fig trees and whites from stone. She accused the whites of corrupting the faith in order to possess the land and its wealth, an act which God would eventually reverse. Her followers believed that she "died" every Friday and went to Heaven "to dine with God and plead the cause of the Negroes, especially the restoration of the Kongo." She was "born" again on the following Sunday.[60]

As time went on, Dona Beatriz came to identify more with the Virgin Mary than with St. Anthony. This brought on her doom:

> She imitated the Virgin and longed to bring into the world a son who would become the saviour of the people, a son born of the intervention of the holy spirit; she wished to be regarded as chaste. A male child was born of whom she said, "I cannot deny that he is mine, but how I had him I do not know. I know however that he came to me from Heaven."[61]

Dona Beatriz was arrested soon after her child was born—a strategic moment for throwing doubt upon her honesty as well as her virginity. The royal council, with some urging from the Capuchin fathers who claimed to be motivated "solely by zeal for the glory of God," pronounced a sentence of death by fire. She was given a chance to recant just before the burning, and Father Laurent de Lucques describes the scene in terms that equate blackness with doom and esthetic undesirability: "[T]he judge appeared. He was clad from head to foot in a black mantle, and on his head wore a hat which was also black, *a black so ugly that I do not believe its like for ugliness has ever been seen*" [italics added].[62] And then the black "virgin" carrying her child was placed on the ground in front of the judge and "now appeared to be filled with fear and dread." Father de Lucques continues:

> We understood then that they had decided to burn the child along with the mother. This seemed to us too great a cruelty. I hastened to speak to the king to see whether there was some way to save him.

This humanitarian intervention did not deter the black king from serving his white god faithfully. Father de Lucques claims that the woman tried to recant as she was led to the stake, but,

> There arose such a great tumult among the multitude that it was impossible for us to be of assistance to the two condemned persons. They were quickly led to the stake. . . . For the rest all we can say is that there was gathered there a great pile of wood on which they were thrown. They were covered with other pieces of wood and burned alive. Not content with this, the following morning some men came again and burned the bones that remained and reduced everything to very fine ashes. . . . The poor Saint Anthony who was in the habit of dying and rising again, this time died but did not rise again.[63]

This priest said that Beatriz died "with the name of Jesus on her lips."

Neither the Franciscans, the Jesuits, nor the Capuchins—and they were all influential in the Kongo kingdom at one time or another— had introduced the cult of the Black Madonna from Europe. When a woman appeared in the flesh claiming to be a black Virgin Mary with a political as well as a religious mission, she, like Joan of Arc, was consigned to the flames. To the monks she represented a horrible caricature of the concept of the Holy Mother.

There is irony in Dona Beatriz's fate. Before the century was over, a great revolution erupted in France that was militantly anti-Roman Catholic. As a part of its assault on what it considered the irrational superstitions of the faith, it burned all of the images of the Black Madonna in central France that its zealots could find. Poetic justice is evident in both France and the Kongo. The numerous shrines of the Black Madonna in France are now tourist attractions. For many decades now, the Church in the Kongo (presently called Zaire) has encouraged artists to carve and paint Jesus and his mother as Negroes—although not as symbols of nationalist rebellion. Dona Beatriz, unlike Afonso the ideal Christian king, has been forgotten by the African masses.

There is a political irony as well. The kings of the Kongo, however subservient they were at times, never allowed Portugal to make a colony of their domain, although Belgium did in the twentieth century. Angola, which became the base for slave raiding, became a Portuguese colony much earlier. Portugal retained it despite constant rebellions until a "war of liberation" defeated the Portuguese forces during the 1960s. Neither in Africa nor Brazil did the Portuguese justify the exploitation of black people with theories that tabooed miscegenation, but White Racism became a support for colonial domination despite official denials of its existence.

CASTILIAN PRIDE AND PREJUDICE

Although they shared the Iberian peninsula, Spain's experience with black people created an ethos markedly different from that of the Portuguese. An Afro-American Latinist scholar has reminded us that in Spain as well as in the British Isles, tendencies toward racial discrimination were already present that could become more elaborate and entrenched in the New World setting. Professor Leslie B. Rout noted that,

> In consolidating their control in the New World, the Spanish attempted to graft onto the newly emerging society the social and philosophical ideas and beliefs then prevalent in medieval Castile. A key concept was that of "purity of the blood." In effect, the nobility, and all those who could claim to have had Christian ancestry, were assumed to have good moral character, and this attribute was passed on through inheritance. Moors, Jews, Africans, and other "new Christians" were assumed to suffer from moral disabilities.[64]

The concept of purity of blood had become salient in the context of the Inquisition, a drive authorized in 1478 to ferret out heretics.[65] The fanatically Christian rulers, having finally taken Andalusia from the Muslims, became almost paranoid in their fears of sedition. They were particularly suspicious of *Mozariba* (Moors who became Christians), *Moriscos* (Moors who adopted Spanish language and customs without converting), and *Conversos* (converted Jews). Although some were tried for blasphemy, Blacks were not singled out as targets of persecution.[66] Religion, not skin color, was the mark of the enemy. Hoetink explains:

> The principle of *limpieza de sangre*, purity of blood, showed all the elements of the colour-bar concept, except that the concept of "impure" blood did not have so much to do with hereditary biological traits as with the belief in the supposed obduracy of heretics, even to the extent that heresy was believed to be hereditary.[67]

Since heretics were white, brown, and black, skin color did not function as the sole or certain symbol of evil.

This concept of *limpieza de sangre* underwent a substantial metamorphosis during its passage to the New World. Skin color became not only relevant but determinate, as Rout explains:

> In Spanish America mixed blood came to be regarded as evidence of moral deficiency and intellectual inferiority. Socially and politically, the Spanish government lumped all the mixed bloods together and identified them as *castas* . . . systems delineating the status of the individual *casta*, based on the degree of Caucasian blood he supposedly possessed, came into use. . . . The effect of these socioracial categorizations was essentially to enforce the idea of white supremacy, while propagating the belief that African heritage was evil.[68]

What the Spanish call *castas* are not similar to East Indian castes, for as this author notes,

> during the eighteenth century some blacks made conspicuous socioeconomic advances . . . the number of black and mulatto militia officers increased significantly . . . some mulattoes were able to enter certain craft guilds and, through hard work, to enrich themselves. . . . Moreover, if the prosperous mulatto could pay, decreeing him "white" was a means of securing his loyalty.[69]

White Racism did not decisively fix an individual's status in Latin America. Neither legal *castas* nor customary mechanisms for moving upward through mixed-blood status groups existed in American colonies of British origin. Both Iberian and British cultures in the Americas transmitted the belief that "black blood" and "Indian blood" contributed a "taint" in individual heredity. The British colonies in the Americas did not provide what Carl Degler has called a "mulatto escape hatch."[70]

A Look at Spanish History

When the Muslim conquest of the Iberian peninsula began in the eighth century A.D., a tier of Christian kingdoms remained just south of the Pyrenees that included Leon, Aragon, Castile, and the northern part of Portugal. The rest of Spain was organized as Andalusia, which by the end of the ninth century A.D., covered over two-thirds of the peninsula. On the northern border with France, two Christian kingdoms, Leon and Castile, became the spearhead of what historians call the Reconquest, the expulsion of the Muslims by the Christians. It took seven hundred years for the Christians to complete the Reconquest, a conflict that left a strong imprint on Spain, where most of the fighting took place.

As we have seen in our discussion of the Muslim world, that culture made a deep impression on the Spanish culture in ways ranging from architecture to literature. Race relations and attitudes toward "blackness" and Negroes were also affected. Blacks, including Africans from south of the Sahara, became involved at many levels in the complicated politics of the Iberian peninsula. Not all of them were slaves. Those who were profited from a relatively benign system of Islamic slavery.

Ferdinand III of Castile scored the decisive success of the Reconquest with the capture of Cordova and Seville by the middle of the thirteenth century. It was agreed that the Moors could retain a kingdom around the city of Granada, in return for paying regular tribute to Castile. An old policy of mutual tolerance that had been disregarded was revived. Meanwhile the Christians prepared for a final expulsion of all Moors.

Toledo, under a Christian archbishop, became famous as a center where Christian, Jewish and Arab scholars translated each others' works of literature and philosophy, as well as Greek manuscripts. All European scholars profited from this contact with the more sophisticated Muslim culture.[71] Arabs and Moors passed on the accumulated knowledge of the East. Among some of the specific items was the Hindu invention of the zero, as well as Arabic numerals, which made it possible to dispense with the clumsy Roman system of alphabetical numbers. The study of medicine was revolutionized, and Constantine the African transmitted valuable translations of the Greek physician, Galen.[72]

Blacks and mulattoes must have taken part in this intellectual activity, although few scholars are so described. Certainly, European scholars were exposed to the names of earlier Blacks who had made contributions to literature and the arts in Muslim lands, such as the writer and historian al-Jahiz, whose works were available, and the musician Ziryab, who had been the reigning cultural pacesetter of Muslim Andalusia under al-Rahmin II.

Despite this period of friendly intercourse, rulers of Christian Spain came to hate the Moors they had struggled so long to expel. But the hatred did not imply any lack of respect or even admiration for the learning and skill of the enemy. Even then, pejorative remarks about the enemy's skin color are rare. Sylvia Wynter, an Afro-Caribbean scholar specializing in Hispanic literature, has commented on the text and illustrations of the eleventh-century *Cántigas*, in which a Christian king vilifies the enemy by using the skin-color contrast as a metaphor. Wynter writes:

> The black Moor is portrayed as the opposed term to the Christian religious metaphor. Like the other Moors, he is cast in the dread role of infidel, invader and defiler of Christian altars. The Moor, "black as pitch," was not only the opposed religion; his color was the opposite of "white," symbol of Christianity . . . the relation of the black Moor, symbolically, to the Devil was a relation which sprang from a reality in which the Mohammedan was the dominant power.[73]

Wynter notes an important point made by an Afro-American scholar who has analyzed the *Cántigas*, Miriam DeCosta. She stresses that "the black Moor was not denigrated (or feared as the case may be) because of his color, but because of his religion." Blackness was a symbol of Infidel power, not of Negro inferiority.[74]

Attitudes Toward Blacks and Slavery

The literature of the Christian Spaniards involves a rejection of the Negro physical type on esthetic grounds. However, as in the case of the classical Greeks, a decided preference for their own somatic norm image did not signify the imputation of a cognitive deficit to Negroes. Attitudes toward black slaves were compounded of noblesse oblige and Christian charity, as modified by Islamic values and practices.

By the thirteenth century, when Castile had become the most important Christian kingdom on a peninsula still divided between Muslims and Christians, a codification of Christian laws on slavery was made, *las siete partidas*. Professor Franklin Knight, in his study of slavery in Cuba, calls this "an extremely liberal slave code without equal among the other European nations. The legal basis for slavery was defined, the personality of the slave received recognition, and the right of all men and women to freedom was affirmed." Knight cited a portion of the code: "It is a rule of law that all judges should aid liberty, for the reason that it is a friend of nature, because not only men, but all animals love it."[75] Knight stresses the point that as Castile did not include either plantations or a wild frontier, a liberal code did not interfere with the operation of the prevailing economic system. Keeping any ethnic group in permanent subjection was alien to the law's intent. It was not formulated to deal with a Negro slave majority, but Blacks profited from it.

A change in the source and use of slaves during the fourteenth and fifteenth centuries made the relatively mild color prejudice in the Iberian culture more serious. Muslims from North Africa who had been captured in wars predominated. After Portugal had discovered Africa as a source of labor power, these black slaves were used in both Spain and Portugal on plantations recaptured from the Moors. Wynter talks about the change:

> After the establishment of the slave trade by the Portuguese, the dominant fact of black existence in Spain and Portugal was his existence not as a black, but as a slave . . . To be a Negro was to be a slave.[76]

However, the duties and rights of slaves were still controlled by the blending of Islamic and Christian law and custom. The idea that being a slave was the only proper status for a Negro was completely alien, as was the idea that all slaves should be black.

By the middle of the fifteenth century, Castile, and Aragon in alliance with it, had become the dominant military force on the Iberian peninsula. Castilians, proud to the point of arrogance, led in the Spanish exploration and settlement of the Americas. Although the majority of the individuals and families in Hispanic America may not have been from the kingdom of Castile, the values of the upper strata of that kingdom prevailed.[77]

Research is still needed on the institutionalized divisions among Negroes and mulattoes that Spanish colonists made according to the "purity" of their blood. In some parts of the Latin American Diaspora the elaboration of terminology for the degrees of mixture and/or physical types became so elaborate as to constitute an obsession.

In the Spanish system, three generations of absorbing "white blood" extinguished the "taint," bred it out, so to speak. An octoroon was born white. There was no such belief in British racial theory. However, from a black perspective even these "looser" attitudes toward miscegenation and mixed-blood progeny are sometimes labeled "racist." Implicit in the Spanish colonial system is extreme derogation of "Negroidness," and pressure for co-optation through miscegenation.[78] Professor Rout, summarizing his comparative study of Latin American nations, stated in 1975:

> Nominally all the Spanish American republics accept their black citizens as full-fledged participating members of the body politic, but the one universal truth is that black physical traits—kinky hair, thick lips, dark skin—are prized in no Spanish-American country. Even if the black individual succeeds against these odds and becomes wealthy and powerful, he is encouraged to mate with someone lighter-complexioned than himself in order to sire progeny

who will be more "acceptable." The racism inherent in this kind of social practice should be patently obvious.[79]

Using the terms employed in our analysis, we would call this skin-color prejudice that falls short of being racism. We would argue that it is essentially prejudice against "Negroidness," and not against dark skin-color generally or even black skin-color if not associated with Negro features and hair. It also allows for black upward mobility through wealth. Rout notes that:

> a blatantly discriminatory system such as that long in vogue in the southern United States was hardly possible in a miscegenated Spanish America, but the ambiguous acceptance of some mulattoes in no way negates the fact that race and color prejudice have always been trenchant aspects of the Spanish cultural heritage.[80]

Magnus Mörner, in *Race Mixture in the History of Latin America*, calls attention to causative factors:

> the Crown on the whole opposed intermarriage with the African element. One of the reasons for this attitude was that slaves were to be prevented from obtaining freedom for their children or even for themselves in this way. . . . The stigma of slavery and the fear of Moslem contamination were also present.[81]

In 1806 the Council of the Indies made explicit what had been implicit for centuries in Hispanic-American policies toward Blacks. The Council left us a classic statement on aristocratic justification of colonial color discrimination:

> The different hierarchies and strata are of greatest value to the monarchical state because their gradual and connected links of subordination and dependence support and substantiate the obedience and respect of the lower vassal towards the King. This is so not only because of the greater distance from the throne but because of the great number of people who by their vicious origin and nature cannot be compared with simple people in Spain and do constitute a very inferior species. It would be utterly reprehensible if those known to be sons and descendants of slaves sat down with those who derive from the first conquistadores or families that are noble, legitimate, white and free from any ugly stain.[82]

Although intermarriage with Africans was discouraged in Spain in a policy opposite to that in Portugal, having progeny by concubines was not tabooed either in Motherland or colonies.

It might be suggested that in both Spain and Portugal, and in their peripheral subcultures, the attitude toward unmixed Negroes is more similar to that of the Central Islamic Lands than to that of medieval Christendom. A demographic situation in which subordinated Blacks often outnumbered both whites and mixed-bloods tipped the scales away from the universalism of both Christian and Muslim values toward values and behavior necessary to protect the socioeconomic system and privileged strata within it.

The transfer of the sugar-growing complex from the African offshore islands to the New World accentuated tendencies toward *racial* slavery that were not typical of Iberian slavery. Because of the presence of ladinos in the system in Europe—Christianized and acculturated, and not all slaves—as well as white slaves, color prejudice was tempered. Values associated with slavery in the homeland made it difficult for a Latin American system to reduce Negroes to a completely degraded position. In fact, from the outset, some ladinos were treated with a substantial degree of trust and respect, as evidenced by Estevanico, who explored the area where the Pueblo Indians in the United States now live. About twenty years elapsed between the time Columbus made his first voyage and the first slaves from Africa were brought directly to the Caribbean.[83] Before that, at least one black sailor was with Columbus. Another was with Cortés when he explored Mexico, and others accompanied Balboa and Pizarro.

Blacks in the Literature of the Golden Age[84]

During the sixteenth century, African slavery became gradually institutionalized in Spain's American colonies. A steady diet of demeaning stock characters would be created in New World Hispanic literature. Some derogatory images arose in Spain, too. The literature of the Golden Age (1516-1681) includes a stereotype of the Negro as a buffoon, illiterate, uncouth, and prone to mangle the Spanish language. A prime example was Francisco Gómez de Quevedo's burlesque of a black wedding party, in his poem *Boda de negros*.

Nevertheless, the culture at home remained somewhat isolated from the colonial situation. Some favorable images of black people from Muslim Spain remained imbedded in Iberian culture after the Christian Reconquest. Black and brown faces were familiar in tapestries and illuminated manuscripts as a part of Iberian history that Castilian pride did not obliterate. Christian Spain also developed favorable images of its own, among them the Black Madonna of Montserrat and the black Wise Man, Balthasar. Some of these positive medieval images remained as a counter to derogatory propaganda spread by Spanish planters in the Americas. Writing at the time of New World explorations, the dramatist Lope de Vega turned the black Wise Man into King Melchor and placed a black queen and a black priest at his side.[85]

For the Spanish, black history did not begin with the unloading of slaves from Guinea on the wharfs of Cadiz and Lagos. Moorish romances and "frontier" stories became popular in the sixteenth and seventeenth centuries.[86] These were replete with black heroes. One book by Ginés Pérez de Hita told about Captain Farax, a black Moor who fought the Christians near Lorca, killing and enslaving many. He was eventually captured by the Christians, who tried to burn him alive, but Farax escaped to Africa. Another play portrayed him as a valiant and gallant foe.

The Moorish hero could also undergo a structuralist transformation. In one of Claramonte's dramas, the heathen hero is replaced by a Christian who covers himself with glory as he rises from private to general. In a drama by Lope de Vega, the hero is a Negro son of the king of Algeria, married to "an extraordinarily attractive black princess." Suspecting him of Christian sympathies, his father sends him to assist the Turks in their assault on the Christian island of Sardinia. As his father feared, the son defects and helps the Christians to a resounding victory over the Infidels. In another play, the black hero, Juan de Mérida, is stripped of his Muslim past and transformed into a black Christian general.

Writers of the Golden Age, as well as the literary Renaissance (1406-1516) that preceded it, evidently assumed their audiences would find nothing incongruous about the black queens and princesses in their stories. Thus, Calderón de la Barca writes about Persina, the black Queen of Ethiopia, and de Saba tells of a black Queen of Sheba. The story of the Amazons, "black with exquisite figures," who assisted the Turks in an assault on Constantinople is obviously taken from the African/Muslim tradition. But there is no Muslim element to be seen in a long poem on Granada by José Galardo that mentions a mulatto lady, Catalina de Soto, who was famous for her needlework, along with a black Dominican friar and the noted black scholar Juan Latino. Cervantes, familiar with both the Muslim and Castilian traditions, included two black female *servants* and four white slave girls in his *The Jealous Estremadurian*.

As time goes on, Spanish literature reflects the loss of self-esteem that black people began to suffer after the Reconquest. In the play, *Eufemia, the Dark Domestic*, a woman is trying to bleach her hair and skin to please her Spanish lover. He reassures her that no white face could be dearer than hers, that her body is smooth as velvet, though her face is dark.[87] But the need for reassurance reveals the general devaluation of dark skin color.

Afro-American scholars from the time of Carter Woodson in the 1920s have been interested in a critical examination of Spanish literature. Dr. Martha Cobb, writing in 1972, states that such works often express duality of concept: the stereotyping of Blacks as illiterate, uncouth buffoons, but also expressions of compassion for them because they are enslaved; exposure of their contemporary degradation, but also portrayals as they were during the heroic age of Muslim Spain or in early Christendom. There is consciousness of a lower-class group that mangles pure Castilian Spanish into *negroide*, but the recognition, too, of brilliant exceptions. This literature was produced after Castile and Aragon had completed the expulsion of the Moors from Andalusia.

The Black Experience in Christian Spain

Ruth Pike, in writing a book about the *conversos* [converted Jews] in sixteenth-century Seville, devoted some attention to the status of Negroes in this city of about 50,000 people. At least 10,000 of them were Africans and people of whole or partial African descent. Her work gives us a glimpse of the type of relations between black and white people that existed in Iberian cities during the period of the initial settlement of the Americas. Pike notes of the ladino population that:

> Competition for jobs strained relations between freedmen and the white Sevillian laborers. The whites showed their contempt for Negroes with the customary sidewalk jeer (*estornudo*). On the individual level, however, Negroes and whites mixed freely and contacts were friendly. Miscegenation and common-law unions were frequent. Many Sevillians, including members of the clergy, maintained illicit relationships with female household slaves and in some instances recognized their illegitimate children. Among the servant class miscegenation was common practice and mixed marriages were not unknown. . . . The very willingness of Negroes to become Christians and to remain faithful to their new religion facilitated their popular acceptance. In addition, their incorporation into the social and ritual activities of the church accelerated the process of their Hispanization.[88]

Pike notes that Negro, Moorish, and Morisco slaves made up a sizeable and conspicuous part of the population of Seville during the sixteenth century. Despite absorption through miscegenation, the city contained several barrios that "were especially noted for their numerous Negro residents."[89] In 1475, Juan de Valladolid, a royal servant popularly known as "the Negro count," was appointed *mayoral* of the Seville Negro community. Free persons of color, as well as slaves, lived in these sections. Pike describes one of them:

> Slaves who worked at outside jobs to support themselves and their owners usually did not reside in their masters' homes. Although they were scattered throughout the poorer sections of Seville, their traditional quarter was the parish of San Bernardo, located outside the city walls in a swampy region dominated by a foul-smelling stream called the Tagarete. This was a poor parish inhabited by working people—gardeners employed in the nearby Alcázar, employees of the municipal slaughterhouse, and bakers who worked in the many baking establishments in the district. It was also a high crime area and was known for its numerous ruffians and bullies, many of whom occasionally worked at odd jobs in the slaughterhouse.
>
> By the last quarter of the century the population of San Bernardo had increased so greatly that church and municipal authorities decided to divide San Bernardo and to create the new parish of San Roque. The chapel of the Hospital of Our Lady of the Angels was chosen to serve as a temporary parish church for San Roque, and, maintained by the Negro religious confraternity, it remained the center of the district's religious life until the completion of the church of San Roque in 1585. Nine years later, the confraternity purchased three lots opposite the new church and built a chapel that they occupied in the last years of the century.[90]

According to Pike, the church plaza was a favorite meeting place:

> Among the Negroes who assembled in the Plaza de Santa María la Blanca were many freedmen and women. Although most Sevillian Negroes were slaves, the city also contained a significant free Negro population. Enfranchisement was not a step toward economic and social betterment, however, for Negroes and mulattoes, whether slaves or freedmen, remained on the lowest rungs of the social ladder. Ex-slaves continued to work in unskilled and menial jobs and to reside in the same neighborhoods as before their emancipation. *A combination of discrimination and unfavorable economic conditions prevented freedmen from rising in society.* The artisans feared Negro competition and jealously excluded them from the few skilled positions which the inadequate Sevillian industry afforded. Even unskilled jobs were at a premium in Seville because of the steady flow of landless peasants from the countryside into the town. Chronic unemployment and severe food shortages were the realities

of life for the majority of Sevillians throughout the sixteenth century [italics added].[91]

One type of discrimination was the understandable rule erected by the guilds that no slave craftsmen, black or white, could belong to them. The use of slave labor was an obvious threat to their welfare. Pike observes that Blacks could still be employed by master craftsmen in their shops, and that in some cases craftsmen purchased slaves to work in their establishments, sometimes as apprentices.[92] It would seem that social and political considerations, not White Racism or abstract notions of "blackness," accounted for the barrier to guild membership.

There was, however, some institutionalized separation of Blacks and whites, and even between Blacks and mulattoes. Thus, one Seville parish contained "enough mulattoes . . . to justify the creation of a religious confraternity" that had its own chapel and a separate door opening on the "Street of the Mulattoes." These patterns were reinforced by the doctrine of "purity of blood" that characterized Seville society. The institution of confraternities was transferred to Hispanic America. Division of the society into segments based on color laid the basis for social stratification in the Americas that has been dubbed by one scholar a "pigmentocracy."[93]

Some stereotypes from Spain were transferred to the Americas. In the "Motherland" slaves were used in all sorts of domestic service, in the handling of horses and carriages, and in some "odd jobs in connection with their masters' business." Pike also notes, significantly for later stereotypes, that:

> Another especially desirable quality in a slave was the ability to sing, play and dance, as music and dancing were popular pastimes during the period. Negroes showed particular fondness and aptitude for both music and dance and were often in great demand as entertainers at private parties and public celebrations.[94]

Another form of slavery also existed in Seville, and throughout Andalusia: the systematic exploitation of slave labor for profit. Many Sevillians considered slaves a capital investment and a profitable—sometimes exclusive—source of income. These black slaves were sent out to the workplace.

> They were a common sight on the Seville waterfront, where they worked as stevedores. Many performed menial tasks in the famous soap factories or in the public granary. Others earned a living as porters, street vendors, and bearers of sedan chairs. There is also

some evidence that they served as *corchetes* (constables), a rather unpopular calling in sixteenth century Seville.[95]

Blacks and mulattoes from Seville sometimes went to the Americas. One case reveals the confidence and trust occasionally placed in an individual slave, not unlike a pattern prevalent in the Muslim world.

> As early as 1502, the Sevillian trader Juan de Córdoba sent his Negro slave and two other agents to sell merchandise for him on the island of Hispaniola. Seven years later Juan de Zafra, a Negro slave, was commissioned by his master, the well-known Sevillian physician Dr. Alvarez Chanca, to sell goods in the New World. Zafra remained in America for several years, and until his death in 1515 he acted as a commission agent for his master. Most famous of all the Negro traders in America was Pedro Franco, who was freed by his master Franco Leardo, a wealthy and prominent Genoese merchant of Seville, just a few months before he left for America. Leardo gave him 300 ducats and sent him to Panama as his agent, probably under the usual four-year partnership contract (compañía). Several other Sevillians besides Leardo entrusted him with merchandise to be sold in the New World. Unfortunately, Pedro Franco was not able to fulfill the terms of his contract with Leardo, for he died within a year after his arrival on the Isthmus. In his last will and testament he left all of his property to his former master.[96]

Although Pike makes no reference to ladinos returning to Spain after making their fortunes in the New World, she does mention some free Negroes, presumably ladinos, seeking their fortunes in the Americas. She notes that

> If it was difficult for freedmen to improve their status in Seville, they might seize the opportunity to emigrate to the New World. The registers of the Casa de Contratación indicate that many Negro freedmen crossed the ocean to America during the sixteenth century. Most of these emigrants were single men and women with young children and of family groups.[97]

Seville was only one of a number of Iberian cities that had a black and mulatto population living within Christendom after the fourteenth century. If accepted as typical of urban race relations, it must be recognized that there were significant variations. However, in the present state of research on the Black Experience in these urban situations, a comparative statement is impossible. Among literate people throughout Christian Spain there was, however, a common stock of ideas and practices that included some mild color prejudice existing side by side with relationships, conceptions, and attitudes that ignored it. As in Muslim Spain some slaves and ex-slaves became upwardly mobile by virtue of exceptional talent.

Some Blacks penetrated the upper reaches of "the hierarchic, estate based corporative society of late Medieval Castile." This was a pattern that could not be transferred to the New World, where social systems were based upon a broad stratum of subordinated Blacks. In 1528, a young West African woman and her twelve-year-old son became slaves in the household of the daughter of a famous Spanish general in Cordova. When the family moved to Granada a few years later, the black boy became guardian of his mistress's six-year-old son. He joined his ward at the Cathedral School and then at the University of Granada. As Janheinz Jahn phrases it, he was "so outstanding in Latin that he renounced his slave name Juan de Sessa and called himself Juan Latino."[98]

Juan Latino received his bachelor's degree at about the age of thirty. He played the organ, lute, and guitar, and began to move about with the stylish young set of Granada. He married a girl he had been employed to tutor. In 1557, Juan Latino became a professor at the University of Granada, a post he held until ill health brought his retirement in 1586. Over the years, he was a confidant of Don John of Austria and the Duke of Sessa, and published a considerable body of poetry.

Critics agree that Juan Latino's verses show "the erudite academic style of the period, the zealous Spanish Catholicism and patriotism, interspersed with countless classical allusions."[99] His career is proof that being black was not an insuperable barrier to movement, via talent and education, into the ranks of the Spanish aristocracy. The epitaph on his tombstone, however, shows that his origins were never forgotten, although this is seen as consciousness of cultural and religious differences rather than an expression of color prejudice:

> To Master Juan Latino
> Professor of Granada and Dona Ana de Carlobal
> his wife and his heirs MDLXXIII
> Scholar of famous Granada and teacher
> of brilliant young students,
> Orator pious in speech, outstanding in doctrine
> and morals.
> Offspring and son deep black with black
> Ethiopian forebears.

He learnt as an innocent child the precepts
 that lead to salvation.
He sang in the fair Latin tongue the
 illustrious Austrian's glories,
Under this pillar he lies, he will
 rise with his wife well beloved.[100]

That Juan Latino was honored in Granada should come as no surprise, for that city had always given free expression to the talent of both Blacks and Jews. More significant is the fact that he was embraced as part of the emerging national culture. Lope de Vega, the dramatist, referred to Juan Latino in his play *La Dama Boba*, and Diego Ximénez de Encisco wrote a play about him in his *Comedias Escogidas*. The great Cervantes, in a poem prefixed to *Don Quixote*, spoke of "black Latino's gift of tongues."

Dr. Martha Cobb evaluates Juan Latino's career from a modern Afro-American black esthetics perspective:

> He wrote like a white Spaniard, with no central theme that concerned itself with his African origins nor with the condition of slavery that he not only must have witnessed but must himself have been subjected to. . . . The success of Juan Latino was achieved despite the fact that he was African. The price exacted was that he convert to Christianity, cut loose from his African origins, and adopt the Spanish way of life. By Spanish standards, therefore, he was judged a worthy individual.[101]

MISCEGENATION AND ACCULTURATION IN THE BRITISH ISLES

Sixteenth-century Britain had neither an intellectual inheritance nor a body of experience based on contact to prepare it for intimate relations with Africans. Its cities had no large population of slaves as did Seville and Lisbon. Britain had no literature and folklore favorable to Blacks as did the Iberians. When the first British ships sailed along the coast of Africa and into the Caribbean, the people of the Iberian Peninsula were just ending almost eight hundred years of prolonged contact on their own soil with Africans in varied roles and at many levels of social status. In contrast, black and brown people were few and far between in the British Isles. Yet, before the end of the seventeenth century, Britain had become the primary source of information and speculation about the assumed proclivities and capabilities of Africans. We shall concentrate upon examining interpersonal relations in Britain involving esthetic and erotic evaluations, as revealed in literature.

Britain vied with Holland for the monopoly in the buying and selling of black slaves during the seventeenth century. What impact did this introduction to Africa and Africans via slavery and the slave trade have on race relations in Britain itself? It must have been significant because it was in London, not Seville or Lisbon, that the following words appeared in 1788, in what was said to be "perhaps the most popular and influential English-language periodical of the day"—*Gentleman's Magazine*. A stereotype of "The Negro" was being propagated here that eventually overwhelmed all competing images of the black personality and character:

> The Negro is possessed of passions not only strong but ungovernable; a mind dauntless, warlike and unmerciful; a temper extremely irascible; a disposition indolent, selfish and deceitful; fond of joyous sociality, riotous mirth and extravagant shew. He has certain portions of kindness for his favorites, and affections for his connections; but they are sparks which emit a glimmering light through the thick gloom that surrounds them, and which in every ebullition of anger or revenge, instantly disappear. Furious in his love as in his hate; at best, a terrible husband, a harsh father and a precarious friend. A strong and unalterable affection for his countrymen and fellow passengers in particular seems to be the most amiable passion in the Negro breast. . . . As to all other fine feelings of the soul, the Negro, as far as I have been able to perceive, is nearly deprived of them.[102]

This is not *le bon éthiopien* of medieval Europe, an image Britain never shared.

For the next century, Anglo-Saxons in England, North America, and the Caribbean would claim to be the "experts on 'The Negro.'" In the sixteenth century, however, the stereotype of "The Negro" had not yet crystallized, although elements of it were present in the varied images then current, some from the medieval heritage and some being created by the Elizabethan and Jacobean dramatists.

English voyagers did not touch the shores of West Africa until after 1550 and almost a hundred years elapsed before they became heavily involved in the slave trade. Before that period, they did, however, carry on commerce in other commodities in West Africa, where the Portuguese were trying to maintain a trading monopoly. A number of books about Africans appeared in Britain.[103] There is an oft-quoted legend that the captain of a British ship sailing off the African coast in the early sixteenth century was offered a cargo of slaves. "I made answer we were a people who did not deal in any such commodities, neither did wee [sic] buy or sell one another, or any that had our own shapes," was his legendary reply.[104] This was true then, but it would not always be so. Nor had it been.

A Look at British History

The English people had known slavery at a time when Europeans, not Blacks or any other colored ethnic group, were enslaved in Britain. From early in its history, the British Isles had experienced slavery as an element in the system of social organization and had used people as a medium of exchange. There were some who profited from the European slave trade that preceded the trade in Africans. Marc Bloch mentions that "great Britain furnished many slaves to the continent as far away as Provence and Rome, torn as she was by frequent wars between the Anglo-Saxon kings or against the Celtic peoples who were themselves prey to internal strife."[105]

The Norman invasion of Britain during the eleventh century brought additional British slaves to the continent. In the Domesday Book, the Normans documented the fact that slavery still flourished in England. The French invaders provided a model of feudal relations that eventually replaced slavery throughout the British Isles.

After an intensive comparative study, Bloch concludes that "England was definitely the country where slavery, properly so-called, kept an important place in economic life to the longest time in all of Europe."[106] Even in the twelfth century, when Western and Central Europeans had generally banned the enslaving of fellow Christians, that rule was ignored in Britain:

> A continual guerrilla war raged there between the Saxons and Celts, who were Christians of course, but were adversaries willingly considered foreign to Roman orthodoxy. It is not an accident if we can see so many slaves and freedmen there carrying Celtic names or surnames such as "Scot."[107]

Bloch adds that

> the Anglo-Saxon conquerors of the English island used their word for "Welsh" also to mean "slave." The internal slave market as distinct from enslavement of prisoners of war ended in Britain by the middle of the eleventh century, but export of large numbers of boys and girls had been taking place during the tenth and eleventh centuries to Italy and Ireland, and perhaps Spain. The girls were sometimes fattened in order to increase their market value. *This trade was virtually wiped out as the Germans pressing eastward on the*

continent flooded the market with Slav prisoners of war after the twelfth century [italics added].[108]

Slavery within Britain disappeared during the fourteenth and fifteenth centuries, as the wars against France and numerous peasant revolts strengthened the position of both the yeoman class and serfs. Also, an emerging sense of national consciousness was inconsistent with slavery. This emphasis on "freedom" eventually ended the enslavement of fellow Christians. Until the sixteenth century, Britain would have no contact with "infidels" or "pagans" who could be enslaved. There had been no code specifically designed to protect slaves as in Spain and Portugal. Nor did Blacks assume the position in religious iconography that they did on the continent.

Britain remained somewhat isolated from the culture of Western Europe that produced positive images of blackness and black people during the Middle Ages, such as Black Madonnas and the cult of St. Maurice. There were no pilgrimages or stained glass cathedral windows to keep alive the concept of black dignity and worth. Blackness as a concept, and *black* people, did appear in British folk drama and in those productions known as Mystery Plays that were staged by guilds. To the English, black people were "strangers" when contact with them began in the sixteenth century.

Mythological Blacks did not carry a benign aura inherited from the Greek tradition or medieval European Christianity. One scholar claims that, from the period of the Crusades, "blackness" had been a standard characteristic of Satan, who was occasionally even referred to as an "Ethiopian."[109] Devils were also sometimes, but not always, presented as black in the Mystery Plays, which began after 1300 and thus may have reflected continental influences that reached England with the Norman conquest.[110] One such drama cycle referred to Lucifer as a "devil full dark who was an angel bright" before being cast out of heaven for his defiance of God.[111]

While the British peasants and city folk were depicting the Devil as black in the Mystery Plays, it is reported that in folk festivals not sponsored by the Church, "the early sword dancers used to blacken their faces with the festival fire."[112] This medieval folk festival is considered to be a pagan survival. There was probably a direct line of cultural transmission between ancient fertility cults and the mummers who performed the Morris Dance on some occasions, although the dance itself was most likely a Moorish dance introduced into England from Spain by way of France.[113]

On the continent, "It was the custom in good societies for a boy to come into the hall when supper was finished, with his face blackened, his forehead bound with white or yellow taffeta, and bells tied to his legs. He then proceeded to dance the Morisco dance."[114] In England, by Shakespeare's time, the Morris dance had become a popular May festival featuring the characters of Robin Hood, Maid Marian, Friar Tuck, and other outlaws of Sherwood Forest.[115] Only the bells on the ankles remained, and the dancers no longer blackened their faces. A favorable black image of Moors borrowed from the continent had disappeared.

Meanwhile, participation in the far-off wars of the Crusade against the Infidel Muslims had made Moors symbols of the devil for Englishmen as the battles of the Reconquest had done for the Spaniards. There was a tendency to make the equivalence: Satan = Black = Moor. (The Devil was sometimes referred to as "Mahamet.") "Ethiopians" were recognized as another kind of black person, and were no longer considered equivalent to evil, thanks to Protestant biblical exegesis and the Prester John mythology, but *The* Negro was sometimes given a demonic significance, nevertheless.

Attitudes Toward Blacks and Slavery

Winthrop Jordan is convinced that a Manichaean black-white contrast was present in the British symbol system prior to the fifteenth century:

> In England, perhaps more than in southern Europe, the concept of blackness was loaded with intense meaning. Long before they found that some men were black, Englishmen found in the idea of blackness a way of expressing some of their most ingrained values. . . . Black was an emotionally partisan color, the handmaid and symbol of baseness and evil, a sign of danger and repulsion. . . . White and black connoted purity and filthiness, virginity and sin, virtue and baseness, beauty and ugliness, beneficence and evil, God and the devil.[116]

Jordan does not explain why the affective response associated with "black" was so much greater in England than on the continent. But he insists that this aversion to the color black "carried over" to the skins of people in the first contacts between Englishmen and Africans. Jordan feels that contact with black people had a shock effect on the British:

> In this respect the English experience was markedly different from that of the Spanish and Portuguese who for centuries had been in

close contact with North Africa and had actually been invaded and subjected by people both darker and more highly civilized than themselves. The impact of the Negro's color was the more powerful upon Englishmen, moreover, because England's principal contact with Africans came in West Africa and the Congo where men were not merely dark but almost literally black; one of the fairest-skinned nations suddenly came face to face with one of the darkest peoples on earth.[117]

Jordan says that the first West Africans seen in London probably arrived in 1554 in the persons of five young men brought over to learn the language so they could be helpful to British merchants trading on the Guinea coast.[118] Within fifty years, Blacks were present in Britain as cooks, house servants, common laborers, and even as clerks. English historian James Walvin describes them as "everyday sights" in seventeenth-century Britain, "assimilated almost to the point of equality with white Englishmen particularly in religious and sexual matters."[119] This occurred despite intensely negative attitudes toward the color black, if Jordan is correct. It also tends to refute the Degler-Gergen thesis linking derogation of blackness in the symbol system with attitudes toward black people.

The original group of Africans living in Britain in the sixteenth century, and their descendants, did not enter the social system as slaves, and there was no relationship between race and servitude. Within a century, however, other black people living in North America and the Caribbean under the British flag would be subjected to a very harsh form of *racial* slavery developed in connection with the cultivation of sugar.

Winthrop Jordan indicates how British attitudes toward black people may have originated:

> Elizabethans were not in the business of modeling themselves after Spaniards. Yet, from about 1550, Englishmen were in such continual contact with the Spanish that they could hardly have failed to acquire the notion that Negroes could be enslaved . . . from the first, Englishmen tended to associate, in a diffuse way, Negroes with the Portuguese and Spanish. The term *negro* itself was incorporated into English from the Hispanic languages in mid-sixteenth century and *mulatto* a half century later.[120]

After some hesitation, Queen Elizabeth granted permission for British ships to engage in the slave trade. When Britain broke Spanish sea power with the defeat of the Armada in 1588, Elizabeth promptly granted certain favored merchants exclusive rights for ten years to supply slaves to Spanish colonies in the New World. Like the Spanish sovereign before her, she received a "cut" for each black body delivered. In 1618, thirty London merchants, the Company of Adventurers, were granted the slaving concession. They were followed by the Royal Adventurers of 1660 and the Royal African Company in 1672.

Commerce in black bodies rapidly became big business. In 1713, England secured the *asiento* that gave her traders a monopoly on supplying slaves to Spanish colonies, with a rebate, per head, to the Spanish Crown. Moreover, Britain now had its own colonies in the New World, with plantations that required cheap labor.

At home in Great Britain, the public had viewed Africans as interesting human beings; now, many thought of black people only as slaves. From the beginning of British involvement in the African slave trade, a distinction was drawn between the buying and selling of slaves—or even their possession—by Englishmen in the colonies, and the keeping of Negroes—or any other people—in slavery within the British Isles. A few slaves were present in Britain in various capacities, but there was uneasiness about that situation.

As the British public learned to sing a boastful song, "Rule Britannia, Britannia rules the waves/ Britons never, never, shall be slaves," some Englishmen also insisted that *any* slave, British or otherwise, black or white, should be automatically freed by setting foot on British soil. Those who knew their country's history of slavery insisted that such un-British activity occurred long before Britain had evolved into a bastion of freedom. By the middle of the seventeenth century, some Protestant religious sectarians, especially Quakers, were questioning the righteousness of slavery, even when they were unsure about the capabilities of black men or the status they should have in a white society.[121]

The Philosophical Debate

It is clear from the literature of the last half of the sixteenth century that some educated Englishmen did not believe that all Blacks were intended to be slaves by nature or Providential Design. Older concepts of slavery as a social condition resulting from accidents of warfare or birth into an enslaved family still prevailed. The causes of slavery were discussed quite apart from the causes of differences in physical appearance among the peoples of the world. Very few Englishmen were involved in buying and selling Africans, and virtually none owned them as slaves. There was nothing in law or tradition about how Englishmen should deal with slaves. These would become matters for debate in the eighteenth and nineteenth centuries.

In the seventeenth, the basic intellectual concern was simple curiousity about black people. Englishmen had read about them in the Bible and classical sources, but they now began to appear in the flesh in Britain. Questions about Blacks that puzzled Englishmen were not on the minds of people in Spain and Portugal, where environmental explanations of race from the the Islamic tradition were still widely accepted.

George Best, an English explorer and man of letters, became obsessed with the question of why black people are black. Environmental theories that the sun blackened their skin and curled their hair failed to explain something else he had observed in the 1500s:

> Therefore to returne againe to the blacke Moores, I my self have seene an Ethiopian as blacke as a cole brought into England, who taking a faire English woman to wife, begat a sonne in all respects as blacke as the father was, although England was his native countrey, and an English woman his mother: whereby it seemeth this blacknes proceedeth rather of some natural infection of that man, which was so strong, that neither the nature of the Clime, neither the good complexion of the mother concurring, coulde any thing alter, and therefore, wee cannot impute it to the nature of the Clime.[122]

In view of developments associated with the emergence of racism, it is significant that George Best expresses no racially motivated indignation over the black man "taking a faire English woman to wife," although his reference to "good complexion" reveals an esthetic judgment.

Best was not only wondering why the couple had such a dark child, he was puzzled, too, by the fact that dark people had lived for centuries in northern climes without bleaching out. Fifth-century Athenians had raised similar questions. To account for the "blackness" of Africans, he went back to what he believed were the original ancestors:

> the most probable cause to my judgement is, that this blackenesse proceedeth of some naturall infection of the first inhabitants of the Country, and so all the whole progenie of them descended, are still polluted with the same blot of infection. Therefore it shall not bee farre from our purpose, to examine the first originall of these blacke men, and howe by a lineall discent they have hitherto continued thus blacke.[123]

He stated his belief that Noah's son Ham had "used the company with his wife" while on the Ark, in defiance of Noah's command, and for this sexual sin, God decreed that his son Chus (i.e., Kush or Cush) and "all his posteritie after him should be so blacke and lothsome, that it might remaine a spectacle of disobedience to all the worlde. And of this blacke and cursed Chus came all these blacke Moores which are in Africa. . . . Thus you can see that the cause of the Ethiopians blacknesse is the curse and the naturall infection of blood."[124]

Old beliefs, neglected and not widely known, now became functional. Apparently, George Best had discovered the Babylonian Talmud version of the Ham story, and he was using it, instead of the more familiar biblical story, to bolster his theory about the origin of the Negro's skin color.[125] He was using it, too, to reinforce a stereotype of black hyper-sexuality that was already prevalent in some British circles, but not to justify enslavement of Blacks. A stereotype had not yet become the basis for an ideology.

The first British colony in North America was not established until about twenty-five years after George Best wrote, and the colonies in Barbados twenty-three years after that. A need for justifying slavery had not yet begun to shape British thinking about black people. Soon after the acquisition of Barbados, opposition to slavery and the slave trade arose. Thus, a quarter of a century after Englishmen began to use Africans to cultivate cane in the West Indies, and sixty-eight years after George Best's repetition of the Talmudic version of the Ham story, Sir Thomas Browne attacked prejudice against Blacks in his "Enquiries Into Vulgar and Common Errors."

By then, apologists for slavery were using this version of the Ham story to elaborate anti-Negro ideology. Browne dismissed the Ham story as "sooner affirmed than proved," and said that it carried with it "sundry improbabilities." He pointed these out by suggesting that in taking the Hebrew stories at their face value, (i.e., as affecting all descended from Ham) the curse might be extended even to Italy![126]

The most significant aspect of Sir Thomas's remarkable discussion was his closely reasoned argument against a standard of beauty that would condemn all black people as ugly, and his comment on "blackness" that

> Whereas men affirm this colour was a Curse, I cannot make out the propriety of that name, it neither seeming so to them, nor reasonably unto us; for they take so much content therein, that they esteem

deformity by other colours, describing the Devil, and terrible objects, white.[127]

Sir Thomas was writing in the tradition of al-Jahiz of Basra, who took up cudgels in the ninth century against proponents of the inferiority of the "Zanj" under Islam in Mesopotamia. As Jordan has pointed out, there was a persistent attempt in Britain, throughout the sixteenth and seventeenth centuries, to define Africans as "ugly" and as "apelike," the latter designation implying certain immoral qualities as well as lack of physical beauty. Sir Thomas took up the case on the side of the Africans:

> . . . if we seriously consult the definitions of beauty, and exactly perpend what wise men determine thereof, we shall not apprehend a curse, or any deformity therein. For first, some place the essence thereof in the proportion of parts, conceiving it to consist in a comely commensurability of the whole unto the parts, and the parts between themselves: which is the determination of the best and learned writers. Now hereby the Moors are not excluded from beauty: there being in this description no consideration of colours, but an apt connexion and frame of parts and the whole. Others there be, and those most in number, which place it not only in proportion of parts, but also in grace of colour. But to make Colour essential unto Beauty, there will arise no slender difficulty: For Aristotle in two definitions of pulchritude, and Galen in one, have made no mention of colour.[128]

Having discussed the esthetic question as a philosophical issue, Sir Thomas then took an anthropological approach:

> For Beauty is determined by opinion, and seems to have no essence that holds one notion with all; that seeming beauteous unto one, which hath no favor with another; and that unto every one, according as custome hath made it natural, or sympathy and conformity of minds shall make it seem agreeable. Thus flat noses seem comely unto the Moor, an Aquiline or hawked one unto the Persian.[129]

Sir Thomas made a telling argument for convincing the British upper class when he reminded his readers that "horses are handsome under any colour, and the symmetry of parts obscures the consideration of complexions." Arguing by analogy, he concluded that "likewise the Moors escape the curse of deformity."[130]

By the middle of the seventeenth century, in England, the lines were already drawn between some scholars who denigrated Africans and others who defended them (the "vindicationists"); between those who were elaborating a derogatory stereotype of "the Negro" and those who not only refused to participate in the process but who also insisted that the stereotype did not reflect complex reality. It is significant that this type of debate did not take place in Spain. Familiarity with black people made it unnecessary. The equivalent there was a debate among theologians about American Indians.[131]

While intellectuals discussed the origin of black people and evaluated their esthetic and cognitive condition, ambivalent popular images about black people were also in evidence. New World slavery favored the survival of derogatory images of Blacks. Some positive images also existed in Britain, although favorable images were not so prevalent as on the continent. The British masses had not had the exposure to "blackness" that continental Catholics had through pilgrimages to shrines of black religious figures.

Black People on Stage

One clue to popular conceptions of black people is provided in presentations of Moors on the Elizabethan and early post-Elizabethan stage. Shakespearean plays were designed to appeal to mass audiences. They were not court dramas.[132] They were written to please the groundlings as well as the people in the boxes. A comparison of two of Shakespeare's plays is illuminating.

In *Titus Andronicus*, produced as early as 1594, the Moor is presented as a sinister and repulsive character. *Othello*, depicted on the stage a decade later, in 1604, is a "noble Moor." Either Shakespeare or his audience—or both—had changed during that short period. If Walvin is correct that Blacks were accepted as equals by ordinary people during the seventeenth century, Shakespeare had correctly taken the pulse of his public. Empathy was possible. The "Moor" had been an abstraction for most Londoners when the first play was written, but many black people were living in England by the time *Othello* was produced.

Titus Andronicus is so "coarse" a melodrama that some scholars do not believe Shakespeare wrote it. The hero is an elderly Roman soldier of a noble family who has returned home after victories against the barbarian Goths. Among the prisoners of war is the queen of the Goths, who marries the emperor of Rome as part of the peace-making process.

Her faithful attendant and clandestine lover is Aaron the Moor, whose presence among the Goths is never explained. Aaron, whose makeup included an "intense black face,"[133] is a villain who seduces the queen to his will and immediately sows dissension. When the queen bears a black baby, her attendants want to kill it. This Aaron will not allow, proudly defending his "blackness." The Moor dies, but not before conspiring to have several relatives of Titus Andronicus maimed and slaughtered. There is even an episode involving cannibalism, but it is the white Goths, not Aaron, who prepare the meal and eat it.

The Moor is characterized by adultery, deceit and murder, which must have aroused considerable dislike and suspicion of "blackamoors" among those who saw *Titus Andronicus*. According to one Shakespearean critic, Aaron the Moor is "the antithesis of all Christian goodness. He is willful wickedness incarnate."[134]

An entry in the Stationer's Registry of London may explain how Shakespeare thought up this story and why he thought it would appeal to a London audience. The request dated July 22, 1570, asks for a license to print "a history intituled a strange and petiefull novell dyscoursunge of a noble Lorde and his Lady, with theyre tragicall end of them and thayre 11 children executed by a blacke morryon." *The Tragical History of Titus Andronicus* was published anonymously in England with a note, "Newly Translated from the Italian Copy printed at Rome." It was presumably widely read in London. The synopsis refers to "a bloody Moor" and "the wicked Moor." This figure is unnamed in the Italian story, and the plot differs from Shakespeare's in many significant details.

Othello was another adaptation of an Italian tale, but in this case Shakespeare's genius transformed the story into a dramatic tragedy about "the noble Moor." Shakespearean scholars believe that the plot of *Othello* was taken from a work available in French as early as 1584, the *Hecatommithi* of Giovanbattista Giraldi Cinthio. One section contains several stories about "The Unfaithfulness of Husbands and Wives," including the tale of "a Moor who was very valiant and a handsome person" married to an Italian girl. They lived in peace and harmony in Venice. The malevolent Iago convinces the husband that his wife has fallen in love with another man because, as he tells him, "she has taken an aversion to your blackness." The Moor kills his wife and is denounced as a "barbarian." He is told "you Moors are of so hot a nature that every little trifle moves you to anger and revenge." The Moor does not commit suicide, but is banished from the Italian city.[135]

A British Shakespearean scholar suggests that Cinthio's purpose in telling the story was "to warn young ladies against disproportioned marriages," and to impress on them that "they should not link themselves to such against whom Nature, Providence, and a different way of living have interposed a bar." This sounds like a British assessment of an Italian's mind. Neither does it seem to have been Shakespeare's intent, though critics find varied meanings in *Othello*.[136]

Lemuel Johnson suggests that Shakespeare deliberately avoided making Othello a devil, as he had almost done with Aaron in *Titus Andronicus*.[137] He notes, too, that even when casting Aaron in the villain's role, a "'black-is-beautiful' inversion is expressed sometimes with a surprising lyrical tenderness that is startlingly incongruous in a play that thrives on horrifying perversions." Aaron's defense of his infant son illustrates this point. Other critics feel that the youthful Shakespeare "was trying to outdo some of his predecessors" in inventing horrors, but that he was a more mature man when he created "the noble Moor." Johnson, himself, suggests that "we may look upon *Othello* as the sober restatement of some of the perspectives on the Negro seen in *Titus Andronicus*." At the end of *Othello*, in his opinion, "there seems to be a more reasoned and enlightened perspective."

In Johnson's interpretation, the literary text of *Othello* functions primarily as a vehicle for consideration of the nature of good and evil. In that case, "the Negro's color offered the most visible and dramatic means of contrastive evaluation. . . . Thus, the Negro, insofar as he was 'cole-black,' became a most apt representative of the devil."[138]

This interpretation should be accepted with caution. Throughout Shakespeare's work, black as a verbal value symbol remains derogatory and pejorative, the legacy of centuries of negative attitudes deeply embedded in the culture. But Shakespeare does not use black inherited traits to account for the behavior of his characters. Nor does he condone skin-color prejudice, although he presents some of his characters as doing so.[139] Moreover, the Mystery Plays were being replaced in Shakespeare's time by Morality Plays in which *Vice*, *Lust*, and other sins were replacing the *Devil* in importance. There is nothing to suggest that Vice was portrayed as black. When the devil appears in Morality Plays, he is sometimes black, but he is the clever busybody, the practical joker, the best-loved character in the play.

Much ink has been spilled over the question of whether Shakespeare meant Othello to be a "tawny Moor" or a "blackamoor." There was no such debate during the sixteenth and seventeenth centuries. Indeed, only the most strained interpretations could twist the word black to mean "merely dark" or "brunette" in the play. Moreover, Rodrigo calls Othello "thick lips."

Yet, one critic wrote in 1825 that "It is very probable that the popular notion of a Moor was somewhat confused in Shakespeare's time," and another wrote that "most surely as an English audience was disposed in the beginning of the seventeenth century, it would be something monstrous to conceive this beautiful Venetian girl falling in love with a veritable Negro."[140] These reactions were recorded at a time when racial slavery was transforming generalized British racial prejudice into White Racism.

The transformation of Othello into a "tawny Moor" did not occur suddenly. The role was being played in black-face in 1770, and Garrick played it that way in 1831. John Quincy Adams, a former U.S. president who opposed slavery, quixotically denounced Desdemona for marrying "a rude unbleached African!" not Shakespeare for creating the role.[141] Yet, during the same year that Garrick was playing the role in black-face, John Galt was writing in his *Lives of the Players* that Shakespeare had made a mistake, for "Can we imagine him so utterly ignorant as to make a barbarous negro plead royal birth, and, at a time, too, when negroes were not known except as slaves?"[142] Coleridge some years later insisted that Shakespeare didn't know what a Moor was.[143] Edmund Keane, the great nineteenth-century tragedian, is said to have considered it a "gross error" for an actor "to make Othello either a negro or a black." He "altered the conventional black to the light brown" which, he claimed, characterized the Moors by virtue of their descent from the Caucasian race.[144] This resistance to the concept of a black Othello reveals an inability of later generations to understand the ethos of British culture before White Racism emerged. Color prejudice there was in Shakespeare's time, but White Racism was yet to come.

The blind spot concerning the color of Othello is, of course, related to a racist reaction to sexual relations between black males and white women that grew up along with racial slavery in the Americas. Also, in both the British and Italian versions of the Othello tale, ethnic anti-Moorish stereotypes are expressed, and, in both, antiblack prejudice is also manifested by some characters, although not by all. The American literary critic Louis Auchincloss has recently reminded us, however, that

> . . . it is necessary to make clear that the play is not involved with racism as we conceive of it in America in 1968. Many of the characters make it brutally clear that they find Othello's blackness physically repusive, but none of them consider him a social inferior. They regard him as Victorian Englishmen might have regarded some splendid Maharajah. Othello is of royal birth; he is the military

savior of the Venetian state; he dines on equal terms with the greatest senators and is well known to the Doge. But he is always a complete foreigner. The Venetian aristocrats will never admit him to their innermost society, and they certainly do not want their daughters to marry Moors. But then they probably would not marry their daughters outside of fifty families along the Grand Canal.[145]

In other words, esthetic preference, class prejudice, ethnic prejudice, and antiblack prejudice were intermingled, but institutional racism did not exist.

Shakespeare's presentation of Moors, in *The Merchant of Venice* as well as the two plays we have discussed in some detail, assumes the existence of a stereotype of "The Moor" among his audiences, and a certain amount of fascination with the subject. In the popular mind, Moors were equated with Muslims and those are generally "enemies of Christendom." Battles with the followers of Mohammed were still taking place as Shakespeare wrote. But the stereotype was not always connected with negative attitudes.

Another Elizabethan dramatist wrote a play that was performed at the same time as *Othello*. This was John Webster's *The White Devil*,[146] a title that Elizabethan specialist Hazelton Spencer says refers to "a devil disguised under a fair appearance." The play is significant not only because the devil is so designated, but because it presents a Moor who is neither villainous or heroic, but simply an interesting and exotic part of Florentine society. An attractive and intelligent Moorish maidservant appears in the play, along with a male Moorish servant. The duke of Florence disguises himself as a Moor. Expressions such as "black slander" and "a black concatenation of mischief" appear in the play, reminding us of the symbolic and metaphoric usage of the period. But the word is not used to vilify people. Webster displays no moralizing interests. Moors simply make for good drama.[147]

After Shakespeare, black human beings on the stage, with rare exceptions, cease to be a matter of interest to dramatists in Britain.[148] While Negroes are disappearing from both the folk plays and the stage, a sentimental interest is gradually evolving in actual black people in British lands overseas, the oppressed slaves on Caribbean plantations.

Black People in Britain

The first sustained face-to-face contacts between Africans and people from the United Kingdom occurred during the early years of the sixteenth century as the "sea dogs" captured cargoes from

Spanish and Portuguese ships that included both ladinos and unacculturated Africans. These were few in number, and when some were landed in Britain, they were viewed as curiosities.

It soon became fashionable in aristocratic circles to have "black-o-moor" boys as pages. There was no tradition in Britain of black men as soldiers or eunuchs invested with authority, although educated people who read about Islamic lands knew that they currently played such roles there as they had in the past. Insofar as they were exotic, Blacks in Britain had an erotic aura about them, but this carried nothing of the high emotional load present in Islamic societies.[149] In fact, the few seventeenth-century Blacks living in Britain seem to have been accepted merely as human beings with unusual bodies by the servant classes with whom they had the most regular and intimate contact, as James Walvin has shown in *Black and White: The Negro in English Society, 1555-1945*.

Walvin tells us that, by the early eighteenth century, "Visitors to England were forcibly struck by the number of blacks to be seen in town and country alike." Walvin notes that some black servants were "firm favorites in wealthy households" and aristocratic circles, where Blacks were present as butlers, waiting men, and in various other capacities, including an occasional African prince who was being treated as an equal. Two Blacks—a page and a dwarf—were part of Elizabeth's court. The Stuarts' court entertained with minstrels and "Masques of Blackness" in which the ladies blackened their faces and real Africans took part. Favorable stereotypes were emerging, too.

In his definitive volume *Black and White in Britain*, Walvin presents an excellent chapter on "The Black Community, 1700-1800." He notes that:

> On the fringes of English society in the eighteenth century there existed Negroes who defy any neat analysis along social or occupational lines. These men moved in the world of popular entertainment, using their blackness or unusual colour and talents, their strengths and their oddities, to live out a stereotyped role which has stuck with Blacks to this day. A popular myth, finding its origins in a misunderstanding of the role of music in West Indian and West African society, was, to use the words of John Wesley, that Negroes have an "ear for music."[150]

The alleged "ear for music" may have been more of what Gordon Allport calls a "well merited reputation" than a stereotype. In any event this doctrine of "special gifts" offset to some extent the efforts of others to depict "*The* Negro" as an undesirable savage. It may, however, have also inspired beliefs about Blacks that served to cut them off from opportunities to function in the other areas of British life. It may have created a self-fulfilling prophecy, functioning as the British equivalent of the American dictum, "That's why darkies were born." (A similar "self-fulfilling" prophecy had been present in Muslim Spain.)

Walvin is also impressed by the presence of black working people, as household servants in middle class homes and doing menial tasks in shops and businesses. Others "were totally independent of white masters, living as humble but propertied Englishmen."[151] These individuals interacted easily with white people of their own socioeconomic level.

From the beginning, however, some Englishmen considered Blacks a problem. Professor Winthrop Jordan in *White Over Black* has written with considerable insight, using rich documentary material, on "First Impressions: Initial English Confrontations with Africans." He attempts to explain why British intellectual leaders, moralists, and theologians became concerned about the presence, for the first time, of black people in the British Isles and the North American colonies. Lack of previous contact meant there were no customary behaviors to structure their relations with Blacks. Except among the literate who absorbed attitudes from their reading, there were no ethnic stereoptypes, favorable or unfavorable.

Then, during the sixteenth century, sailors reporting upon what they had seen and heard along the west coast of Africa began to feed a mass of contradictory observations and hearsay reports into the British cultural stream. These formed the basis for mostly negative stereotypes about Negroes—thieves, cannibals, ritual murderers, idolators, sex-obsessed women as well as men, both naked, but also kind, lovers of children, and not hostile to white men unless mistreated. There were events in Britain that reinforced derogatory evaluations of black people.

The sixteenth century was characterized by extreme social and economic internal tensions. Five years before the first groups of West Africans came to London, an uprising had been mercilessly crushed during a period of widespread unemployment and inflation. During the middle of the century, Catholic-Protestant conflict erupted with such fury that three hundred men and women were burned at the stake for heresy between 1555 and 1558. After an armed rebellion against Queen Mary I, who tried to restore Catholicism, Elizabeth came to the throne in a victory for the Protestants.

Queen Elizabeth signed an order in 1557 to deport "black-o-moors," explaining that "her own liege people were annoyed with them" and that there were too many of them in view of the fact that the British population was increasing rapidly and that a near famine had occurred in 1556.[152] How and by whom the alleged annoyance was being expressed is not clear in the documents. Nor is there any evidence that the order was ever enforced.

As Jordan has said, the middle classes were seeking a secure sense of their own national identity, a fragile construct that had emerged recently after centuries of conflict among Scotch, Welsh, Irish and English. The sixteenth century was a crucial one in Britain's development of a will and a purpose vis à vis European nations, and national unity was imperative. Blacks were aliens, and highly visible ones.

Middle-class leaders were also anxious to protect the morals of the masses—and particularly the women—from "immoral blacks." Jordan points out that an upsurge of Puritanism was taking place at the time slavery and the slave trade in the West Indies were developing. He feels that, "it is scarcely surprising that Englishmen should have used people overseas as social mirrors and that they were especially inclined to discover attributes in savages which they found first but could not speak of in themselves."[153] Unbridled sexuality was the master symbol.

The growth of Protestant sectarianism with a Puritan bias was Bible-based, and the King James version produced in 1611 must have resulted in a widening of the circle of people familiar with the Scriptures. While Bible reading reinforced Puritan values, it could not stimulate any anti-Negro sentiments, for as we have seen, the biblical image of Blacks is on the whole favorable. Yet with increasing literacy, negative symbols from folk traditions became embedded in the popular mind and were given a theological underpinning. It is likely that one book may have had as much influence as any single work in reinforcing the image of an equivalence between the Devil and the Negro, John Bunyan's The Holy War, published in 1682. Mansoul battles against the Devil, Diabolus, who is specifically described as being a Negro.[154]

By the end of the seventeenth century, an equivalence was being widely made in Britain among people who took religion seriously: NEGROES=BLACKNESS=NUDITY=SEXUAL SIN=PHYSICAL AND SPIRITUAL UGLINESS.[155] It should be stressed that not all Englishmen were Puritans, and that matters for soul-searching among middle-class and highly literate peoples may not have bothered the masses at all. There were some non-Puritans of the middle classes among whom a more liberal attitude on race, religion and sexuality prevailed.

Samuel Pepys, in his diary, gives us a glimpse of this viewpoint.[156] A Cambridge-educated bibliophile, government official, and royal court-watcher, he modeled his sexual behavior to some extent upon what he observed there, although with occasional expressions of guilt. Pepys, who in his diary says, "musique and women I cannot but give way to, whatever my business is," records numerous instances of his kissing and fondling the maids in his own household and those of friends. He had constant fantasies about women, noting, for instance, that he wanted "to have a bout" with them and commenting on the faces and bodies of women at King Charles's court, those in the new profession of actress who fascinated him, shopgirls, fellow workers, wives, and prostitutes. In 1666, a black shopgirl named Nan caught his roving eye. Pepys had begun to write music in his leisure time when not busy at the naval office. He needed some specialized materials for pursuing his hobby, and wrote:

> April 13: Called upon an old woman in Pannier Ally to agree for ruling some paper for me and she will do it pretty cheap. Here I found her have a very comely black mayde to her servant which I liked very much.

Five days later, the diarist records:

> April 18: Coming home called at my paper ruler's and there found black Nan which pleases me mightily, and having saluted her again, away home and to bed.

On April 20, Pepys records a reconciliation with his wife "who gives me more and more content every day," but within the week he jots a note in the diary, "So abroad to my ruler's of my books, having God forgive me! a mind to see Nan there which I did."

Despite occasional pangs of conscience—and fears his wife would find out—Pepys had been having an affair with a married woman and was trying to seduce a carpenter's wife. But on May 2, he recorded for the day: "Among other stops went to my ruler's house and there staid a great while with Nan idling away the afternoon with pleasure." What Pepys often described as "dalliance" ran the gamut from kissing and breast-fondling to "bedding the wench." How far he went with Nan he does not say. The "dalliance" went on for five months at least, the last entry being made on July 25: "I did this afternoon call at my woman that ruled my paper to bespeak a musique card, and there did kiss Nan."

Pepys was probably not unusual insofar as "dalliance" by middle-class males with black servants was concerned (and white ones as well). There was little opportunity for such "dalliance" between wives and unmarried women of this stratum and black males, however, for there were few such men in these households. (Incidentally, Pepys was very suspicious of his wife's conduct with her music teacher, who was white.) Rumors of "dalliance" between black men and white women of the aristocracy were rife.

At the level of the working classes, relationships between black men and white women were the most typical. By the end of the eighteenth century the black population in Britain had increased greatly, males being in the great majority. As Walvin points out:

> A majority of black males would find it impossible to form perma-
> nent relations with women of their own colour and inevitably many
> settled down with local white women of the class the blacks were
> closest to—the poor whites. Sexual relations between black and
> white flourished, a fact which alarmed and angered white commen-
> tators [who were of higher class levels].

Walvin mentions, too, that "More unusual but not uncommon, were marriages between Englishmen and black women . . . Such happy unions were held up by white humanitarians as the ideal for racial harmony." He adds: "There can be no doubt, however, that by a substantial and influential section of English society, miscegenation was regarded as a threat to that society." It became the rallying point for vituperative eighteenth-century press treatment of Blacks that whipped up antiblack racism.[157]

The elite perspectives of British history usually provided by scholars offer only the aristocratic view. Most historians do not analyze, by class, beliefs about Negroes and behavior toward them. There is much evidence that racial and ethnic attitudes and sanctions controlling interracial behavior have been class-linked in Britain since the sixteenth century.[158] As Walvin describes it:

> Relations between the poor whites and the poor Blacks form a
> curious contrast to the relations between the white master class and
> the Blacks, which were generally based on fear, distrust or a
> mutually acceptable paternalism. With the poor whites, the Blacks
> shared the dirt and the hunger of London's poor districts. There were
> few signs of the tensions and resentments between the two sides
> that one associates with similar situations in a more modern

context. The reasons for this may be complex, but a simple answer lies in the appalling conditions shared by everyone. Life was so hard and enjoyments so few that it could scarcely be claimed that immigrant Blacks were taking anything from the whites; there was nothing to take in the first place. Poor whites and Negroes looked on each other with friendly cooperation. The best example of this was the traditional shelter given by many poor whites to runaway slaves, preventing the masters from claiming their human property.[159]

That racial prejudice in Britain was class-linked is also stressed by J. Jean Hecht, who in a revealing social history stresses the harmonious relations between black and white domestic servants and the frequency of miscegenation between them, noting that black men were especially favored by English women. Walvin states that

For centuries past, sexual relations with Negroes had been overlaid by the myth of black sexual prowess. This belief shared by both white men and women became something of an institution in the course of the eighteenth century and was used to explain, or deride, mixed unions. The strength of, and widespread support for, this myth was perhaps one of the most powerful factors in moulding the racial attitudes between the two sides.[160]

But it was not the decisive factor in the growth of derogatory stereotypes about Blacks. The myth had been present in the sixteenth and seventeenth centuries, too, with no virulent display of racism. The decisive factor was the rapid growth of slavery in the colonies and their export of racist attitudes back to Britain.

The issue of slavery in Britain itself became a matter for concern as a few Blacks from the New World came to live in the United Kingdom with West Indian planters who were visiting or had retired. When attempts were made to take some of them back to the West Indies, they resisted. Others, with the help of British friends, raised the question of whether it was legal to hold them as slaves in Britain. This matter was not settled until the latter part of the eighteenth century when the famous Mansfield decision was handed down, declaring that no one could be held in slavery on British soil and that a slave brought to Britain was automatically freed.

A century would pass before the English plantation owners in colonies of the Caribbean would accept Parliamentary action that emancipated the slaves.

Summary

Beginning in the sixteenth century, Western European Christendom became the economic center of an international periphery that included the Americas.[161] The cultural aspect of the economic world system can be viewed as an extension of selected values and customs of Christendom into Africa, Asia, Oceania, and the Americas through merchants, soldiers, missionaries, seamen, and other culture bearers. Among the social structures that crossed the Atlantic was the lucrative sugar plantation with the use of black slaves to work it.

In Europe, the linkage between sugar cultivation and the use of black slaves had been made gradually. The rise of the Ottoman Turks had simultaneously moved the sugar plantations west to islands offshore of Africa and shut off the traditional sources of white slaves just as the Portuguese were beginning a trade in West African slaves.

There had been slaves in Europe for hundreds of years, and as the Middle Ages waned, the number of black slaves increased in southern Europe. But the form slavery took throughout the Western Hemisphere, regardless of the European culture that created the colony, was *racial slavery*. At first the Indians were enslaved, but soon after the cultivation of sugar began, only black slaves were used. The widest consensus supported the principle that no men or women defined as "white" were to be held as slaves. No southern European system used black labor exclusively.

Soon the New World's economic existence depended upon slave labor in plantation areas. Between 1500 and the middle of the nineteenth century, at least ten million Africans were transported to the Caribbean and to North and South America as slaves. The bulk of these were employed on plantations, but not all. By 1550, the slave trade had acquired considerable momentum with Portugal as the major supplier. During the seventeenth century, Britain and Holland displaced Portugal. During the eighteenth century, England became the dominant country supplying the market with African manpower.

When African slavery became dominant, prejudice against Negroidness, which we have described in various forms from antiquity, became a bulwark for this unique system. We saw how color prejudice in Romanized Egypt during the early Christian era was a strong element in making the skin color of black Ethiopians a symbol of sin. Later, prejudice against Negroidness, rather than black skin color itself, was common throughout Muslim lands. But in these areas, individual Blacks sometimes rose to positions of considerable power and influence, even if their appearance continued to draw negative esthetic judgments.

As old prejudices against Negroes were mustered to the defense of *racial* slavery, doctrines of White Racism were formulated to strengthen them. Stories about a curse of Noah that were never included in the Old Testament now came forward in various versions that turned the enslavement of Blacks into a punishment for sexual sins. A myth of black supersexuality, with roots extending back at least to Roman times, added to the emerging stereotype of *The* Negro. Alleged relationships between blackness and uncivilized behavior or unrestrained emotion or cognitive deficit, which had enjoyed limited audiences or covered only specific groups in the past, were now generally applied to all sub-Saharan Africans.

While White Racism was developing in the colonies of the New World, positive images of Blacks, and some degree of opportunity for black people, continued to exist in the exploring nations of Portugal, Spain and Britain. As time went on, however, racial prejudice in the homelands of Western Europe would increase due to continuous feedback of the stereotypes and attitudes developed in the slave societies of the colonial periphery. This degradation of the status of black people coincided with the Renaissance and Reformation and continued as one aspect of a rapidly expanding mercantilist capitalism. It constituted a sharp break with the concepts and practices of medieval European Christendom regarding Negroes, as we have seen.

When English, Dutch, and French joint stock companies began to lay out plantations in the New World using African slaves that would grow tropical staple crops for the European market, the Spanish and Portuguese settlers in the Americas had already been operating social systems there for over a century, based upon the cardinal principle that no white men and women should be held as slaves. (The definition of "white" was somewhat elastic, however.) The northern Europeans did not invent *racial* slavery, but they developed the most elaborate racist ideologies for defending it.

Looking back, we can see that the institution of *racial* slavery had been taking shape in the Mediterranean islands and African "offshore" islands for almost a century before 1510 when Charles V of Spain authorized the first direct importation into the Caribbean of Blacks from Africa. Considered in the widest socio-political setting, the enslavement of Blacks in the New World came at a period when the favorable images of St. Maurice had faded away, when the last remnants of Black Power in West Africa had been smashed, and when attempts at acquiring Western technology by the rulers of the Kongo that might have made that kingdom competitive were rebuffed. And as Baudet reminds us Prester John lost prestige at the same time that the Portuguese who had once searched for him were opening up the slave trade that replaced all other forms of trade with Africa. This was the nadir in the Black Experience, and this situation was functionally related to other important power shifts that were occurring throughout the world. What Black Nationalists call the "white-out" of black history was about to begin.

EPILOGUE

Seven events during the sixteenth century were experienced as almost apocalyptic by the people involved in them, and they had worldwide repercussions. All had significance for subsequent black history.

1521   the conquest of Montezuma's empire in North America by Spanish troops under the leadership of Cortés

1523   the conquest of the Inca empire in the South American highlands by Spanish troops under the leadership of Pizarro

1542   the Portuguese victory over the Muslims in defending the Abyssinian highlands of East Africa

1571   the defeat of the Turks at the Battle of Lepanto by an alliance composed of Spain, Venice, Genoa, and the Papal States

1578   the defeat of Portugal by the Moors at the Battle of Alcazar in North Africa

1588   the defeat of the Spanish Armada

1591   the destruction of the Songhay Empire in West Africa by the Moroccans

The Spanish Conquests of the Aztecs and Incas

With the defeat of the two most highly developed civilizations in the Americas, Spain began to extract great wealth in the form of gold and silver, much of which was shipped back to the European "Mother Country." Some of it, however, was used to make life comfortable and attractive for the *criollos* who became the settled population on the *encomiendas* and in the newly built cities. Although the native Amerindians formed the basic labor force at first, this wealth also bought African slaves for use as domestic servants and in a wide variety of artisan and laboring pursuits,

293

including mining. Africans were used, too, in the Antilles and on coastal plantations for the growing of sugar.

These two military victories created a market for African bodies as well as the means for buying them. The Spanish shattered the most complex societies of the Amerindians and brought into being new caste-like structures with Spaniards at the top, African slaves and Indian peons at the bottom, and mestizos, mulattoes, and zambas in between. Theories that had linked "pure Castilian blood" to religious orthodoxy in Spain now tied skin color not just to moral deficiency but also to cognitive inferiority.

The Portuguese Victory over the Muslims in Ethiopia

One hundred years before the empires of the Incas and the Aztecs fell to the Spaniards, the Portuguese had won some areas in Africa by force and made alliances with kings in West Africa and the Kongo region. They also tried to subvert the authority of the king of Monomotapa in eastern central Africa.

They fought only one large-scale war of conquest in Africa, in which they captured the coastal city of Malindi on the Indian Ocean. Nevertheless, the Portuguese military presence there blasted Muslim hopes of destroying the Christian kingdom in the highlands of East Africa. The Portuguese pushed inland and found the kingdom that the Arabs called Abyssinia. They were sure that its king was Prester John, and their embassy referred to him as such. This land, being Christian and under attack by its Muslim neighbors, was promised support as an ally against the Infidel.

The coming of the Portuguese at this specific point in time had an element of the "miraculous" to it in the minds of the African Christian rulers. Portuguese intervention turned the tide against the Muslims at the historic Battle of Lake Tsana in 1542. Subsequent invasions failed. Abyssinia resisted the Ottoman Turks as vigorously and as successfully as it did the Arabs from across the Red Sea. Abyssinia (now called Ethiopia) remained independent for the next four hundred years.[1]

Defeat of the Turks at Lepanto

When the sovereigns of Castile and Aragon united to form the Spanish nation, Aragon had already extended its power over several Mediterranean islands, including Sicily. Along with the Italian states, this kingdom faced constant pressure from the Ottoman Turks, who moved steadily westward by sea in the Mediterranean and on land in North Africa and the Balkans. If Turks and Moors could have composed their differences and combined in an invasion of Spain and Portugal, the Muslims might have reversed the gains of the Christian Reconquest. This was not to be.

When Pope Pius V sponsored a Christian League, at the request of Venice, to fight the Turks, Spain joined. On October 7, 1571, about thirty years after the Portuguese helped to keep the Muslims out of Ethiopia, the Christian League checkmated the Muslims by destroying the Turkish Mediterranean fleet at Lepanto. Over five hundred ships under the command of Don John of Austria (the friend and patron of the black poet, Juan Latino) constituted the Christian naval forces. It was reported that 25,000 Muslims were killed and a very large number wounded. Over 15,000 Christians were then liberated from galleys where they were being held as prisoners. The Christian League reported 8,000 of its own forces killed and 16,000 wounded.

The implications of the victory at Lepanto for the black world were profound. The Ottoman Turks now gave up their attempts to conquer Africa west of Egypt, and began to intensify their push southward into the African areas southeast of Egypt. With the "Turkish menace" checked, the Spaniards and Portuguese could devote their attention and resources undisturbed—except for occasional attacks by Algerian and Moroccan pirates—to buying or capturing Africans and transporting them across the Atlantic for developing their colonies in the Americas.

Defeat of Portugal by the Moors at Alcazar

Portugal had occupied a coastal area south of the mouth of the Kongo River in Angola, from which it exported slaves. Its kings were not content with this, however. They were also anxious to eliminate the Moroccan middlemen in the trade of horses for slaves. Control of Morocco also meant control of the trade routes that brought gold and slaves North across the desert. Seven years after Spain led the Christian forces that defeated the Turks at Lepanto, King Sebastian of Portugal decided to invade Morocco, now that the threat of a Turkish alliance was lessened.

With fanatical zeal and foolish arrogance, King Sebastian took to the field with a mass of camp followers, who were planning to enjoy what the king had promised was certain victory. A force of 16,000 soldiers clad in steel armor disembarked and proceeded to march south with colors flying. Coaches and wagons accompanied the cavalry and foot soldiers. E. W. Bovill notes that

> It was not until this strange column took the road that men realized
> the full measure of the King's stupidity in encumbering his army as
> he had. At every step it was hindered by thousands of non-combat-
> ants and the wildly extravagant and useless impedimenta which had
> been deemed necessary to the dignity and well-being of Portuguese
> chivalry in the field. The hundreds of priests and the horde of pages,
> musicians, servants, negroes, mulattoes, wives, serving women and
> prostitutes, instead of being left aboard [the ships that brought them]
> were still with the army, and probably their children as well. They
> numbered as many as the fighting men.[2]

Moving slowly through the almost unbearably hot sun, the column
marched into an ambush and was cut to pieces. Prince Sebastian was
killed, although for centuries Portuguese peasants would not believe
it and the myth of his eventual return persisted.

The debacle at Alcazar resulted in the extinction of Portugal as a
nation for the sixty years between 1580 and 1640 and its rule by
Philip II of Spain. When it regained independence, Portugal began to
concentrate much of its energy upon giving support to settlers who
were establishing plantations in Brazil, using black labor from its
African colonies to grow sugar. The port of Luanda in Angola became
a major center for exporting slaves to North and South America and
the Caribbean.

Britain played a clandestine role in helping Morocco defeat a
European power. Throughout the fifteenth century a steady demand
for sugar had grown among the British people, and Moroccans in the
province of Sus near the Sahara Desert began to supply it, trading
sugar for military supplies. The plantation labor in Sus was almost
exclusively Negro, although white slaves were used in various other
capacities. On the eve of the Portuguese invasion, Queen Elizabeth's
emissary persuaded a Moroccan sultan to add saltpeter, a crucial
item in the manufacture of gunpowder, to the items Morocco would
trade for needed weapons. For a Christian power to arm a Muslim
power was considered an unfriendly act by other Europeans. Portugal
saw it as particularly offensive, because her sailors had been
systematically capturing Moroccan coastal ports since 1415.

The Defeat of the Spanish Armada by England

If the defeat of the Portuguese at Alcazar in 1578 dealt a fatal blow
to Portugal's stature as a world power, Britain began to finish off
Spain a decade later. In 1585 the two powers went to war, although

Queen Elizabeth had tried to avoid an outright conflict with the great Catholic power. British privateers had been at war with Spain ever since that country scored its victories in Mexico and Peru, but the fiction was propagated that the government did not approve, that the "sea dogs" were undisciplined pirates. The gold and silver and other commodities being sent home on Spanish galleons were the constant prey of British privateers who gave a share of the loot to the Crown.

In the year 1573 alone, Drake (Francis before he became a "Sir") stole 40,000 British pounds worth of silver, gold and pearls from Spanish ships. During the first year of the war with Spain he sacked and burned the cities of Santo Domingo and Cartagena. Sugar, hides, silver, gold, rare woods, and pearls were the prizes systematically looted from Spanish ships and towns by British pirates for nearly a century before the Spanish fleet decided to sail into the English Channel to do battle against the British.

Drake and the British men-of-war, aided by a devastating storm, decimated the Spanish Armada in 1588. Britain gave the the coup de grace to Spanish naval power around 1600 and became master of the seas after defeating the Dutch during the next century. The British made no attempt to capture any of Spain's possessions on the American continents. Sharing the island of St. Kitts with France and occupying the uninhabited island of Barbados, England had a more profitable goal in mind, taking over fertile Caribbean islands. Wealth through growing sugar was the British objective. In 1655, Britain snatched an island prize from Spain, Jamaica. Soon thereafter, England secured the coveted *asiento*, the sole right to sell slaves to Spanish possessions in the Americas.

The defeat of the Spanish Armada set Britain on the road to maritime dominance of the world in the long run, and to a virtual monopoly of the slave trade north of Angola in the short run. Attitudes toward black people in the future would be shaped to a great extent by the British, not by the Iberians.

The Destruction of the Songhay Empire by the Moroccans

If the defeat of Spain's armada in 1588 marked a climax in European history that affected the black world profoundly, an event in West Africa three years later marked a climax in black history of great symbolic import. The Songhay empire, largest and most stable of the black Sudanic kingdoms, was defeated by Morocco in 1591 and disintegrated into a group of small warring states. The way was thus opened for eventual French and British imperial penetration.

The decisive battle in West Africa was fought in 1591 and was, in one of its aspects, a victory of a new technology over an old one. Britain had armed Sultan al-Mansur of Morocco in exchange for saltpeter, and, as one historian phrases it, "The guns of the Moroccans triumphed over Songhai cavalry and bowmen."[3]

Any danger of a Portuguese attack in the rear had ended with Alcazar. The first military probe was made soon after, when the victorious sultan sent troops in 1581 to occupy two important Sahara oases. Then in 1583 a larger army tried to cross the Sahara and was lost in the desert. Nevertheless, the next year the rich salt mines close to the borders of Songhay were captured. Then came the successful invasion of the extensive black kingdom. This thrust into the sub-Saharan black lands must be seen within the context of the other events that have been described.

During 1587, the year before the defeat of the Spanish Armada, according to Bovill, "El-Mansur was demanding from England a certain war with Spain." During the year of the Armada debacle, he tried to negotiate a formal alliance with England against the unified kingdom of Spain and Portugal which Elizabeth as a Christian queen could not consider. As a result, "by the end of the year the Shereef had forbidden the export of saltpetre, but he was still obtaining arms from England."[4] After all, he was a counterweight against Britain's Iberian foes that Britain must not alienate.

Bovill emphasizes the continuous flow of munitions into Morocco at a time when both Turkey and Morocco's European enemies were so busy elsewhere that they constituted no danger to the Shereef's domain. He paints a picture of a young, ambitious Moroccan ruler wanting to use his arms and munitions somewhere but too prudent to provoke the Turks or Spain. Therefore, "the Shereef was forced to contemplate the forbidding wastes of the Sahara as the only direction in which imperial expansion was possible."[5] Harry A. Gailey, Jr. takes a less romantic view of Mansur's motives, commenting that with a strong Europe and Turkey to the north, the sultans of Morocco became more concerned with controlling as much of the rich trans-Saharan trade as possible.[6] An additional hypothesis might be advanced, namely, that the Shereef of Morocco moved to prevent the Europeans from diverting all of the rich trade away from the desert trails to the Atlantic coast. If Morocco controlled Songhay it would also benefit from any new European connections that the merchants of Timbuctoo, Gao, and Jenne made with traders on the Guinea coast.

Bovill points out what a prize Songhay was, and why it is significant from a black perspective:

> Far away on the south, beyond the desert, lay the rich negro countries of Western Sudan the wealth of which was known to every merchant in the Maghreb. The ancient caravan traffic in gold and slaves, ivory and ostrich feathers, which the Moors bartered for the salt of Taghaza, had for centuries been the life-blood of the Barbary coast. All down the centuries a score or more of ports on that rugged shore had been crowded with Christian shipping lading precious cargoes from the heart of Africa.
>
> In El-Mansur's time the rise of the powerful negro state of Songhai with its twin capitals, Gao and Timbuktu, both on the Niger had given to the Western Sudan a strong central government and with it unwonted tranquillity. This had attracted to these remote countries large numbers of merchants from North Africa whose activities had greatly stimulated the caravan traffic of the Sahara. Of this trade the most important element was gold, but what none of the foreign merchants could discover was the mysterious country of Wangara where the negroes [sic] were believed to get their gold.
>
> In the previous century this ancient trade had inspired Prince Henry the Navigator to explore the coast of Guinea in search of the unknown source. El-Mansur resolved to achieve by land what Prince Henry had failed to do by sea. He would seek out the hidden wealth of the negroes. But Songhai had first to be reckoned with. The need would therefore be, not for an exploring expedition, but a military force strong enough to crush the powerful negro state and yet capable of crossing the forbidding and almost limitless wastes which separated the kingdom of Morocco from the Sudan.[7]

Mansur placed the expedition in the hands of a Spanish eunuch, Judar Pasha, who had grown up in Morocco and had the reputation of being an excellent general. He took 3,000 highly trained men armed with the latest European firearms and managed to cross the desert with a minimal loss of life. His troops defeated a numerically superior force at Gao and then moved on to sack Timbuctoo. Bovill states that these invaders brought "untold misery to the negroes of the Sudan." Vast quantities of wealth were carried back to Morocco. Bovill notes that before the death of Sultan Mansur,

> Jasper Tomson, a member of an influential English commercial house and a witness of Judar Pasha's return to Marrakech from the Sudan, reported that the magnificent present which the Pasha brought for the Shereef [of Morocco] included thirty camel-loads of timber, which was what they called unrefined gold, which he valued at 604,800 [British pounds]. Even as late as 1607, when the anarchy

in Morocco and the Sudan which had followed El-Mansur's death must have adversely affected the amount of treasure flowing northwards across the desert, a Frenchman reported from Marrakech the expected arrival of 4,600,000 livres of gold from Gao and Timbuktu. . . .

But gold was only part of the wealth El-Mansur was obtaining from the Sudan. When Mahmud Pasha, another of his generals, returned he brought the Shereef 1,200 slaves, civet and civet cats and many loads of ebony, in addition to quantities of gold. Besides his thirty camel loads of gold, Judar brought "great store of pepper, unicorn's horns, a certain kind of wood for dyers to some 120 camel loads . . . 50 horses, and a great quantity of eunuchs, dwarfs, and women and men slaves, besides 15 virgins, the king's daughters of Gao, which he sendeth to be the King's concubines."[8]

Bovill makes an acute observation on the international significance of the invasion of Songhay:

English interest in the wealth which Morocco was deriving from the Sudan was not limited to its direct benefit to their Barbary trade. It was awakening wider aspirations. The English would have been dull indeed had not the sight of these golden streams pouring into Morocco awakened in them the same desire to discover the hidden gold-fields of Wangara that had first inspired the great discoveries of Prince Henry. The trade of the English with the Guinea coast had been resumed and expanded, and the opportunities it offered for penetrating the interior suggested the possibility of diverting to the sea El-Mansur's gold at its source. What Hakluyt called "the searching and unsatisfied spirit of the English" might succeed where Prince Henry and El-Mansur had failed. The enterprise crystallised out in 1618 with the formation in London of the Company of Adventurers for the Countries of Guinney and Binney (Benin) for the Discovery of the Golden Trade of the Moors of Barbary.[9]

Bovill's observation on who did and did not profit from Morocco's plundering of Songhay is relevant to a consideration of the situation of the masses of Britain and Songhay as well as those of Morocco:

The common people benefited little from their country's newfound wealth which was of course largely concentrated in the hands of the Shereef and his favourites. Although the degrading poverty of the masses went unrelieved, the merchants reaped large profits in satisfying the needs of the court. The unprecedented demand for European goods brought prosperity to the foreign merchants and to none more than the English.[10]

Only insofar as it gave a stimulus to the Industrial Revolution did the exploitation of Africa's wealth benefit the ordinary people in Britain any more than those in Morocco. As to the masses in Songhay, most became pawns in power struggles of what the Africanists call "the successor states" to that empire. They retained slavery as a part of their own social systems but did not integrate their kingdoms into the great slave-trading operation of the Islamic world. When some of these states became aware of new trading partners wooing them on the Atlantic coast, the descendants of some of the "negroes of the Sudan"—though by no means most— found themselves being marched to the Gulf of Guinea, whence to make the Middle Passage on the slave ships that carried millions of Africans across the Atlantic Ocean during a period of 350 years. There they would experience a new form of bondage—*racial* slavery.

A Watershed in the Black Experience

The sixteenth century was marked by these climactic events in the history of the Western world. In the history of the Black Experience it was an important watershed. On one side is an epoch extending back almost five thousand years during which esthetic prejudice against the Negro phenotype can be documented in a few situations where prestige-conscious elites in southwestern Asia and northern India have left a record revealing their skin-color prejudices. That such feelings were not universal has been demonstrated in the case of ancient Egypt, classical Greece, pre-exilic Palestine, and medieval European Christendom. Highly stratified social systems within the Muslim world defined Negroes as the Pagan Other, but "toleration" and "tokenism" became characteristic of relations with Blacks who accepted Islam when residing as minority peoples within areas under Arabic, Berber, and Turkish dominance.

We have suggested that certain passages of the Babylonian Talmud and some references in the Midrash contributed toward pejorative anti-Negro stereotypes and attitudes. However, these evaluations would have remained highly localized in Mesopotamia had not the predominantly Persian intellectuals of the Abbasid period spread them widely among literate Muslims. Negroes, not dark-skinned people in general, were defamed. In a number of situations we note that culture could override negative reactions to the Negro phenotypes. In medieval European Christendom (as compared with medieval Islam) Blacks, known only through biblical and Greco-Roman references among elites, and through depictions of Black Madonnas and the heroic St. Maurice, had a highly favorable image. The sixteenth century marked the beginning of a reversal. The African slave trade and a very demeaning form of slavery in the Americas, as Baudet points out, destroyed the mystique surrounding a legendary unseen Christian king in Africa, Prester John. Indians replaced Ethiopians as the focus of Christian concerns.

On the other side of the sixteenth-century watershed lies the modern era during which *racial* slavery emerged to replace the old historic types of enslavement in southern Europe and on the Mediterranean islands, which involved a variety of racial types. Modern *racial* slavery meant that all slaves were Negro and no whites were slaves. Its center was in the periphery, in the Caribbean Islands and Latin America. After the abolition of slavery in the nineteenth century, the White Racism that had buttressed racial slavery did not disappear but became the ideology supporting color-caste systems and systems of color-class with non-whites at the bottom. Africa continued to be a supplier of eunuchs and soldiers, concubines and prostitutes, to the Middle East with certain Arab groups becoming the raiders and merchants; but in the sixteenth century, a new feature was added to the enslavement of Africans— the cruel Middle Passage across the Atlantic into the systems of chattel slavery in the New World. The plantations of the New World depended upon slave labor for their very existence and the result was a degree of harshness of control that was very rare in the Middle East.

In the plantation economies of the Americas the supervising whites were a minority group in societies they built up. According to Herbert Blumer extreme racial prejudice is bred in such situations due to the fears of the superordinate group. Indeed, from the outset in the Caribbean, resistance to subordination and attempts at dehumanization broke out in the form of slave revolts and *marronnage*. The pattern of resistance was repeated in North and South America until slavery was abolished during the nineteenth century.

Acculturation in these slave societies included the co-optation of mixed-blood individuals by the master class in order to implement a policy of "divide and rule." In the colonial societies of Africa forms of resistance ranged from the so-called revitalization movements, (Dona Beatriz was a founder of one in the Kongo) through strikes and outright warfare.

The complexities of the African Diaspora into the Western Hemisphere that began during the sixteenth century can only be understood if placed in the context of vast movements of people from many European areas journeying to the Americas as indentured servants or adventurous free men and women seeking expanded political and economic opportunity. For many of these Europeans, their interests and those of investors were best served by having a sector in the new socioeconomic system where essential labor could not participate in the scramble for free land on the frontiers and could be bound permanently to the plantations that were growing sugar, indigo, rice, and other profitable commodities. In many parts of Asia exploitation of the resources was best carried out by reducing the indigenous people to some form of peonage. A world system was emerging that has been skillfully portrayed by sociologist Immanuel Wallerstein.[11] Forms of labor that had disappeared in the European center were revived and perpetuated in the peripheries. The implications of this evolving global system for Africa and its inhabitants are being continuously analyzed from varied theoretical and ideological perspectives. It is generally agreed, however, that the enslavement of Africans during the fifteenth and sixteenth centuries was part of a worldwide process that has been described by Karl Marx in his usual biting sarcastic tone:

> The discoveries of gold and silver in America; the extirpation of the indigenes in some instances; their enslavement or their entombment in the mines in others; the beginnings of the conquest and looting in the East Indies; the transformation of Africa into a precinct for the supply of the negroes who were the raw material of the slave trade— these were the incidents that characterized the rosy dawn of the era of capitalist production. These were the idyllic processes that formed the chief factors of primary accumulation.[12]

Feudalism in Europe was dying. Modern mercantilist capitalism was being entrenched. African slavery became an integral part of the new system emerging. The Black Diaspora in the Americas was one result of this great historic transformation.

NOTES

PREFACE

1. Carl Degler's ideas are put forth in *Neither Black nor White: Slavery and Race Relations in Brazil and the United States* (New York: Macmillan, 1971). Kenneth J. Gergen presents his views in "The Significance of Skin Color in Human Relations," *Daedalus* 96, 2 (Spring 1967). It was republished in *Color and Race*, ed. by John Hope Franklin (Boston: Houghton Mifflin, 1968), pp. 112–128.

CHAPTER 4

The basic reference used in discussing the status of black people in the Greco-Roman period is the definitive book by the Afro-American classical scholar, Frank Snowden, *Blacks in Antiquity* (1971). Its very readable style is complemented with 82 pages of not to be ignored endnotes that discuss Latin and Greek sources, some of which he, as a classics professor at Howard University, was able to translate for comparison with other translations. A decade later, Snowden extended his discussion to include ancient Palestinian Jewry and provided a theoretical explanation for cases of sporadic color prejudice, in a book whose ironic title, *Before Color Prejudice* (1983), would be more accurate if called *Before White Racism*.

Snowden has contributed a chapter to volume 1 of the magnificently illustrated (in polychrome) work sponsored by the Menil Foundation, *The Image of the Black in Western Art* (New York: William Morrow and Co., 1979). In volume 2, two sections, "Notice" and "Introduction," set the theme of the book. Highly relevant to our discussion and to Snowden's two books is the result of an exhaustive search of the sources: Jean Marie Courtès on "The Theme of 'Ethiopia' and 'Ethiopians' in Patristic Literature." The discussion contains surprising conclusions about the attitudes of some early Church Fathers toward blackness and black people. A valuable contribution—well-documented with photographs as well as pertinent citations—is Jean Devisse's essay on "Christians and Black" with sections on "An Ambiguous Iconography," "The Black Unknown, the Black Dishonored," and "White God and Dark Devil" (black to purple).

Serious students might wish to supplement our use of the King James version of the Old Testament for studying attitudes toward blackness and black people by examining other versions of the English Bible and some of the many translations in other languages.

Doubleday and Co., in publishing *The Anchor Bible* book by book, has released a volume of special relevance to our inquiry, Marvin H. Pope's *Song of Songs: A New Translation: With Introduction and Commentary*. This scholar pinpoints what he calls "melainophobia" as the source of biased interpretations and even mistranslation of words referring to skin color. His erudite scholarly discussion, tinged with wit, sarcasm, and irony, is a pleasure to read.

Of all the references in our notes to the Talmudic and Midrashic stories, the most interesting, objective and sophisticated are Robert Graves and Raphael Patai, *Hebrew Myths: The Book of Genesis* (1944) and Louis Ginzberg, *Legends of the Bible* (1966). For a recent publication that summarizes rabbinical comment from Europe, the Middle East and East Africa on Ham, Noah, Ebed-Melech, et al., see Menahem M. Kasher, *Encyclopedia of Biblical Interpretation* (1955).

A voluminous body of literature has appeared since 1960 dealing with "black theology." Dr. Ben Jochannon's books are the most provocative: *The Black Man's Religion: The Myths of Genesis and Exodus* and *Extracts and Comments from the Holy Black Bible.* (He had published *We the Black Jews* in 1949.) A well-educated Protestant minister, Dr. Albert B. Cleage of Detroit, after establishing the Shrine of the Black Madonna, published *Black Messiah* in 1968 (New York: Sheed and Ward). Dr. James Cone, in *Black Theology and Black Power* (New York: Seabury, 1969) rejects Cleage's ethnic exclusiveness but asserts that black people have a special "redemptive mission."

The most systematic exposition of the doctrine that there is a "salvation" in "blackness" and not for black people alone, is by a Filipino Catholic philosopher who once taught at an Afro-American college: Eulalio R. Baltazar's *The Dark Center, A Process Theology of Blackness* (New York: Paulist Press, 1973). His critical reaction to Gergen's *Daedalus* article is similar to mine, which was expressed in Volume 1. Baltazar accepts Snowden's idea that holding a symbolic Manichaean opposition of "white" to "black" does not necessarily "carry over" to human relations. He devotes one chapter to "Black as a Symbol of Reality and Truth," and another to "Black as a Positive Christian System." As he reads the Bible, black is "a symbol of the divine and of goodness," but its role in Christian history is expressed in chapters on "Black as Ambivalent Cross-Cultural Symbol" and "Black as Ambivalent Symbol of Experience."

1. According to tradition, the High Priest Eleazer in Jerusalem sent seventy translators to Alexandria in Egypt in 288 B.C. to begin preparing a Greek version of the Pentateuch, Prophets, and Hagiographa for use by Jews living in the Egyptian diaspora who no longer understood either the ritual language, Hebrew, or the Palestinian vernacular, Aramaic. From the seventy, it was named the Septuagint; this Greek translation of the Old Testament became the basic document of early Christianity. Meanwhile, in Palestine, rabbis in synagogues continued to hand down oral commentaries on the scriptures. Over a span of about a thousand years, priests, rabbis, and Prophets produced a written literature based on oral tradition—the Torah—and then an extensive commentary on it—the Oral Law. Concurrently, there emerged another body of oral tradition, the Midrash, which provided comments on and explanations of the Oral Law. This is rich with folklore and with varied and colorful comment by teachers and rabbinic scholars. Eventually the oral comments on the Oral Law were written down and referred to as the Mishnah. A rich body of colorful folklore and comments on it by rabbis formed the Haggadah. The Mishnah and Haggadah were collated and systematized into the Jerusalem Talmud and the Babylonian Talmud between A.D. 300 and A.D. 600, the word "talmud" being based on a Hebrew root word that means "instruction." See the article entitled "Talmud, Babylonian" in *Encyclopedia Judaica* for a detailed discussion and assessment of the worldwide impact of this

compilation, which was completed during the sixth century A.D. In the same source, see also the essay entitled, "Talmud, Jerusalem." This talmud was completed about a century earlier but never became as influential.

2. Genesis 1-10, King James version (as throughout this volume). There are numerous variations of the origin myth in the Babylonian Talmud. A popular belief was that Adam had been made from brown, black, yellow, white, and red earth. Another was that when Cain killed his brother Abel, the mark placed upon him was the whiteness of leprosy, not black skin as taught by the Mormons in the United States. See the first hundred pages of Louis Ginzberg, *Legends of the Bible* (New York: Jewish Publication Society of America, 1966); and "Glosses on the Creation Story" and "Earlier Creations," in Robert Graves and Raphael Patai, *Hebrew Myths: The Book of Genesis,* (New York: Doubleday, 1944), pp. 40–46. See also Louis Ginzberg, *The Legends of the Jews* (Philadelphia: Jewish Publication Society, 1938) vol. 1, pp. 54–60; vol. 4, p. 143. In *Legends of the Bible* Ginzberg selects and synthesizes from varied sources to produce a very interesting narrative.

3. See, e.g., Harold Isaacs, "Blackness and Whiteness," *Encounter* (August 1963). This scholar believes that such an opposition does exist. A learned discussion of the semantic complexities involved in interpreting the use of color terms in Hebrew and Arabic has been presented by a scholar who believes that where rain is highly valued, black will be valued, because it is associated with clouds that promise rain. He also noted that nomadic Semites prized the night and used the term "black" to praise its virtues. There was sometimes a metaphoric carry-over to gods and people. But in certain contexts white was cherished, too. See Ignác Goldziher, *Mythology Among the Hebrews* (New York: Cooper Square, 1967), pp. 133–197.

4. For a discussion of the meanings of hue, brightness, and saturation, as students of color use the words, see Eleanor Irwin, *Colour Terms in Greek Poetry* (Toronto: Hakkert, 1974), pp. 9–12. Biblical writers express more concern with brightness than with hue, but still only two books in the Bible concentrate on the contrast between "light" and "darkness" as a metaphor of human experience: Job in the Old Testament and John in the New. It is implicit, however, in a number of other places.

5. See, e.g., 2 Kings 5:27, Leviticus 13:8 and 14:2, and 2 Chronicles 26:21, as well as numerous New Testament references to leprosy. When Miriam complained about Moses marrying an Ethiopian woman, the biblical account states that "she became a leper, white as snow" (Numbers 12:4-10).

6. The tabulations used here are based on *Complete Concordance of the Revised Standard Version Bible,* compiled under the supervision of John W. Ellison and published by Thomas Nelson and Sons, New York, 1970. Similar results were obtained from a study of *Young's Analytical Concordance* (1982) based on the King James version, also published by Nelson and Sons. A perceptive student of this subject has warned analysts of the Bible that "frequency of use or occurrence should not be the criterion for determining the color symbolisms of black and white. The more objective criterion is the degree of importance of the object symbolized. It is the object symbolized that gives true meaning and importance to the symbol." This scholar made some very insightful remarks, based upon a selected sample of passages, in "The Religious Basis of Western Color Symbolism" and "Transference of the Religious Symbolism to Skin Color" Eulalio R. Baltazar, *The Dark Center: A Process Theology of Blackness,* argues that "on the authority of the Bible black is a positive symbol, the symbol of the divine and of goodness."

7. Isaiah 1:18.

8. Jeremiah 13:23.

9. The biblical references to Zerah are 2 Chronicles 14:9-14, 16:18. The well-known contemporary Jewish scholar, Immanuel Velikovsky, in *Ages in Chaos* (New York: Doubleday, 1952), pp. 208–211, attempts to demonstrate that Zerah was actually Amenhotep II of the XVIIIth Egyptian Dynasty, whose Negro physiognomy led the Jewish chroniclers to call him an Ethiopian. However, his evidence is purely circumstantial and conjectural.

10. Ezekiel 29:2-5.

11. Isaiah 36:6. Professor William F. Albright of Johns Hopkins University has noted that soon after the kingdom of Israel was annihilated, "Judah was now the sole heir of the glories of David and Solomon. Hezekiah (circa. 714-686 B.C.), lured by promises of Ethiopian aid, attempted to resist Assyria but was defeated and compelled to pay a crushing tribute" (see the article entitled "Palestine" in *Encyclopedia Britannica*, vol. 17 [1963]). Jeremiah is depicted as advising strongly against any reliance on Egypt and Ethiopia.

12. Nahum 3:8-10, 18.

13. Jeremiah 46:17, 20, 25-26. These are statements made during a long diatribe against Necho, one of the Egyptian Psammetichi kings who fought against the Babylonian armies and who referred to the Ethiopians among his troops. The reference is to Necho II. His successors ceased to use Ethiopian troops.

14. For a vivid cataloguing of "whoredoms," see Ezekiel 23. Jeremiah 44 adds the worship of "the pagan Queen of Heaven" to the list when assailing the wives of the men of Judah, who preferred to take refuge in Egypt rather than remain in Palestine under the rule of a king appointed by Nebuchadnezzar of Babylon. A Babylonian victory over Judah was interpreted as Jehovah's "chastening rod" for the people's sins.

15. Ezekiel 30:16, 25, 26.

16. Ezekiel 29:13-15.

17. Psalms 68:31. This verse, so treasured by modern black Christians, has been interpreted by some scholars to mean that the psalmist is exulting over the day when Ethiopians as well as Egyptians will come to Jerusalem bearing gifts for the rulers of Judah, who have been restored to power as their overlords. The 1981 edition of the New World Translation of the Holy Scriptures, published by the Watchtower Bible and Tract Society of New York (Jehovah's Witnesses), reads: "Because of your temple at Jerusalem kings will bring gifts to you . . . Bronzeware things will come out of Egypt, Cush itself will quickly stretch out its hands [with gifts] to God." The emphasis here is on gifts for the temple, not a restored Hebrew monarchy. (The brackets were supplied by the translator.)

18. In Zephaniah 2:12 and 3:10, in the midst of the prophet's message about Jehovah's promise to destroy Assyria, there is a suggestion that Ethiopia is holding war captives who are to be "delivered"; "You also, you Ethiopians, you yourselves will be people slain by my sword"; "From the region of the rivers of Ethiopia, the ones entreating me, the daughter of my scattered ones will bring a gift to me." It is intimated that some of the Jews will be forgiven of their sins and will remain in Ethiopia. It is Amos who, in the midst of a discussion of punishments visited upon the enemies of the Jewish people and of Jehovah's deliverance of them and others, makes the enigmatic statement whose meaning is not clear from the context (Amos 9:7). Ginzberg, in *Legends of the Jews*, vol. 6, p. 412, notes that some rabbis interpreted this passage not as expressing friendliness to Ethiopians but instead as

reflecting God's intent that just as Ethiopians had been wicked and punished, so Israel would be. Ginzberg gives this as one of several examples of the use of the rhetorical device of antiphrasis, which according to this scholar explains a number of texts that are ostensibly favorable to Blacks. They mean the opposite of what they say, he argues.

19. Hinduism was emerging between the sixth and second centuries B.C. An English translation of the Rig Veda, the oldest of the works that Brahmins were copying, editing, and collating, includes a hymn about the great Indian god of thunder: "Indra who is invoked by many, and is accompanied by his fleet companions, has destroyed by his thunderbolts the Dasyus and Simyus who dwelt on earth and then he distributed the fields to his white-complexioned friends." Another translation reads: "He, Indra, flays the enemy of his black skin and kills him and reduces him to ashes" (Rig Veda, book 1, 130, 8); and, "Plaguing the lawless he gave up to Manu's seed the dusky skin." Indra also called the Dasyus the "Krishna Yonis," or those with black vaginas. Dr. Ambedkar, in a critical study of these references, points out that they are very few and that it is not clear whether they represent the attitudes of Indo-Europeans invading northern India two millenia ago or of Brahmins consolidating their own position in the fifth century B.C. and reading their own color prejudices back into antiquity as they compiled the Rig Veda.

20. Jeremiah 38, 39:15-18. Ebed-melech was a figure of considerable interest to rabbinic scholars as Ginzberg, in *Legends of the Jews*, indicates (see vol. 4, pp.299–300, 318–319; vol. 5, pp. 96, 169; vol. 6, pp. 385, 387, 389, 412). One Hebrew pseudepigraphic work was entirely centered around Ebed-melech: "Ebed-melech, the Ethiopian, the Friend of the Prophet," in *The Paralipomena of Jeremiah* (cited in Ginzberg, *Legends of the Jews*, vol. 6, p. 387). Discussion went on among rabbis cited in the Talmud as to whether or not Ebed-melech was one of the nine pious men who never tasted of death, according to Ginzberg, *Legends of the Jews*, vol. 6, p. 412. Here Ginzberg states that some sources insist that references to Ebed-melech as an Ethiopian are "antiphrastic." Thus, when he was called "black," it really meant the opposite. This was said because he was the only "white" man (i.e., good man) at the court. The antiphrastic interpretation could be an unconscious, almost automatic attempt to explain away blackness! (For a list of the nine men who were said to have entered Paradise alive, including Elijah, see *Derech Eretz Zuta*, chap. 1, p. 102, in *Hebraic Literature* [London and Washington D.C.: Classics Library, 1902] with a special introduction by Maurice H. Harris.)

Another explanation that is equally antiphrastic involves a Talmudic reference to Michal, David's first wife, as "the daughter of Cush." She was the daughter of Saul, first King of Israel, who, according to one tradition, was called "the Ethiopian" (or Cushite). Ginzberg, in *Legends of the Jews*, vol. 7, p. 274, says this meant that "Saul was as distinguished for his beauty as the Ethiopian is for his color." The antiphrastic argument seems more plausible here than in the case of Ebed-Melech, but it is still open to the charge of explaining away or denying blackness in a biblical Jew.

Also, some nonbiblical sources insist that compilers of the book of Jeremiah confused the "holy man," Baruch, with Ebed-melech (see *Encyclopedia Judaica*, vol. 4 [1960], p. 266, citing Sif. Num., 12:1, a Talmudic source).

21. A valuable source is *The Genuine Works of Flavius Josephus, the Jewish Historian*, trans. William Whiston (Cincinnati: Applegate, 1850), which includes *The Antiquities of the Jews*, a work we shall cite frequently. The writings of

Flavius Josephus contained considerable speculation about the influence of the Egyptians on Jewish thought and culture, as well as on the origin of the Jewish people—his own ethnic group. He accepted the now discredited theory that the original Jews were the Hyksos invaders of Egypt. If the consensus view is accepted, the Jewish people experienced Egyptian culture at one of its peaks, during the reign of Rameses II, when black and mixed-blood rulers, court officials, and attendants were prevalent.

During the 1940s, Sigmund Freud, the founder of psychoanalysis and himself a Jew, in his book, *Moses and Monotheism* (New York: Knopf, 1939), put forward the view that Moses was not a Jew but was an Egyptian believer in the teachings of the black religious reformer, Akhenaten, of the Eighteenth Dynasty. After the priestly reaction against Akhenaten, during the disorders following the death of Tutankhamen's successor, Horemheb, Moses, according to this theory, led an ethnically mixed group (what Exodus 12:38 calls "a mixed multitude") out through the Sinai desert to Canaan. Thus Freud comes to the surprising conclusion that the Jews received their monotheistic teachings from the black pharaoh (although he makes no mention of Akhenaten's race). But Freud goes even further. He suggests that many Jewish customs, including circumcision and the eating of kosher foods, are also of Egyptian origin.

22. Numbers 12:4-10 tells the story, including how Miriam was punished with leprosy for criticizing Moses.

23. Recent English-language publication of a body of Jewish legends and folklore reveals stories that attribute color prejudice to some of the male residents of Jerusalem and the surrounding area during the sixth century B.C., after the Persian rulers allowed some of the Jews to return from their exile in Mesopotamia. One of these stories states:

> When the Jews returned from Babylon their wives had become brown, and almost black, during the years of captivity, and a large number of men divorced their wives. The divorced women probably married black men, which would, to some extent, account for the existence of Black Jews (Samuel Rapaport, *A Treasury of the Midrash* [New York: KTAV Publishing House, 1968], p. 71, summarizing data from Genesis Rabbah 18).

This story raises a number of crucial questions about how such a change could have occurred, questions with no ready answers. The suggestion of a bias in favor of lighter women on the part of Palestinian males, if it existed, could be an esthetic preference with, perhaps, some status-allocating implications. It does not necessarily mean that skin color functioned to assign a lower status to all black people in the Judean social system.

There is no explanation of how enough black men happened to be in Israel to marry the women, or how the women became dark when the husbands were away. Is this another case of peasant women becoming dark-skinned because they worked outdoors, thus losing status because their color marks them as being different from women of higher status levels? We use the case simply to indicate that color awareness was present among the ancient Hebrews and that at some point it seemed to become socially salient either in the compilers' minds or actually among the people they were writing about.

24. The allegorical interpretations are summarized in Frank Snowden, *Blacks in Antiquity: Ethiopians in the Greco-Roman Experience* (Cambridge, Mass.: Belknap Press of Harvard University Press, 1971). All of Chapter 4 relies heavily on this definitive but low-key "vindicationist" work by a distinguished Afro-

American professor of classics at Howard University, for data about attitudes of Greeks, Romans and early Christians toward black people. Professor Snowden works from original Greek and Latin sources and combines this kind of research with observation and analysis of art styles. Interested readers might wish to consult Snowden's eighty-two pages of citations and critical annotations.

For the Church Fathers, see Origen, pp. 199–200; Gregory of Nyasa, p. 200; Jerome, pp. 200–201; Arator, p. 204; and Augustine, p. 204. See also from Snowden's extensive endnotes, pp. 331–333. One scholar (not a Negro), in discussing Origen in detail, notes that his "attitude toward negritude is not wholly positive" and that he "goes on to plaster his supposed positive attitude toward negritude with a whitewash of highly questionable quality" and accuses him of "fancy exegetical footwork" (Marvin H. Pope, *Song of Songs: A New Translation With Introduction and Commentary* [Garden City: Doubleday, 1977], p. 310–311).

25. Song of Solomon 1:5-6. The revised standard version reads, "I am dark *but* . . . "; the early Greek version reads, "I am dark *and*. . . . " The headings for each chapter in the King James version interpret the Song of Solomon as a prophetic allegory referring to Christ and his church. The mystical Jewish work, *The Zohar*, cites an esoteric interpretation made by Rabbi Judah of the Roman Empire period, in which the girl symbolizes the community of Israel "who is 'black' [i.e., depressed and desolate] because of her captivity and 'comely' because of the Torah and good works" (see *The Zohar*, vol. 1, trans. Harry Sperling and Maurice Simon [London: Soncino Press, 1933] p. 43). See also "The Spiritual Canticle," in *The Poems of St. John of the Cross*, trans. John Frederick Nims (Chicago: University of Chicago Press, 1979). This sixteenth-century Spanish Christian mystic uses the poem as a metaphor for the love existing betweeen a person and God. The poet implies that God, like Solomon, is a "respecter of persons," however, for the girl says that the man (i.e., Solomon) loved her "but thought me, cheek and brow, a shade too Moorish" (from "The Spiritual Canticle" in *The University of Chicago Magazine* 73, 1 [Autumn 1979]:18).

26. The biblical story of Noah, the Flood, and the aftermath is given in Genesis 6-10. See Ginzberg, *Legends of the Jews*, pp. 159–164, for other versions of the legend along with rabbinic comments. The version of the Noaic genealogy most widely available to people in Christendom, i.e., the "Table of Nations," is this one given in Genesis, 10-12. The fact that in this genealogy, some of the sons of Cush are placed in the Fertile Crescent and Arabia and some in Africa has been considered a problem by modern biblical students. Some solve it by arguing that translators have missed the point, that Cush is a name used to designate two quite different kinds of people; others adopt the idea that a dark-skinned population once covered the entire area. Rabbinic scholars eventually agreed that "Cush" and "Cushite" should be used with reference to Ethiopia and then devoted their skill to proving that biblical references to individuals cited as Cushitic were either antiphrastic or metaphorical, i.e., that persons referred to as Cushites were not really black (See the article entitled "Cush" in *Encyclopedia Judaica* [1960], pp. 394–395).

27. Josephus, *The Antiquities of the Jews*, pp. 6-7. This work, written in A.D. 93, is useful for studying variations on stories found in the Bible. In addition, comparisons with the Babylonian Talmud reveal differences of emphasis between the rabbinic tradition of the Mesopotamian diaspora, three centuries after Josephus wrote, and the views of this sophisticated intellectual living in Jerusalem at the time of the destruction of the Temple. Data pejorative to black

people appears in the Babylonian Talmud but not in the writings of Josephus, a Hellenized Jew.

Throughout Isaiah, Ezekiel, and Jeremiah, when the terms "Cush" or "Cushite" appear in the text, there is no doubt about their application to Nile Valley kingdoms. However, because the Genesis story mentions non-African as well as African peoples in the line of Ham and Cush, biblical scholars perceived a contradiction that had to be resolved. There is now a tendency to feel that some of the early transmissions by oral tradition confused the word "Kassites," a Mesopotamian people, with the word "Cushite," and that the Old Testament referent is sometimes one and sometimes the other, knowledge of the context being necessary for a determination. However, it sometimes seems more likely that racist prejudices enter into the decision to call a specific person a Cushite, i.e., an African Cushite (See the article entitled "Ham" in Encyclopedia Judaica, vol. 7, p. 1216; and in The Jewish Encyclopedia [New York: Funk and Wagnalls, 1904], p. 186). Rabbinic scholars of an earlier period solved the "problem" by accepting the idea that the dark-skinned sons of Cush built cities in Mesopotamia and ruled the area before the Semitic peoples won control of the area (See Ginzberg, Legends of the Jews, vol. 5, pp. 198, 199, 201, 211, and vol. 1, pp. 177–178). By the time Josephus wrote (circa A.D. 90), "time has not at all hurt the name of Chus; the Ethiopians over whom he reigned are even at this day, both by themselves and by all men in Asia, called Chusites" (p. 7).

28. Josephus, The Antiquities of the Jews. The legends surrounding Nimrod must have accumulated during the period prior to the writing of the book by Josephus. These legends later found a place in the Haggadic literature and were incorporated in the Babylonian Talmud. The fanciful nature of many of these stories led the more serious scholars to reject them, whereas the popular synagogue exhorters used them and they later became part of what is known as the Midrashic literature and the Gemara portion of the Talmud. It is obvious that Josephus was aware of some of these stories, although he does not elaborate upon them. For instance in speaking of the Tower of Babel, he states, "Now it was Nimrod who excited them to such an affront and contempt of God. He was the grandson of Ham, the son of Noah, a bold man, and of great strength of hand." The Old Testament stresses only that he was a "mighty hunter." In his index to Legends of the Jews, Ginzberg lists 195 citations through the sixth century A.D. that refer to Nimrod, in contrast to only forty-five that refer either to Cush, Cushites, Ethiopia, or four important personalities associated with these names. Most of the references in the legends refer to Nimrod as arrogant, impious, and wicked, and several speak of him as becoming "ruler of the world" after he established the "first monarchy." Early legends attribute the disaster at the Tower of Babel to him, and post-exilic legends blame him for teaching sorcery and fire worship to the Persians. This emphasis on the wickedness of Nimrod, son of Cush, is a Mesopotamian diaspora counterpart to the Palestinian emphasis upon Canaan, the son of Ham. Some versions of the Nimrod legend refer to him as a son of Cush, the son of Ham, giving rise to the belief, in some quarters, that "black people" once ruled the entire Middle East.

29. Curiously Josephus classified the Persians as kinsmen of the Jewish people through Shem. Today they are, by consensus of Orientalists, classified along with the Medes as Indo-Europeans. Neither the Old Testament nor Josephus provides an ancestral line for the inhabitants of India, China, or Japan. The Scythians, Medes, and Persians represent the northeastern and southeastern limits of the

peoples to whom Josephus felt the "Table of Nations" referred (Magog, Madai, and Elam in the original table). His assumption that Gomer referred to Gauls presupposed knowledge, on the part of the compilers of the Pentateuch, that would have been unavailable in their lifetimes. His inclusion of Thodel as an ancestor of the Iberians was also an obvious "updating." Both the original makers of the "Table of Nations" and Josephus tried to include all of the people of "the known world," but that "world" was constantly expanding through exploration and conquest. And there were, of course, still vast areas of the world "unknown" to the Middle Eastern and Mediterranean contemporaries of Josephus.

Some scholars still classify languages as Semitic (after Shem), Hamitic, and Japhetic, long after doubt has been thrown upon the usefulness of the Noaic genealogy for securing accurate knowledge about actual relationships between various racial and ethnic groups.

30. See Genesis 12:46–50 and Genesis 15, 17 for one account of Abraham and the Covenant. For a list of references to Abraham in the nonbiblical Jewish tradition, see Ginzberg, *Legends of the Jews*, vol. 7, pp. 6–13. The literature on the early history of the Jewish people is voluminous. Specific details relating to events and personalities can be found briefly stated from the point of view of liberal Jewish scholars in *Encyclopedia Judaica* (1960). Various scholars contributed an excellent article in the 1963 edition of *Encyclopedia Britannica*, vol. 13, pp. 42E–58, under the title "Jews." The Old Testament, of course, tells the story from the point of view of Jewish participants in the events, persons with a pronounced ethnic bias. Egyptian records do not refer at all to their sojourn in the country or to Joseph, Moses, and the Exodus. In recounting the story of the breakup of the Solomonic kingdom and subsequent events, much of the biblical account is presented from the point of view of the southern kingdom, Judah. It has been heavily edited to favor the Prophets in their controversies with kings and priests, a fact discussed in the introduction to Graves and Patai's *Hebrew Myths*. For the most generally accepted account of Abraham's wanderings and his concept of a covenant with Jehovah, see Genesis 12:46–50 and Exodus 1–18.

31. The basic story is told in Genesis 9, 10. The curse is specifically laid on Canaan in Genesis 9:25. This story has been the subject of constant rabbinic elaboration and Christian theological speculation. See Ginzberg, *Legends of the Jews*, vol. 7, pp. 78–79, 202. Compilations of rabbinic comment over the centuries reveal the use of Noah as an example of the evil effects of imbibing too much alcohol. One of the most recent efforts at making some of these comments available to the English-speaking public is to be found in Menahem M. Kasher, *Encyclopedia of Biblical Interpretation* (New York: American Biblical Encyclopedia Society, 1955), pp. 68–70. One comment declared, "degrading indeed is drunkenness, for it is compared to idolatry." Another observed, "When a man drinks one glass he is like a lamb, humble and meek. When he drinks two he waxes brave as a lion, speaks truculently and boastfully, 'Who is like unto me.' And when he drinks three or four he becomes like a swine, wallowing in filth and mire." Kasher, editor of the *Encyclopedia*, writes, in his own commentary, "Scripture shows how even a righteous man like Noah could be degraded through drunkenness." The most ingenious interpretation stated that Noah was the first man to make wine and, in so doing, gave mankind something to offset the curse laid on Adam whereby he had to earn his living by the sweat of his brow. It was a beneficent discovery, but Noah had to learn by experience how devastating it could be if misused. For a comment by an early Protestant theologian, see John Calvin, *Commentaries on*

the First Book of Moses Called Genesis (Grand Rapids, Mich.: W. B. Eerdman's, 1948), pp. 300-307. Like the rabbis, Calvin used the story of Noah to emphasize the evils of excessive drinking, saying, "I rather suppose that we are to learn from the drunkenness of Noah what a filthy and detestable crime drunkenness is." Calvin notes that drunkenness can make fathers "become laughing stock to their own children." As to Ham, Calvin calls him a "lascivious youth" deserving of punishment. So "God held the whole seed of Ham as obnoxious." Calvin did not, however, mention Ham's descendants as being condemned to serve other people as slaves.

32. See a statement attributed to a rabbi in the fourth century A.D., included in the Babylonian Talmud and the Midrash, cited in Kasher, Encyclopedia of Biblical Interpretation, p. 72, note 66. See also Ginzberg, Legends of the Jews, vol. 5, p. 196. The curse on Canaan was also justified by some Talmudic commentators on the grounds that Canaan had originally taken land that Noah allotted to Shem. This claim of usurpation justified the warfare against Canaan after the Exodus, according to Ginzberg, Legends of the Jews, vol. 3, p. 220. The story was used before the Ptolemaic era by the Carthaginians, according to one Talmudic legend, in order to assert their claim to Palestine. They sent a deputation to Alexander the Great informing him that Judea had been allotted to the sons of Canaan after the Flood and that the Phoenicians, who established Carthage, were Canaanites. They asked Alexander to return the land to their sovereignty. But the Jewish leaders then informed Alexander of the curse that gave them title to the Jews, so he denied the Carthaginian claim.

33. There are several nonbiblical variations of the Noah-Ham story stating that it was only Ham himself who was punished, not any of his specific descendants. Insofar as it was generally believed that Ham's descendants were all of those dark-skinned people who settled northern and eastern Africa, and that the word Ham had similar origins to those of the Egyptian word Chem and meant both "hot" and "black," it is possible that from time to time, it was to some group's interest to apply the presumed curse on some people presumed to be descendants of Ham.

   One allegorical interpretation of the Ham story by some rabbis is undoubtedly more recent than the interpretations justifying the conquests of Canaan's cities and farmlands. It could not be older than the eighth century B.C., when devastating military attacks on Israel and Judah were made by the Assyrians, and some of the kings, against the advice of the Prophets, sought alliances with Ethiopia and Egypt. The story of Shem and Japheth walking backward to cover their father's nakedness is presented as having "prefigured" an event that was to occur centuries later: "naked the descendants of Ham, the Egyptians and the Ethiopians, were led away captive into exile by the king of Assyria while the descendants of Shem were not 'exposed'" (Isaiah 20:4). This time, Africans, not the Canaanites, were the targets of disapproval. There is no necessary imputation of either esthetic unpleasantness or cognitive deficiency to the Africans, however. Consequences of the acts of ancestors were simply working themselves out with supernatural inevitability (as in the great Greek tragedies).

34. Rabbi Dr. I. Epstein, in his Foreword (p. xvii) to Rabbi Dr. H. Freedman and Maurice Simon, eds., Midrash Rabbah. Rapaport in A Treasury of the Midrash, and Graves and Patai in Hebrew Myths stress the point that some of the legends and comments on them are very old. However, Rapaport points out that many stories from the Midrash were elaborated during the periods of Roman attacks on

Palestine during the reign of the Roman emperors Titus and Vespasian. This may have some relevance to comments about Ham and his descendants.

35. Martin McNamara, *Targum and Testament* (Shannon, Ireland: Irish University Press, 1972), p. ii.

36. Babylonian Talmud, trans. I. Epstein et al., (1935-60), Sanhedrin 70a, p. 477. This section gives an account of the difference of opinion between Rabbi Rab and Rabbi Samuel over whether castration or sodomy was the sin committed by Ham. The sodomy accusation was evidently not reported in the earliest versions of Ham's offenses.

37. This version has the flavor of a folktale with explanatory intent, and is related along with a number of other stories about how the animals behaved and misbehaved on the Ark (see chapter 20, "The Deluge," in Graves and Patai, *Hebrew Myths*). The legends are delightfully retold. By the time they were written in the Midrashim they may have been circulating for centuries among the illiterate folk. Any stories about black skin being a result of sexual delinquencies would no doubt have become the basis for stereotyped conceptions of existing black people.

38. The sodomy story, "in one Midrashic passage . . . has been added to Ham's crimes," according to Graves and Patai, *Hebrew Myths*, p. 122. See also Ginzberg, *Legends of the Jews*, vol. 2, p. 166; vol 5., pp. 188, 191, citing the Babylonian Talmud.

39. During the twentieth century, Henrietta Szold of Hadassah (the American Jewish women's organization), anthropologists Paul Radin and Raphael Patai, and Hebrew studies experts Louis Ginzberg, Micha Bin Gorin, and Samuel Rapaport have been making available in English a body of Jewish legends and folklore that was in existence for centuries only in Hebrew, Aramaic, and Yiddish. Some were stories collected and edited with rabbinic comments between the time of the destruction of the Temple in Jerusalem in A.D. 72 and the completion of the Jerusalem Talmud around A.D. 400 and the Babylonian Talmud a century later.

40. In this reference the sources are cited by Professor Ephraim Isaac in standard conventional abbreviated form: Bek. 45b; Num. R. 16; 22; Cant. R. 1:6:3; P.R.E. 24; Cant. 5:11; Yalkut Shim'oni 1238; M. K. 16b; Sifre 12:1(99); Targum Onkelos: Num. 12:1; Suk. 34b, B.B. 97 B; B. Suk. 53a. See also *Midrash Rabbah*, Genesis, chapter XXXVI.7, "And Noah awoke from his wine," p. 293.

41. Rapaport, *A Treasury of the Midrash*, p. 96.

42. In an unpublished memorandum entitled, "The Curse of Ham—A History of a Misunderstanding," Professor Ephraim Isaac criticizes Graves and Patai. In *Hebrew Myths*, published in 1964, they had collapsed a number of Talmudic and Midrashic statements about Ham and his descendants into a single paragraph. The impression was conveyed that the expression "born black and ugly" was connected with this Midrashic description of Canaan. See p. 13 of the memorandum, written in the early 1970s while Professor Isaac was a member of the faculty in Afro-American Studies at Harvard University, and kindly made available to the author. Graves and Patai (*Hebrew Myths*, p. 121) cite two tractates of the Babylonian Talmud: B. Sanhedrin 72a-b, 108b and B. Pesahim 113b; three Midrashic sources: Tanhuma Buber Gen. 48-50; Tanhuma Noah 13,15; and Gen. Rab., 341.

43. This version is from Louis Ginzberg, *Legends of the Jews*, p. 169. See also Ginzberg, *Legends of the Bible*, for same version, p. 80. Graves and Patai present a version that is identical but with an additional clause, "and their male members

shall be shamefully elongated" (*Hebrew Myths*, p. 121). Ephraim Isaac, in the memorandum referred to in the previous note, points out that Graves and Patai were working from a fourth century A.D. Midrashic work, Tanhuma Noah 13. He retranslates the passage from the Levy-Epstein Hebrew edition of Tanhuma Noah and renders the final clause as "His prepuce became stretched." He translates "twisted curly hair" as "the hair of his head and his beard became singed," noting also that the curse was said to have applied to Ham only and not specifically to Canaan. He notes that an 1885 edition of Tanhuma Noah does not contain this particular passage at all!

44. Graves and Patai, *Hebrew Myths*, p. 121.
45. Kasher, *Biblical Interpretation*, vol. 2, pp. 79-82, 91-98. This detailed account of Nimrod is summarized from H. Polano, trans., *The Talmud: Selections from the Contents of the Ancient Books, Its Commentaries, Teachings, Poetry, and Legends* (London: Warnean and Co., n.d.), pp. 26-29. This translator and editor has presented a version stating that some of the malefactors who built the Tower of Babel were turned into people who looked like apes. Another version of the story said that *all* were turned into apelike humans (Eleazer ben Ashar ha-Levi, *The Chronicles of Jerahmeel* [New York: KTAV Publishing, 1971], p. 69). The *Encyclopedia Judaica*, pp. 1176-1177, presents a comprehensive summary of the nonbiblical legends about Nimrod, with a citation for each separate legend. This includes a story that tells of Nimrod killing Abraham and casting him into a fiery furnace, as well as one in which Nimrod is eventually defeated in a conflict with Abraham. The editors suggest that there was probably an ancient epic about Nimrod that included some of these incidents. Among the many legends is one that reverses the basic story and makes Nimrod a son of Shem. This lends some credence to the idea that an ancient conflict between Semitic speakers and their non-Semitic predecessors in Mesopotamia is the underlying subject of the Nimrod story, and that details will vary depending upon the era from which a specific version comes. For a full list of the references in the nonbiblical sources, with critical comments, see citations listed under "Nimrod" in Ginzberg, *Legends of the Jews*, vol. 7.
46. These comments are not based upon the Septuagint version of the Old Testament, which used the expression, "black *and* comely." The word "but" is essential to the rabbinic comments. Since the Vulgate version of the Old Testament, which uses "but" instead of "and," was not available until A.D. 405, the question is raised of when the Midrash on the Song of Solomon was written and what language the compiler's source used.
47. Freedman and Simon, *Midrash Rabbah*, Esther, The Song of Songs, vol. 9, I.5, 1, "I am black, but comely." pp. 51-53. Rapaport in *A Treasury of the Midrash*, pp. 166-167, presents relevant comments in a chapter on "Midrash Song of Songs."
48. Freedman and Simon," *Midrash Rabbah*, Esther, The Song of Songs, vol. 9, I.5, 1, "As the tents of Kedar," pp. 54-55.
49. Ibid., p. 51, 51n. Pope, *Song of Songs*, pp. 307-309. The author is not only erudite, but is also witty and sensitive to attempts to "talk away" blackness. In discussing "black and/but beautiful," he notes that the Septuagint used the Greek word, *melaina*, but that in the case of writers using Latin, effort was made to mitigate the blackness with the rendering *fusca*, "dark," rather than *nigra*, "black," as reflected in citations by early Christian expositors, which waver between *nigra* and *fusca*, between "and" and "but" (*et/sed*), and in the terms for beauty, *pulchra/speciosa/formosa*. Jerome's Vulgate rendering, *Nigra sum sed formosa*, has been followed in

most vernacular versions of the Bible, along with a "but" instead of an "and." Pope points out that the Revised Standard Version, however, changes "black" to "very dark," translating the Hebrew *sahor* in this fashion. But except for this Song of Solomon passage, *sahor* is translated as "black." He concludes that "the unprejudiced rendering 'black and beautiful' is understandably favored by persons who value their own blackness, real or imagined." He recognizes what he calls "melainophobia" in the traditional exegesis.

50. Isaac, "The Curse of Ham," an unpublished manuscript, pp. 29–30.
51. *Mimekor Yisrael, Classical Jewish Folktales*, ed. Emanuel Bin Gorion (Bloomington: Indiana University Press, 1976), vol. 3, pp. 327–328.
52. Ibid., "Eldad ha-Dani (The Danite)," first version (168) pp. 330–332; quotation is from p. 330.
53. Ibid., p. 330.
54. Ibid., p. 331.
55. Ibid., "Dan and His Brother Tribes," (No. 165) pp. 324–325. Quotation from p. 325.
56. Ibid.
57. Ibid.
58. Ginzberg, *Legends of the Jews*, vol. 1, p. 169.
59. It is possible that negative images of Blacks were excluded from the Old Testament and later from the Jerusalem Talmud for reasons of state. When the texts of the Pentateuch and the Prophets were being standardized during the fourth century B.C., post-exile national life was being restored in Judea and renewal of traditional ties with Egypt and Ethiopia may have been envisioned. Recording folk prejudices against Blacks, even if they existed, would not have been wise national policy: alliances with Egypt/Ethiopia might be needed in the future.
60. Bernard Lewis, *Race and Color in Islam* (New York: Harper & Row, 1971), pp. 33–36.
61. In Palestine, the Greeks and the Romans were viewed as "the enemy" defiling sacred soil. Those who imitated them or fraternized with them were traitors. There was never a large stratum of people in Judea who were Hellenized or Romanized. Yet, as *Encyclopedia Judaica* (1971, p. 40) points out in its article on "Babylonia," during the first century A.D. when Jews in Palestine were being punished for their revolts against the Romans, "among Babylonian Jewry was a class of native-born aristocrats, who probably acted like other Parthian nobles, as local strong men." The Sassanians, according to the same article, "throughout the whole period of their rule . . . made extensive use of the Jews in international politics and trade." The story of Queen Esther, who married the Persian king, symbolizes the extent to which some Jews were able to acquire power and prestige under the Persians. The Feast of Purim celebrates that situation. This improved state of affairs continued throughout the Hellenistic period and under the Seleucid rulers who took power after the death of Alexander, with a period of some persecution between. Under these circumstances parts of the Jewish community became involved in the importation and exploitation of "Zanj" labor in southern Mesopotamia. Insofar as the landed upper class followed the ancient Babylonian pattern, it would have been a slaveholding class. And it is likely that some of the farmers and tradesmen held slaves as well. The Jewish people were also represented in commerce, in manufacturing, and in the ownership of vessels that traded in the Persian Gulf and the Indian Ocean, where they were in direct contact with "Zanj." Some historians emphasize the importance of social-class stratification within the Mesopotamian Jewish community, pointing out that

even some of the rabbis came from among the wealthy class. The Talmud naturally reflected these class interests. See the article entitled "Babylonia" in *Encyclopedia Judaica* (1971), pp. 34–43.

62. Ibid.

63. Not all of the stories in the published folklore about Blacks deal with Israelites rampaging among cannibalistic Rumrum or imposing themselves upon industrious and prosperous communities in "civilized" areas of Kush. Some tell of relations between Hebrew masters and black servants in either Palestine or Mesopotamia. That these stories were accepted as credible by rabbis who used them as parables in teaching is a significant index to both the behavior of Blacks and attitudes toward them. Two of the stories are about self-assured Ethiopian female bond servants, each of whom insists that the master of the house loves her better than he does his wife. In one case, the servant makes this claim to the wife's face; in the other she tells another servant that her master has promised to divorce his wife and marry her. Another story deals with an Ethiopian male servant who tries to seduce the wife of his absent master. The matter-of-fact tone without racially pejorative comment is in sharp contrast to tales about relations with Blacks living in their native habitat in Kush, as related by Eldad.

64. In the famous speech attributed to St. Paul in Acts 17:18-31, the inference is that he was acquainted with the disputes between Greek philosophers. Snowden (*Blacks in Antiquity*, p. 117) makes reference to a tradition that Paul had been influenced by Menander. See also the article entitled "St. Paul" in the *Encyclopedia Britannica* (1963) for a discussion of the likelihood that Paul received some education in Greek modes of thought even though his basic training came from Jewish scholars.

65. Alice Elizabeth Kober, *The Use of Color Terms in Greek Poetry*, (Geneva, N.Y.: W.F. Humphrey Press, 1932), p. 35.

66. Irwin, *Colour Terms*, pp. 177, 178.

67. Kober, *Use of Color Terms*, p. 34.

68. Ibid., p. 34.

69. Kober, *Use of Color Terms*, pp. 25–26.

70. Further semantic difficulties appear in certain metaphoric usages and in references to gods rather than to people. Sometimes the word for white is used to signify brightness, which does not refer to hue but rather to another dimension of visual effect. Likewise, black sometimes means darkness, i.e., absence of light. In general, however, the Greeks did not use *melas* and its derivatives to refer to the opposite of brightness. For instance, another term was used to describe "darkness of night" and "darkness of the underworld." Presumably, here the associations did not carry over to people, but they could apply to supernatural beings. Referent and context determine the choice of word for designating "black" or "dark" persons, places, or things.

71. Irwin, *Colour Terms*, "The Gods: Olympian and Chtonian," pp. 182–186.

72. Ibid., "Notes on Etymology," pp. 217–219, 219–220.

73. Ibid., pp. 151–152.

74. Ibid., pp. 155–156. See also an analysis of the positive associations with blackness in ancient Hebrew religions, in Goldziher, *Mythology Among the Hebrews*, pp. 146–157.

75. See Snowden, *Blacks in Antiquity*, pp. 102, 103, 122, 181. He cites evidence pointing to consideration of Eurybates as a Negro. The case of Eurybates illustrates the measure of disagreement that often exists between white and black

scholars over the interpretation of data. Snowden, a cautious and conservative black scholar, states that "Eurybates, the herald of Odysseus, who had accompanied him from Ithaca to Troy, was black-skinned and wooly-haired," and that "a black-skinned, wooly-haired individual, we have seen, was to the Greeks an Ethiopian" (p. 102). In another passage he notes that "a high esteem for Ethiopians appears as early as Homer, whose black, wooly-haired Eurybates won the high respect of Odysseus" (p. 181). A recent work by a highly competent white scholar insists, however, that the description has nothing to do with race. The word that Snowden translates as "black" she translates as "dark-skinned." She goes on to say, "But Odysseus himself has wooly hair as a mark of beauty . . . Wooly hair then need not be foreign, and since Eurybates . . . is from Ithaca, it is likely that he, like Odysseus, was a Greek" (Irwin, *Colour Terms*, pp. 113–114). One scholar, in translating the *Odyssey* for modern English and American readers states as a general principle that "too faithful a rendering defeats its own purpose; and if we put Homer straight into English words neither message nor manner survives." He describes Eurybates as having "a dark complexion and curly hair" (Homerus, *The Odyssey*, trans. E.V. Rieu [London: Penguin Classics, 1953]).

76. Homerus, *The Odyssey*, trans. Rieu, pp. 25–26, 185, 294.
77. The unsigned article entitled "Memnon" in vol. 15 of the 1963 edition of *Encyclopedia Britannica*, with a hint of incredulity, states that "as an Ethiopian Memnon was described as black, but [sic] was noted for his beauty." This account mentions the legend that Aurora, or Eos, wept for her son and that the ancients said her tears are the dew seen at dawn. The merging of solar myths with legends about heroes was widespread in antiquity and may have sometimes had metaphorical significance. The early versions of the story that place the home of Memnon in Elam, east of Babylon, locate him for the Greeks on the horizon where the sun rose. Both Strabo and Diodorus tried to reconcile a contradiction in the story that had arisen by imperial Roman times: was Memnon's Ethiopia in Elam near Babylon or in the Nile Valley? That both locales were mentioned in the legends lends some credence to the idea that in antiquity it did not seem strange to consider the possibility that the inhabitants of parts of Mesopotamia were once black (cf. Nimrod legends).
78. Snowden, *Blacks in Antiquity*, pp. 151–153, points out that among the early poets, Memnon was considered an Asian who came to Troy from Elam, in what is now southeast Iran. During the fifth and sixth centuries, however, Athenians, by consensus, located Ethiopia in the upper Nile Valley, and Memnon became a Negro rather than an unspecified type of black man. On the same pages, Snowden discusses other Ethiopians who played prominent parts in Greek mythology, including the Perseus-Andromeda story and the legend of the Ethopian woman who was the mother of Danaus's fifty daughters. Both chapters 6 and 8 of his book are also relevant to this theme.
79. Snowden, *Blacks in Antiquity*, p. 180.
80. Ibid., p. 179. Snowden, in *Before Color Prejudice: The Ancient View of Blacks* (Cambridge: Harvard University Press, 1983), written a decade later, extends his dicussion of black as an "ominous" color. He writes, "Although the Greek and Roman association of the color black with death and the Underworld had in origin nothing to do with skin color, the introduction of dark-skinned peoples into such contexts was a natural development." In other words, he believed that attitudes toward blackness in the symbol system can carry over to skin, and black people then become an ominous symbol. But he hastens to say that "it is unlikely

that the association of dark-skinned peoples with omens of evil in the early
Roman Empire had an adverse impact on day-to-day reactions to Blacks." He cites
both Degler and Gergen to defend this position and also to buttress his argument
that negative reactions to people of a different color on first contact are likely to
disappear as such people become used to each other. Snowden ignores Degler's
contention that aversion to black skin color is a universal trait.

81. Snowden, *Blacks in Antiquity*, pp. 272–273. This author mentions the baleful
effect of seeing a black person in certain situations (pp. 179–180), but discussed
the belief in the apotropaic powers at some length.

82. Snowden, in discussing "Negro roles" in Greek satiric plays and Negro representations in masks, does not deny the element of caricature in these uses (See *Blacks
in Antiquity*, pp. 160–161). For a critique by Joseph Harris, see *Africans and Their
History* (New York: New American Library, 1972), pp. 12–13.

In his later work, *Before Color Prejudice* (1983), pp. 82–83, Snowden uses H.
Hoetink's concept of somatic norm image to comment that " . . . like other
people, white and black, in their expressions of esthetic preference the Greeks and
Romans used their own physical traits as a yardstick" but "the somatic norm
image was not always observed [i.e., by artists]." He believes that "some scholars
have read non-existent antiblack sentiment into Greco-Roman preferences which
in fact merely reflected the prevailing norms and were no more racist than the
preferences of blacks for their own ideals of beauty." Snowden admits that "Some
Negroes, but far from the majority, appeared in scenes that may be rightly
classified as comic or caricatural . . . Still there is no reason to conclude that
classical artists who pictured Blacks in comic or satirical scenes were motivated
by color prejudice. Whites of many races—even gods and heroes—appeared in
comic or satirical scenes. Why should blacks have been excluded?" See the
forceful statement that Greek arists caricatured Blacks made by Professor
Orlando Patterson, an Afro-Caribbean scholar in the Sociology Department at
Harvard, in *Slavery as Social Death*, (Cambridge: Harvard University Press), pp.
177–178.

83. Snowden, *Blacks in Antiquity*, pp. 181–182.

84. Ibid. See plates 21, 23, 40, 95, 97, 100.

85. Ibid. See, e.g., p. 93, plate 70; p. 96, plate 72; p. 249, plate 115.

86. Ibid., pp. 192–195.

87. Serge Sauneron, *The Priests of Ancient Egypt* (New York: Grove, 1980), chapter on
"The Sacred Wisdom."

88. Cheikh Anta Diop has stated the case for Greek cultural indebtedness to Egypt
from the perspective of a West African physical scientist and man of letters (See
Cheikh Anta Diop, *The African Origin of Civilization: Myth or Reality* [Westport,
Conn.: Laurence Hill and Co., 1971], pp. 230–235). George G. R. James, a Caribbean
professor teaching at a black college in the United States, presents a credible case
for extensive borrowings but interprets the data as evidence of a conspiracy to rob
Egyptians of credit for cultural elements borrowed. See his *Stolen Legacy* (New
York: Philosophical Library, 1954; reprinted in 1976 by Julian Richardson
Associates of San Francisco). French Egyptologist Serge Sauneron analyzes the
areas in which he thinks Egypt's impact was greatest as compared with those in
which it was less important. He notes that so high was the prestige of Egypt's
learning that biographers of early Greek philosophers attributed an Egyptian
period of training to them, even if it was apocryphal. For Pythagoras a period of
Egyptian study is almost certain, but for Plato it is very problematical. See

Sauneron, *The Priests of Ancient Egypt*, the chapter on "The Sacred Wisdom." This is an excellent source, including as it does direct quotations from ancient documents. The definitive work on this subject is Martin Bernal's *Black Athena* (Rutgers, N.J.: Transaction Press, 1987). The author is a distinguished British classical scholar. See also John A. Wilson, "The Intellectual Role of Egypt," and Henry and H. A. Frankfort, "The Emancipation of Thought from Myth" in Henri Frankfort, Mrs. H. A. Frankfort, John A. Wilson and Thorkild Jacobsen, *Before Philosophy* (Baltimore: Pelican, 1949), pp. 130–131, 237–262.

89. For evidence of black soldiers at Marathon, see Snowden, *Blacks in Antiquity*, pp. 123, 125, and his discussion of sources on pp. 291, 293, notes 13, 16.

90. Ibid., pp. 123, 143.

91. Ibid., p. 170.

92. Ibid., pp. 128–129.

93. Ibid., p. 105.

94. Ibid., p. 109.

95. Ibid., p. 108.

96. Snowden notes that "Greek mercenaries, perhaps Egyptian-born and children of the mercenaries who had served under Psammetichus, had been employed by Psammetichus II (594-588 B.C.) in his Nubian campaign" (*Blacks in Antiquity*, p. 104).

97. For an excellent discussion, see M. Rostovzeff, *The Social and Economic History of the Roman Empire* (Oxford: Clarendon Press, 2nd ed., 1957), vol. 1, "City and Country in Egypt," pp. 273–298, and "City and Country in Nubia," pp. 299–307.

98. Snowden, *Blacks in Antiquity*, pp. 184, 186.

99. William Westermann, *The Slave Systems of Greek and Roman Antiquity* (Philadelphia: American Philosophical Society, 1955), p. 23.

100. Ibid., p. 97.

101. For a summary of Aristotle's views, see the article entitled, "Slavery" in *Encyclopedia Britannica*, vol. 20 (1963), p. 775. In *Slave Systems* (p. 40), Westermann notes that "the Hellenistic theorists abandoned the racial-genetic approach characteristic of Aristotle which rested its explanation of slavery upon the acceptance of ideas of the national inferiorities and superiorities." Aristotle had considered slavery to be "not only natural but also necessary for the maintenance of the type of democratized city-state community, with its privileged body of citizens, in which [he] lived." He, like Euripides, considered Greeks to be free men and "barbarians" to be natural slaves. Belief in the influence of climate, environment, and the inheritance of acquired characteristics were basic to such a theory. For an excellent discussion of these philosophers and others see Snowden, *Blacks in Antiquity*, pp. 170–182.

102. Ibid., pp. 170–171.

103. A.N. Sherwin-White, *Racial Prejudice in Imperial Rome* (Cambridge: Cambridge University Press, 1967), p. 60. See also the comments on pp. 57-60 about reactions of Romans to the size, hairiness, and other anatomical traits of some of the European barbarian tribes, and about Strabo's reaction to the alleged existence of cannibalism among the Celts of Gaul, the Lusitanians, and the Germanic Cimbri as a feature of cult ceremonies.

104. Ibid., p. 99.

105. Snowden, *Blacks in Antiquity*, p. 174.

106. Quoted in ibid.

107. Bernard Braxton, *Women, Sex and Race* (Washington D.C.: Verta Press, 1973), p. 62.
108. Raymon de Becker, quoted in ibid., p. 63.
109. Ibid., p. 63.
110. Snowden, *Blacks in Antiquity*, p. 179, citing Aristotle's *Physiognomonica*. 6.812a.
111. Quoted in ibid., p. 176. Snowden refers to a tradition that St. Paul was influenced by the poet Menander. When both mentioned the Scythians, they were referring to a European people who were believed to be not only the counterparts of Ethiopians as the "remotest of men" but cannibals as well. Origen also associated cannibalism with Ethiopians (See Snowden, *Blacks in Antiquity*, p. 196).
112. Ibid., p. 180.
113. Quoted in ibid., p. 175.
114. Paul emphasized the "second coming" and the resurrection of the dead. (See 1 Corinthians 4:5, 11:26, 15:23, and the entire two epistles to the Thessalonians. The apocalyptic eschatology was implicit in Paul's letters but was fully developed by John in Revelations between 81 and 96 A.D. in the references to a "new heaven" and a "new earth."
115. See 1 Corinthians 15 for a discussion of the change from "corrupt" bodies to "incorrupt" bodies.
116. Snowden, *Blacks in Antiquity*, p. 171–178, summarizes the Greco-Roman philosophers' views about slavery and ethnic traits. Snowden indicates the existence of stereotyped beliefs about various ethnic groups or nations. These were not symbolized by differences in color, nor were they thought to be inherited in such a fashion that they could not be modified. See also Sherwin-White, *Racial Prejudice*, p. 60.
117. Insofar as Christianity was considered a threat to the security of the eastern borders of the empire, it was persecuted. Failure to accept Augustus Caesar as divine and criticisms of his successors constituted a challenge. The Roman rulers after Augustus favored the Isis-Serapis cult, whose followers were believed to have killed St. Mark in A.D. 68, during the reign of Nero. Between A.D. 81 and 96, the Emperor Domitian even accorded the cult a special place in Rome, but it met strong resistance in Egypt, where the ordinary people had always considered it an alien imposition and had clung to the worship of Isis and Osiris, not Isis in an invented syncretic religion, as devotion to other gods in the Egyptian pantheon faded away. Some scholars consider the high status accorded the Madonna and Child in Roman Catholicism to be a transformation of the Isis-Horus myth.
118. See Genesis for discussion of the line of Cain, which invented musical instruments, worked in iron and brass and began living in cities.
119. For a discussion of the distinction between hue, value (i.e., brightness), and chroma, see Irwin, *Colour Terms* pp. 7–13. See also *Philo*, trans. and ed., G. H. Whitaker and F. H. Colson, (London: William Heinemann, 1930) 10 volumes, Books I and II, pp. 155–161, 169–173, 134–135; and Book III, pp. 174, 540–541; 378; and Jean Laporte, "Philo in the Tradition of Biblical Wisdom Literature," in *Aspects of Wisdom*, ed. Wilken, pp. 103–142. Philo was interested in color symbolism. For instance, he associated white linen with the earth and black with the air. He made no connection between this scheme and human beings. Descendants of Ham are referred to as evil doers, but there is no reference to blackness being the result of a curse.

120. See Rabbi Epstein's "Foreword" to Freedman and Simon, eds., *Midrash Rabbah*, p. xx. Rapaport in *A Treasury of the Midrash*, and Patai, in *Hebrew Myths*, both remind the reader that collections of folklore and legends, as well as rabbinic comment on them and biblical passages, were compiled between 100 A.D. and 400 A.D. in Palestine as the basic core of what became the Midrash. This material was used regularly in sermons and other forms of public discourse. It was more popular than less entertaining expositions of the law as given in the Mishnah. Midrash Rabbah Genesis was the first volume of this genre to be compiled.

121. The quotation is from Westermann, *Slave Systems*, p. 150. There is some confirmation of the class composition of the converts in the early congregations in the writings of one eminent sociologist, but he makes no mention of race and ethnicity. See a discussion of the social strata from which the first Christians were recruited in Greece and Asia Minor in Max Weber, *The Sociology of Religion* (Boston: Beacon Press, 1963; first published in Germany in 1922), chapter 6, "Castes, Estates, Classes and Religion," pp. 81, 83, 85; chapter 7, "Religion of Non-Privileged Classes," pp. 95–96, 99, 115.

122. Snowden, *Blacks in Antiquity*, pp. 216–217.

123. Colossians 3:11.

124. Joel A. Rogers, *Nature Knows No Color Line: Research into the Negro Ancestry in the White Race* (New York: Helga M. Rogers, 1952), p. 10 (quoting from a translation of *Works of Emperor Julian*, vol. 3, "Against Galileans," p. 357). Rogers, a self-trained and self-published Jamaican scholar, was a pioneer in investigating the origins of anti-Negro sentiments and behavior in human history, putting forward his explanation in chapter 1 of *Nature Knows No Color Line*, "Where Did the Color Problem Originate?" This short but seminal essay draws too heavily upon Gerald Massey's *A Book of the Beginnings* and Godfrey Higgins's *Anacalypsis* to inspire complete confidence, but it does have a solid grounding in conventional source material that cannot be ignored. He discovered a number of basic sources that all subsequent scholars addressing themselves to this problem have "rediscovered" and found essential to any serious research on the subject of the origin of anti-Negro stereotypes. These are, most notably, the Babylonian Talmud and the Midrashic literature.

125. Quoted in Snowden, *Blacks in Antiquity*, p. 205, from the Loeb edition of Augustine's *De civitate Dei*.

126. Snowden, *Blacks in Antiquity*, p. 4.

127. Ibid., p. 204.

128. Ibid.

129. Ibid., pp. 198–209.

130. Ibid., pp. 198, 200, 211, 212.

131. E. A. Budge, ed. and trans., *The Book of the Saints of the Ethiopian Church* [The Ethiopic Synaxarium] (Hildesheim and New York: George Verlag, 1976), p. 1031.

132. Snowden, *Blacks in Antiquity*, p. 210.

133. Budge, *Book of the Saints*, p. 1031.

134. In *Blacks in Antiquity*, Snowden gives considerable attention to the case of Father Moses: on pages 5, 18, 197, 198, 201, 209–211. Twelve years later, in *Before Color Prejudice*, the same author devotes less than a page to this black ascetic! Snowden concedes that the story might be "completely apocryphal" but suggests that this account and others "are an important part in the formation of the early Christian image of Ethiopians" (note 237, p. 149). Thus, he avoids the necessity of defending this ascetic's obsequious behavior vis à vis a white archbishop.

In *Before Color Prejudice*, Snowden cites a 1978 article in the *Harvard Theological Review* (vol. 71, pp. 304–311) on "Anti-Black Sentiment in the *Vita Patrum*" that draws the same conclusion about the treatment of Father Moses that I do. J. M. Courtès, who published on the theme of Ethiopia and Ethiopians, is referred to frequently. Courtès states that the Father Moses story should be interpreted allegorically. The views expressed by these scholars, and published after his earlier work, may have been a factor in Snowden's decision to abandon Father Moses' case as "an interesting application of the Christian imagery that was accepted by black converts who found it inoffensive to their blackness."

135. See articles in the 1963 edition of *Encyclopedia Britannica* entitled, "Mani," "Manichaeism," "Gnosticism," and "Zoroastrianism." It is not possible to date the initial impact of the Persian religious and philosophical concepts upon Jewish thinkers, although there is strong evidence of its presence during the fourth and fifth centuries A.D. One scholar states that the Babylonian Talmud "freely incorporated the folklore and popular demonology of its time, the latter under the influence of Zoroastrianism" (Morris Adler, *The World of the Talmud* [New York: Schocken, 1963], p. 56). This would have been too late to affect the earliest Church Fathers, and the historic record indicates that it was the Manichaean variety of Persian thought that was having the greatest impact on the Christians at the time. Professor Cyrus Gordon, an American Near Eastern scholar, feels that the dualistic Manichaean pattern is much older in Jewish thought than most of his fellow scholars hold. In speaking of how, in the New Testament and the Dead Sea Scrolls, "the forces of good (or light or God) are pitted against the forces of evil (or darkness or Satan)," he mentions that "this is frequently attributed to borrowing from Zoroastrianism." In his opinion, however, "the myth of the dualistic battle was deeply entrenched in Canaan from pre-Hebraic times. The myth of the conflict was absorbed by the Hebrews along with language, literature, and lore of Canaan from the very start of Hebrew history in Canaan." If this is true, the absence of anti-Negro sentiments in the Old Testament may indicate the lack of any necessary carry-over of this Manichaean dichotomy to social relations. This scholar makes the "heretical" suggestion that "all the available evidence points to the spread of this dualistic myth from the Semitic to the Iranian sphere, not vice versa" (Cyrus H. Gordon, Professor of Old Testament, Brandeis University, on "Canaanite Mythology, in Samuel Noah Kramer, ed., *Mythologies of the Ancient World* [New York: Doubleday Anchor Book, 1961], p. 201).

136. See the article entitled "Mani" in *Encyclopedia Britannica* (1963).

137. George Sarton, *Galen of Pergamum*, (Lawrence, Kan.: University of Kansas Press, 1954); and Benjamin Farrington, *Greek Science: Theophrastus to Galen* (Harmondsworth, England: Penguin, 1949), pp. 155–161.

138. Quoted in Lewis, *Race and Color in Islam*, p. 34, citing a quotation from Galen in Mas'udi, *Muruj al-dhahab*, ed. and trans. into French by Charles Pellat (Paris, 1962), p. 69.

139. One of the most distinguished and influential of the Church Fathers, Tertullian (A.D. 155–222), was probably acquainted with the Galen stereotype because not only was he well-read in all of the philosophical literature but he also had a special interest in medicine. His basic attitudes were undoubtedly influenced most profoundly, however, by the Stoics, whom he admired, and by the Pauline Christianity he professed as well as by other Greek influences shaping early Christianity. If Tertullian shared Galen's belief in the intellectual inferiority of

Blacks, he did not mention it in his work; nor did he mobilize nonbiblical Jewish folklore to reinforce Galen. Of course, he may have accepted the idea and combined it with either the Greek belief in environmental causation or with a curious kind of theology that has surfaced in modern times: i.e., becoming a "new man in Christ Jesus" tones up the mind as well as the soul and offsets environmental and genetic deficits! See the article entitled "Tertullian" in *Encyclopedia Britannica*, vol. 21 (1963).

Some research by Professor Frank Snowden suggests caution in assuming, as I do, that some of the Church Fathers may have been exposed to Galen's belief in a black cognitive deficit. In *Before Color Prejudice* (pp. 114–115), Snowden comments on the reference to ten traits characteristic of black males, which is attributed to Galen by Mas'udi, a tenth-century Arab scholar. Snowden states that he has not found this passage "in any extant work of Galen or any other author of the Greco-Roman period." He suspects that Muslim reports about "Zanj" in Mesopotamia and East Africa were attributed to Galen. The Arabist Bernard Lewis uses the Mas'udi passage without questioning its authenticity. My assumption of Galen's influence on early Christian theologians may be invalid if Snowden's suspicion of a later Arab attribution is correct.

140. Romans 1:26-31 and 13:15. Early Christian leaders who were familiar with the writings of Plato must have found the discussion of love at the famous banquet offensive. Aristophanes casually discussed "boy-lovers," Alcibiades told of his attempt to seduce Socrates, and Socrates discussed what Diotema, a wise woman, had said to him about male homosexuality. *Great Dialogues of Plato*, trans. Eric H. Warmington and Philip G. Rouse (New York: New American Library, 1956), pp. 87–88; 105–106; 110–113. See the article entitled "Dionysus" in *Encyclopedia Britannica*, vol. 7 (1963); James George Frazer, *The Golden Bough*, vol. 1 (New York: Book League of America, 1929).

141. R. E. L. Masters, *Eros and Evil* (New York: Lancer Books, 1969), p. 15. Ephraim Isaac quotes the passage on "Cushi" from Jerome's *Homily 3* in the unpublished memorandum referred to previously.

Snowden, in *Before Color Prejudice* (pp. 100–101), states that "Early Christian writers referred to Ethiopians and blackness primarily in two major contexts, demonological and exegetical." Snowden states without equivocation that "In apocryphal and patristic literature black was the color of the devil and of some demons who tempted early Christians or troubled them in visions and dreams." Snowden feels that the color of demons who annoyed Christians is "obviously related to the Greco-Roman associations of black with evil and the Underworld." This symbolism "does not seem to have had a negative effect on the generally favorable view of blacks dating back to the Homeric poems, or to have given rise to a serious anti-black sentiment." I suggest that the symbolism was more likely due to proximity to black pagans south of Egypt whose "lust" was being deplored.

142. Klaus Wessel, *Coptic Art* (New York: McGraw-Hill, 1965) pp. 234–235.

143. Ibid., p. 54.

144. Ibid.

145. See Harry A. Gailey, Jr., *History of Africa from Earliest Times to 1800* (New York: Holt Rinehart and Winston, 1970), "Carthage and Rome in North Africa," pp. 41–48.

146. Wessel, *Coptic Art*, p. 55.

147. Ibid.

148. Ibid., p. 56.
149. Ibid.
150. For many years the standard English translation was Rowland Smith, ed., *The Greek Romances of Heliodorus, Longus, and Achilles Tatius, Comprising the Ethiopica* (London: G. Bell and Sons, 1912), pp. 188–300. A translation preceding that of Smith has been recently reprinted in the United States (Thomas Underdowne, ed., *Heliodorus: An Aethiopian Romance* [Darby, Pa.: Arden Library, 1979]). Two decades before this edition, the University of Michigan Press at Ann Arbor published (1957) a new translation prepared by Moses Hadas. The quotations in this book are from that text.
151. *An Ethiopian Romance: Heliodorus*, trans. with an introduction by Moses Hadas (Ann Arbor, Mich.: the University of Michigan Press, 1957) p. ix. See also Snowden, *Blacks in Antiquity*, pp. 143, 148, 152, 154, 164, 181, 188, 194.
152. Hadas, *Heliodorus*, pp. 193, 232.
153. Ibid., p. ix.
154. Westermann, *Slave Systems*, p. 161.
155. Alexander Badawy, *Coptic Art and Archaeology: The Art of the Christian Egyptians from the Late Antiquity to the Middle Ages* (Cambridge, Mass.: MIT Press, 1978) pp. x, 33–67; Wessel, *Coptic Art*, pp. 65–68.
156. For a succinct discussion of the early history of the church in Egypt, see Badawy, *Coptic Art and Archaeology*, pp. ix–xii (chronological summary) and 1–14 (historical outline). Wessel, in *Coptic Art*, presents a clear, informative account emphasizing distinctions between the Greek church in Egypt and the indigenous Coptic church. See especially his chapters entitled "Origins" and "Egypt under the Roman Empire." Both books contain extensive bibliography.
157. Budge, *The Book of the Saints*, p. 1031.
158. Ibid., p. 1032.
159. Snowden, *Blacks in Antiquity*, p. 21.
160. The excavations by Michalowski, a Pole, are described by William Y. Adams, in *Nubia* (Princeton: Princeton University Press, 1977), pp. 482–484.
161. Westermann, *Slave Systems*, p. 161.
162. Snowden, *Blacks in Antiquity*, pp. 145–146, citing Homer and Diodorus.
163. Westermann, *Slave Systems*, p. 23.
164. See the articles entitled "Mani" and "Manichaeism" in *Encyclopedia Britannica* (1963).
165. Winthrop Jordan, in *White Over Black* (New York: Penguin, 1968), pp. 17–21, discusses the adoption of the Ham story by Europeans and quotes a version of the curse: "Your seed will be ugly and dark-skinned." Jordan's sources are Freedman and Simon, *Midrash Rabbah*, vol. 1, p. 293; and Maurice Simon, trans., *The Zohar*, vol. 1, p. 246. The Afro-American scholar, Joseph E. Harris (*Africans and Their History*) summarizes the sixteenth-century debate in England on pp. 17–19, 35–37, 54, 56; and in New England on pp. 200–201; with other references on pp. 245–246, 308.
166. Alfred J. Butler, *The Arab Conquest of Egypt* (Oxford: Oxford University Press, 1902) pp. 256–257.

CHAPTER 5

The literature on the Muslim world is vast, including the source material—primary and secondary—in the Arabic language. I have used only a small portion of the literature available in French and English secondary sources for supplying the minimal amount of background knowledge about Islam needed for a discussion of attitudes toward black as a color and toward black people. Two valuable small volumes are Bernard Lewis, *The Arabs in History* (1964 edition) and Alfred Guillaume, *Islam* (Penguin, 1956). Both men are distinguished Arabists. An authoritative source on Islam in varied geographical contexts can be found in the two-volume *Cambridge History of Islam* (1970) edited by P. M. Holt, Ann K. S. Lambton, and Bernard Lewis. I have found the multi-volume *Encyclopedia of Islam* (1913, 1960) to be especially useful. Gustav von Grunebaum, in *Medieval Islam*, provides perceptive interpretative comment. An interesting account of the life of Mohammed and the spread of Islam, beautifully illustrated with paintings by Turkish artists and text by a well-educated devout Muslim, is *Mecca the Blessed, Medina the Radiant* by Emil Esin, printed by Crown Publishers, New York, 1963. For many years the self-trained Afro-West Indian historian Joel A. Rogers compiled biographical profiles for his two-volume *World's Great Men of Color* (1947, 1967). A number of these are Muslims and his documentation, including ancient and modern sources, is a useful guide for serious students. There is no comprehensive treatment of Blacks in the Muslim world available in English other than the highly informative and remarkably succinct *tour de force* presented as a Harper Torchbook, Bernard Lewis's *Race and Color in Islam* (1970). The footnotes reveal the author's exhaustive search into Arabic, German, and French sources. He mentions one article in Arabic on "The Blacks in Arabic Life and Literature," but states that "The place of the black in Arab-Islamic society was extensively studied in an excellent German doctoral thesis by G. Rotter, *Die Stellung des Negers in der Islamisch-arabischen Gesellschaft bis zum XVI Jahrhundert* (Bonn: 1967), which deserves a wider circulation. I have profited greatly from this work." I have profited greatly from Lewis's work as the references below show.

Lewis confines his discussion to the role of Blacks in the Middle East, North Africa (including Egypt) and Muslim Spain. Vast areas of the Muslim world in Asia and Oceania should eventually be examined for comparison with the areas studied by Lewis. J. Spencer Trimingham has written several definitive works on Islam in sub-Saharan Africa, and a few studies exist of Islamic communities in East Africa, South Africa, and the Caribbean, where East Indians and Javanese are in economic and political competition with Blacks.

Most useful of the very few analyses in English of the status of Blacks in contemporary Islamic societies in northern Africa is Leon Carl Brown, "Color in Northern Africa," (*Daedalus* 96, 2 [Spring 1967]) and Robert A. Fernea, *Nubians in Egypt* (Austin: University of Texas, 1973), especially chapter 7. Interviews with Africans and Afro-Americans who have lived and worked in Islamic lands would constitute a useful first step in assessing the extent to which color prejudice is expressed, suppressed, obscured, denied or ignored by various social strata.

The *Autobiography of Malcolm X* is a moving account of how identification with the Islamic world functioned as a mechanism of personality integration for a highly intelligent young Afro-American with leadership potential. He was assassinated before he had an opportunity to probe beneath the surface of the apparent absence of skin-color prejudice in the Muslim world, or to ask why in some Muslim lands, the egalitarian ideals of Mohammed do not prevail. The euphoria induced by the pilgrimage to Mecca inhibited him from posing these questions. Honesty demands that they be raised.

    1. See "Zamzam" in *Encyclopedia of Islam* (1913). See also John Lewis Burckhardt, *Travels in Arabia*, (London: Henry Colburn, 1829), pp. 143, 145, 163. See also chapter 29, "Ishmael," in Graves and Patai, *Hebrew Myths*, pp. 156–160.

2. Alfred Guillaume, *Islam* (Baltimore: Penguin, 1956), p. 30.
3. The titles of two chapters in Emil Esin, *Mecca the Blessed, Medina the Radiant* (New York: Crown, 1963), indicate those to whom Mohammed's message was primarily directed: "The Apostle of the Portionless" (p. 98) and "The Fragile Ones" (p. 103).
4. Guillaume, *Islam*, pp. 60–62.
5. Ibid., p. 33.
6. *Encyclopedia of Islam*, 2nd edition, 1961, has an entry for Ham. By the tenth century A.D., as Bernard Lewis notes (*Race and Color in Islam* [New York: Harper, 1970], pp. 66–67), Muslim authors were explaining that slavery was a natural state for black people because "the ancestor of dark-skinned people was Ham the son of Noah who (according to Muslim legend) was damned black for his sin. The curse of blackness, and with it that of slavery, passed to all the black peoples who are his descendants." The way in which they acquired the legend is not made clear by any Arabists.
7. For references to Bilal see Lewis, *Race and Color*, pp. 94–96. See also *Encyclopedia of Islam* (1960), article "Bilal." Informative, too, are G. I. Kheirallah, *Islam and the Arabian Prophet* (New York: Islamic Publishing Co., 1938), p. 34; and Esin, *Mecca the Blessed*, pp. 82, 94, 121. Rogers presents some interesting legends about Bilal in *World's Great Men of Color* (Collier Macmillan edition), vol. 1, pp. 143–147, including one about a contemptuous rebuff by the Byzantine Christian general in Syria who refused to negotiate with what he referred to as "this black slave." Bilal is said to have punished him by imposing severe surrender terms.
8. See Kheirallah, *Islam and the Arabian Prophet*, pp. 38–40, "The Flight to Abyssinia," and John A. Williams, ed., *Islam* (New York: George Braziller, 1961), pp. 64–65.
9. Eric R. Wolf, "The Social Organization of Mecca and the Origins of Islam," *Southwestern Journal of Anthropology* 7 (Winter 1951): 330–355.
10. Bernard Lewis, *The Arabs in History* (New York: Harper Colophon Books, 1967), pp. 42–43.
11. One source says Bilal was looked upon by Meccans "with horror and disgust" after the return to Mecca from Medina. D. S. Margliouth, *Mohammed and the Rise of Islam* (New York: G. P. Putnam's Sons, 1905), p. 387. See also note 7.
12. Guillaume, *Islam*, pp. 41–42; 72.
13. Lewis, *Arabs in History*, pp. 42–43; see also Koran, Suras II and V. The edition of the Koran that is used throughout is a translation by George Sale, published circa 1726 by Frederick Warne and Co. of London.
14. Guillaume, *Islam*, pp. 42–43; 45.
15. Ibid., pp. 45–51, and Esin, *Mecca the Blessed*, p. 109.
16. Lewis, *Arabs in History*, p. 46.
17. Guillaume, *Islam*, p. 40.
18. "One of Mohammed's last expeditions was directed against the Syrians," Guillaume (*Islam*, p. 53) notes. He points out with regard to the Byzantine and Sassanid areas that "neither of the great powers of the time was in a position to offer an effective resistance to the new enemy (p. 78)."
19. Guillaume, *Islam*, pp. 78–80; Lewis, *Arabs in History*, pp. 57–59; Esin, *Mecca the Blessed*, p. 97. See also Lewis, *Race and Color*, p. 27.
20. Lewis, *Arabs in History*, p. 54.
21. Rogers, *World's Great Men of Color* (Collier edition, 1967), "Bilal, the First Muezzin and Treasurer of Islam," vol. 1, pp. 143–147.

22. Ibid., p. 147.
23. Lewis, *Arabs in History*, pp. 55–58.
24. This is an inference from poetry written by Negroes which was considered pre-Islamic until the 1920s, when its antiquity was questioned. According to a distinguished scholar, "The controversy is still far from closed." James Kritzeck, *Anthology of Islamic Literature* (New York: New American Library, 1964), p. 53.
25. Lewis, *Race and Color*, pp. 11.
26. Ibid.
27. On page 7 of ibid., Lewis has expressed his doubts about the existence of pre-Islamic racial prejudice in Arabia: "The evidence of the Qur'an on the lack of racial prejudice in pre-Islamic and the earliest Islamic times is borne out by such fully authenticated fragments of contemporary literature as survive." The contradiction may lie in his making color prejudice synonymous with *racial* prejudice. An extreme derogation of "Negroidness" could have existed in pre-Islamic Bedouin society without the incipient racism that would develop later.
28. Bernard Lewis suggests that the theme of the wonderful exploits of 'Antar as a great mulatto hero was developed by Kharijite sectarians as propaganda for equality of mixed-bloods with Arabs. The most readily accessible source of information on 'Antar is the *Encyclopedia Britannica* (1963), on "'Antarah ibn Shaddad al-'Absi." Two articles in the *Encyclopedia of Islam* (second edition, 1960) are scholarly and authoritative: "'Antara" and "Sirat 'Antar," (the Romance). The latter discusses the massive body of oral tradition that had begun to take written form by the twelfth century A.D. and evolved into a complicated cycle of tales with many "layers" of material from various times and places. Through it all 'Antar is a hero whose daring deeds and romances make him an attractive popular figure. As the legend grew, his mother, the black girl from the Sudan enslaved by the Arabs, was transformed into a romantic figure, and in the XVIIIth book of the romance, it is revealed that she was the daughter of an Abyssinian king. Terrick Hamilton published a four-volume work in English in 1820 with the title *Antar, a Bedoueen Romance*. The first edition of the *Encyclopedia of Islam* states that 'Antar was "the son of Zabiba, a black slave girl" who "like a true upstart . . . refers to black slaves in somewhat contemptuous terms." See also Lewis, *Race and Color*, pp. 11–14, 26. For a detailed discussion of 'Antar and a short bibliography, see Rogers, *World's Great Men of Color*, vol. 1, pp. 138–142. Cedric Dover, a Eurasian man of letters, published a tribute to 'Antar in the Afro-American journal, *Phylon* (15, 1-2 [1954]) in which he states that the poet's troubles came from his being "black, illegitimate, and once enslaved." Dover calls 'Antar's literary output, "the first classical work concerned with color prejudice." 'Antar died in 615 A.D., before Mohammed announced his revelations.
29. See detailed discussion of slavery in article "'Abd" in *Encyclopedia of Islam* (1960), by R. Bronschvig. It should be noted that the root "'abd" appears in many proper names such as Abdullah, where it carries the meaning of "servant" rather than "slave." In some Central Islamic Lands, particularly Arabia, "'abd" means black slave or Negro, not slave as a general term. Incidentally, Lewis, *Race and Color*, p. 27n states that "Slavery in the Islamic world still awaits a comprehensive study."
30. Rogers, *World's Great Men of Color*, vol. 1, p. 93.
31. References to black concubines are frequent in the literature. Travelers in northern Africa refer to Arab and Berber leaders who had Negro concubines in addition to the four wives permitted under Islamic law.
32. Lewis, *Race and Color*, p. 19.

33. John A. Williams, *Islam*, pp. 83–84.
34. Lewis, *Race and Color*, pp. 91, 92. Mohammed, according to one tradition, was supposed to have said, "Do not bring black into your pedigree."
35. The *Cambridge History of Islam* (Cambridge: Cambridge University Press, 1970) pp. 6–12, 16–18.
36. Mas'udi, *Les Prairies d'Or* (Paris: Société Asiatique, 1965), chapter xxxvii, "Les Adites et leurs Roi," vol. 2, pp. 349–350.
37. *The Arabian Nights* (Modern Library edition, pp. 435–436; 465–467). The reference to "Habash" having once held others under the yoke is significant. In one story in *The Arabian Nights* there is recognition of the fact that African kingdoms once played important roles in human history, and that Islamized black kingdoms existed in Africa. The Caliph in Damascus sends an expedition to "North-Western Africa" to search for some magical objects, existing from Solomonic times. The searchers find the spot that gives the story its name, "The City of Brass." Graven tablets tell the story of how supernatural powers helped Solomon to wipe out the city because of an insult by its ruler, Kush (ancestor of the Blacks), the son of Shaddad, who once "ruled mankind, and over all earth, upheld dominion, until the turns of Fortune and the chance of Change." One inscription refers to people "who Zanj and Habash once bound beneath the yoke" and to Nubia's once great power. The glory of "the City of Brass" was gone, but nearby a black king ruled over a tribe living in caves, speaking an unknown tongue, and wearing skins. The expedition was not sure, at first, as to whether they were human beings or *jinns*, but the king told them that "we also are children of Adam, of the lineage of Ham, son of Noah," who had been converted to Islam. The black king knew where some of the much wanted "curcubites" from Solomon's time were, and presented them to his co-religionists, who " . . . took leave of the Black king, and setting out on their homeward journey, travelled till they came to Damascus."
38. For context, see Henry Cassels Kay, trans. and ed., Najm ad-Din 'Umarah ibn 'Ali al-Hakami, *Yaman: Its Early Mediaeval History* (London: Arnold, 1892). See discussion of Abraha in Mas'udi, *Les Prairies d'Or*, vol. 2, pp. 385–387. For a biography of Abraha based upon European scholarly accounts see Rogers, *World's Great Men of Color* (1947 edition, privately printed), pp. 109–111. This Abraha is not to be confused with the Ethiopian king of the same name, described by Rogers, in a chapter entitled "Abraha, Emperor of Ethiopia Whose Adoption of Christianity Changed the Face of the World" (circa A.D. 350), pp. 107–108.
39. Mas'udi, *Les Prairies d'Or*, vol. 2, pp. 387–388.
40. Ibid., p. 387.
41. This discussion of Sura CV in the Koran is written by the translator, George Sale, circa 1736; see Guillaume, *Islam*, pp. 21–22, for a detailed discussion of this Abraha's activities.
42. Koran, Sura CV. The following statement appears in the article "Ahabish" in the new edition (1960) of *Encyclopedia of Islam*: "Lammen (1928) [a distinguished Arabist] put forward the view that the Ahabish consisted of Abyssinian and other negro slaves attached to a core of nomadic Arabs; and further held that the power of Mecca in the early 7th century A.D. rested upon these mercenaries." This idea has been rejected by other scholars who are cited in the article. If such slave-soldiers did exist among the Bedouins it is likely that attitudes toward Blacks may have had both negative and positive aspects depending upon the nature of intertribal relations in which these soldiers were involved. If these soldiers were

when Abraha tried to conquer Mecca, black soldiers would have been fighting on both sides, just as they were when the jihad armies entered Egypt.

43. When the Arabs invaded Egypt and moved southward into Nubia, the resistance was so great that a negotiated peace seemed desirable to the Arab leaders. The agreement lasted for 600 years. The Nubians agreed to furnish a specified number of slaves per year—the *bakt*—and the Arabs promised not to invade. For an account of the agreement, see Adams, *Nubia*, p. 88. For a criticism, see Chancellor Williams, *The Destruction of Black Civilization* (Chicago: Third World Press, 1971), pp. 153–156.

44. Kay, *Yaman*, pp. 83–87. The ruler referred to is Husayn ibn Salamah, whose life is discussed in detail on pp. 8–9.

45. Ibid., p. 21, for the episode about the wealthy Abyssinian. Mention is also made (p. 124) of a prominent mahdi who was "an eloquent man of prepossessing appearance, dark-complexioned." A reference to "Lower orders of people" appears on p. 82. Also Mas'udi, the tenth-century Arab traveler, referred to a Yemenite who refused to eat meat butchered by a Zanj (East African Negro) because he said "the Zanj was a distorted creature." Cited in Lewis, *Race and Color*, p. 99. The episode of the angry traveler and the wealthy Abyssinian is presented under the title "Faraj as-Sahrati, the Benefactor" in Graham W. Irwin, *Africans Abroad* (New York: Columbia University Press, 1977), pp. 60–61. Ibn Khallikan (*Biographical Dictionary*, vol. 1, p. 347) recounts in some detail the story of as-Sulaihi, who took over all of Yemen as leader of a rebellion. In the year A.D. 1080 he set out to make the pilgrimage. In addition to Yemenite troops he was accompanied by five thousand Abyssinian spearmen on foot. When a political opponent killed him on the way to Mecca, his Abyssinians changed sides and helped to pillage as-Sulaihi's camp. In 1089, the sheik who killed as-Sulaihi was himself killed in an uprising. Ibn Khallikan does not mention the behavior of the Abyssinians in this revolt.

46. Lewis, *Arabs in History*, p. 54.

47. Guillaume, *Islam*, p. 113.

48. Lewis, *Arabs in History*, pp. 72–73.

49. Ibid., p. 79. The black banners were in mourning for troops who died in establishing the caliphate in Baghdad.

50. Roland Oliver and J.D. Fage, *A Short History of Africa* (Baltimore: Penguin Books, Inc., 1962), p. 77–78.

51. Quotations and citations from Ibn Khaldun in this chapter are from a recent translation of his *Muqaddimah* from Arabic into French, published as *Discours sur l'Histoire Universelle* (Beyrouth: UNESCO, Commission Internationale pour le Traduction des Chefs d'oeuvre, 1967), vol. 1. This reference is to pp. 165–175 (quotation from p. 172). The standard English translation was published a decade earlier: Ibn Khaldun, *The Muqaddimah*, trans. by Franz Rosenthal (Princeton: University of Princeton Press, 1958).

52. Lewis, *Race and Color*, p. 28. Snowden, on the other hand, emphasizes the prevalence of black slaves in the Greco-Roman world. Since neither had statistics the impression is related to the argument being made.

53. There are graphic accounts by travelers, from Ibn Battuta through the nineteenth century, of women being marched across the desert for sale in the markets of North Africa. Constant reference is made to their preponderance in the caravans.

54. Eunuchs were used as keepers of harems and as confidential officials in high places in many areas. It was constantly rumored that women in harems and some adulterous housewives cherished the presence of the type of black eunuchs whose

virility had not been destroyed but who could not impregnate them. A number of tales about black eunuchs in the Muslim world, some no doubt apocryphal, are given in Allan Edwardes and R. E. L. Masters, *The Cradle of Erotica, A Study of Afro-Asian Sexual Expression and an Analysis of Erotic Freedom in Social Relationships* (New York: The Julian Press, Inc., 1966), pp. 141–144. See also Bernard Braxton, *Women, Sex and Race*, p. 63. For a vivid description of the influential black eunuchs of Mecca and Medina in the early nineteenth century see Burckhardt, *Travels in Arabia*, pp. 158–161; 178; 342–345. Orlando Patterson presents incisive and insightful comments on eunuchs as having power but being without "honor" in the Muslim world, criticized and often despised (*Slavery and Social Death*, pp. 312–324). The caliph in Baghdad was reported to have had seven thousand black and four thousand white eunuchs at the beginning of the tenth century (Lewis, *Race and Color*, p. 68, and note 83 on pp. 68 and 69).

55. See Roland Oliver and Gervase Mathew (eds.), *History of East Africa* (Oxford: Oxford University Press, 1963), pp. 99, 101. Professor Mathew states that the Sassanian (Persian) rulers built up "considerable seapower" in the fourth century and that "It is probable enough that the late Sassanian kings bought slaves from East Africa to be their Mamelukes . . . There is evidence for a considerable population of black warrior slaves from East Africa" (p. 101).

56. Lewis, *Race and Color*, pp. 69–75; Tulun (tenth century Egypt) had twenty-four thousand white and forty-five thousand black troops.

57. Rogers, *World's Great Men of Color* (Collier edition), pp. 164–165; Irwin, *Africans Abroad*, p. 76.

58. Lewis, *Arabs in History*, p. 147, and Patterson, *Slavery and Social Death*, pp. 308–310.

59. Lewis, *Arabs in History*, pp. 97–98. See also "The Islamic Ghilman" in Patterson, *Slavery and Social Death*, pp. 308–314.

60. Lewis, *Arabs in History*, pp. 146–147.

61. Miskawaihi, "Experiences of the Nations," included in *Eclipse of the Abbasid Caliphate*, trans. by H. F. Amedroz and D. S. Margoliouth (Oxford: Basil Blackwell, 1921), vol. 4, p. 337.

62. On one occasion, four hundred soldiers from the Dailemite tribe deserted. The vizier sent a group of black infantrymen into the barracks where the deserters had barricaded themselves. The black soldiers killed them all, cut up their bodies, put the pieces in sacks, and dumped them into the Tigris River, as recorded in *Eclipse of the Abbasid Caliphate*, vol. 5, pp. 227–228.

63. Lewis, *Race and Color*, p. 70.

64. In the eleventh century, the caliph sent Dailemite forces to garrison a town that was resisting the payment of taxes. Miskawaihi reports that "the rabble of Shiraz with some of the negro infantry and the slaves of the farmers precipitated themselves when the Dailemites were scattered about the bazaars and killed some seventy of them." The story is told in "Experiences of the Nations," included in *Eclipse of the Abbasid Caliphate*, vol. 4, p.337.

65. Lewis, *Race and Color*, p. 69.

66. Ibid., pp. 68–69.

67. The *Cambridge History of Islam*, pp. 178–180.

68. See "Egypt" in *Encyclopedia Britannica* (1963), vol. 8, p. 60; Rogers, *World's Great Men of Color* (1947 edition), vol. 1, pp. 108–215; and "Kafur" in Ibn Khallikan, *Dictionary*.

69. See article "Egypt" in *Encyclopedia Britannica* (1963), vol. 8, p. 60.

70. Oliver and Fage, *A Short History*, p. 79.

71. Lewis, *Race and Color*, pp. 70–71.

72. Ibid., p. 71n. Nubian soldiers were not the only people accused of cannibalism during famines in Egypt. Lewis, citing Stanley Lane-Poole, *A History of Egypt in the Middle Ages* (London: Methuen, 1901), p. 146, reports that "in 1096, owing to the low Niles of several years preceding, food was so scarce that the people began to eat each other . . . Human flesh was sold in public." A case of soldiers eating human flesh for quite different reasons has been cited in an 1148 A.D. case. A rebel soldier was captured after his escape from prison and decapitated, then "His body was cut into little pieces and devoured by the young soldiers, in the belief that they would thus assimilate his pith and courage." Fifty-three years later there was another famine in Cairo and "the people in Cairo were driven to eat dead bodies . . . " (Ibid. p. 169).

73. Lewis, *Race and Color*, p. 71.

74. Ibid., pp. 71–72.

75. Ibid., p. 72.

76. Ibid., p. 73. Maqrizi, an Arab historian, claimed that black soldiers had been arrogant and murderous, so "when their outrages were many, and their misdeeds increased, God destroyed them for their sins." Lewis, *Race and Color*, p. 73, quoting from Khitat, II, p. 19.

77. Ibid., p. 73.

78. Adams, *Nubia*, p. 456.

79. Oliver and Fage, *A Short History*, p. 94.

80. "Shadjar al-Durr" in *Encyclopedia of Islam* (1913).

81. A short account of Shadjar al-Durr appears in the article, "Egypt," in *Encyclopedia Britannica* (1963). See also *Recueil des Historiens des Croisades* (Paris: Imprimerie Nationale, 1872), pp. 126–129, which presents translations from Arab historians to the effect that Shadjar al-Durr was either Turkish or Armenian and that the Sultan's mother was a "negress."

82. Lewis, *Race and Color*, p. 74.

83. Ibid. A similar ritualization of African kingly power occurred in Brazil many centuries later (Donald Pierson, *Negroes in Brazil*, [Chicago: University of Chicago Press, 1938], pp. 95–100). This substitution of ritual activity for actual power is a recurrent phenomenon among suppressed ethnic groups.

84. Lewis, *Race and Color*, pp. 75–76, 77.

85. Ibid. For facts helpful in interpretation of the Farajallah incident see David Ayalon, *Gunpowder and Firearms in the Mamluk Kingdom* (London: Valentine, Mitchell, 1956).

86. For a well-researched sophisticated discussion of the role of eunuchs in Muslim societies, see Orlando Patterson, *Slavery and Social Death*, pp. 314–331. Patterson states that some adult slaves had themselves castrated in order to increase their power over masters who wanted to be sure their officials would have no descendants!

87. The revolutionary significance of armored cavalry is analyzed in detail by William H. McNeill in *The Rise of the West* (New York: Mentor, 1963), pp. 434–437; 540–546. He stresses the role of the Turkish people in introducing this mode of warfare into Mesopotamia and Persia. See also P. M. Holt, Ann K. S. Lambton, and Bernard Lewis, eds., *Cambridge History of Islam* (Cambridge: Cambridge University Press, 1970), pp. 229.

88. Lewis, *Race and Color*, pp. 75–76, citing the Arabic writer Ansari.

89. Oliver and Fage, *A Short History*, p. 71.
90. Research into the available records of Makuria and Nubia might shed some light on the question of whether or not a push northward against Asian invaders was ever discussed by the rulers of these kingdoms after the reign of Saladin in Egypt.
91. An illuminated manuscript has kept alive the tradition that Negroes were in Tarik's army of invasion in A.D. 711. See Bradley Smith, *Spain: A History in Art* (New York: Simon and Schuster, 1966. pp. 58-59. No special mention of them is made in the histories of Andalusia by Anwar Chejne, Evariste Lévi-Provençal, Reinhart Dozy, Jan Read, J. A. Conde, and others cited below. However Conde makes frequent mention of Blacks in the armies of subsequent groups of Berbers who invaded Spain (J. A. Conde, *History of the Dominion of the Arabs in Spain* [London: Bohn, 1844]). Rogers, however, includes Tarik in vol. 2 of *World's Great Men of Color*, and cites sources for his claim of Tarik's Negroid ancestry in his *Sex and Race* (New York: privately published, 1942], vol. 1, 2nd edition, p. 286.
92. Black troops were used to quell disorders in Seville, Cordova, and Toledo. Of the palace guard in Toledo, one historian comments that they were "men whom they [i.e., the citizens] considered to be the ever-ready instruments of their oppressors." Conde, *History of the Dominion*, p. 283.
93. Conde, *History of the Dominion*, pp. 127-285, and Reinhart Dozy, *Histoire des Musulmans d'Espagne, jusqu'à la conquête de l'Andalousie par les Almoravides* [Paris: E. J. Brill, 1932], pp. 595-679. With regard to the Almoravid invasion, Conde (p. 214) describes Yusuf, the leader, as "a dark brown caliph, but he had comely features." The Christian king, Alfonso, confronted him with Turkish archers. At the decisive moment, Yusuf threw in "four thousand fresh troops of his negro [sic] guard equipped with shields of hippopotamous hide and Indian rapiers." A. R. Nykl, *Hispano-Arabic Poetry and its Relations With the Old Provencal Troubadours* (Baltimore: J. H. Furst, 1946), p. 71, reports that the invading African army used drums to frighten the horses of the Spanish cavalry. Vivid descriptions of this Battle of Zallaca are given by Conde (pp. 269-284) who mentions in a footnote on p. 276 that "a negro slave belonging to King Jusef [Yusuf] wounded Alfonso in the thigh with his curved scimitar."
94. Of one Shiite ruler of Cordova it was said that he brought peace to his realm and that "all went well until he organized negro [sic] regiments for his protection, thus irritating the Berbers." Nykl, *Hispano-Arabic Poetry*, p. 12.
95. All of the histories of Muslim Spain cited discuss the role of the so-called "Slavs"—the saqalibah—in some detail. See especially, Anwar G. Chejne, *Muslim Spain: Its History and Culture* (Minneapolis: University of Minnesota Press, 1974), pp. 36, 38, 46, and 114-115; Reinhart Dozy, *Spanish Islam: A History of the Muslims in Spain* (London: Chatto and Windus, 1913), pp. 429-430; and Evariste Lévi-Provençal, *Histoire de l'Espagne Musulmane* (Leiden: Brill, vol. 3, 1953), pp. 29, 53, 131. Not only did *saqalibah* males become prized as soldiers and administrators by Andalusian rulers, but also in the erotic and esthetic domains, "Female saqaliba with fair skin and blue eyes were eagerly sought as concubines. The price could be very high, depending upon a girl's talents as a dancer or singer and upon her physique" (Chejne, *Muslim Spain*, p. 135).
96. See comments by al-Jahiz, quoted by Rogers, *World's Great Men of Color* (1947 edition), p. 94.
97. Lewis, *Arabs in History*, p. 104.
98. Ibid., p. 86. Irwin, in *Africans Abroad* (pp. 77-79), presents a long excerpt from Theodore Nöldeke's *Sketches From Eastern History* (trans. by John Sutherland

Black [London: A. and C. Black, 1892]). This is the most thorough account in English of the Zanj rebellion, detailed, and dramatic as well. The author notes that "with the saltpeter workers were undoubtedly associated many fugitive slaves from the villages and towns, and probably all sorts of fairskinned people as well, but apparently few representatives of the urban proletariat." Class superceded race in this instance.

99. Lewis, *Race and Color*, p. 66.
100. *Encyclopedia of Islam* (1913) states that the black slaves were "hopeless and homeless" and worked in gangs of five hundred to five thousand along with peasants (See article on "Zanj," p. 1213). Lewis, *Arabs in History*, p. 104, reports mention of a gang of fifteen thousand!
101. Irwin, *Africans Abroad*, p. 70.
102. Ibid. For a detailed account of this revolt, see MM. Gaudefroy-Demombynes and Platonov, *Le Monde Musulman et Byzantin Jusqu'aux Croisades* (Paris: Boccard, 1931), p. 445–449. The authors mention the activities of Soleiman. For a succinct account of the rebellion see Lewis, *Race and Color*, pp. 65–67. H. A. R. Gibb in an article, "Caliphate," in the 1963 edition of the *Encyclopedia Britannica* (vol. 4, p. 651), puts the revolt into its wider context as does Lewis in *Arabs in History*, chapter 6, "The Revolt of Islam." This source gives a comprehensive view of the widespread social unrest throughout the Caliphate during the ninth century. Detailed discussion of the period, treating the Zanj rebellion *inter alia*, but making possible an estimate of its importance at the time, is presented in the *Cambridge History of Iran* (Cambridge, England: Cambridge University Press, 1968), pp. 79–119. Irwin, in *Africans Abroad* (pp. 73–107), presents documents written by several people.
103. Lewis, *Arabs in History*, p. 105. According to Nöldeke, cited in Irwin, *Africans Abroad*, p. 86, the rebels were supplied with food by Bedouins.
104. Lewis, *Arabs in History*, pp. 105–106.
105. Lewis, *Race and Color*, p. 169.
106. Gaudefroy-Demombynes and Platonov, *Le Monde Musulman*, pp. 445–449.
107. *Encyclopedia of Islam* (1974 edition), p. 1213.
108. Gustav von Grunebaum, *Medieval Islam* (Chicago: University of Chicago Press, 1953), p. 210.
109. Lewis, *Arabs in History*, p. 104.
110. I have followed the account given by Rogers, *World's Great Men of Color* (Collier edition), vol. 1, "Ibrahim Al-Mahdi, Islam's Greatest Songster and Caliph of Bagdad," pp. 148–162, citing Ibn Khallikan's *Dictionary* in Slane's translation, H.H. Palmer's *Haroun Al-Raschid*, vol. 4 of Zotenberg's *Works of Tabari*, and vol. 7 of Mas'udi's *Prairies d'Or*. The Slane translation of Ibn Khallikan states that "being of a dark complexion which he inherited from his mother, Shikla or Shakla (who was a Negress) and of a large frame of body, he received the name of al-Tinnim (the dragon)" (p. 62). Ibn Khallikan was writing in the thirteenth century and does not discuss his sources. Apparently, there are differing traditions about Shikla's race. Bernard Lewis does not accept Ibn Khallikan's version of the Ibrahim al-Mahdi story even though he cites him as a major source. Lewis states that Ibrahim " . . . was of swarthy color, so much so that some sources—mistakenly it would seem—say that his mother was black" (*Race and Color*, pp. 94–95). Lewis's claim that Ibrahim's mother was "a Persian lady," white in color, not black, needs clarification.
111. Love of music was frowned upon by some devout Muslims.

112. Lewis, *Race and Color*, pp. 94-95.
113. His father and the royal family had objected to the cultivation of Ibrahim's interest in music because it was "considered far beneath the dignity of the high born. Slaves were chiefly the singers of those days." Some singers objected to Ibrahim's competing against them. The royal family tried to restrict his entertaining to court circles, but he eventually became a public singer with his own troupe of entertainers (Rogers, *World's Great Men of Color* (Collier edition), vol. 1, pp. 150-151 and 157).
114. Lewis, *Race and Color*, p. 128.
115. Ibn Khallikan's *Biographical Dictionary* lists less than a half dozen black scholars or caliphs. Among them was Zu'n-Nun al Misri, referred to as "the first person of his age for his learning, devotion, communion with the divinity, and acquaintance with literature." See vol. 1, pp. 534, 513, 293; vol. 3, pp. 615-626; vol. 4, p. 345, for others.
116. See Chejne, in *Muslim Spain* (pp. 20, 152, 163, 225, 267, 300, 372-373) for detailed discussion. He mentions the movement of intellectuals from the Middle East to Andalusia under 'Abd ar-Rahman II, and calls Ziryab "the most important emigre." Bernard Lewis makes a similar judgment in *Arabs in History*, p. 124. Lévi-Provençal, *Histoire de l'Espagne Musulmane*, vol. 1, 1950, p. 88, states that Ziryab was run out of Egypt for singing one of 'Antar's songs, "If my mother were as black as a crow," although the significance of the hostility to the song is not discussed (pp. 62-63). I accept Chejne's statement about Ziryab, that before coming to Andalusia "he was a black slave of the famous musician Ibrahim al-Mawsili, the leading musician of the day, who trained him in the arts of music and singing." He cited as his source Ibn 'Abd Rabbihi's *Al-'Iqd al-Farid*, vol. 6, p. 34. Chejne's footnotes indicate that he was familiar with other sources that were not so explicit. See also Nykl, *Hispano-Arabic Poetry*, p. 27. One of the most extensive accounts available in English of Ziryab's impact on Andalusia is a discussion of his career under the designation 'Ali ibn Nafi' in *The History of the Muhammedan Dynasties in Spain*, by Ahmed Ibn Mohammed Makkari (trans. by Pascual de Gayanjos [Johnson Reprint Co., 1943] vol. 1, pp. 121, 410-412 and 2, pp. 116-121). This source does not refer to him as a Negro, but mentions that he was given the name Ziryab in his youth, after a well-known bird, because of his "dark complexion" and his sweet voice. See also S. M. Imamuddin, *Some Aspects of the Socio-Economic and Cultural History of Muslim Spain, 711-1492 A.D.* (Leiden: E. J. Brill, 1965), pp. 31, 178. Some modern scholars, including Lewis, either do not feel that Ziryab's race or color merit mention or they deliberately place the accent elsewhere. For instance, Jan Read (*The Moors in Spain and Portugal* [London: Faber and Faber, 1974], pp. 71, 89) calls him an Iraqi and does not mention his color. Another scholar discusses him at some length as an almost legendary figure "of Persian origin" (Dozy, *Histoire*, pp. 711-1110). Ibn Khaldun praised Ziryab for his musical accomplishments and referred to him as a "servant" but said nothing of his race, a significant omission in view of Ibn Khaldun's keen interest in that subject. For black vindicationists, the question of Ziryab's race is of great importance; for others it has very little significance.

Most accounts of Ziryab lean heavily upon al-Maqqari's (i.e., Makkari's) *Analectes* I and II. A study of this and other Arabic works might throw some light on a now not-too-well-illuminated point, viz., whether in conflict situations in Andalusia—interpersonal or group—between Whites and Blacks, skin-color and race became "counters in the game." We know this was true in Egyptian politics between the seventh and the sixteenth centuries. The cultural situation in Andalusia around which the question might be raised is stated by Immamuddin, *Some Aspects*, pp. 178–179: "Hakam I patronised musicians . . . 'Alun and Zarqun were invited to Spain from the East and were famous for their music, but Ziryab came later from Baghdad and wrested the laurels from them and laid the foundations of an organized musical art. . . . " Chejne outlines the consequences of this triumph (*Muslim Spain*, p. 225): "Ziryab seems to have aroused the jealousy of many, among them the poets Ibn Habib and al-Ghazzal. . . . Likewise, the satirist Yahya b. al-Hakam, known as al-Ghazzal by virtue of his extreme beauty, composed venomous satire against Ziryab. These satires earned him exile. He went to Iraq. . . . " Al-Maqqari discusses al-Ghazzal in his *Nafh al-Tib*, vol. 1, p. 449. Nykl presents some of his work in *Hispano-Arabic Poetry* (p. 23). Chejne also cites 'Abbas, *Tarikh al-adab al-Andalusi: 'asr siyadat Qurtubah*, pp. 157ff. These sources should be inspected to see whether or not his somatic image and his ancestry were used in the attacks on Ziryab. If they were not, this is of some significance in relation to our inquiry about function of skin color in specific situations.

117. Chejne, *Muslim Spain*, pp. 372–373.
118. Lewis, *Race and Color*, p. 65. Given the fact that so many other scholars refer to Ziryab as black, Lewis's description in *The Arabs in History* (p. 124), is puzzling: "One of the most noteworthy figures among them was *a Persian musician* driven from the court of Harun ar-Rashid by the jealousy of his teacher" [italics added].
119. Lévi-Provençal, *Histoire*, vol. 1, p. 189.
120. Chejne, *Muslim Spain*, p. 225.
121. In *Race and Color* (pp. 16–18) Lewis suggests, not very convincingly, that al-Jahiz's defense of the Blacks was written tongue-in-cheek as a parody of Persian attempts to defend themselves against Arab derogation; that it was an attempt to use the literary device of *reductio ad absurdum*. But the excerpts of *The Boast of the Blacks* reprinted by Rogers have the ring of passionate sincerity and display a knowledge of the role of Blacks in Islamic history that is far out of proportion to the amount of research one might undertake to score a veiled point on behalf of the Persians against the Arabs. See Rogers, *World's Great Men of Color* (1947), vol. 1, pp. 89–95.
122. Lewis, *Race and Color*, p. 17.
123. Ibid., p. 16.
124. Ibid., p. 94.
125. Ibid., p. 80. An interesting legend illustrates the extent to which the status "slave" and "black man" were conceptually separated on some occasions. Two poets were having an audience with the caliph in Baghdad. The Arab recited but did not praise the caliph. The black poet praised him. The caliph said, "He is the best poet of his race, but the best poetry comes from men of noble race. The worst proceeds from slaves." He then bought the black man and freed him. He was still a Black but no longer a slave (Ibn Khallikan, *Biography*, vol. 3, p. 643). The Arabist Lammens stated that there were many slaves in Mecca before the Hegira. They were "a plentiful commodity" being mostly "coloured people of Ethiopian origin and the nucleus of the Meccan militia" (article "'Abd," *Encyclopedia of Islam* (1960), vol. 2, p. 19).
126. Lewis, *Race and Color*, pp. 64–65.
127. Von Grunebaum, *Medieval Islam*, p. 78.
128. Joseph E. Harris, *African Presence in Asia* (Northwestern University Press, 1971),

pp. 178 and 87-90. The quotation is from Joseph E. Harris, "The Black Peoples of Asia," in World Encyclopedia of Black Peoples (St. Clair Shores, Mich.: Scholarly Press, 1975), vol. 1, p. 269.

129. Harris, "The Black Peoples of Asia," p. 269. See also Irwin, Africans Abroad, which includes a section on "Africans in India," composed of extracts from Cambridge History of India, John Briggs's History of the Rise of Mohammedan Power in India, and a long extract translated from W. Coolhaas (ed.), Pieter van den Broeke in Azie. Rogers presents a profile of "Malik Andeel, Benevolent Sultan of Bengal India," in World's Great Men of Color, pp. 173-176. Harris in African Presence discusses a number of other prominent individuals of African descent in Indian history.

130. Irwin, Africans Abroad, "Africans in India," pp. 137-167, especially p. 152 for Irwin's comments on the story of the dynastic marriage.

131. Lewis, Race and Color, p. 76.

132. Rogers, World's Great Men of Color, pp. 225-231, "Yakub Al-Mansur, Greatest of the Moorish Rulers of Spain."

133. Ibid., pp. 228-229. Eight years after the Almoravid invaders won the Battle of Zallaca, they took the city of Lisbon, thus adding Lusitania to their Andalusian conquests. Self-serving contemporary reports state that the invaders from Africa were welcomed at first by "the common people" but that they lost their allegiance because of the Almoravid's attempt to enforce drastic puritanical laws. Another African Muslim group, the Almohades, eventually replaced them. The Berber who led this second invasion had a group of black soldiers as a palace guard but, according to some accounts, distrusted them (Jan Read, The Moors in Spain and Portugal pp. 125-127). See also Conde, History of the Dominion, pp. 314, 317, 337-338, and 346-349. The Almohade leader has been described as "dark olive" in complexion (p. 385). See Chejne, Muslim Spain (pp. 80-95) for details of the development of the Almohade movement in Africa.

134. Rogers, World's Great Men of Color (Collier edition), pp. 232-234. Quotation is from p. 233.

135. Ibid., pp. 232-233.

136. Ibid., p. 233.

137. Ibid., pp. 257-264, "Mulai Ismael, Most Extraordinary Ruler of the Eighteenth Century."

138. Rogers, World's Great Men of Color (1947), pp. 146-148, quoting D. Busnot, Histoire Regne de Mouley Ismael (Rouen, 1714).

139. Basil Davidson, Lost Cities of Africa (Boston: Little Brown and Co., 1959), pp. 90-92.

140. Said Hamadun and Noel King, Ibn Battuta in Black Africa (London: Rex Collins, 1975), pp. 28-30.

141. See Gailey, History of Africa, pp. 48, 63-65.

142. Oliver and Fage, A Short History, pp. 80-81, and Lewis, Arabs in History, pp. 145-146.

143. George Peter Murdock, Africa: Its People and Their Culture History (New York: McGraw Hill, 1959), pp. 388-403.

144. Lewis, Race and Color, p. 61. See also J. Spencer Trimingham, A History of Islam in West Africa (Glasgow: Oxford University Press, 1962), pp. 34-103, "West Sudan States."

145. Murdock, Africa, pp. 132.

146. Trimingham, West Africa, p. 21. There is some evidence that some Negroes were

living among Berber groups north of the desert at the site of what became the northern terminus of the caravan trail that led southward to the black state, Ghana. The northern terminus was Sijilmasa. A Negro settler seems to have been the founder of this town. He was accepted as a chief by the nomadic Berbers before the Arab invasion in the eighth century A.D. He had been deposed before that by the Berbers. For an interesting examination of the tradition by a Boston University professor, see Daniel F. McCall, "The Traditions of the Founding of Sijilmasa and Ghana," *Transactions of the Historical Society of Ghana*, vol. 5, part 1, 1961.

147. Murdock, *Africa*, p. 403.
148. Summarized from L. C. Briggs, *Tribes of the Sahara* (Cambridge, Mass.: Harvard University Press, 1960), Chapter 3, "The Sedentary Populations," pp. 63–105.
149. Ibid., p. 101–102. Briggs's informative analysis is concerned with the sedentary peoples of the Sahara. The central Sahara has been dominated by a nomadic tribe, the Tuaregs, or "people of the veil," which is worn by the men, not the women. The Tuaregs roam over a 1.5 million-square-mile area. They extract tribute from the oasis people, mostly black, who grow dates and have sheep and goats. They guide some caravans across the desert and raid others. They are color-conscious, calling Negroes "blue," the dark-brown Hausa people "black," the Arabs "white," and themselves "red." Tuareg preference for an idealized light somatic norm image and esthetic prejudices against Negroidness have never been so strong as to inhibit the highest status group in Tuareg societies from taking black concubines or even marrying Negro women. However, over the centuries some correlation between color and social status has persisted. The lowest status group, *Imghad* or serfs, are of two types, one Negroid, the other resembling the "nobles." Both nobles and serfs have traditionally held slaves.

The *ikelan*, or household slaves, are virtually all black. They are a sedentary group living on oases and concerned with cultivation. The so-called "outdoor slaves" (*bela, buzu*, or *bugadie*) are not an exclusively black group. They travel with the camel nomads and do all of the hard work connected with the march. The Tuareg have constantly harassed the black villagers within Mali and Songhay and dominated the city of Timbuctoo at one time.

150. Ibid., p. 102–103.
151. Ibn Khaldun, *Histoire des Berbères* (Paris: Librairie Orientaliste, 1969), vol. 1, p. 263, quoted in Trimingham, *West Africa*, pp. 49.
152. Trimingham, *West Africa*, pp. 55, 57–60.
153. Quoted in Ibid., p. 21, note 1.
154. Ibid., pp. 51–52.
155. Ibid., pp. 52–54.
156. Ibid., p. 22.
157. Ibid., p. 22.
158. Ibid., pp. 23–24.
159. Ibid., p. 55.
160. Ibid., pp. 29–31.
161. Ibid., p. 62. Cf. with Dutch naming of a people in southern Africa "Hottentots" in deriding their language.
162. As quoted from al-Idrisi in Trimingham, *West Africa*, p. 63.
163. This episode is recounted in ibid., pp. 61–62.
164. See discussion of Mali in ibid., pp. 62–69.
165. Ibid., pp. 63–66.

166. Ibid., pp. 67–69.
167. Quoted in Oliver and Fage, *A Short History*, pp. 91.
168. Hamadun and King, *Ibn Battuta in Black Africa*, pp. 28–29.
169. Oliver and Fage, *A Short History*, p. 91.
170. Hamadun and King, *Ibn Battuta in Black Africa*, p. 51.
171. Trimingham, *West Africa*, p. 80.
172. Ibid., p. 68, note 1.
173. Joseph E. Harris, *Africans and Their History*, p. 54.
174. Ibid., p. 55.
175. Trimingham, *West Africa*. See chapter 2, "The Songhay Empire of Kawkaw," pp. 85–103.
176. Ibid., p. 98n.
177. Ibid., p. 63.
178. Ibid., pp. 61–62 and 64.
179. Joseph Harris, *Africans and Their History*, pp. 51–56.
180. H. A. R. Gibb, *Mohammedanism: An Historical Survey* (London: Oxford University Press, 1953) pp. 157–158.
181. Harris, *Africans and Their History*, p. 55.
182. See the following articles in Rhoda L. Goldstein, ed., *Black Life and Culture in the United States* (New York: Crowell, 1971): Colin A. Palmer, "The Slave Trade," pp. 87–102 and L. Drewry, "Slavery and the Plantation," pp. 103–130.
183. See, e.g., Mas'udi, *Prairies d'Or*, vol. 2, pp. 251, 349, 357, and 433.
184. Ibn Khaldun, *Discours*, pp. 167–168; 71–72 citing previous writers.
185. Lewis, *Race and Color*, pp. 34n. In *An Introduction to Islamic Cosmological Doctrines* (Cambridge, Mass.: The Belknap Press of Harvard University Press, 1964), pp. 268–269, Seyyed Hossein Nasr relates Ibn Sina's system to that of other scholars who developed the idea of the seven climates and the concept that " . . . there is a profound relation between the flora, fauna, men and climatic conditions of a region . . . and the civilizations and religions which rise in those climates. Just as the amount of sunshine influences the color of the skin of the people living in a certain zone, so do these subtle or psychic aspects of Nature influence the soul of the people living in a particular climate" (p. 83).
186. Lewis, *Race and Color*, p. 99.
187. Ibid., p. 92.
188. Ibid., pp. 35, 36.
189. Ibid., p. 36.
190. Nasr, *Cosmological Doctrines*, p. 268.
191. Aristotle, *Physiognomy*; for a relatively recent argument in favor of physiognomy, see 15th edition, published in 1878, of John Caspar Lavater, *Essays on Physiognomy* (London: William Tegg and Co.).
192. Kai Kaus, "The Purchase of Slaves," in James Kritzeck, *Anthology of Islamic Literature* (New York: New American Library, 1964), pp. 160–161.
193. Ibid., p. 161.
194. Ibid., p. 162.
195. Ibid., p. 162.
196. Ibid., p. 165.
197. Mas'udi, *Prairies d'Or*, vol. 2, p. 197.
198. Ibid., p. 337.
199. Ibn Khaldun, *Discours*, vol. 1, pp. 93–106.
200. Ibid., p. 172.

201. Ibid., p. 170.
202. Ibid., p. 173.
203. Ibid., pp. 166–167; 170–174.
204. Ibid., pp. 482n and 1045–1046. See Koran, Sale's eighteenth-century translation into English with notes. Sura XXXI is Mohammed's tribute to the sage. The Englishman, Sale, notes that some Arab writers said he was " . . . of black complexion . . . with thick lips and splay feet." He said that, for these reasons, "some call him an Ethiopian." Sale, coming from a society dominated by White Racism, found it difficult to accept this explanation of his physical traits and said, "He must have been deformed enough!" Rogers discusses Loqman in vol. 1 of *World's Great Men of Color*, pp. 67–72. In addition to Sale and another edition of the Koran, Rogers cites J. L. Marcel, *Fables de Loqman* (Cairo: 1799) and Mas'udi, *Prairies d'Or*.
205. Ibn Khaldun, Discours, vol. 2, pp. 515; vol. 3, pp. 990, 1213, 1249n., 1259, 1263. Ibn Khaldun frequently refers to Mas'udi as a source. Not only does the latter refer to al-Jahiz and his book, "Sur l'excellence des Noirs et leur comparison avec les Blancs," but he accepts it as a serious defense (vol. 1, p. 70). Despite Mas'udi some modern Arabists think Jahiz wrote with "tongue in cheek."
206. Ibid., vol. 1, pp. 117, 166.
207. See Ibn Khaldun, *Histoire des Berbères*, vol. 2, pp. 105–116, and *Discours* vol. 1, pp. 166–170.
208. Lewis, *Race and Color in Islam*, pp. 7–8.
209. Nykl, *Hispano-Arabic Poetry*, p. 87.
210. Goldziher, *Mythology*, pp. 219–224; 55–57; 146–150. His primary point is that nomadic peoples did not fear the night. Belief in the universality of such a fear is crucial to the Degler-Gergen analysis.
211. Nykl, *Hispano-Arabic Poetry*, p. 297.
212. The extent to which themes derogatory to black males existed among unlettered people should be assessed by a careful study of folklore among the varied ethnic groups within the Muslim world.
213. *The Arabian Nights*, pp. 1–13. See Lewis, *Race and Color*, p. 4, for a summary of E. W. Lane's 1859 version of the story that speaks of twenty male black slaves taking part with the white female slaves in the episode. Burton, whose version we are using, changes the race of the males to white. A reprint of the Lane translation published in 1913 by Holby of Philadelphia retained the interracial character of the event as did the John Payne translation done in London in 1914 for "subscribers only."

The opening story is a Persian tale, not an Arab one, and this may be responsible for the sharp "Manichaean" distinction between white people and black people and the attribution of evil characteristics to blackness as in the case of a jinn described as "black and frightful" with "the shape of a giant." He had used his magical powers to seduce a beautiful white woman. The opening episode is placed in Turkestan and Persia and involves the wife of a Persian king. A sanitized version of Burton that retains the interracial character of the Lane translation relates the incident as follows:

A secret gate of the sultan's palace suddenly opened, and there came out of it twenty women, in the midst of whom walked the sultaness, who was easily distinguished from the rest by her majestic air. This princess, thinking that the king of Tartary was gone a-hunting with his brother the sultan, came with her retinue near the windows of his apartment. For the prince had so placed himself that he could see all that passed in the garden without being perceived himself. He observed that the persons who accompanied the sultaness threw off their veils and long robes, that they might be more at their ease; but he was greatly surprised to find that ten of them were black men, and that each of these took his mistress. The sultaness, on her part, was not long without her gallant. She clapped her hands, and called Masoud, Masoud, and immediately a black descended from a tree, and ran towards her with great speed.

214. *The Arabian Nights,* p. 6. The husband's statements suggest that sexism not racism was the dominant reaction in these cases. This attitude is deeply embedded in Islamic cultures and has found extreme expression in purdah, the veiling of women, and the custom of using eunuchs to guard the harem. It has Indian as well as Arabic roots. Sindbar, of Indian origin but writing in Arabic, published *Book of the Wiles and Deception of Women* in the eleventh century (also called *Book of the Ten Wise Men*). It consisted of twenty-six stories "showing the deceit and cunning of women" (Chejne, *Muslim Spain,* p. 408). Some observers imply that this attitude of suspicion and distrust of wives is widespread in contemporary Arabia where the old traditional norms and values are still strong. One nineteenth-century source claimed that there was a realistic basis for such suspicions when he wrote because of the prevalence of adultery and lesbianism, with Blacks frequently being the partners. For instance, the authors state that women in Saudi Arabia—Muslim, Jewish and Indian—"chase after Hamites and Negroes" (Edwardes and Masters, *The Cradle of Erotica,* pp. 175-178). However without more evidence than that of Jacobus, Burton and one or two other sources, and these now nearly a century old, any such generalizations should be taken with more than a grain of salt. But if husbands believe that these delinquencies exist, attitudes toward both women and black males will be affected.

215. This theme calls for psychoanalytic interpretation as well as sociological explanation.

216. Ibid., p. 4.

217. Ibid., pp. 41-42.

218. Ibid., pp. 477-516.

219. Ibid., p. 507.

220. Ibid., p. 517. See also pp. 112-121 for reference to black women.

221. See "The Arabian Nights," in *Encyclopedia Britannica* (1963).

222. Lewis, *Race and Color,* "A Variety of Stereotypes," pp. 96-101. Lewis abstracted these traits from the works of Arabic writers. Other people, too, were stereotyped. One writer dealing specifically with Muslim Spain notes that Galicians were "treacherous and dirty." They were said to bathe only once or twice a day "even then with cold water"; and "they never wash their clothes." The population of Brittany was defined as "ugly, have bad character, and count among them many thieves" (Chejne, *Muslim Spain,* p. 286.)

That positive, favorable, stereotypes about Blacks could emerge in some situations is suggested by this and other sources. Thus, in the Arabian shrine cities of Mecca and Medina, a favorable stereotype was in existence during the nineteenth century of the pious, industrious, free Negro who had come to Arabia on the pilgrimage. One student of life in Arabian cities during the latter part of the nineteenth century comments on black pilgrims from Nigeria in West Africa and from the Sudan, stating that: "Few negroes, or Tekayrne, as they are called, come to Mekka [i.e., Mecca] without visiting Medina also, a town even more venerable in their estimation than Mekka. The orthodox sect of Malekites to which they belong, carry, in general, their respect for Mohammed further than any of the three other sects; and the negroes, little instructed as they usually are, may be said to adore the Prophet. . . . They approach his tomb with a terrified and appalled conscience, and with more intense feelings than when they visit the Kaaba." These pilgrims believe that any prayers made at the tomb will certainly be answered. Impressed as this observer was by the devotion of the Blacks, he was even more impressed by their disciplined orderliness and willingness to work. In contrast to pilgrims from India, he stated that "very few of them are beggars" and that they cut and sell wood, serve as carriers and porters, and make small mats and baskets, living together in a community "till they have earned money enough to their service home." A similar pattern of industry by Blacks was reported for Jiddah and Mecca where "they also make clay coffee pots, serve as water carriers, and prepare an intoxicant called bouza." This European contrasts them favorably with the elderly black eunuchs ogling the prostitutes in the shrine cities. These comments are from Burckhardt, *Travels in Arabia*, p. 120 (a reprint of the 1829 edition).

223. Lewis, *Race and Color*, p. 99.
224. J. S. Trimingham, *The Influence of Islam Upon Africa* (London: Longman, 1968), pp. 42, 62–65.
225. H. A. R. Gibb, *Modern Trends in Islam* (Chicago: University of Chicago Press, 1947), p. 20.
226. Trimingham, *The Influence of Islam*, pp. 57, 60, 83–84.
227. Ibid.
228. H. Hoetink, *Caribbean Race Relations: A Study of Two Variants* (London: Oxford University Press, 1967), Part 4, "The Somatic Norm Image," pp. 120–152. No systematic comparative study has been made of what black esthetic norms exist in various parts of the world. Exciting perspectives are opened up by Dr. Sylvia Ardyn Boone, an Afro-American professor at Yale, who has been a participant-observer among the Mende people in West Africa. Her book, published in 1986 by the Yale University Press, includes a beautiful group of photographs: *Radiance From the Waters: Ideals of Feminine Beauty in Mende Art*.
229. *The Arabian Nights*.
230. Kai Kaus, "The Purchase of Slaves," in Kritzeck, *Anthology of Islamic Literature*, p. 163.
231. Ibn Khaldun, *Discours*, p. 342n.
232. Max Weber, *Sociology of Religion*, p. 238.
233. Lewis, *Race and Color*, p. 35.
234. Ibid., pp. 27–29.
235. Gordon W. Allport, *The Nature of Prejudice* (New York: Doubleday, 1938), pp. 85–86; 104; 123; 211.
236. Lewis, *Race and Color*, p. 101, note 143; see also p. 37, note 65.
237. Ibid., p. 30.
238. See note 7.
239. Al-Jahiz, quoted in Rogers, *World's Great Men of Color* (1947 edition), p. 90.
240. The poet Mutannabi ridiculed Kafur in scurrilous verses but he had to flee into exile. In a similar case in the city of Granada in Muslim Spain, the black ruler of the city forced into exile a poet who referred to him as a black slave.
241. Quoted in Rogers, *World's Great Men of Color* (1947 edition), p. 94.

242. Lewis, *Race and Color*, p. 95.
243. Ibid., pp. 92–93. Al-Jahiz boasted of how black troops, after a specific battle, became "stallions" as they took the women. Rogers, *World's Great Men of Color* (1947 edition), p. 92.
244. Ibid., pp. 82–83.
245. Von Grunebaum, *Medieval Islam*, p. 226.
246. Ibid., p. 209.
247. Lewis, *Race and Color*, pp. 31–35, 96–97, 100.
248. Ibid., p. 96–97.
249. Trimingham, *West Africa*, p. 44, note 2.
250. Lewis, *Race and Color*, p. 98.
251. Ibid., p. 100.
252. Ibid.
253. Nykl, *Hispano-Arabic Poetry*, pp. 107–109.
254. Lévi-Provençal, *Histoire de L'Espagne Musulmane*, vol. 3, pp. 178–179. One Arabist claims that black women as concubines had "high honor" in Muslim Spain and were "prized" as wives. Blacks in Spain were not Zanj. Yet class-linked esthetics put them at a disadvantage. Lévi-Provençal noted that royalty tried to find French and Circassian women for wives. Their blondness was the attraction.
255. Edward William Lane, *Arabian Society in the Middle Ages* (London: Curzon Press, 1883, reprinted in 1971), p. 273.
256. Koran, Sura IV, "Women."
257. Von Grunebaum, *Medieval Islam*, pp. 209–210.
258. Chejne, *Muslim Spain*, p. 176–177.
259. Mas'udi, *Prairies d'Or*, vol. 1, p. 69.
260. Von Grunebaum, *Medieval Islam*, pp. 176–177.
261. Lewis, *Race and Color*, pp. 27–28.
262. Ibid., pp. 36–68.

CHAPTER 6

Henri Baudet's small volume, *Paradise on Earth: Some Thoughts on European Images of Non-European Man*, contains an excellent introduction to a study of changes in European attitudes toward black people during and after the period of the Crusades. However, his view that contact with people of color in the Middle East resulted in generally favorable attitudes toward black and brown people is not accepted by all scholars. Baudet's emphasis upon the role of the Prester John myth in stimulating positive attitudes toward Ethiopians is not denied by medievalists, but is not stressed. The discovery of the New World with its Amerindian population shifted attention away from Africans and fixed it upon the Amerindians. Baudet fails to assess the importance of the transatlantic African slave trade as a factor in depressing the status of black people.

Themes introduced by Baudet are investigated in greater depth by Paul H. D. Kaplan in *The Rise of the Black Magus in Western Art*. He explores the interrelationships between the Prester John stories and the prevalence of the belief that one black Wise Man was among the three Magi. The legends about the Queen of Sheba and the Shulamite girl in the Song of Solomon are examined with regard to the specific time periods when these women achieved iconographic significance in Europe as black personalities. Kaplan's most distinctive contribution, however, is his convincing and well documented account of the way in which the cult of St. Maurice became an integral aspect of the Hohenstaufen kings in their quest for power in Saxony and the Holy Roman Empire.

The most useful source for studying medieval views about blackness and black people is an extended essay by Jean Devisse in *The Image of the Black in Western Art*, vol. 2, sponsored by the Menil Foundation and published by William Morrow, New York, in 1979. Sections of the essay are devoted to "Christian and Black," "The Black and His Color From Symbols to Reality" and "A Sanctified Black: Maurice." The essay is illustrated by numerous color photographs of illuminated manuscripts and of paintings and sculpture in cathedrals. Generalizations are documented with extensive references to Latin as well as vernacular sources. Byzantine Christian paintings are presented for comparison with Western illuminated mansuscripts. The one weakness of the volume is the absence of any discussion of Black Madonnas in Europe. The discussion of Maurice, coupled with Kaplan's, leaves little room for additional research. On some of the other topics Devisse points out the need for further investigation.

These three books, for reasons that are not clear, do not discuss the prevalence of the cult of the Black Virgin in parts of Europe. No comprehensive studies of this phenomenon are available in English. However, students will find M. Durand-Lefebvre's volume useful, *Etude sur l'origine des Vierges Noires* (1937). An illustrated book about Black Madonnas in one area of France has been utilized in our discussion, Madame F. Vialet's *Iconographie de la Vierge Noire du Puy* (1983). This work has been supplemented with Jean Ajalbert's *L'Auvergne*.

These books and others they refer to in their bibliographies or text decisively document the fact that blackness and black people are not, in all times and places, in all social contexts, "looked down upon." These works are primarily concerned with the *religious/mystical* domain, and to a lesser extent the *erotic* and *status-allocating* dimensions of race relations. Three of the four books make effective use of photographs in developing their arguments. They attempt to specify factors involved in differential evaluations of blackness and black people that occur over time within specific geographical areas.

The editor of the Menil Foundation volume that contains the Devisse essay states that "This book is a beginning, a groundbreaking, an invitation to look further, to be curious." Our chapter should be evaluated in the same way.

1. See article "Halle," in *Encyclopedia Britannica* (1963) for details of the conflicts within this diocese between the social classes and Protestants and Catholics. The naming of churches for Moritz (i.e. Maurice) is described.
2. Hans-Joachim Kunst, *The African in European Art* (Bad Godesberg: Internationes, 1967), p. 14.
3. Rogers, *World's Great Men of Color*, vol. 1.
4. Charles Verlinden, *L'esclavage dans l'Europe Mediévale: Péninsule Ibérique et France* (Brugges: De Tempel, 1955).
5. Henri Baudet, in *Paradise on Earth: Some Thoughts on European Images of Non-European Man* (New Haven, Conn.: Yale University Press, 1965), finds that the figure of Prester John, a mythical African Christian king, appealed to the popular imagination in the late Middle Ages and was "closely in tune with the time" (pp. 20–21).
6. William H. McNeill, *History Handbook of Western Civilization* (Chicago: University of Chicago Press, 1953), pp. 379–380.

7. Paul H. D. Kaplan, *The Rise of the Black Magus in Western Art* (Ann Arbor: UNI Research Press, 1983), "The Development of the Black Prester John," pp. 43-46.

8. Jean Devisse, "From the Demonic Threat to the Incarnation of Sainthood," in Ladislas Bugnar, *The Image of the Black in Western Art* (New York: William Morrow, 1979), pp. 37-147.

9. McNeill, *Rise of the West*, pp. 431-432.

10. Kaplan, *The Black Magus*, pp. 8, 23, 59-83.

11. Faber Birren, *The Story of Color: From Ancient Mysticism to Modern Science* (Westport, Conn.: The Crimson Press, 1941), p. 45.

12. Ibid., pp. 325 and 22.

13. Ibid., p. 57.

14. Ibid., pp. 66 and 69-73.

15. Ibid., p. 31.

16. Johan Huizinga, *The Waning of the Middle Ages: A Study of the Forms of Life, Thought and Art in France and the Netherlands in the XIVth and XVth Centuries* (New York: Doubleday, 1954), p. 120. This is a paperback edition of a book first published in 1924 in English translation by F. Hopman of Leiden.

17. Ibid., p. 270.

18. Ibid., p. 271. After mid-fifteenth century, the colors black and white were out of favor in France, with blue and yellow becoming popular.

19. See chapter 15, "Symbolism and Its Decline," in Huizinga, *The Waning of the Middle Ages*.

20. Rogers, *Nature Knows No Color Line*, pp. 79-80. The evidence cited by Rogers is folkloric and onomastic. Some archaeological evidence is presented in Peter Fryer, *Staying Power: the History of the Black People in Britain* (London: Pluto Press, 1984), p. 2.

21. Rogers, *Nature Knows No Color Line*, pp. 69-71.

22. Scholars disagree about the origin of the "Black Knight" legend and its assimilation to Arthurian legends. See *Morien, A Metrical Romance* (London: David Nutt, 1901), pp. 1-16.

23. William Graham Sumner, *Folkways* (Boston: Ginn and Co., 1906), pp. 16-18, 49, 346.

24. See "Roland, Legends of" in *Encyclopedia Britannica*, (1963), unsigned but with adequate bibliography. Two readily accessible basic documents in English are Gerard J. Brault, *The Song of Roland: An Analytical Edition* (University Park: Michigan State University Press, 1978), and *The Song of Roland*, trans. with an introduction by Frederick Goldin (New York: W. W. Norton, 1978).

25. Brault, *Roland/Analytical*, pp. 119-197.

26. Saladin, the Muslim sultan, assigned a church in Jerusalem to Ethiopian Christian pilgrims who came regularly (See note 79, chapter 5). At least one record is in existence that speaks of Blacks in the armies against which Crusaders fought in Palestine between A.D. 1095 and 1127. An observer at the taking of Jerusalem and other battles reported that when the Crusaders took the Holy City, "some Turks and Arabs and about five hundred black Ethiopians were allowed to depart with their lives from the Tower of David" when they agreed to give up money that they had sequestered in that building. When a "multitude of Turks, Arabs and Ethiopians" tried to retake Jerusalem on August 12, 1099, a historic battle was fought at Ascalon. After the Crusaders had won a skirmish, the observer said he saw "the ground thickly covered with shields and bucklers, daggers and quivers, bows and arrows, with Saracens and Ethiopians either dead or wounded, with

Franks, too, but not as many." Egypt (referred to as Babylon in the record) sent an army to help take Ascalon back from the Crusaders. This time "Arab horsemen and Ethiopian footmen" were backed up by over a thousand Turkish archers. The Muslims were defeated and many Ethiopians were "slaughtered in the fields." In a battle at Joppa "the Ethiopians held shields in their hands and, thus covered, protected themselves." After five days the Crusaders won. Meanwhile the besieged Christian defenders of Jerusalem were becoming exhausted. The chronicle states that whenever some of them ventured out of the city into surrounding areas, "they are captured or killed by Ethiopians in ambush in ravines and forests." The image of Ethiopians carried back to Europe by these Crusaders was not calculated to win sympathy for them. Sculptures and paintings began to portray Blacks as executioners of the righteous extending back as far as the beheading of John the Baptist and as wielders of whips as Christ bore the cross to Calvary where he was crucified. The image of *le bon éthiopien* was in competition with these negative images. However, at the end of the Crusades the more benign image had triumphed. This was due to political forces within Europe led by Frederick II who, incidentally, had himself been a Crusader. See Fulcher of Chartres, *A History of the Expedition to Jerusalem, 1095-1127* (Knoxville: University of Tennessee Press, 1969), pp. 124, 125, 158, 183, 186, 187, 241, 278. See also Bugnar, ed., *The Image of the Black in Western Art*, pp. 72–80.

In the latter work, Jean Devisse presents extensive pictorial evidence to establish his point that from the fourth century A.D. through the fourteenth, blackness "was merely a symbol and synonym of evil" and did not apply exclusively or even primarily to black *people*. Nor were all demons depicted as black although some were. A spectacular illustration from a British illuminated manuscript is presented in which the demons coming out of the Gadarene swine are very dark but not Negroid. Usually the dark demons were not Negroid. Among learned men and women of the monasteries, however, stories must have circulated about the temptations and torments that some distinguished Church Fathers reported that they suffered at the hands of either gigantic black men or little black imps who harassed them in visions. However, Lucifer, the Prince of Hell, usually appeared in the form of a red Fallen Angel. In western Christendom, women, not men, seem to have been the main targets of black demons. During the "witch mania" period, many women on the continent confessed, when tortured, to having had sexual relations imposed upon them (often in lurid variations) by evil spirits, *incubi*. These were frequently black men, and most of the women reported that they did not enjoy these encounters. Since there were so few black men living in Europe, these fantasies were probably fueled by stories told by early Church Fathers of Ethiopians who had harassed them or by Crusaders returning from the East. It is significant that concurrently, some European Christians were elevating Maurice, the black military hero, to a level of veneration that ultimately resulted in his canonization as a saint. What Baudet calls "le bon éthiopien" was emerging as a favorable stereotype of the Christianized black man, "good" in contrast to "evil" Infidel black soldiers. During witchcraft trials in England, although a few women described the devils as black, none reported being seduced or ravished by devils, black or white. See John Ashton, *The Devil in Britain and America* (London: Ward and Downey, 1896), chapters 9-14, which discuss trials for witchcraft in Britain in the seventeenth and eighteenth centuries.

27. Ludovico Ariosto, *Orlando Furioso*, trans. from the Italian by Barbara Reynolds (Harmondsworth: Penguin Books, 1977), pp. 303–311; 327–335; 416–442; 451–475.

28. *Morien*, p. 29. The English prose publication, described at note 22, is translated from the medieval Dutch by Jessie L. Weston. The Dutch manuscript is believed to have been an early thirteenth-century product, based, probably, on a French tale. The critical notes suggest that the Arthurian cycle in which Lancelot played a prominent role developed independently from an old folktale in which the Black Knight was a central character. The emphasis on a black knight in German and Dutch legends may be related to the veneration of St. Maurice.
29. Ibid., p. 31.
30. Ibid., p. 34.
31. Ibid., p. 35.
32. Ibid., p. 36.
33. Ibid., p. 38.
34. Ibid., p. 41. A curious variation of the tale of Morien was circulating on the continent during the first half of the thirteenth century. The hero is not Percival's nephew but rather his father. Wolfram von Eschenbach wrote a book, *Parzifal*, in which Gahmuret, father of Percival and of the black knight of the Morien story, defends the queen of an "eastern country" against her enemies and then lives with her. Their son was born with skin mottled black and white; he became the "ideal type of the pagan knight" whose deeds were rivaled only by those of this half-brother, Parzifal. See *The Image of the Black in Western Art*, p. 164.
35. Ibid., p. 83.
36. Ibid., p. 143.
37. Ibid.
38. Ibid., p. 144.
39. Ibid., p. 145.
40. Ibid., p. 146–147.
41. Many of the Italian tales of this period depict "the Negro" or "the Moor" as the lascivious seducer of women. The black man cast in the role of the sodomite is unusual. An equivalence—Ethiopian=homosexual=monstrosity—is set up by Ariosto hich might have resonated at several mental and emotional levels. The church during this period was stressing the evils of sodomy (for reasons that are not clear), and this might account for the author's choice of this particular practice to exemplify madness and bestiality. The first English translation omitted the reference to sodomy.
42. *Orlando Furioso*, pp. 562–563.
43. This is Allesandro de Medici, first duke of Florence (1510-1537), whose mother was a Negro servant in a prominent family. His father was reputed to be Pope Clement VII, a member of the Medici family who was Allesandro's defender against detractors and arranged a marriage of the Duke to the daughter of Charles V. Allesandro was murdered at the early age of 27, but had been a reasonably good ruler of an Italian city-state while he lived. Yet one jealous member of the Medici family is reported to have shouted "Negro" and "bastard" at him from time to time. Portraits of the Duke make no attempt to conceal his Negroid features and dark skin color. See Rogers, *World's Great Men of Color*, vol. 2, pp. 302–309, and his sources.
44. "The Dream of Heroism and of Love," in Huizinga, *The Waning of the Middle Ages*, chapter 5, pp. 77–84.
45. Kunst, *Africans in European Art*, p. 21.
46. Rogers, *Nature Knows No Color Line*.
47. Huizinga, *The Waning of the Middle Ages*, p. 143.

48. Kunst, *Africans in European Art*, pp. 18–19.
49. Ibid., p. 19.
50. Ibid., p. 25.
51. Ibid., p. 20.
52. Bastide erroneously states that the Black Magus is always displayed in a subordinate role. See photographs in Kaplan, *The Black Magus*.
53. Hannes Vatter, *The Devil in English Literature* (Berne: Francke Verlag, 1978).
54. R. E. L. Masters, *Eros and Evil* (New York: Lancer Books, 1969), p. 37
55. John Ashton, *The Devil in Britain and America* (London: Ward and Downey, 1896).
56. Arturo Graf, *The Story of the Devil* (New York: Macmillan, 1931), pp. 29 and 269.
57. William Rose, ed., *The History of the Damnable Life and Deserved Death of Dr. John Faustus* (New York: E. P. Dutton, n. d.), p. 107.
58. Masters, *Eros and Evil*, pp. 36–42.
59. Bugnar, ed., *The History of the Black in Western Art*, pp. 37–80.
60. Carl Jung, the psychoanalyst, in writing of his childhood experiences and dreams, comments on one specific episode that he never forgot, saying: "The fear of the 'black man' *which is felt by every child*, was not the essential thing in that experience." Years later, while traveling in East Africa Jung said, "Only once during the entire expedition did I dream of a Negro." It was a man with a red-hot curling iron "intending to make his hair 'kinky.'" Jung comments, "I took this dream as a warning from the unconscious . . . At that time I was all too close to 'going black!'" Occasionally he suffered fear especially when among one group who were "the blackest Negoes I had ever seen" (C.G. Jung, *Memories, Dreams, Reflections* [New York: Vintage Books, 1961], pp. 14, 270–273). Jung's belief that all children fear "the black man" did not apply specifically to Negroes; in fact it included men in black clothing such as Jesuits! Another scholar, after discussing portrayals in stained glass windows of churches that cast Negroes in the role of executioners of saints and torturers of Jesus Christ, gave a psychoanalytical interpretation as a partial explanation of negative attitudes toward black people in Europe: "Ignorance and prejudices arising from many sources created an assortment of cliches on Africa and its peoples that were reinforced by an extraordinarily crude equivalence imagined by Christians between a color and the most disturbing aspects of the Christian world. *A whole mental structure, unconscious for the most part, was erected to the detriment of the Blacks,* although in some cases and to some degree other facts and other experiences could, as we shall see, modify this state of mind." Devisse, in *The Image of the Black in Western Art*, p. 80.
61. This figure is given in a comprehensive study published in Paris in 1937, Marie Durand-Lefebvre's *Etude sur l'Origine des Vierges Noires*. Madame Frédérique Vialet's monograph, *Iconographie de la Vierge Noire du Puy*, summarizes all of the literature through 1983 that was available on "Black Virgins" or "Black Madonnas" in France, along with a useful bibliographic guide. The most comprehensive summary was stated to be E. Saillens, *Nos Vierges Noires, leurs origines*, published in Paris in 1945, and among the most recent works were P. A. Sigal, *Les marcheurs de Dieu* (Paris, 1974), and J. Huynen, *L'énigme des Vierges Noires* (Paris, 1972). The references to studies of the Black Virgin of the cathedral of Puy-Velay are extensive. For a decade annual expositions in honor of the Virgin have been held there and these have stimulated considerable research for the preparation of brochures, booklets, announcements, and memorabilia. Madame Vialet's work,

published by the Department of Haute-Loire, is in the form of a well-illustrated catalogue for the 1983 Exposition in the Baptistère Saint-Jean of the Cathedral of Puy.

62. The first description of the image at Notre Dame du Puy as black occurred in the fifteenth century. A famous painting by Hieronymus Dumonteilh (see plate 7) portrays the Virgin and Child as definitely Negroid. Votive offerings and jubilee publications in that century and the next gave a similar portrayal. No documentary evidence exists prior to the fifteenth century as to the race or color of the Virgin. Various students have speculated that the image at Puy was dark or black from the tenth century on. See particularly Vialet, *Iconographie*, pp. 30–32. When Ajalbert wrote *L'Auvergne* (Paris: Libraires-Imprimeries Réunies) in 1896, the tradition had been set for over four hundred years. Vialet summarized L. Breiner's (1935) theory of progressive blackening of the statue over this period.

63. J. Ajalbert, *L'Auvergne*, pp. 135–150, 189.

64. Ibid., pp. 143–144.

65. Ibid., pp. 145–149.

66. J. A. Rogers, *100 Amazing Facts About the Negro With Complete Proof* (New York: Helga M. Rogers, 1957), p. 30, quoting from Romain Rolland, *Intermédiaire des Chercheurs et des Curieux*, vol.34, p. 193.

67. Ajalbert, *L'Auvergne*, pp. 135–137.

68. Olivia Bitton-Jackson, *Madonna or Courtesan: The Jewish Woman in Christian Literature* (New York: The Seabury Press, 1982), p. 11–12. The complex interrelationships that emerged among devotees of the Queen of Sheba and the Shulamite woman have been carefully analyzed by Kaplan in *The Black Magus*, pp. 37–38.

69. Vialet, *Iconographie*. See especially "Les Hypothèses de Nos Contemporains," pp. 31–32, and "Nos Conclusions," pp. 30–31. Plates 69, 73, 74, 75, 76, 77, 78, 79, 80, 81 are of particular interest.

70. Ibid., pp. 84–85.

71. Ibid., pp. 25–26.

72. Ibid., p. 30.

73. Marvin K. Pope's study in 1977 of the *Song of Songs* contains a thorough analysis of the Black Madonna phenomenon, evaluating an impressive range of source material. He summarizes Marie Durand-Lefebvre's, *Etude sur l'origine des Vierges Noires*, which spoke of some 275 such madonnas in churches and monasteries of Europe. She discussed five hypotheses that had been advanced to account for their existence: (1) natural cause of discoloration of originally lighter material; (2) choice of "an ethnic type" as a model including a Jewish Virgin Mary presumably darkened by her stay in Egypt; (3) a model of Oriental origin derived from Asia; (4) symbolism from the *Song of Solomon* and other Biblical sources; (5) survival of ancient cults (especially Isis). Some images had been painted black that were not Negroid, and in these cases the color must have some significance. Danita Redd published a long article in the 1985 volume of the *Journal of African Civilization* on "The Black Madonna of Europe: Diffusion of the African Isis." What might have been the definitive article on the subject was marred by her insistence on Isis as the sole source of European representations.

74. Pope, *Song of Songs* (pp. 312–314), presents some very convincing evidence that "there may have been no cause to bring Black Virgins from the East to Rome, since it is likely that they were already there as survivals of ancient pagan cults." Among those worshipped in a black form were *Aphrodite melainis* whose color Pausanias explained as due to the fact that most of mankind usually made love at

night. Other black goddesses were Diana, Demeter, Cybele, Venus, and Isis. Athena was worshipped in both a black and white form. According to Pliny the image of Diana of Ephesus was made of ebony. The original form may have been a black stone. The image of Isis was sometimes black, and R. E. Witt writing in 1971 states that "statues like the one in Paris might stay inside Christian churches without arousing comment" (See Pope, *Song of Songs*, p. 314).

75. Roger Bastide, "Color, Racism, and Christianity," *Daedalus* 96, 2 (Spring, 1967): 316–317. Although he was a professional anthropologist, Bastide presented no empirical data to indicate that any votaries of the Black Madonna held such ideas. He deduced their sentiments from a combination of Freudian and Jungian psychoanalytical theory. It is highly improbable that the tens of thousands of people who stream to these shrines annually share any uniform concepts or emotions about the images. We have no knowledge either of whether any of them conceive of these Madonnas as being racially and ethnically black, as pieces of wood blackened by age, weather, smoke, etc., or simply as black wood. Or do some imagine meanings they think were intended by the assumed maker of the image? A comparative study of the Black Madonnas would make a worthy doctoral dissertation in anthropology. One thorough anthropological study is available of the shrine at Montserrat in Catalonia and enough has been written by journalists to supplement the author's correspondence with two Polish anthropologists to warrant a tentative statement on this matter.

76. William Christian, an anthropologist, lived in the Montserrat area of Catalonia for over two years while observing, interviewing and studying documents. (Some Black Madonnas were for sale as souvenirs in the Barcelona airport in 1955, when the author stopped there. They were in a wide variety of sizes and all were dark brown in color with only slightly Negroid features.) "The Black Madonna: A Religious and Historical Context" was reported on during a symposium on Nov. 8, 1985, at the University of California, Los Angeles, on "The Dark Madonna: Woman, Culture and Community Rituals." Mary Elizabeth Perry also read a paper on "The Black Madonna of Catalonia: Legend, Ritual, and Iconography."

77. From the article "Montserrat" in *Encyclopedia Britannica* (1963).

78. Ibid.

79. Professor Michel Rut, in a letter to the author dated August 27, 1985, writes that Our Lady of Jasna Gora is usually called Madonna of Czestochowa. The name Die Schwarze Madonna (the Black Madonna) is used mostly by Germans. Some think the image became discolored when the Bohemians damaged it in the fifteenth century. Professor Pietranok, another ethnologist, states that there are folktales that state the image became darkened during an attack by heretics. He adds, "The face of the madonna is not black but swarthy, as the faces of many people from the Mediterranean area and the image was painted probably in Byzantium." Our Lady of the Bright Mountain (Jasna Gora) is a name frequently used. It should be noted that this is not the original icon but is a restoration made in the sixteenth century.

80. Professor Rut states that the term *czarna* meaning dark or black is occasionally used in print and visual media and by ordinary people but that the word for mulatto woman or Negress is never used. History books rarely refer to Our Lady of Jasna Gora as *czarna* and in his opinion people attach no special merit to the madonna being czarna.

81. Kaplan, *The Black Magus*, p. 77.

82. Rogers, *World's Great Men of Color*, vol. 1, "St. Maurice of Aganaum," pp. 290–294.
83. Kaplan, *The Black Magus*, p. 76. In referring to the coronation of Charles IV in Rome this scholar writes, "From the early twelfth century part of the standard ritual of imperial coronation had taken place at the altar of St. Maurice in Old St. Peter's, where the Bishop of Ostia had anointed the candidate." He cites the text of the coronation protocol, April 5, 1355, as explicitly mentioning this act. This site for the coronation was chosen before portrayal of Maurice as black by artists and sculptors began.
84. Kunst, *Africans in European Art*, p. 14.
85. Kaplan, *The Black Magus*, p. 10.
86. Ibid., p. 77.
87. Ibid., pp. 76–77.
88. Ibid., p. 78.
89. Ibid.
90. Ibid., p. 79.
91. Ibid., pp. 43–46.
92. Ibid., pp. 61–62.
93. Ibid., Figs. 54, 89, 93, and 94.
94. *Orlando Furioso*, pp. 304–305.
95. The following well-documented discussions are especially valuable: "The Legend of Prester John," "Prester John in Asia," and "The Development of the Black Prester John" in Kaplan, *The Black Magus*, pp. 43–48 and 51–62.
96. Baudet, *Paradise on Earth*, p. 20.
97. Ibid., p. 14.
98. Ibid., p. 14.
99. Ibid., p. 18.
100. McNeill, *History of Western Civilization*, pp. 393–395 and 457–458.
101. Baudet, *Paradise on Earth*, pp. 16–18.
102. Bastide, "Color, Racism, and Christianity."
103. Bishop Jerome Osario, *The History of the Portuguese During the Reign of Emmanuel, Containing All Their Discoveries*, trans. by James Gibbs (London: A. Miller, 1752), vol. 1]
104. Baudet, *Paradise on Earth*, p. 19. Baudet discusses the religious roots of the myth of Paradise as well as the exotic primitivism that emerged as one aspect of the Renaissance which led to such concepts, eventually, as "The Noble Savage." His analysis of the psychological needs these utopian ideas satisfied when the medieval period was ending is both enlightening and convincing. Yet he neglected the Protestant millenarianism that burgeoned along with the Reformation. The believers conceived of a sinful world redeemed by an "earth renewal" process that would cause the planet to be turned into Paradise by divine action. See Howard Kaminsky, "Chiliasm and the Hussite Revolution," in Sylvia L. Thrupp, ed., *Change in Medieval Society* (New York: Appleton Century-Crofts, 1964), pp. 249–269.
105. See Richard S. Dunn, *Sugar and Slaves: The Rise of the Planter Class in the English West Indies, 1624-1713* (New York: W. W. Norton, 1972).

CHAPTER 7

1. Charles Sumner includes the John Jay letter in a long footnote in his *White Slavery in the Barbary States* (Boston: Ticknor, 1847), p. 29n. Ibid., pp. 55-57. Sumner quotes a companion of the British Minister to Morocco, who, reporting on an examination of the condition of white slaves in an effort to negotiate ransoms, said, "I am sure we saw several captives who lived much better in Barbary than they ever did in their own country." Sumner cites others who spoke of "slaves who left Algiers with regret" and of some who had become rich and "were often known to become indifferent to freedom and to prefer Algiers to their own country."

2. Since Sumner was attempting to prove that "heathens" in North Africa practiced a milder form of slavery than Christians in the American South, he probably overemphasized exceptions to the general rule that the white slaves wanted to be freed and sent home. But some captives "apostasized" and went ino the service of Muslim shereefs in North Africa. Note, e.g., cases mentioned in E. W. Bovill, *The Battle of Alcazar: An Account of the Defeat of Don Sebastian of Portugal at El-Ksar el-Kebir* (London: The Batchworth Press, 1952), pp. 167-168. For a vivid account of slavery in Barbary that stresses the disabilities and distress even of those who were given considerable privileges, see Norman Robert Bennett, "Christian and Negro Slavery in Eighteenth Century North Africa," *Journal of African History* 1, 1 (1960): 65-82.

3. Consult bibliographies and citations in David Brion Davis, *The Problem of Slavery in Western Culture* (Ithaca: Cornell University Press, 1966); Orlando Patterson, *Slavery and Social Death: A Comparative Study*; and William L. Westermann, *The Slave Systems of Greek and Roman Antiquity*. The discussions of slavery in antiquity by these three authors are comprehensive and definitive. All agree that ancient slavery was not *racial* slavery. Patterson, however, does say that race is not a factor to be ignored in the study of slavery where phenotypic differences exist. Professor M. I. Finley of Jesus College, Cambridge University, England, a distinguished classicist, agrees with Patterson. In an article on "The Extent of Slavery" in Robin W. Winks, ed., *Slavery: A Comparative Perspective* (New York: New York University Press, 1972), Finley takes issue with those who insist that racial slavery is a recent phenomenon, stating that "Prejudices of color, race, nationality, and religion were deeply involved in slavery, not only as ideological justification but also as influences on its institutional development." He feels that "race" in a very loose sense has always been involved when people enslave an outgroup. Finley uses "race" as equivalent to ethnic group or tribe and does not confine it to an anthropometrically defined category. It would have been better if he had said "ethnicity." A. N. Sherwin-White in *Racial Prejudice in Imperial Rome* uses the same concept in a discussion of Roman relations with Britons, Gauls and Germans. What he describes is *ethnocentrism* verging on cultural chauvinism. There is no hint of any theories of inherited inferiority of mind or temperament or even of an application of Greek environmental theories to account for differences. Popular beliefs similar to what we define as "racism" may have existed, but we have no way of knowing.

4. For a thorough, heavily documented, discussion of the transition from slavery to serfdom, see Marc Bloch, *Slavery and Serfdom in the Middle Ages*, trans. from the French by William R. Beer (Los Angeles: University of California Press, 1975),

especially the chapter, "How Slavery Came to an End." For an evaluation of Bloch's views on the relative role of the Church and changes in technology as compared with the views of Lefebvre des Noëttes, see "A Changing Society: Technology, Adaptation, and Invention" in William Carroll Bark, *Origins of the Medieval World* (Stanford University Press, 1958), pp. 89–100. A succinct statement summarizing a wide variety of sources on the relationship between slavery and serfdom in Europe is given on pp. 37–116 in David Brion Davis, *The Problem of Slavery in Western Culture.*

French, Italian, and Iberian states used slaves to man their naval galleys in the Mediterranean until slavery was abolished in the nineteenth century, after which convicts were used for that purpose. Both the Venetians and the Genoese used slaves as domestic servants at home as well as in their colonies on the islands of the Mediterranean. See Charles Verlinden, *The Beginnings of Modern Colonization: Eleven Essays With an Introduction* (Ithaca: Cornell University Press, 1970), pp. 30–32.

Marc Bloch's *Slavery and Serfdom in the Middle Ages* presents an excellent analysis of an etymological shift that took place in designating unfree labor, along with a discussion of the enslavement of Slavs and their transportation to Western Europe. In explaining the origin of the term "slave," he notes that "It is nonetheless striking that the very word slave—a juridical term, but still conveying at the beginning a very strong ethnic flavor—entered the domain of the French language very late. It scarcely appeared in it until the thirteenth century, and was then applied to people of an unfree condition who were perhaps Slavs but who certainly had not been born upon the frontiers of Germany . . . Europe could demand [only] a small amount of slave labor in the Slavic territories that its soldiers were ravaging" (*Slavery and Serfdom*, pp. 28 and 29). For three centuries, slaves from Poland and Russia were used in Europe so that the ethnic term Slav had shifted its meaning to a status term. However, most of the Slavs brought westward had been destined for the Muslim part of southern Europe, which also used Franks and Germans taken in wars against Christians.

5. Davis, *The Problem of Slavery,* p. 100.
6. Bloch, *Slavery and Serfdom,* pp. 28–30, describes the trade in "Slavs," including the "manufacture" of eunuchs after boys reached the lower Rhone Valley in France. He points out a sometimes neglected fact, namely, that the Crusaders were involved in the slave trade. For a dispassionate honest discussion of the participation of Jews in the trans-European slave trade see article on "Slavery" in *Encyclopedia Judaica,* 1960.
7. A group of Venetians came by sea to aid the Crusaders who, under Baldwin I, were establishing the Kingdom of Jerusalem in the twelfth century. They carried slaves back to Italy with them when they raided three islands on the way home that were claimed by the Christian king of Constantinople—Rhodes, Samos, and Chios. They carried off a number of boys and girls into slavery. See Fulcher of Chartres, *A History of the Expedition to Jerusalem,* vol. 3, p. 276.
8. This case is cited on p. 781 of Charles Verlinden, *L'Esclavage dans L'Europe Mediévale: Péninsule Ibérique et France,* vol. 1. This is the definitive two-volume work dealing with the persistence of slavery side by side with serfdom in parts of southern Europe. See especially pages 17–23. See also, by the same scholar, *Modern Colonization,* chapter 2, "Medieval Slavery in Europe and Colonial Slavery in America," pp. 33–51.
9. Verlinden, *L'Esclavage,* vol. 1, pp. 440–455.

10. Verlinden, *Modern Colonization*, p. 40.
11. Verlinden, *L'Esclavage*, pp. 270–271. There is an alternative to the argument that race consciousness was implicit in the act of describing the color of slaves. This practice could have been one of providing information to help describe individual runaways or potential runaways. Color and other anatomical traits assist in describing individuals whose names appear on notices, deeds, wills, etc. On the other hand, the practice might also be indicative of race consciousness present to a degree that involved prejudice and discrimination.
12. Verlinden, *Modern Colonization*, pp. 5, 7.
13. Verlinden, *L'Esclavage*, vol. 1, pp. 321–370. See p. 357 for unflattering references to the people of the Canary Islands. A description of the inhabitants of the Canaries by the first Europeans to visit them and record their impressions can be found in Gomez Eannes de Azurara, *The Chronicle of the Discovery and Conquest of Guinea*, trans. by G. H. Beazley and E. Prestage (London: the Haklyut Society, 1896), vol. 1, chapters 68, 75, and 79 to 83. These Berber Guanche people were depicted as much more "degraded" than the "blacks" or "Negroes" that Azurara referred to on the continent.
14. Verlinden, *Modern Colonization*, pp. 5, 7.
15. Ibid., pp. 79–97.
16. This case is presented in ibid., p. 91. See pp. 82–90 for several others involving black slaves.
17. Ibid., pp. 91, 92.
18. Ibid., p. 22.
19. One of the two most readily accessible accounts of the transfer process is Philip D. Curtin, "The Slave Trade and the Atlantic Basin: Intercontinental Perspectives," in N. I. Huggins, Martin Kilson, and Daniel Fox, eds., *Key Issues in the Afro-American Experience* (New York: Harcourt Brace Jovanovich, 1971), pp. 74–96. See also a definitive article by Verlinden, "The Transfer of Sugar Production from the Mediterranean to the Atlantic," in *Modern Colonization*, pp. 17–26. Curtin's article includes a summary of Verlinden's work as part of a much broader discussion. While Verlinden stressed the supply side, an American anthropologist, Sidney W. Mintz, has recently contributed a superb analysis of the demand side in *Sweetness and Power: The Place of Sugar in Modern History* (New York: Viking, 1987).
20. Fernando Ortiz, *Cuban Counterpoint: Tobacco and Sugar* (New York: Knopf, 1947), p. 276. See also entire section, "On How the Sugar *Ingenio* Has Always Been the Favored Child of Capitalism," pp. 267–282.
21. Ibid. pp. 255, 262, 275.
22. Verlinden, *Modern Colonization*, p. 26.
23. Magnus Mörner, *Race Mixture in the History of Latin America* (Boston: Little, Brown and Co., 1967), p. 26; and H. Hoetink, *Slavery and Race Relations in the Americas* (New York: Harper and Row, 1973), pp. 58–60. Hoetink writes at some length about Spanish women who were sent as "slaves" to Hispaniola to be wives to the colonizers. This seems to contradict our assertion that the most essential diagnostic feature of American slavery was that it was racial slavery. Further research is necessary to clear the question of whether or not these women were slaves in the sense of being "owned," were bound for life, and bore enslaved progeny. Women came to North American colonies as wives "sight unseen," but they were indentured. Were these Spanish women "slaves," or indentured servants, or some other category of "unfree" individuals?

24. Hoetink, *Slavery and Race Relations*, pp. 80, 84-86.
25. Harry A. Gailey, Jr., *History of Africa from Earliest Times to 1800* (New York: Holt Rinehart and Winston, 1970), p. 135.
26. Lewis, *Race and Color in Islam*, pp. 38-64.
27. St. Benedict the Moor who, having been made head of his monastery, chose to work in the kitchen, was introduced to the African slaves in Latin America. St. Maurice, the Christian warrior, was not. Martin de Porres was the only black person canonized in Latin America. His prime virtue, like that of St. Benedict, was humility. This Peruvian slave devoted his life to serving the poor and caring for abused animals. While no Black Madonnas made the transatlantic passage Mexican peasants enshrined their own "Dark Vigin," Our Lady of Guadalupe, who became more popular than a competing virgin in Mexican hagiography who was not "dark." The concept diffused without the specific black content. See Victor Turner, *Image and Pilgrimage in Christian Culture* (New York: Columbia University Press, 1978) for references to Our Lady of Guadalupe.
28. Ethiopian was used by the Church Fathers with two referents: Blacks living south of the Sahara, and all Negroes everywhere. Blacks immediately south of Egypt were gradually Christianized as were the inhabitants of the Abyssinian highlands.
29. See Kaplan, *The Black Magus*, pp. 48-51.
30. Suriname in South America institutionalized a very severe form of slavery under Dutch rule; the Dutch who colonized New Amsterdam (now New York) introduced a very benign form of slavery. British slavery in Jamaica as compared with slavery in Virginia was extremely harsh while slavery in New England was mild as compared with Virginia slavery. Obviously the determinants were not the types of European culture the settlers brought with them but, rather, the structure of the colonial situations.
31. Hoetink, *Caribbean Race Relations*, p. 31.
32. Ibid.
33. A classic study supporting the generalization that type of economy is the crucial variable is Franklin Knight, *Slave Society in Cuba During the Nineteenth Century* (Madison: University of Wisconsin Press, 1970). See especially "Introduction," pp. xv to xxi.
34. See especially Carl Degler, *Neither Black Nor White*, (New York: Macmillan, 1971).
35. Gilberto Freyre, *New World in the Tropics* (New York: Knopf, 1959), pp. 54-56.
36. Leslie B. Rout, Jr., "History of the Black Peoples of Spanish America," in *World Encyclopedia of Black Peoples*, Conspectus vol. 1 (St. Clair Shores, Mich.: Scholarly Press, 1975), p. 262.
37. Azurara, *Chronicle of Guinea*, pp. 80-81.
38. Ibid., pp. 83-84. There is no clue as to whether distinctions were made between whites, mulattoes, and those "black as Ethiops" when individual matings were being arranged. There is some evidence from a later period that mulattoes were being favored in Iberian societies. Both the positive attitude toward miscegenation and the negative esthetic appraisal of "Negroidness" revealed in Azurara's account of the Lagos incident were carried into Africa, Asia, and Brazil. The culture bearers were explorers, soldiers, settlers and administrators not all of whom approved of the Crown's encouragement of racial intermarriage in overseas areas as one way to "civilize" and Christianize. In Portugal the approved marriages were of African men to Portuguese women; in the overseas situation this was generally taboo. Approved matings involved Portuguese men and "native"

women, very few white women being available as wives and consorts. However, there was little disapproval of miscegenation without marriage. Norms brought from Portugal assigned a higher value to *morena* (brown) phenotypes than to *preto* (black). It is not surprising to find one governor in India reluctantly carrying out the Crown's policy of intermarriage while showing his personal preference for more Caucasoid physical types instead of "the black women of the Malabar coast." In the Brazilian colony where the white sex ratio eventually became balanced, various combinations of Indian, African, and Portuguese traits were prized in mistresses and prostitutes although not in wives. The colonizers' attitudes were demeaning to all women of color despite ties of affection that were frequently present.

The presence of progeny from mixed matings was useful in implementing a policy of divide and rule during rebellions and in ensuring a loyal group of soldiers when colonial settlers were at war with surrounding tribes and states—an endemic situation in Angola. One government official in Africa who disapproved of pressure from the Crown to encourage intermarriages, nevertheless wrote: "The soldiers of the garrison and other European individuals father many black children of the black ladies for want of white ladies with the result that there are many mulattoes and coloureds. The sons of these unions make great soldiers, chiefly in the wars in the backlands against the heathen inhabitants. Many of them become great men." In settling large areas of Mozambique Portuguese men were encouraged to marry African women who inherited land. Such titles to inherited land were only ruled valid by the colonial government if the women married Portuguese males! Despite positive attitudes toward miscegenation, in overseas situations power remained in the hands of white males. It was co-optation by incorporation and often coincided with brutal treatment of "heathen" Blacks or enslaved Blacks. See Carl Degler's very valuable study of Brazil, *Neither Black Nor White*, and "The Portuguese Racial Legacy," by David M. Abshire in Abshire and Michael A. Samuels, *Portuguese Africa* (New York: Praeger Publishers, 1969). See also Basil Davidson, "Slaves or Captives? . . . " in Huggins, Kilson, and Fox, eds., *Key Issues in the Afro-American Experience*, pp. 65–66.

39. Azurara, *Chronicle of Guinea*, vol. 1, pp. 84–85.
40. Ibid., pp. 82–83. These were not the first slaves seen by the Portuguese; it was the first time they had seen a mass of imported slaves landed and treated in this brutal fashion. They were shocked. This was something new in their experience.
41. Freyre, *New World in the Tropics*, p. 55.
42. For a brief but informative discussion of slaves in Portugal, see Verlinden, *L'Esclavage*, vol. 1, pp. 835–840. In 1620 there were 10,470 slaves in Lisbon. Conditions had been favorable for assimilation beginning in the sixteenth century (p. 839).
43. Ibid.
44. Ibid.
45. Bovill, *The Battle of Alcazar*, p. 5.
46. For a thorough analysis of the Portuguese impact on the people near the mouth of the Kongo River, see Georges Balandier, *Daily Life in the Kingdom of the Kongo From the Sixteenth to the Eighteenth Century* (New York: Pantheon Books, 1968). This book is as interesting as it is informative. The quotation is from p. 42.
47. Ibid., p. 43.
48. Ibid.
49. Ibid., p. 48.

50. Ibid., pp. 54–58.
51. Ibid., p. 84.
52. Ibid., p. 82.
53. Ibid.
54. Ibid., pp. 80–81.
55. Ibid., pp. 68, 72–75.
56. Ibid., p. 256.
57. See Anthony Wallace, "Revitalization Movements," *American Anthropologist* 58 (1956):264–281.
58. Balandier, *Daily Life in Kongo*, p. 257.
59. Ibid., p. 258.
60. Ibid., p. 259.
61. Ibid.
62. Ibid., p. 262.
63. Ibid., p. 263.
64. Rout, "Black Peoples of Spanish America," p. 230.
65. Portugal complied reluctantly, Spain with enthusiasm.
66. In 1579, thirty-eight sentences were passed by the Inquisition in Seville, among them one on Juan de Color, "a black." He confessed to having "reviled the name of our dear Lady" and other saints. The judge gave him two years in prison. Juan Corineo, a Moor, had contended that "our Lady" did not "conceive as a virgin," for which he had to pay with a hundred strokes of a whip. Among six cases of bigamy one involved a Moor who was punished with a hundred strokes and ten years enslavement on a galley. Two mulattoes and two other individuals were among a half dozen persons who insisted that it was "no sin to copulate" without being married. See *The Fugger Newsletters*, edited by Victor von Klarswell and published in London by John Lake in 1924, First Series, pp. 10 and 30–33.
67. Hoetink, *Caribbean Race Relations*, p. 5. When upper-class Castilian Spaniards spoke of "keeping the blood pure," pride of lineage within Christendom was as important as revulsion against incorporating Jewish, "Moorish infidel," or Spanish "heretic" blood. Status consciousness as well as religious prejudice was involved. Color became the symbol of status. The transformation from religious to racial conceptualization was easy in the American social milieu.
68. Rout, "Black Peoples of Spanish America," pp. 249–250.
69. Ibid., p. 251.
70. Degler, *Neither Black Nor White*, pp. 226–232.
71. David Knowles, *The Evolution of Medieval Thought* (New York: Vintage, 1962), pp. 188–189.
72. Ibid., pp. 82, 154. See also "Constantinus" in *Encyclopedia Britannica* (1963).
73. From Sylvia Wynter, "The Eye of the Other: Images of the Black in Spanish Literature," in Miriam DeCosta, ed., *Blacks in Hispanic Literature: Critical Essays* (Port Washington: Kennikat Press, 1977), p. 11. This is the introductory essay in an important volume by a group of Afro-American scholars. Sylvia Wynter, using a sophisticated variety of semiotic analysis grounded in a modified Marxist approach, provides a valuable context for understanding the other essays, all of which are of high quality. Her choice of the Miriam DeCosta quotation is particularly apt.
74. Ibid., p. 11.
75. Knight, *Slave Society in Cuba*, p. 124.
76. Wynter, "Eye of the Other," p. 10.

77. Morner, *Race Mixture in Latin America*, p. 111.
78. Rout, "Black Peoples of Spanish America," p. 262.
79. Ibid.
80. Ibid.
81. Morner, *Race Mixture*, p. 111.
82. *Colección de documentos para la formación social de Hispanoamerica, 1493-1810* (Madrid, 1953-62), vol. 3, p. 825.
83. Rout, "Black Peoples of Spanish America," pp. 242-243. For the black sailor who accompanied Cortez, see Peter Gehard, "A Black Conquistador in Mexico," *Hispanic American Historical Review* 58 (1978): 451-459.
84. Martha Cobb, "The Afro-Arabs, Blackamoors and Blacks: An Inquiry into Race Concepts Through Spanish Literature," in DeCosta, ed., *Blacks in Hispanic Literature*, pp. 20-27; see p. 26.
85. DeCosta, *Blacks in Hispanic Literature*, pp. 40-41.
86. Cobb, "The Afro-Arabs," pp. 20-27.
87. Ibid., pp. 24-25; also in DeCosta, *Blacks in Hispanic Literature*, Howard M. Jason, "The Negro in Spanish Literature to the End of the Siglo de Oro," pp. 33-34.
88. Ruth Pike, *Aristocrats and Traders: Sevillian Society in the Sixteenth Century* (Ithaca: Cornell University Press, 1972), pp. 187-188. The section on "Slaves and Freedmen" is well-documented. In 1565 there were 6,327 slaves in a population of 85,538, the largest slave population of any Spanish city. See also P.E.H. Hair, "Black Slaves at Valencia, 1482-1516: An Onomastic Inquiry," *History in Africa,* 7 (1980): 120-139.
89. Ibid., p. 186.
90. Ibid., p. 185-186.
91. Ibid., p. 187.
92. Ibid.
93. Alejandro Lipschütz, *El indoamericanismo y el problema racial en las Américas* (Santiago de Chile, 1944), p. 75, and other works by the author.
94. Pike, *Aristocrats and Traders*, p. 178.
95. Ibid., pp. 183-184.
96. Ibid., pp. 184-185.
97. Ibid., p. 189.
98. Jahneinz Jahn, *A History of Neo-African Literature* (London: Faber and Faber, 1966), pp. 30-34, "Juan Latino a Renaissance African." Jahn calls him "a 'home made' Christian Moor." Incidentally his hero Don John about whom he wrote poetry won great renown for his military victories over the Moors, especially at the Battle of Lepanto.
99. Not one of the following anthologies considered any of Juan Latino's work significant enough to include: Eleanor Turnbull, ed., *Ten Centuries of Spanish Poetry* (Baltimore: John Hopkins Press, 1955); Seymour Resnick and Jean Pasmantier, eds., *An Anthology of Spanish Literature in English Translation* (New York: Ungar, 1958); E. A. Peers, ed., *A Critical Anthology of Spanish Verse* (New York: Greenwood Press, 1968); Willis Barnstone, ed., *Spanish Poetry: An Anthology* (New York: Oxford University Press, 1970); and John A. Crow, *An Anthology of Spanish Poetry* (Baton Rouge: Louisiana University Press, 1979). However, at least one Spanish critic, Antonio Marin Ocete, lauded him in an essay in 1925 (See G. K. Osei, *History of the African People* [London: 1971, vol. 2] pp. 43-44).
100. Jahn, *Neo-African Literature*, pp. 33-34.

101. Cobb, "The Afro-Arabs . . . and Race Concepts," p. 26.
102. Quoted in James Walvin, *Black and White: The Negro and English Society, 1555-1945* (London: Allen Lane, the Penguin Press, 1973), p. 160.
103. See footnotes to chapters 1 and 2 in Winthrop Jordan, *White Over Black, American Attitudes Toward the Negro.*
104. Jordan, *White Over Black*, p. 60.
105. Bloch, *Slavery and Serfdom*, p. 3.
106. Ibid., p. 25.
107. Ibid., p. 25.
108. Ibid., discussion on pp. 26 and 28.
109. Vatter, *The Devil in English Literature*, p. 88. References to the devil as an "Ethiopian" were probably restricted to certain scholarly circles in which it was common knowledge that St. Andrew of Scythia (died circa A.D. 940) had visions of fighting against "a multitude of Ethiopians under the guidance of a gigantic Moor" as he struggled to remain "pure." They knew, too, that five centuries earlier, St. Anthony of Egypt reported that he was "harassed by black giants in his dreams" and that "More than one anchorite of the Thebaid [i.e., monks in Upper Egypt near Thebes] beheld the demon in the form of an Ethiopian" (Graf, *The Story of the Devil*, pp. 28, 208, and 250-355). No Jungian archetype theory or modern Manichaean analysis is necessary to explain why the devil took on the guise of blackness for these early Church Fathers. Chapter 4 explains that their battle against African paganism made it almost inevitable. Graf is apparently making the same point and generalizing broadly from the concrete case when he states that "Black appears as the native color of the demons from the very earliest centuries of Christianity and the reasons for assigning it to them are self-explanatory so obvious are they and natural . . . the demon conforms himself to the times and places around which he moves."

     The hypothesis might be advanced that as Puritan ideas became strong in some segments of the British middle class an equivalence between the Negro and the Devil, or between the Negro and sexual sins, became prevalent because of the association that the more Puritanical segment of this class made between Negroes and the revels and sexual dalliance of the aristrocracy. Not only were black masked balls held at court during the sixteenth century, but Negroes actually participated at times. Poems had titles such as "The Blackamoor and Her Loves" or "A Fair Nymph Scorning a Black Boy Courting Her." John Bunyan in the next century in his book, *The Holy War*, depicts Satan as "King of the Blacks or Negroes." See discussion of the erotic appeal of, as well as expressed aversion to, sexual relations with Blacks during the sixteenth and seventeenth centuries in Rogers, *Nature Knows No Color Line*, pp. 156-176 and 221.
110. Vatter, *The Devil in English Literature*, p. 98.
111. Ibid., p. 71. See also note 307.
112. Ibid., p. 88.
113. "A Dissertation on the Ancient English Morris Dance" in Francis Douce, *Illustrations of Shakespeare and of Ancient Manners with Dissertations* (London: no publisher named, 1807, vol. 2), pp. 431-482.
114. Ibid., p. 437. Church wardens were reporting the Morris Dance in a form similar to the continental dance as late as the reign of Henry VIII just prior to the Elizabethan Age.
115. Ibid., p. 436.
116. Jordan, *White Over Black*, p. 7. This definitive volume shows the same weakness

in the discussion of blackness in the British symbol system that most liberal analysts reveal. They are impressed (and somewhat shocked) by the discovery of the high degree of negative affect associated with the idea of blackness. They do not give sufficient attention, however, to the polysemic nature of the verbal symbol "black," and to differences in use and meaning due to social class subcultures and changes over time. For instance, in Britain, the devil was not always depicted as black and blackness did not always have the connotation of evil, contrary to the impression given by Jordan.

117. Ibid., p. 6, minimizes earlier contacts that some English individuals had with Negroes or knowledge gained by Crusaders or through constant close trade relations with Portugal. There is, for instance, a credible report of an African slave running away from London to Portugal during the fifteenth century and asking the king of that country for asylum. See Verlinden, *L'Esclavage*, vol. 1, p. 630. For an excellent account of the impact of the five Africans who arrived in 1554, with comments about a few who were certainly in England and Scotland before that date, see Peter Fryer, *Staying Power*, pp. 1-8. His account of John Hawkins trafficking in slaves within a decade after the first five arrived documents the involvement of Queen Elizabeth I in the slave trade.

118. Jordan does not mention that two African women were baptized in Scotland in 1507 and like one of the king's minstrels, were attached to the court. See a brief mention by Edward Scobie in *Black Britannia* (Chicago: Johnson Publishing Co., 1972), p. 8, and a longer discussion in Fryer, *Staying Power*, "Africans in Scotland," pp. 2-4. See also James Walvin, "Black Slavery in England," *Journal of Caribbean History* (November 1973).

119. Walvin, *Black and White*, p. 10.

120. Jordan, *White Over Black*, p. 60.

121. The antislavery movement began as one aspect of the Protestant sectarian upsurge in the sixteenth and seventeenth centuries, insistently questioning the righteousness of social arrangements and with a significant number of people determined to try to "live free from sin." The milieu out of which this religious question came is vividly revealed in the personal history of the founder of the sect that took the leadership in opposing slavery, the Religious Society of Friends (Quakers). It is significant that when Fox was first confronted with slavery on a visit to Barbados in the West Indies in 1671, his initial reaction was to advise masters to treat them kindly and to change their status to that of indentured servants, freeing them "after a certain number of years." During the next century Quakers became proponents of emancipation. See George Fox, *Autobiography* (Philadelphia: Ferris and Leach, 1919), p. 495. It is significant that the colony of Rhode Island passed a law in 1657 making it illegal to hold Negroes in bondage beyond a period of ten years.

122. See "George Best, Discourse, 1578" in James Walvin, *The Black Presence: A Documentary History of the Negro in England, 1555-1860* (London: Orbach and Chambers, 1971), pp. 34-37. For a careful evaluation of this concern with the color of Africans, see Walvin, *Black and White*, pp. 16-28.

123. Walvin, *The Black Presence*, p. 35.

124. Ibid., p. 35.

125. Ibid.

126. "Sir Thomas Browne, Enquiries Into Vulgar and Common Errors, 1646," in Walvin, *The Black Presence*, pp. 37-47.

127. Ibid., p. 44. The idea that Africans thought of the devil as white became

widespread during the sixteenth century. It is an assertion the sources of which have not been researched carefully. It seemed reasonable to people who were trying to imaginatively take the role of the other. A study of the prevalence of this idea merits research.

128. Ibid., p. 44.
129. Ibid., p. 45.
130. Ibid.
131. Note that Baudet, *Paradise on Earth*, p. 18, actually refers to "canonization of the Negro by continental intellectuals." Charles V summoned a junta of theologians to debate the question of whether wars against the Indians were just. Father Juan Ginés de Sepúlveda, basing his argument upon Aristotle, insisted that the Indians were slaves "by nature" and conquest of them was good for their souls as well as profitable for the Spaniards. Father Las Casas made an eloquent affirmation of the equality of all races. The judges were unable to agree, but the wars of conquest continued. For excerpts from the arguments, see Benjamin Keen, ed., *Readings in Latin American Civilization, 1492 to the Present* (Boston: Houghton, Mifflin, 1955), pp. 89–91.
132. Alfred Harbage, *Shakespeare's Audience* (New York: Columbia University Press, 1941), chapter 3, "What Kind of People?" pp. 53–91. His answer was unequivocal—"It was predominantly a workingclass audience." A sixteenth-century document presented in G. B. Harrison, *England in Shakespeare's Day* (London: Methuen, 1928), pp. 29–30, refers to the London masses as "The Rascal Multitude." John Dover Wilson stressed the heterogeneity and liveliness of contemporary audiences in his *Life in Shakespeare's England* (London: Harmondsworth: Penguin, 1913, 1949). Charles Dudley Warner in *The People for Whom Shakespeare Wrote* (New York: Harpers, 1897) comments that "there prevailed an insatiable curiosity for seeing strange sights and hearing strange adventures." The stage catered to that interest, which was reinforced by gossip and rumor, for "London swarmed with soldiers, adventurers, sailors who were familiar with all seas and every port, men with projects, men with marvelous tales . . . " (pp. 139 and 142). Warner stresses the fact that "this people had a taste for blood, took a delight in brutal encounters . . . nor were they fastidious in the matter of public executions" (p. 148). The murder, mayhem, and constant warfare in Shakespearean tragedy fitted the temper of the times!
133. Roland Mushat Frye, *Shakespeare's Life and Times: A Pictoral Record* (Princeton: Princeton University Press, 1967), Section 32, "Titus Andronicus," Section 34, "Titus Andronicus on Shakespeare's First Printed Play," and Section 35, "Titus Andronicus on the Elizabethan Stage." One English critic calls the play "a drama depicting sadism quite frankly . . . a play of unrelieved horror. . . . " but states that the play was "a great favourite with Elizabethan audiences and had a considerable vogue for many years . . . " (J. H. E. Brock, *Iago and Some Shakespearian Villains* [Cambridge, England: W. Heffner and Sons, 1937], pp. 31, 32). Another English critic suggests that the playwright Kyd had helped to prepare Elizabethan audiences for murderous villains with *The Spanish Tragedy* (G. B. Harrison, *Shakespeare Under Elizabeth* [New York: Henry Holt, 1933], pp. 17–19). See also Eldred Jones, *Othello's Countrymen: The African in English Renaissance Drama* (London: Oxford University Press, 1965).
134. For a sensitive reaction to this plot and to Shakespeare's treatment of it see Lemuel Johnson, *The Devil, the Gargoyle and the Buffoon: The Negro as Metaphor in Western Literature* (Port Washington, N.Y.: Kennikat, 1971), pp. 40–

44. It is significant that Shakespeare used alien Moors as depicted in Italian stories not the European Moors of Andalusian Spain.

135. Horace H. Furness, *A New Variorum Edition of Shakespeare—Othello* (Philadelphia: Lippincott, 1886), p. 380.

136. Ibid., p. 372. One modern critic, perhaps reading more recent Anglo-Saxon attitudes back into the Elizabethan and Jacobean periods agrees that Shakespeare was trying to make a point about the "unnatural" character of the marriage, stating that he was defining it as a "Beauty marries the Beast" situation (See Kenneth Muir, *Shakespeare's Sources*, [London: Methuen, 1957], pp. 122–140]. Even if the marriage is appraised as "unnatural," the question is whether it is being considered such because Othello is a black Moor or because he is a non-Christian. The Beauty/Beast metaphor may tell us more about the mind of the critic than that of either Brabantio, Shakespeare, or the Elizabethan audience. Incidentally Jungians would argue that the Desdemona/Othello contrast represents Shakespeare's recognition of an archetype being expressed in this case through a racial/cultural contrast.

137. Johnson, *Devil, Gargoyle, and Buffoon*, p. 44. Most of the critical appraisals of *Titus Andronicus* have been made by white critics. An Afro-American point of view is presented in this perceptive book. Calling attention to Peele's play about the Battle of Alcazar, as he does, Johnson focuses attention where it should be—on British attitudes toward Moors as conceived of as heathen enemies not as enslaved Blacks. For a discussion of a black Moorish ruler who was defined for public consumption as a particularly reprehensible person as early as 1581, through pamphlets sold in London, see chapter 3, "Mulai Mohammed," and chapter 6, "Queen Elizabeth's Secret," in Bovill, *The Battle of Alcazar*.

An American literary critic suggests the presence of rather precise stereotypes about Moors—that is North African Muslims—some of whom were tawny and some black. In his view, Shakespeare regarded Othello's jealous passion as " . . . a basic characteristic of Moors, who were considered to be a very violent people, quite different from Englishmen or even Italians" (Louis Auchincloss, *Motiveless Malignity* [New York: Houghton Mifflin, 1969], p. 6).

138. Johnson, *Devil, Gargoyle and Buffoon*, p. 37. This author stresses the use by Shakespeare and others of his time of the black/white contrast as moral metaphors. This did not necessarily mean that an individual black person symbolized evil or called to mind a devil or Satan, the Prince of Devils, whatever the subliminal effects of making the contrast at the abstract level may have been. Nor did the Moor=Devil equivalence control all thinking and action involving black and white people. During the sixteenth and seventeenth centuries, not only were distinctions drawn between "tawny" Moors and "black-o-Moors," but also between "Moors" and "Negroes," the latter, presumably, being Blacks from West Africa, pagan not Muslim. Queen Elizabeth's 1601 deportation order specified both "Negroes" and "black-o-moores" who were a menace to the realm. As late as 1731, a proclamation of the Lord Mayor of London ordered that "no Negroes or other blacks be suffered to be bound apprentices" (Walvin, *The Black Presence*, pp. 64 and 65). It appears that Englishmen were making distinctions between various kinds of Blacks on the basis of amount of pigmentation, ethnicity, religion, occupation, and social status. At the same time, they could laugh at black devils clowning in Morality Plays and at characters on the stage berating each other in color terms.

J. A. Rogers has presented a documented, illustrated essay on the use of variations of the term "Moor" in British and European heraldry and patronyms which indicate the complexity of the problem of deciding upon the meanings and affect connected with the words. One thing is clear—there was no blanket pejorative attribution, even if Rogers' tendency to emphasize actual acceptance of Moorish ancestry by prominent British families is open to question (Rogers, *Nature Knows No Color Line*, pp. 69–110, "The Negro as 'Moor'—Negro Ancestry in Aristocratic European Families").

139. For a complete listing of passages in which the word "black" occurs, see Bartlett's *Shakespeare Concordance*. Note also the pejorative use of the word by Desdemona's father in Othello.

140. Furness, *Variorum/Othello*. The quotation is from an extensive section on "Othello's Colour," p. 390.

141. Ibid., p. 391.

142. Ibid., p. 390.

143. Ibid., p. 389.

144. Ibid., p. 390.

145. Auchincloss, *Motiveless Malignity*, pp. 6–7.

146. John Webster's play, *The White Devil or Vittoria Corombona*, with his note "To the Reader," and with extensive comments by the editor, Professor Hazelton Spencer of Johns Hopkins University, is available in *Elizabethan Plays Written by Shakespeare's Friends, Colleagues, Rivals, and Successors* (Boston: Little, Brown and Co., 1933). One of the seventeen playwrights included was Christopher Marlowe, whose *Tamburlaine* included favorable references to "the mighty Christian-priest/Called John the Great." This Ethiopian, Prester John, is a contrasting black heroic type to the two Moors—the pagan Aaron and Othello. For an excellent annotated discussion of a Florentine mulatto, Alessandro de Medici, see chapter on "First Reigning Duke of Florence" in Rogers, *World's Great Men of Color*, vol. 2, pp. 24–33, picture included.

147. A judgment based on reading John Webster's play.

148. Vatter, *The Devil in English Literature*, pp. 66 and 92–105.

149. Hoetink, *Caribbean Race Relations*, discussion of exoticism and race relations, pp. 59–60, 61, and 131–132.

150. Walvin, *Black and White*, p. 70.

151. Ibid.

152. This abortive attempt of Elizabeth's Council to deport the Africans is described in detail with supporting documentation in Walvin, *Black and White*, pp. 7–10 and notes on p. 14. See also Walvin, *The Black Presence*, pp. 64–65, "Royal Proclamation of 1601, Licensing Caspar van Sendar to Deport Negroes." Walvin mentions, but does not stress, the economic interest that the queen herself had in allocating a contract to a Dutch businessman to round up and deport these Blacks in Britain. This was in conflict with her sentimental interest in specific black individuals who were connected with the court. While ordering "Negroes," presumably from Guinea, deported, the Queen was having close political and economic relations with Moroccans of the Negroid Marrakesh area. See Bovill, *The Battle of Alcazar*, "Queen Elizabeth's Secret." Fryer points out that a painting in 1570 depicted the queen being entertained by seven black musicians and three dancing Negro youth. While questioning the caption on the picture, the author states that "such a group was by now a standard feature of every self-respecting European court," and that "to disguise themselves as black women in

masquerades became a favorite pastime among the queen's ladies-in-waiting." (He cites a critical study published in 1963 and quotes Ben Jonson's comments on his *Masque of Blackness* [1604-05]). Fryer then discusses Elizabeth's deportation order, quoting it in a version that adds to her economic defense of the action and popular complaints against them that " . . . most of them are infidels, having no understanding of Christ or his Gospel" (Fryer, *Staying Power*, pp. 9–12). They were referred to as "those kinds of people" who "may be well spared in this realm."

153. Jordan, *White Over Black*, p. 40.
154. John Bunyan, *The Holy War*, (Oxford: Clarendon Press, 1980), p. 9; first published in 1682.
155. Jordan, *White Over Black*, pp. 40–43, "The Blackness Within," and other parts of the chapter that are relevant.
156. *Selections From the Diary of Samuel Pepys, 1660-1669* (New York: Books, Inc., n.d., Art-Type Edition of the World's Popular Classics). Shakespeare's Sonnets 130 and 131 have been interpreted as referring to one of his lovers, the so-called "Dark Lady." Unlike Pepys who is writing for his diary, Shakespeare, writing for a sophisticated public, is defensive and apologetic. Defending the woman as beautiful in his eyes if not in the eyes of others, he virtually ridicules her hair and lips. For a comment on this case see Rogers, *Nature Knows No Color Line*, p. 171.
157. Walvin, *Black and White*, pp. 48, 52–55.
158. Ibid., "The Black Community: 1700-1800," pp. 46–73. Walvin presents convincing evidence to support the proposition that racial prejudice against black people in Britain was rooted in a segment of the middle class and was deliberately fostered by those with economic interests to be served. The ordinary people, on the other hand, not only had congenial and friendly relations with black people but took to the streets, upon occasion, to protect runaways from being captured and re-enslaved. See also Fryer, *Staying Power*, pp. 71–72.
159. Walvin, *Black and White*, p. 57.
160. Walvin, *Black and White* p. 53. Details on the prevalence of widespread fraternization between domestic servants across racial lines are given in J. Jean Hecht, *The Domestic Servant Class in Eighteenth Century England* (London: Routledge and Kegan Paul, 1956). She calls attention to the fact that black men were especially popular with the women in these circles. See also Walvin, *Black and White*, for an informative and significant chapter on "The Black Community, 1700-1800." See Hogarth cartoon of black male servant embracing white female servant in Nigel File and Chris Power, *Black Settlers in Britain, 1555-1958* (London: Heinemann, 1981), p. 53. The same photograph appears in Rogers, *Nature Knows No Color Line*, p. 160.
161. Verlinden, *Modern Colonization*, 30.

EPILOGUE

1. See article on "Ethiopia" in *Encyclopedia Britannica* (1963), vol. 8, p. 785.
2. Bovill, *The Battle of Alcazar*, pp. 101–102.
3. Gailey, *History of Africa*, p. 73.
4. Bovill, *The Battle of Alcazar*, p. 172.
5. Ibid., p. 173.

6. Gailey, *History of Africa*, p. 74.
7. Bovill, *The Battle of Alcazar*, p. 172.
8. Ibid., p. 173, 178.
9. Ibid., p. 179.
10. Ibid., p. 178.
11. Immanuel Wallerstein, *The Modern World System: Capitalist Agriculture and the Origins of the European World Economy in the Sixteenth Century* (New York: Academic Press, 1974), vol. 1: "Slavery," pp. 43–44, 86–90, 94, 99–100, 103–104, 121, 126, 187, 280, 326, 332, 339, 341; and "slave trade," 89, 188, 193, 335, 339.
12. Karl Marx, *Capital (A Critique of Political Economy)* (New York: E. P. Dutton, 1930), vol. 2, p. 832; originally published in German in 1882.

INDEX

St. Clair Drake was Professor Emeritus at Stanford University, where he taught anthropology and sociology and organized and directed the African and Afro-American studies program from 1969 until his retirement in 1976. He also taught at Dillard University, Roosevelt University, the University of Chicago, Boston University, Columbia University, and the University of Liberia. From 1958 to 1961 Drake was head of the sociology department of the University of Ghana. While doing field work in England and Wales for a dissertation on race relations in Britain, he met and worked with the organizers of the Pan-African Federation, among them George Padmore and Kwame Nkrumah.

Drake's works include *Black Metropolis* (1945, 1962, and 1970), which he co-authored with Horace Cayton, *Race Relations in a Time of Rapid Social Change* (1966), *Our Urban Poor* (1967), and *The Redemption of Africa and Black Religion* (1970). He contributed numerous poems and articles to professional journals and other publications. In 1973, he received the American Sociological Association's Du Bois-Johnson-Frazier Award. He was elected an Honorary Fellow of the Royal Anthropological Institute of Great Britain and Ireland in 1986, and he was senior scholar at the W.E.B. Du Bois Institute of Harvard University in 1987, the year Volume 1 of *Black Folk* was published.